JOURNAL FOR THE STUDY OF THE NEW TESTAMENT
SUPPLEMENT SERIES

268

Editor
Mark Goodacre

To my father and mother,
Chul Soo and Jung Ha
and
my wife, Hee Sub
and
my two sons,
Suh Joong and Young Joong

The Significance of Clothing Imagery in the Pauline Corpus

Jung Hoon Kim

T & T CLARK INTERNATIONAL
A Continuum imprint
LONDON • NEW YORK

Copyright © 2004 T&T Clark International
A Continuum imprint

Published by T&T Clark International
The Tower Building, 11 York Road, London SE1 7NX
15 East 26th Street, Suite 1703, New York, NY 10010

www.tandtclark.com

British Library Cataloguing-in-Publication Data
A catalogue record for this book is available from the British Library

Library of Congress Cataloguing-in-Publication Data
A catalogue record for this book is available from the Library of Congress

Typeset by ISB Typesetting, Sheffield
Printed on acid-free paper in Great Britain by
Antony Rowe Ltd, Chippenham, Wiltshire

ISBN 0-567-08246-6

CONTENTS

Part II
THE CLOTHING IMAGERY IN THE PAULINE CORPUS

ACKNOWLEDGMENTS

Praise be to God, who has filled my needs with all manner of blessings on my long and difficult journey through the wilderness of academia, in pursuit of my MA at the University of Durham and my PhD at the University of Glasgow, the result of which is this volume. During my period of research, as I faced many frustrations, serious illness, and academic and financial difficulties, he has provided me with superfluous grace through many different people for the completion of this thesis. Without their help, fulfillment of this writing task would not have been possible. I wish to express my gratitude to them all, only some of whom I can name here. First of all, I greatly appreciate the guidance of my supervisor, Dr Joel Marcus. Without his patient direction, this study would not have reached its end. His perceptive critiques and comments provided a highly valuable challenge and a stone to sharpen ideas relevant to the thesis. I also thank Dr John Barclay, who cared for my work when Dr Marcus was on his study leaves. He provided very profitable comments to point out the way. I extend my thanks to Mr John Bradley for his thoughtful help and to Mrs Johnston, the secretary for postgraduates in the Department of Biblical Studies, for her kind consideration of my various requests.

I wish to give my profound thanks to Professor Bok Yoon Shin, the president of the Hapdong Graduate School College of Theology, who has given me considerable encouragement since I embarked on my research. Special thanks should be dedicated to Professor Chi Mo Hong, my former teacher at the University of Chongshin, who has bestowed great help with love and concern. I also wish to send my gratitude to Dr Yung Ki Yu, who has provided helpful guidance not only at the outset but also at the final stage of my research. The most significant gratitude should go to Dr Ho Duck Kwon, my Christian brother, who has patiently supported me for years and years; the same gratitude goes to the churches which have sent financial support through him. My sincere gratitude also goes to Rev. Seo Kyu Yang, Dr Byung Soo Cho, Dr Sang Won Lee and Rev. Chang Yoon Oh, who as college-fellows have showed brotherly friendship and generosity.

Over the last years, my family and I have experienced the wonderful provision of God, who has lavishly supplied all things of which we have needed through his faithful servants. I wish to give my warmhearted gratitude to Rev. Myung Hyuk Kim and the Kang-Byun Church, Rev. Byung Shik Park and the Song-Pa-Jeil Church, Rev. Yung Sun Park and the Nam-Po Church (which provided the Lamp scholarship), Rev. Hong Joon Choe and the Pusan Sae-Joong-Ang Church, and Rev. Sun Kyu Park and the Jun-Won Church.

I am so greatly indebted to Rev. John and Mrs Susan Harding, who have given great Christian love. Mr Harding's loving care as well as his godly inspired prayer, and Mrs Harding's flowers of encouragement from her garden and her modesty, consideration and wisdom will be long cherished. In particular, Mrs Harding bestowed unsparing effort in order to correct my English, and this was a truly efficient and concrete aid. I also thank the members of the Shettleston Free Church for their prayer, kindness and concern. It was a great joy to see them at the church every Lord's day. They silently showed me what presbyterian saints' piety is.

The memory of the fellowship with Mr Brian and Mrs Brenda Norton will be lasting. Their devotion to God has resulted in the edification of the Durham Evangelical Presbyterian Church, where I have been privileged to participate in the eldership. Brenda's considerate love and Brian's discreet care and his preaching, which is full of an evangelical boldness and conviction, and his exemplary life which exerts a sacrificial effort for the supply of human needs, will constantly be remembered as a ministerial example. Specifically, the prayer meeting at Mrs Freda Blunt's house in Pittington and the Bible meeting at the home of Mr David and Mrs Glenys Brewis, will be continuously left in my heart as a happy memory. The fellowship with Mrs Helen Cook and her children will also not be forgotten.

I am also grateful to Professor Kyu Nam Jung, the president of the University of Kwang Shin, who has been a significant source of encouragement whilst rounding off the thesis.

Finally, I would like to record a personal note. Without my parents' endless love and prayer, it might not have been possible to proceed with the research. Their sacrificial love has caused me to exclaim, 'Parents are indeed wonderful!' I also thank my sisters and brothers, Yong Sook, Jung Sun, Yoon Soon, Sang Hoon and Choong Hoon, and their spouses. Above all comes my inestimable debt to my wife, Hee Sub, whose loyal support has been magnificent throughout the period of this study and to my two sons, Suh Joong and Young Joong, who have shared every difficulty with their parents and who are our special joy. When we arrive at the Land of Morning Calm (Korea), we will remember the sound of Suh Joong's Grade 5 violin playing and Young Joong's keyboard at the Eagle Hights flat in Sighthill. I dedicate this thesis to my parents, my wife and my two sons, and thereby give all glory to God.

ABBREVIATIONS

1. *General Items*

A	Codex Alexandrinus
ℵ	Codex Sinaiticus
aor.	*aorist*
AV	Authorized Version (= KJV)
B	Codex Vaticanus
C	Codex Ephraemi Syri
D	Codex Bezae
f.	female
Gk.	Greek
HB	Hebrew Bible
IVP	Inter-Varsity Press
JB	Jerusalem Bible
KJV	King James Version (1611) = AV
Lat.	Latin
LXX	Septuagint
m.	male
MS(S)	manuscript(s)
MT	Masoretic Text (of the OT)
NASV	NEW AMERICAN STANDARD VERSION
n.d.	no date
NEB	NEW ENGLISH BIBLE
NIV	NEW INTERNATIONAL VERSION (1978)
NJB	NEW JERUSALEM BIBLE (1985)
NT	New Testament
OT	Old Testament
par(s).	parallel(s)
pl.	plural
RSV	REVISED STANDARD VERSION (NT 1946, OT 1952, Apoc. 1957)
RV	REVISED VERSION, 1881-85

2. *Commonly Used Reference Works, Journals and Serials*

AB	Anchor Bible
ABC	F.C. Eiselen *et al.* (eds.), *The Abingdon Bible Commentary* (New York: Abingdon, 1929)
ABD	*Anchor Bible Dictionary*
ABRL	Anchor Bible Reference Library
AGAJU	Arbeiten zur Geschichte des antiken Judentums und des Urchristentums
AJT	*American Journal of Theology*
AnB	Analecta Biblica

AOT	H.F.D. Sparks (ed.), *The Apocryphal Old Testament* (Oxford: Clarendon, 1984)
APOT	R.H. Charles, *The Apocrypha and Pseudepigrapha of the Old Testament* (2 vols.; Oxford: Clarendon, 1913)
BAGD	W. Bauer, W.F. Arndt, F.W. Gingrich and F.W. Danker (eds.), *Greek-English Lexicon of the NT and Other Early Christian Literature* (Chicago and London: University of Chicago, 2nd edn, 1979)
BBC	Broadman Bible Commentary
BETL	Bibliotheca Ephemeridum Theologicarum Lovaniensium
BFT	Biblical Foundations in Theology
BHT	Beiträge zur historischen Theologie
BKAT	Biblischer Kommentar: Altes Testament
BLG	Biblical Language Greek
BM	*Benediktinische Monatsschrift*
BNTC	Black's New Testament Commentary
BZNW	Beihefte zur Zeitschrift für die neutestamentliche Wissenschaft
CBAA	Catholic Biblical Association of America
CBC	*Cambridge Bible Commentary on the New English Bible*
CBNS	Century Bible New Series
CBNTS	Coniectanea Biblica New Testament Series
CBQ	*Catholic Biblical Quarterly*
CBQMS	*Catholic Biblical Quarterly Monograph Series*
CC	Calvin's Commentaries
CCCS	Concordia Classic Commentary Series
CCWJCW	Cambridge Commentaries on Writings of the Jewish and Christian World: 200 BC to AD 200
CECNT	Critical and Exegetical Commentary on the New Testament
CGTSC	Cambridge Greek Testament for Schools and Colleges
CHB	*A Commentary on the Holy Bible by Various Writers*
ComC	The Communicator's Commentary
CQ	*Classical Quarterly*
CQNS	*Classical Quarterly New Series*
CRAI	*Comptes rendues à l'Académie des inscriptions et belles-letters*
CTJ	*Calvin Theological Journal*
DB	*A Dictionary of the Bible*
DBAT	*Dielheimer Blätter zum Alten Testament*
DPL	*Dictionary of Paul and His Letters*
EB	Eichstätter Beiträge
EDNT	*Exegetical Dictionary of the New Testament*
EEC	*Encyclopedia of Early Christianity*
EGGNT	Exegetical Guide to the Greek New Testament
EGT	*The Expositor's Greek Testament*
EKKNT	Evangelisch-katholischer Kommentar zum Neuen Testament
EPC	Epworth Preacher's Commentaries
EPIB	Editrice Pontificio Instituto Biblico
EQ	*Evangelical Quarterly*
ERET	Eine Reihe von der Evangelischen Theologie
EVGB	Evangelisch Verlagsanstalt GmbH Berlin
ExpT	*Expository Times*
FLTP	*Fontana Library of Theology and Philosophy*
FRLANT	Forschungen zur Religion und Literatur des Alten und Neuen Testaments

FzB	Forschung zur Bible
GSC	Geneva Series Commentary
HBC	*Harper's Bible Commentary*
HC	Householder Commentaries
HCCB	Hermeneia—A Critical Commentary on the Bible
HTKNT	Herders Theologischer Kommentar zum Neuen Testament
HTR	*Harvard Theological Review*
HTS	Harvard Theological Studies
HUCA	*Hebrew Union College Annual*
IASH	Israel Academy of Sciences and Humanities
IB	*Interpreter's Bible*
IBCTP	Interpretation: A Bible Commentary for Teaching and Preaching
ICC	International Critical Commentary
Int	*Interpretation*
IOCB	*The Interpreter's One-Volume Commentary on the Bible*
JBL	*Journal of Biblical Literature*
JE	*The Jewish Encyclopedia*
JHUSA	The Johns Hopkins University Studies in Archaeology
JJS	*Journal of Jewish Studies*
JSPSup	Journal for the Study of the Pseudepigrapha Supplement Series
JJTP	*Journal of Jewish Thought and Philosophy*
JQR	*Jewish Quarterly Review*
JSJ	*Journal for the Study of Judaism*
JSNT	*Journal for the Study of the New Testament*
JSNTSup	Journal for the Study of the New Testament Supplement Series
JSOT	*Journal for the Study of the Old Testament*
JSOTSup	Journal for the Study of the Old Testament Supplement Series
JSP	*Journal for the Study of the Pseudepigrapha*
JTS	*Journal of Theological Studies*
JTSNS	*Journal of Theological Studies New Series*
KEKNT	Kritisch-Exegetischer Kommentar über das Neue Testament
LCL	Loeb Classical Library
LEC	Library of Early Christianity
MoffNTC	Moffat New Testament Commentary
MThS	Münchener theologische Studien
NBD	*New Bible Dictionary*
NCBC	New Century Bible Commentary
NCCHS	*A New Catholic Commentary on Holy Scripture*
NICNT	New International Commentary on the New Testament
NIGTC	New International Greek Testament Commentary
NJBC	*New Jerome Biblical Commentary*
NovT	*Novum Testamentum*
NTD	Das Neue Testament Deutsch
NTG	New Testament Guide
NTM	New Testament Message
NTS	*New Testament Studies*
NTSR	New Testament for Spiritual Reading
NTT	New Testament Theology
ODCC	*The Oxford Dictionary of the Christian Church*
OTP	J.H. Charlesworth, *The Old Testament Pseudepigrapha* (2 vols.; vol. I, London: Darton, Longman & Todd, 1983; vol. II, New York: Doubleday, 1985)

PCB	Peake's Commentary on the Bible
PIASH	Publications of the Israel Academy of Sciences and Humanities
P. Oxy.	B.P. Grenfell, A.S. Hunt *et al.* (eds.), *Oxyrhynchus Papyri* (1898–)
SB	*Studia Biblica*
SBLDS	Society of Biblical Literature Dissertation Series
SBLSCSS	Society of Biblical Literature Septuagint and Cognate Studies Series
SBLSPS	*Society of Biblical Literature Seminar Papers Series*
SBM	Stuttgarter biblische Monographien
SBS	Sources for Biblical Study
SBU	Symbolae Biblicae Upsalienses
SE	*Studia Evangelica*
SHR	Studies in the History of Religions
SIHC	Studies in the International History of Christianity
SJLA	Studies in Judaism in Late Antiquity
SJT	*Scottish Journal of Theology*
SJTOP	Scottish Journal of Theology Occasional Papers
SNT	Studien zum Neuen Testament
SNTIW	Studies of the New Testament and Its World
SNTSMS	Society for New Testament Studies Monograph Series
SPS	Sacra Pagina Series
NovTSup	*Novum Testamentum*, Supplements
TB	*Tyndale Bulletin*
TDNT	G. Kittel and G. Friedrich (eds.), *Theological Dictionary of the New Testament* (trans. G. Bromiley; 10 vols.; Grand Rapids: Eerdmans, 1964–1976)
THKNT	Theologischer Handkommentar zum Neuen Testament
TNTC	Tyndale New Testament Commentaries
TS	*Texts and Studies: Contributions to Biblical and Patristic Literature*
TU	*Texte und Untersuchungen*
TUGAL	Texte und Untersuchungen zur Geschichte der Altchristlichen Literatur
TWOT	*Theological Wordbook of the Old Testament*
UBS	K. Aland *et al.* (eds.), *The Greek New Testament* (New York: United Bible Societies, 4th edn)
USQR	*Union Seminary Quarterly Review*
WBC	Word Biblical Commentary
WC	Westminster Commentaries
WUNT	Wissenschaftliche Untersuchungen zum Neuen Testament
ZAW	*Zeitschrift für die Alttestamentliche Wissenschaft*
ZB	Zürcher Bibelkommentare
ZNW	*Zeitschrift für die Neutestamentliche Wissenschaft*

3. *Old Testament Pseudepigrapha and Apocrypha*

Apoc. Abr.	*Apocalypse of Abraham*
Apoc. El.	*Apocalypse of Elijah*
Apoc. Mos.	*Apocalypse of Moses*
5 Apocry. Syr. Pss.	*5 Apocryphal Syriac Psalms*
Asc. Isa.	*Martyrdom and Ascension of Isaiah*
1 Bar.	*1 Baruch* (Apocrypha)
2, 3 Bar.	*2, 3 Baruch*, i.e. Syriac, Greek *Apocalypse of Baruch*
Cave Tre.	*Cave of Treasures*

1, 2, 3 Enoch	Ethiopic, Slavonic, Hebrew *Enoch*
4 Ezra	*4 Ezra, or 2 Esdras*
Gk. Apoc. Ezra	Greek *Apocalypse of Ezra*
JA	*Joseph and Aseneth*
Jud.	*Judith* (Apocrypha)
Jub.	*Book of Jubilees*
Ladd. Jacob	*Ladder of Jacob*
1 Macc.	*1 Maccabees* (Apocrypha)
Pss. David	*More Psalms of David*
Pss. Sol.	*Psalms of Solomon*
Quest. Ezra	*Questions of Ezra*
Sib. Ora.	*The Sibylline Oracles*
Sir.	*Book of Sirach*, or *Ecclesiasticus* (Apocrypha)
Test. Levi	*Testament of Levi*
Vita	*Vita Adae et Evae*
Wisd. Sol.	*Wisdom of Solomon* (Apocrypha)

4. *Qumran Writings, Dead Sea Scrolls*

| 1 QpHab | Commentary on Habbakuk |
| 11 Qps[a] | Psalms Scroll a from Qumran Cave 11 |

5. *Classical and Hellenistic Sources*

Apuleius
    Metam.   *Metamorphoses*

Josephus
    Ant.   *Jewish Antiquities*

Cicero
    Amic.   *Amicitia*
    Epis. Att.   *Epistulae ad Atticum*
    Orat.   *De Oratore*
    Philipp.   *Philippics*
    Pis.   *In Pisonem*
    Sest.   *Sestio*

Ovid
    Fasti   *Fasti*

Philo
    Abr.   *De Abrahamo*
    Aet. Mun.   *De aeternitate mundi*
    Agr.   *De Agricultura*
    Cher.   *De Cherubim*
    Conf. Ling.   *De confusione linguarum*
    Decal.   *De Decalogo*
    Ebr.   *De Ebrietate*
    Flac.   *In Flaccum*
    Fuga   *De fuga et inventione*
    Gig.   *De gigantibus*

Ios.	*De Iosepho*
Leg. Al.	*Legum Allegoriae*
Leg. Gai.	*Legatio ad Gaium*
Mig. Abr.	*De migratione Abrahami*
Mut. Nom.	*De mutatione nominum*
Op. Mun.	*De opificio mundi*
Praem.	*De Praemiis et Poenis*
Quae. Gen.	*Quaestiones et solutiones in Genesim*
Quod Det.	*Quod deterius potiori insidiari soleat*
Quod Deus	*Quod deus sit immutabilis*
Sacr.	*De Sacrificiis Abelis et Caini*
Som.	*De Somniis*
Spec. Leg.	*De Specialibus Legibus*
Virt.	*De Virtutibus*
Vita Mos.	*De vita Mosis*

Plato
Crat.	*Cratylus*
Gorg.	*Gorgias*

Pliny
Epis.	*Epistulae*

Plutarch
Is. Osir.	*De Iside et Osiride*

Seneca
Epis.	*Epistulae*

Suetonius
Claud.	*Claudius*

6. *New Testament Apocrypha and Early Christian Literature*

Act. Thom.	*Acts of Thomas*
Apos. Trad.	Hippolytus, *Apostolic Tradition*
Cate. Myst.	Cyril, *Catechesis Mystagogica*
Contra Cels.	Origen, *Contra Celsum* (*Against Celsus*)
Epis. Fab.	Jerome, *Epistle to Fabiola*
Gos. Phil.	*Gospel of Philip*
Gos. Thom.	*Gospel of Thomas*
HPrl	*The Hymn of the Pearl* (in *Act. Thom.*)
Herm. *Sim.*	Hermas, *Similitudes* (one part of the *Shepherd* of Hermas)

7. *Targums, Mishnaic and Talmudic Literature, and Other Rabbinic Works*

Targums
Tg. Ps.-J.	Talgum *Pseudo-Jonathan*
Tg. Yer.	Targum *Yerušalmi*

Mishnaic and Talmudic Literature
b. B. Bat.	Babylonian Talmud *Baba Batra*

b. Ber.	Babylonian Talmud *Berakot*
y. Ber.	Jerusalem Talmud *Berakot*
'Ed.	*'Eduyyot*
Ḥagi	*Ḥagiga*
Kelim	*Kelim*
Meg.	*Megilla*
b. Menaḥ.	Babylonian Talmud *Menaḥot*
Pesaḥ.	*Pesaḥim*
Šabb.	*Šabbat*
b. Soṭa	Babylonian Talmud *Soṭa*
b. Yebam.	Babylonian Talmud *Yebamot*

Other Rabbinic Works

'Abot R. Nat.	*'Abot de Rabbi Nathan*
Cant. Rab.	*Canticles Rabbah*
Gen. Rab.	*Genesis Rabbah*
Lam. Rab.	*Lamentations Rabbah*
Lev. Rab.	*Leviticus Rabbah*
Num. Rab.	*Numbers Rabbah*
Pesiq. Rab Kah.	*Pesiqta de Rab Kahana*
Pirqe R. El.	*Pirqe Rabbi Eliezer*
Yal.	*Yalquṭ*

GENERAL INTRODUCTION

In the Pauline corpus the imagery of clothing is both significant and worthy of the attention of any serious biblical student. It occurs in most of the major Pauline[1] letters, viz. 1 Thess. 5.8 (ἐνδυσάμενοι); Gal. 3.27 (ἐνδύσασθε); 1 Cor. 15.49 (ἐφορέσαμεν), 53 (ἐνδύσασθαι [twice]), 54 (ἐνδυσάμενοι [twice]); 2 Cor. 5.2 (ἐπενδύσασθαι),[2] 3 (ἐνδυσάμενοι), 4 (ἐπενδύσασθαι); Rom. 13.12 (ἐνδυσώμεθα); Col. 3.9-10 (ἀπεκδυσάμενοι/ἐνδυσάμενοι), 12 (ἐνδύσασθε); and Eph. 4.22-24 (ἀποθέσθαι/ἐνδύσασθαι), 6.11 (ἐνδύσασθε), 14 (ἐνδυσάμενοι). Of these passages, the clothing images in 1 Thess. 5.8, Rom. 13.12 and Eph. 6.11, 14 refer to a believer's spiritual armour and therefore seem to be a different metaphor from that of the other passages, which focus either on a decisive change in a believer's identity (Gal. 3.27; Rom. 13.14; Col. 3.9-10, 12; Eph. 4.22-24) or in his or her mode of existence (1 Cor. 15.49, 50-54; 2 Cor. 5.1-4). The present study concentrates on the clothing imagery in these latter passages rather than that in the armour passages.

The texts which we intend to deal with are significant theologically. In Gal. 3.27, Rom. 13.14, Col. 3.9-10 and Eph. 4.22-24, the clothing imagery probably describes the baptismal[3] change in a Christian's nature from the perspective of the typology of Adam and Christ.[4] Furthermore, the contextual emphases in each passage affect the significance of the imagery. For instance, in Gal. 3, soteriological elements are dominant in the clothing imagery in 3.27, and eschatological elements are important in the passages before and after 3.26-29.[5] In Rom. 13.11-14, eschatological and ethical elements are emphasized.[6] In Col. 3.9-10 both eschatological and ethical elements are influential.[7] In Eph. 4.22, 23 ethical elements are repeatedly underlined.[8]

---

1.   For the purpose of this thesis, in which I intend to deal with the clothing imagery in Gal. 3.27, Rom. 13.14, Col. 3.9-10, Eph. 4.22-24, 1 Cor. 15.49, 50-54 and 2 Cor. 5.1-4, the adjective 'Pauline' will be used in the sense of 'of Paul's thought' or 'suggesting the name of Paul as the author'. Current scholarship accepts Galatians, Romans, and 1 and 2 Corinthians as authentic, but there is debate about the authenticity of Colossians and Ephesians. Concerning the problem of the last two epistles' authorship, see Chapters 9, §§2.1 and §§3.1, where I express my own view. All biblical citations, unless otherwise stated, are taken from the RSV.

2.   It would be reasonable to regard this word ἐπενδύω in 2 Cor. 5.2, 4 as belonging to the same category to which the word ἐνδύω in other passages also belongs. Ἐπενδύω seems to bring a specific theological nuance, concerning which, see Chapter 10, §§3.3.2 and 3.3.3.

3.   See Chapter 8, §§2.3.2 and 3.3.2; 9, §§2.3.2 and 3.3.2.

4.   See Chapter 8, §§2.3.5 and 3.3.4; 9, §§2.3.4 and 3.3.3.

5.   See Chapter 8, §2.4.

6.   See Chapter 8, §§3.4.2 and 3.4.3.

7.   See Chapter 9, §2.4.

8.   See Chapter 9, §3.4.2.

In 1 Cor. 15.49, 50-54 and 2 Cor. 5.1-4, clothing imagery delineates the eschatological transformation of the Christian's body into a glorious resurrection body. Behind these Corinthian passages the Adam–Christ analogy seems to operate.[9]

Our brief observation of the passages from these six Pauline letters implies that the clothing imagery is of profound consequence in Pauline theology. The imagery relates to the entirety of the Christian's life, as it speaks of a baptismal change in his identity, an ethical change in his practical life, and the resurrection transfiguration of his mode of existence.

Despite this importance, however, no comprehensive study of the Pauline clothing imagery has yet been undertaken. The references to this imagery are only found in commentaries, dictionaries, short articles, and various other books, in a summary fashion. Specifically, in his article, 'Theologie des Kleides', E. Peterson attempts to investigate the theological significance of the relationship of a human being with a garment. He asserts that the question of the relationship of man with clothing is not merely an ethical issue but a metaphysical and theological problem.[10] He argues that the biblical story of the original state and fall of Adam and Eve should be a starting point for a theological consideration of the relation of a person to clothing.[11] He believes that the Bible presents Adam and Eve as originally having been clothed with God's glory, which is a comprehensive term for divine justice, innocence and immortality, but that they lost it because of their fall; however, this lost dress is recovered by believers at baptism.[12] On the basis of this hypothesis, Peterson argues that believers are restored to the original Adamic state in baptism; he sees Gal. 3.27 as referring to believers' being endued with Christ by participating in his death and resurrection in that liturgical act.[13] Peterson's opinion provides us with significant insight into the Pauline theology of clothing, but he does not note the issue of the believers' resurrection, which must have a bearing on the ultimate recovery of the lost dress of glory. Basically, I agree with Peterson, so I would like to prove his point by scrutinizing the Pauline clothing passages more fully.

Whereas Peterson's essay has not been significantly noted, P.W. Van der Horst's article, 'Observations on a Pauline Expression',[14] is more frequently recognized,[15] although his viewpoint is rarely supported by other scholars. Van der Horst does not believe that the origins of the Pauline clothing metaphor can be found in the mystery religions or gnosticism; for him, none of the parallels cited from such sources is (1) pre-Christian, (2) identical with the Pauline putting off/on metaphor, which refers to 'dying and rising with Christ in baptism', or (3) has *man* as the

---

9. See Chapter 10, §§2.3 and 3.3.
10. E. Peterson, 'Theologie des Kleides', *BM* 16 (1934), pp. 347-56 (347).
11. Peterson, 'Theologie des Kleides', pp. 347-48.
12. Peterson, 'Theologie des Kleides', pp. 349-50, 353.
13. Peterson, 'Theologie des Kleides', pp. 353-57.
14. P.W. Van der Horst, 'Short Studies: Observations on a Pauline Expression', *NTS* 19 (1972–73), pp. 181-87.
15. For example, G. Cannon, *The Use of Traditional Materials in Colossians* (Macon: Mercer University Press, 1983), p. 72; J.D.G. Dunn, *The Epistles to the Colossians and to Philemon* (NIGTC; Grand Rapids: Eerdmans, 1996), p. 220.

object of the putting off/on. The second point is a valuable insight.[16] But the first one is not entirely valid, since even later sources can reflect the ideas of an earlier era. Concerning the third point, it should be remembered that the Pauline clothing verbs do not always take a person as their object. Drawing attention to the ancient story of Pyrrho (c. 360–270 BC) and the dog,[17] Van der Horst imagines that it is probably a source for the expression of putting off and putting on in Colossians, which describes baptism.[18] His understanding of the Colossians passage itself seems to be quite correct, but his argument that Pyrrho's anecdote is its origin is scarcely right. Pyrrho's saying 'putting off the man' indicates eliminating the contradiction caused by human weakness rather than a fundamental transfiguration from the old nature to a new one through being united with a different being.[19] Moreover, in Pyrrho's saying neither the baptismal element nor the concept of 'putting on' is found.

M. Thompson's *Clothed with Christ*[20] would seem, by its title, to concentrate on uncovering the meaning of the Pauline metaphor of putting on Christ. But in this monograph, in fact, Thompson's major concern is with clarifying whether and how the so-called Jesus tradition serves Paul's ethics particularly in Rom. 12.1–15.13. He, therefore, assigns only a few pages to the concept of putting on the Lord Jesus Christ (13.14), and even in them he does not focus on clarifying its significance.[21] For the most part he refers only to parallel passages, specifically Gal. 3.27, Col. 3.12, as well as to 1 Cor. 15.53, 54 and 2 Cor. 5.3. He seems to be correct when he argues that 'behind the two ways of life contrasted in [Rom.] 13.12-13 stand two dominions that war against each other—the old reign of sin through the flesh that leads to death, and the Lordship of Christ which through the Spirit breaks the power of sin and leads to life in this age and in the age to come (Rom. 6-8; Gal. 5)'.[22] But Thompson does not speak of how this ethical aspect affects the significance of putting on Christ (Rom. 13.14). He does not suggest a probable connection of this metaphor with baptismal ideas in 6.1-6 or with the reference to the analogy between Christ and Adam in 5.12-21.[23]

Thompson stresses that Rom. 13.11-14 has to be understood not only from an eschatological and baptismal outlook (cf. 12.1-2) but also from a christological viewpoint. This opinion itself sounds reasonable, but he does not properly present

16. Van der Horst, 'Observations on a Pauline Expression', pp. 181-82.
17. See R.D. Hicks (trans.), *Diogenes Laertius*, II (Cambridge: Harvard University Press; London: William Heinemann, 1970), pp. 475-79. This document contains the following story: one day a dog attacked Pyrrho, the founder of the Skeptic school, who fled into a tree, behaviour at odds with his convictions. When he was ridiculed by those who had witnessed this contradictory behaviour, he admitted his failure and excused himself by saying, 'χαλεπὸν εἴη ὁλοσχερῶς ἐκδῦναι τὸν ἄνθρωπον' ('it was not entirely easy to strip oneself of human weakness').
18. Van der Horst, 'Observations on a Pauline Expression', pp. 184-87.
19. See Chapter 9, §2.3.
20. M. Thompson, *Clothed with Christ: The Example and Teaching of Jesus in Romans 12.1–15.13* (JSNTSup, 59; Sheffield: JSOT Press, 1991).
21. Thompson, *Clothed with Christ*, pp. 149-58.
22. Thompson, *Clothed with Christ*, p. 149.
23. A detailed discussion on this issue will be given in Chapter 8, §§3.3.2 and 3.3.4.

what the christological understanding of the passage is. Only by suggesting a link between Rom. 13.11-14 and Gal. 3.27 and Col. 3.10 (cf. Eph. 4.24) does he imply that the 'clothing with Christ' imagery in Romans is connected with baptism and the Adam–Christ contrast. However, when Romans itself contains these implications, appealing to parallels in other epistles does not seem to do justice to the pericope. But despite the deficiencies of his approach, he is led to a notable conclusion: 'Given Paul's tendency to exalt Christ (cf. 1 Cor. 1.30), the meaning of "putting on Christ" should not be limited to one particular expression, but in view of the verb's background, when used figuratively it surely points to adoption of his mind, character and conduct—distinguished from mere imitation by the presence and work of his Spirit'.[24]

At any rate, we do not find a sufficient treatment of the significance of the Pauline clothing imagery from these writings, though they do contain highly valuable insights. This underlines the necessity for a deeper and more detailed consideration of pericopes in the Pauline corpus which include clothing imagery. As has already been implied, the present study intends to unveil the significance of the Pauline clothing imagery by focusing on the following six passages: Gal. 3.27; Rom. 13.14; Col. 3.9-10; Eph. 4.22-24; 1 Cor. 15.49, 50-54; and 2 Cor. 5.1-4.

To achieve this goal, in Part I we will first examine the history-of-religions background to the Pauline imagery of clothing. A scrutiny of the imagery's origin may illuminate its significance. As the clothing imagery in the Pauline corpus involves a number of significant ideas,[25] it would be inappropriate to attempt to discover a single source for all of them. Rather, it is likely that the imagery emanates from many different sources. Accordingly, it is necessary to explore how the clothing image is used in many different documents of antiquity.

First of all, we will concentrate on the meaning of clothing images in the Old Testament, specifically the traditions about Adam's clothing (which is seen in Gen. 3.21), the priest's clothing (which is found chiefly in various places in Exodus and Leviticus and in Ezek. 42.13-14; 44.19; Zech. 3.3-5), God's clothing (which appears in Judg. 6.34; 1 Chron. 12.18; 2 Chron. 24.20) and cosmological clothing (which is found in Ps. 102.26; Isa. 51.6; cf. Heb. 1.11-12). This investigation will give us invaluable insight into clothing imagery in the Pauline corpus. Secondly, we will examine the significance of clothing imagery as used in several later Jewish documents. For this, we will attempt to explicate the meaning of clothing imagery in *1* and *2 Enoch*, *The Books of Adam and Eve*, Philo and rabbinic literature. Thirdly, we will look into *Joseph and Aseneth*, which contains expressive clothing images depicting Aseneth's conversion to Judaism. Fourthly, we will also attempt to elucidate the significance of various clothing images in *The Hymn of the Pearl*, which is a small section of *The Acts of Thomas*. Fifthly, we will attempt to clarify the meaning of the clothing imagery in the mystery religions, especially as these are

24. Thompson, *Clothed with Christ*, p. 158.
25. E.g. putting on Christ by being baptized into Christ (Gal. 3.27), putting on the armour of light and of Christ (Rom. 13.11, 14), putting on the new man (Col. 3.10; Eph. 4.24), putting on Christian virtues (Col. 3.12), putting on the full armour of God (Eph. 6.11-17) and putting on the resurrection body (1 Cor. 15.49, 50-54; 2 Cor. 5.1-4).

reflected in Lucius Apuleius' *Metamorphoses* (XI), which employs several clothing images to describe the protagonist's anthropological transformation. Sixthly, we will briefly consider the Roman apparel, the *toga virilis*. Finally, we will investigate the baptismal practices in the primitive church, consulting the earliest materials that include a reference to baptism. All these documents will provide abundant insight into the significance of the Pauline clothing imagery. Each item will be dealt with in a separate chapter.[26]

In dealing with these ancient documents, the late date of them, except for the Old Testament, is problematic.[27] However, as Van der Horst argues, this point should not be pressed, for later documents may reflect earlier traditions.[28] If a theme consistently and repeatedly occurs in intertestamental literature, it is probable that it echoes an earlier tradition, whether this tradition was in oral form or in a document that is now lost. As R. Scroggs argues, the oral tradition of the Jewish community was probably 'both persistent and widespread throughout the centuries surrounding Paul'.[29] If our view of the relation of non-biblical documents to the Pauline corpus is acceptable, the former may be worthy of being considered in probing the latter. Such a viewpoint could be applied even to non-Jewish documents, for example, Apuleius' *Metamorphoses*, which seems to reflect a very ancient practice of Isiac initiation. It is also probable that secular clothing customs of the Graeco-Roman world, such as the wearing of a *toga*, are reflected in Pauline clothing imagery, particularly in the clothing-with-a-person metaphor.

After considering the above-mentioned documents starting with the Old Testament, we will turn, in Part II, to the Pauline clothing passages themselves. In so doing, we will divide these passages into three parts: (1) Gal. 3.27 and Rom. 13.14, which refer to clothing with Christ; (2) Col. 3.9-10 and Eph. 4.22-24, where the concept of putting off the old man and putting on the new man is prominent; (3) 1 Cor. 15.49, 50-54 and 2 Cor. 5.1-4, which speak of being clothed with a resurrection body. Gal. 3.27, Rom. 13.14, Col. 3.9-10 and Eph. 4.22-24 evidently draw from the same fund of ideas. The first two categories share the metaphor of clothing-with-a-person. C.H. Dodd in his comment on Col. 3.10 asserts that the idea of putting on the new man is not very different from the concept of putting on Christ in Gal. 3.27.[30] Moreover, both metaphors share a background in baptism and in the analogy

---

26. The third item (that is, the clothing imagery in *Joseph and Aseneth*) could have been included in the second item. But since it contains many crucial clothing images, it will be treated in a separate chapter.

27. Much of apocryphal and pseudepigraphal documents are contemporary with or later than Paul, and 'no written rabbinic materials existed until probably at least a century after Paul's death'; see R. Scroggs, *The Last Adam: A Study in Pauline Anthropology* (Oxford: Blackwell, 1966), p. 16.

28. Van der Horst, 'Observations on a Pauline Expression', p. 181.

29. Scroggs, *The Last Adam*, pp. 16-17. Scroggs adds that 'Philo's discussion of Adam proves, for example, that he knew rabbinic teaching of which we know nothing from rabbinic literature itself until later' (Scroggs, *The Last Adam*, p. 17).

30. C.H. Dodd, 'Colossians', in F.C. Eiselen *et al.* (eds.), *ABC* (New York: Abingdon, 1929), pp. 1250-262 (1259).

between Adam and Christ.[31] We may, therefore, argue that the four passages express the same theme within the Pauline theology of clothing. In both cases the clothing-with-a-person metaphor describes the believer's inward change in union with Christ.

Yet it needs to be recognized that in nuance the concept of 'clothing with Christ' in Gal. 3.27 and Rom. 13.14 is slightly different from the concept of 'the new man' in Col. 3.9-10 and Eph. 4.22-24. While the former passages stress a believer's union with Christ itself, the latter seems to emphasize what kind of human being he or she becomes when he or she is united with Christ. Gal. 3.27 and Rom. 13.14 use the single metaphor 'putting on Christ', while Col. 3.9-10 and Eph. 4.22-24 use the double metaphor 'putting off the old man/putting on the new man'. It will, therefore, be reasonable to deal with each pair separately.

1 Cor. 15.49, 50-54 and 2 Cor. 5.1-4 deal with the same issue, that is, what the future mode of Christian existence will be, and so belong to the same category. The ideas that form the metaphor of clothing with the resurrection body in 1 Corinthians 15 are different from those in 2 Corinthians. But as these Corinthian chapters concentrate on the same issue, it will be natural to consider them together.

To each of the suggested three categories of the Pauline clothing-with-a-person passages a separate chapter will be assigned.

---

31. See Chapter 8, §§2.3.2; 2.3.5; 3.3.2; 3.3.4; Chapter 9, §§2.3.2; 2.3.4; 3.3.2; 3.3.3.

Part I

Clothing Imagery in its History-of-Religions Background

INTRODUCTION TO PART I

The intention of Part I is to investigate the history-of-religions background to the imagery of clothing. A close inquiry into this will be preparation for the interpretation of the clothing passages in the Pauline corpus. In Chapter 1, we will investigate the clothing imagery in the OT. There is a strong probability that the Pauline metaphor is connected with OT documents that use various clothing ideas, whether literally or figuratively.

In dealing with OT clothing passages, we will divide them into four categories: (1) Adam's garment, (2) priestly garments, (3) God's garment, and (4) a cosmological garment. In relation to Adam's garment, we will focus on Gen. 3.21, where Adam and Eve are clothed with garments of skins. Regarding the priestly garments, we will look into the passages that refer to the ritual of putting off and putting on the priestly garments, for example Exod. 29.4-9 (par. 40.12-15); Lev. 6.10-11; 16.3-4, 23-24; Ezek. 42.13-14; 44.19. We will also look into the contrast between taking off a filthy robe and putting on a new one (Zech. 3.3-5). Concerning God's garment, we will investigate the passages that describe the unity between God and a human being using the concept of God's clothing himself with a specific person (Judg. 6.34; 1 Chron. 12.18; 2 Chron. 24.20). In connection with a cosmological garment, we will briefly examine Ps. 102.26 where the concept of clothing is combined with the idea of change.

In Chapter 2, we will consider various Jewish writings, that is, *1* and *2 Enoch*, *The Books of Adam and Eve*, the works of Philo, and some rabbinic literature. Many parallels between the Pauline clothing metaphors and these Jewish writings suggest that the former also draws on Jewish traditions which subsequently turned up in those documents. In *1 Enoch* 62.15-16 and *2 Enoch* 22.8-10, transformation from an earthly to a heavenly mode of existence is described by the metaphor of a change of clothes.[1] *Apoc. Mos.* 20–21 refers to Adam and Eve's pre-Fall clothing, the motif of which seems to be significant in the Pauline clothing metaphor. Philo, moreover, speaks of a person's being clothed with virtue (cf. *Quae. Gen.* i.53; *Leg. Al.* ii.53, 64; *Ebr.* 7; *Quod Det.* 42).[2] A view of the high priest's garments such as the one found in Philo (cf. *Vita Mos.* ii.131; *Som.* i.214, 215, 218; ii.133, 135) seems also to be reflected in some aspects of Pauline clothing imagery. The idea in rabbinic literature that Adam was dressed with radiance before the Fall seems to

---

1.   This is similar to the way in which the clothing imagery both in 1 Cor. 15 and in 2 Cor. 5 depicts how a believer's present body will be changed at the parousia; see Chapter 10.

2.   This could be compared with the concept of a believer's being clothed with Christian virtue (particularly in Col. 3.12), although the former is linked with a human being's ethical destiny, while the latter is related to the believer's change of nature through being united with Christ.

reflect other ancient Jewish Adam traditions in which the same idea was prominent, and such traditions may also be reflected in the Pauline clothing imagery.

In Chapters 3 and 4, we will consider the clothing imagery both in *Joseph and Aseneth* and in *The Hymn of the Pearl*, where various kinds of garments, which symbolize their wearer's identity, provide useful insights into Pauline clothing imagery.

In Chapter 5 we will investigate the clothing imagery in *Metamorphoses*. The symbolism of Lucius' attire in several scenes seems to reflect the very ancient practice of initiation in the Isis cult.[3] If Paul recognized the symbolic import given to clothing in other religions, it cannot be totally ruled out that he bore in mind just such a ritual of initiation when he created his own clothing metaphor. In *Metamorphoses*, every important step of the initiate's inward change is symbolized by his changing garments; the change culminates in his identification with Isis signified by his being attired in the garb of the goddess shortly after the climactic initiation ceremony.[4]

In Chapter 6, we will look into Roman apparel; the ceremony at which the Roman male, on reaching the age of sixteen, replaced his boyhood garment with one which denoted manhood, is probably also reflected in the Pauline clothing imagery (particularly in Gal. 3.27), because one important aspect of what the latter depicts is a believer's radical change in his or her status. Regarding Gal. 3.27, some argue that the idea of putting on Christ is analogous to the Roman practice of donning the *toga virilis* as a token of the transition from boyhood to manhood.[5]

In Chapter 7, we will examine the practices of baptism in the early church. The Pauline clothing metaphor seems to be significantly connected with the early church's baptismal practice, which is reflected in passages such as *Gos. Thom.* 37, *Apos. Trad.* 21, *Gos. Phil.* 101 and *Epis. Fab.* 19.

All these background materials deepen our understanding of the Pauline clothing metaphors. They provide a number of crucial concepts which are important when seeking the meaning of the Pauline clothing metaphors, although all the concepts are not found in each of the Pauline clothing passages. A detailed investigation of each relevant background passage will bear out these generalizations.

---

3.   Cf. Plutarch, *Is. Osir.* 352 B; Philo, *Fuga* 110.

4.   Apuleius, *Metam.* XI.24.

5.   J.A. Bengel, *Gnomon of the New Testament*, IV (Edinburgh: T. & T. Clark, 1858), p. 30; C.J. Allen (ed.), *2 Corinthians-Philemon* (BBC, 11; Nashville: Broadman, 1971), pp. 102-103; cf. F. Rendall, 'The Epistle to the Galatians', in W.R. Nicoll (ed.), *EGT*, III (London: Hodder & Stoughton, 1917), pp. 123-200 (174); J. Dow, 'Galatians', in F.C. Eiselen *et al.* (eds.), *ABC* (New York: Abingdon, 1929), pp. 1207-221 (1215).

Chapter 1

CLOTHING IMAGERY IN THE OLD TESTAMENT

1. *Introduction*

In the Old Testament the image of clothing occurs extensively in a wide range of books.[1] Its use is sometimes literal and sometimes figurative. It is often formed by 'garment' language with no use of clothing verbs.[2] But in most cases, clothing verbs play a crucial role in forming the clothing imagery. In the Masoretic Text the dominant clothing verb, which the LXX renders ἐνδύω,[3] is לבשׁ in various forms of qal, hiphil, pual, peal, and aphel.[4] In the LXX other major clothing verbs are ἀμφιάζω,[5] ἐνδιδύσκω,[6] εἰλέω,[7] ἐπιτίθημι,[8] περιβάλλω,[9] ζωννύω[10] or περιζωννύω,[11] περιτίθημι,[12] φορέω[13] and ὑποδύω.[14]

---

1. In this chapter we will deal with the clothing passages which come from the Canonical Hebrew OT texts only. The clothing imagery based on the Apocrypha or Pseudepigrapha will be treated separately in Chapters 2 and 3.

2. For instance, Ps. 102.26 and Isa. 51.6 include important clothing imagery, but they do not use a clothing-verb. Regarding the clothing imagery in these passages, see Chapter 1, §5.

3. E.g. Gen. 3.22 [21, HB]; 27.15; 38.19; 41.42; Exod. 28.36-37 [40-41, HB]; 29.5; 40.13-14; Lev. 6.10-11 [3-4, HB]; 16.23-24, 32; 21.10; Num. 20.26, 28; Deut. 22.11; Judg. 6.34; 1 Kgs 17.5, 38; 2 Kgs 14.2; 3 Kgs 22.30; 1 Chron. 12.18; 2 Chron. 6.41; 24.20; 28.15; Esth. 4.1; Job 8.22; 10.11; 29.14; 39.19; Pss. 34 [35, HB].26; 92 [93, HB].1; 103 [104, HB].1; 108 [109, HB].18; 131 [132, HB].9, 16, 18; Prov. 23.21; 31.21; Song 5.3; Isa. 22.21; 49.18; 50.3; 51.9; 59.17; 61.10; Ezek. 7.27; 9.2; 16.10; 23.6; 38.4; 42.14; Jon. 3.5; Zeph. 1.8; Zech. 3.4 [3, HB], 5 [4, HB], 6 [5, HB]; 13.4.

4. D.A. Oepke, 'δύω κτλ', *TDNT*, II (1964), pp. 318-21 (319). Other Hebrew words which are rendered ἐνδύω in the LXX are חָגַר (2 Sam. 6.14), נָתַן (Lev. 8.7) and עָלָה (Ezek. 44.17). There are also examples in which the noun form לְבוּשׁ is rendered by the verbal form ἐνδύω in the LXX Ps. 34 [35, HB].13; Prov. 31.25; Jer. 10.9; see E. Hatch and H.A. Redpath, *A Concordance to the Septuagint*, I (Grand Rapids: Baker, 1987 [orig. Oxford: Clarendon, 1897]), p. 471.

5. E.g. Job 29.14; 40.5 [10, HB]; cf. 31.19.

6. E.g. 2 Kgs 1.24; 13.18; Prov. 31.21.

7. E.g. Isa. 11.5.

8. E.g. Zech. 3.6 [5, HB].

9. E.g. Gen. 24.65; 38.14, 19; 41.42; Est. 5.1; Pss. 70 [71, HB].13; 72 [73, HB].6; 108 [109, HB].19, 29; 146 [147, HB].8; Isa. 4.1a; 59.17; Ezek. 16.10; 27.7; Jon. 3.6; Mic. 7.10; Zech. 3.6 [5, HB].

10. E.g. Isa. 11.5.

11. E.g. Pss. 17 [18, HB].32, 39; 29 [30, HB].11; 64 [65, HB].6, 12; 92 [93, HB].1; 108 [109, HB].19; Isa. 3.24b; Jer. 4.8; 30 [49, HB].3.

12. E.g. Gen. 41.42; Job 13.26; 39.19, 20; Isa. 59.17; Ezek. 16.11; 27.3, 4, 7.

In the Old Testament clothing imagery is used with a number of different meanings. First, it can connote the covering over of Adam and his wife's nakedness, about which they became ashamed after the Fall and which was probably related to their spiritual death.[15] God's clothing of Adam and Eve with garments of skins (Gen. 3.21) belongs to this category. Secondly, it can symbolize a wearer's social status and role.[16] Being attired with royal garments,[17] widow's clothes,[18] mourning clothes,[19] sackcloth,[20] the first-born son's fine raiment,[21] a hairy garment,[22] armour[23] and priestly garments[24] all fall into this category. Thirdly, it can symbolize a wearer's inner or outer characteristics: God's Spirit being clothed with an individual human being,[25] God or man being clothed with honour and majesty, strength, light[26] or salvation[27] and righteousness,[28] shame,[29] glory and splendour,[30] joy,[31] despair,[32] cursing,[33] skin and flesh,[34] terror,[35] gladness[36] and darkness.[37] Fourthly, it can also stand for a wearer's allegiance to the principle of one true God, keeping him/herself separate from all idols and idolatry. Clothing with unmixed fabric[38] is included in this category. Finally, it can also signify a critical change of the cosmos from the

13. E.g. Prov. 16.23.

14. E.g. Ezek. 16.10.

15. This will be dealt with in Chapter 1, §2 in detail.

16. See D.R. Edwards, 'Dress and Ornamentation', in D.N. Freedman *et al.* (eds.), *ABD*, II (New York: Doubleday, 1992), pp. 232-38 (232).

17. E.g. Gen. 41.42; 1 Kgs 22.30 (par. 2 Chron. 18.29); Est. 5.1; Ezek. 16.8-13; 23.6; cf. 23.12.

18. Gen. 38.19.

19. 2 Sam. 14.2.

20. Esth. 4.1; Jon. 3.5.

21. Gen. 27.15.

22. Zech. 13.4: וְלֹא יִלְבְּשׁוּ אַדֶּרֶת שֵׂעָר לְמַעַן כַּחֵשׁ, 'they shall not put on a garment of hair in order to deceive' (my rendering). This means that the deceitful prophets would not put on a prophet's garment of hair in order to conceal their status. This differs from the LXX text: καὶ ἐνδύσονται δέρριν τριχίνην, ἀνθ᾽ ὧν ἐψεύσαντο, 'they shall clothe themselves with a hairy garment, as they have deceived themselves' (my rendering), which probably means that prophets would continue to wear a hairy mantle as a symbol of their status, as they had lied by being dressed in it. Despite this difference, both concur in pointing out the deceptiveness of prophets.

23. 1 Sam. 17.5, 38; Ezek. 38.4.

24. Exod. 28; 29.4-9 (par. 40.12-15); Lev. 6.3-4; 16.3-4, 23-24; Ezek. 9.2 (cf. 9.3, 11; 10.2, 6, 7); 42.14; Dan. 10.5; Zech. 3.3-5.

25. Judg. 6.34; 1 Chron. 12.18; 2 Chron. 24.20. See Chapter 1, §4.

26. Job 40.10; Pss. 93.1a; 104.1// Pss. 18.32, 39; 65.6; 93.1b; Isa. 51.9; 52.1// Ps. 104.2.

27. 2 Chron. 6.41; Ps. 132.16; Isa. 61.10.

28. Job 29.14; Ps. 132.9; Isa. 59.17; 61.10.

29. Job 8.22; cf. Pss. 35.26; 109.29; 132.18; Mic. 7.10.

30. Job 40.10.

31. Ps. 30.11.

32. Ezek. 7.27.

33. Ps. 109.18.

34. Job 10.11.

35. Job 39.19.

36. Ps. 65.12.

37. Isa. 50.3; cf. Ps. 147.8.

38. Deut. 22.11; cf. Lev. 19.19.

present to the future state. The concept of the cosmos' wearing out like a garment and of its being replaced[39] is ascribed to this category.

In addition, the clothing imagery also portrays a human being's escape from the horror of nakedness.[40] For instance, Ezek. 16.7-13; Prov. 31.21 suggest nakedness as a horror, which can be overcome by being covered with clothes. In the Old Testament the horror of nakedness is predominantly associated with shame. Isa. 20.4 combines nakedness with shame; Isa. 47.3 identifies nakedness with shame; Mic. 1.11 juxtaposes nakedness with shame. In some passages,[41] nakedness connotes the shame of defeat or captivity, resulting from God's judgment upon sin. In Ezek. 16.7-8, in particular, the devastating condition of the captivity of Israel is described as being like the nakedness of a vulnerable new-born baby. In Ezek. 16.36; 23.29 the concept indicates the shame of spiritual adultery.

It is beyond the parameters of the present study to deal with every clothing passage in the Old Testament. Attention will be paid only to a limited number of the clothing passages, that is (1) Gen. 3.21, which speaks of Adam's clothing, and other verses in connection with the passage, (2) Exod. 28 (and *passim* in Leviticus); 29.4-9 [par. 40.12-15]; Lev. 6.10-11; 16.3-4, 23-24; Ezek. 42.13-14; 44.19; Zech. 3.3-5, all of which are related to the [high] priest's clothing, and (3) Judg. 6.34, 1 Chron. 12.18, 2 Chron. 24.20, which refer to God's clothing. We will proceed to examine these three categories in turn, and each issue will be treated in a distinct sub-chapter.

2. *Adam's Garment (Genesis 3.21)*

2.1. *Introduction*
As it includes the earliest statement about man's wearing clothes and involves the narrative of his creation and Fall, Gen. 3.21 deserves our careful attention. The passage reads,

וַיַּעַשׂ יְהוָה אֱלֹהִים לְאָדָם וּלְאִשְׁתּוֹ כָּתְנוֹת עוֹר וַיַּלְבִּשֵׁם

And the Lord God made for Adam and for his wife garments of skins, and clothed them.

Adam was created in a state of lack of shame at his nakedness (Gen. 2.25), but after the Fall he became ashamed of being naked and at the same time became afraid of facing God (3.7, 10-11). His response to this calamity was to make and put on a makeshift covering, but in God's eyes this covering was not appropriate. Therefore, God made a garment of skin and clothed him with it.[42] In this process it

---

39. Ps. 102.26.
40. Note that when Adam and his wife fell, they came to feel great fear about their nakedness in the presence of God. For further discussion on the theme, see section 2.3, below.
41. E.g. Isa. 20.2-4; 47.3; Ezek. 16.7-8, 22, 37, 39; 23.29; Hos. 2.3; Amos 2.16 (cf. Isa. 3.17; Ezek. 23.26); Mic. 1.8; Hab. 3.13; Zeph. 2.14.
42. Concerning the close link between Gen. 2.25, 3.7 and 3.21, see S.N. Lambden, 'From Fig Leaves to Fingernails: Some Notes on the Garments of Adam and Eve in the Hebrew Bible and Select Early Postbiblical Jewish Writings', in *A Walk in the Garden: Biblical, Iconographical and*

was the Fall that caused Adam to feel shame at his nakedness. It should also be remembered, however, that his feeling of shame was related to the death which the Fall had brought about. Adam was originally created as a living soul but after the Fall he became subject to death (cf. 2.15). If thus his death is connected with his feeling of shame and this shame is covered over by God's clothing him, it may be inferred that Adam's being clothed has something to do with his being restored to his original life. Bearing this in mind, we will investigate how both Adam's original and fallen state can throw light on the significance of Adam's clothing.

2.2. A Sign of Restoration to the Image of God (Genesis 1.26-27); the Divine Life (Genesis 2.7); Unashamedness (Genesis 2.25)
The sequence of Adam's Fall and his being clothed by God indicates that what we are told about Adam's being created will shed light on what God's clothing him after the Fall signifies. For the creation is followed by the Fall, which is in turn followed by the clothing of Adam. Gen. 2.7 significantly introduces the concept of 'life', as it relates to man's nature. Yet, this concept also seems to have something to do with the concept of 'the image of God' in Gen. 1.26-27. There is no verbal link between the two passages, which may be because they originate in two separate sources.[43] But as the writer of Genesis combines one with the other, the question of what his intention is, is naturally raised. In the present canonical context Gen. 2.7 functions as a supplementary account to Gen. 1.26-27. The former seems to elaborate the way in which man is created in the image of God (1.26-27).[44]

Gen. 1.26-27 reads,

וַיֹּאמֶר אֱלֹהִים נַעֲשֶׂה אָדָם בְּצַלְמֵנוּ כִּדְמוּתֵנוּ... :וַיִּבְרָא אֱלֹהִים|אֶת־הָאָדָם
בְּצַלְמוֹ בְּצֶלֶם אֱלֹהִים בָּרָא אֹתוֹ זָכָר וּנְקֵבָה בָּרָא אֹתָם

Then God said, 'Let us make man in our image after our likeness' ... So God created man in his own image, in the image of God he created him; male and female he created them.

Gen. 2.7 reads,

וַיִּיצֶר יְהֹוָה אֱלֹהִים אֶת־הָאָדָם עָפָר מִן־הָאֲדָמָה וַיִּפַּח בְּאַפָּיו נִשְׁמַת חַיִּים
וַיְהִי הָאָדָם לְנֶפֶשׁ חַיָּה

then the Lord God formed man of dust from the ground, and breathed into his nostrils the breath of life; and man became a living being.

Literary Images of Eden (JSOTSup, 136; Sheffield: JSOT Press, 1992), pp. 74-90 (especially pp. 74-77); G.A. Anderson, 'Garments of Skin, Garments of Glory' (unpublished paper, n.d.), pp. 1-42 (especially pp. 1-3).

43. See J.F.A. Sawyer, 'Notes and Studies: The Meaning of בְּצֶלֶם אֱלֹהִים ("In the Image of God") in Genesis I-XI', *JTSNS* 25 (1974), pp. 418-26 (especially pp. 418-19); R.S. Hess, 'Genesis 1-2 in Its Literary Context', *TB* 41.1 (1990), pp. 143-53 (especially pp. 143-44). For a detailed discussion of the documentary sources of Genesis, see E.A. Speiser, *Genesis* (AB, 1; New York: Doubleday, 1964), pp. xxii-xxxiv.

44. Cf. J.G. Murphy, *A Critical and Exegetical Commentary on the Book of Genesis* (Edinburgh: T. & T. Clark, 1863), p. 92.

Three actions may be detected in Gen. 2.7: (1) God takes the dust (עָפָר) from the ground, (2) God forms man using the dust, and (3) God breathes the breath of life into the man's nostrils, resulting in a living being. The first item speaks of the material of man; the second, of his shape; the third, of his divine vitality.[45] As the two verbs יָצַר ('to form') and נָפַח ('to breathe') elucidate how God transformed the dust to a man, they seem to echo the verbs בָּרָא ('to create') or עָשָׂה ('to make') in Gen. 1.26-27.

In particular, we note that the divine life has been implanted in the 'man-of-dust'. We can imagine that God's creation of man in his own image consisted of God's action of breathing the divine breath into the man-of-dust. In God's creation of man after his own image, the emphasis should be placed on the fact that God's divine life was implanted into man. In fact, the phrase, נֶפֶשׁ חַיָּה ('a living being'), significantly indicates that man is a being who holds God's life within him. When God breathes his breath of life into the man-of-dust, he becomes נֶפֶשׁ חַיָּה,[46] that is, a physical being whom God's life pervades. On this understanding, we can say that Adam's life has two aspects, physical and spiritual.

Accordingly, we argue that the implanting of God's life[47] in man is an essential aspect of his creation of man, and that the divine life in man is a central aspect of the image of God in man. Whilst God's life resides in the first human couple, in other words, whilst the image of God typifies their existence, their nakedness cannot give them a sense of shame (2.25). We, therefore, suggest that Adam's being clothed with a garment of skin in Gen. 3.21 symbolizes that his original life in the image of God has started to be restored to him.[48] The genitive 'of skin' also reinforces our interpretation, because a skin presupposes the sacrifice of a living being.[49] Investiture with a garment of skin may be regarded as being clothed with the life of the sacrificed creature.

As far as Adam's being clothed (3.21) signals his restoration to the original life which is hinted at in Gen. 2.7, it can further signal his restoration to his original

45. Concerning this idea, see the following paragraph.
46. As this term points to man in whom God's breath of life has been breathed in Gen. 2.7, it must be distinguished from its other usage (e.g. Gen. 1.20, 21, 24; cf. 2.19; 9.9).
47. It is significant that God said to Adam that were he to ignore God's commandment, he would be put to death (Gen. 2.17).
48. The garment of skin seems to be contrasted with the makeshift covering of fig leaves in Gen. 3.7. Garments of skin connote suitable, permanent apparel; fig leaves the opposite. The fig-leaf covering was made by sinful human beings; the skin covering was provided by God. *b. Sota* 14a suggests that Gen. 3.21 should be read in terms of God's benevolence: 'R. Simlai expounded: Torah begins with an act of benevolence and ends with an act of benevolence. It begins with an act of benevolence, for it is written, "And the Lord God made for Adam and for his wife coats of skin, and clothed them"; and it ends with an act of benevolence, for it is written, "and He buried him in the valley [Deut. 34.6a]" ' (quotation from I. Epstein, *The Babylonian Talmud* [18 vols.; London: Soncino Press, 1948]).
49. Cf. Murphy, *Critical and Exegetical Commentary*, pp. 148-49; R.A. Oden, 'Grace or Status? YHWH's Clothing of the First Humans', in *The Bible Without Theology: The Theological Tradition and Alternatives to It* (San Francisco: Harper & Row, 1987), pp. 92-105 (especially, pp. 95-96).

kingship; in the light of the motif of the movement from dust to kingship in 1 Sam. 2.6-8, 1 Kgs 16.2 and Ps. 113.7, the concept of being formed 'of dust' into a man of the divine life (Gen. 2.7) seems to be related to the kingship idea.[50] Further, 'the man' appears to be 'the equivalent of the Mesopotamian *lu-gal* (big man) or "king" '.[51] This understanding of Gen. 2.7 can be further supported by the close relationship between the concept of divine life and that of the image of God, which is apparently characterized by man's kingship over non-human beings and all the earth (1.26-28).[52] In verse 26, which is an expression of God's intention for his creation of man, the 'image-dominion' scheme is clear; again in Gen. 1.27-28, which refers to how God's intention has been achieved, the scheme is also definite.[53] Adam's restoration to the divine life can, in a sense, be thought of as his restoration to God's image.[54]

2.3. *A Sign of Restoration from Shame and Fear (Genesis 3.7, 10-11)*
As was already argued, the statement in Gen. 3.7-11 is also of consequence in an attempt to search for the significance of Adam being clothed in 3.21. For the latter is in continuity with the former.[55] Gen. 3.7 tells that

וַתִּפָּקַחְנָה עֵינֵי שְׁנֵיהֶם וַיֵּדְעוּ כִּי עֵירֻמִּם הֵם וַיִּתְפְּרוּ עֲלֵה תְאֵנָה וַיַּעֲשׂוּ לָהֶם חֲגֹרֹת

Then the eyes of both were opened, and they knew that they were naked; and they sewed fig leaves together and made themselves aprons.

50. W. Brueggemann, 'From Dust to Kingship', *ZAW* 84 (1972), pp. 1-18 (especially, pp. 1-5).

51. W. Wifall, 'The Breath of His Nostrils: Gen. 2.7b', *CBQ* 36 (1974), pp. 237-40 (especially pp. 237-38).

52. Cf. Ps. 8.5; *Sir.* 17.1-7; *Jub.* 2.14; 3.1-3, 9, 15-16; *Wisd. Sol.* 7.1; 9.1-3; 10.1-2; Philo, *Op. Mun.* 24-25, 66, 69, 83-84, 88, 148; *4 Ezra* 6.45-46, 53-59; *2 Enoch* 30.10-15; 31.3; 44.1-2; 58.1-3; *2 Bar.* 14.17-19; *Cave Tre.* 2.12-21. D.J.A. Clines, 'The Image of God in Man', *TB* 19 (1968), pp. 53-103 (especially pp. 83-85) points out that in the ancient near-eastern world, the concept of the image of God was frequently applied to the king.

53. Concerning the issue of the dominion of Adam in Genesis 1–3, see D.T. Asselin, 'The Notion of Dominion in Genesis 1-3', *CBQ* 16 (1954), pp. 277-94.

54. J. Jervell, *Imago Dei: Gen. 1, 26f. im Spätjudentum, in der Gnosis, und in den paulinischen Briefen* (FRLANT, 76; Göttingen: Vandenhoeck & Ruprecht, 1960), p. 83 argues that God's image in Adam has been restored in the Sinai event, that is, in Moses' transformed countenance in Exod. 34.29-35. If so, however, this restoration at Sinai is proleptic of the restoration that will take place in the eschatological future, ultimately in the event of resurrection (cf. *Apoc. Mos.* 28 and 41).

55. J. Skinner, *Critical and Exegetical Commentary on Genesis* (ICC; Edinburgh: T. & T. Clark, 1910), p. 87 makes a more or less contradictory comment on the relationship between Gen. 3.7 and 3.21, saying that 'it [v. 21] is, of course, not inconsistent with v. 7, but neither can it be said to be the necessary sequel to that verse'. But a consistent flow of such ideas as unashamedness (2.25), ashamedness after the Fall and covering with a fig-leafed apron (3.7), and being clothed with garments of animal skins (3.21) shows that v. 7 and v. 21 are very closely linked with one other. J.T. Walsh, 'Genesis 2.4b-3.24: A Synchronic Approach', *JBL* 96.2 (1977), pp. 161-77 (170) points out that '2.25 and 3.21 introduce and conclude the development of the motif of "nakedness"'.

This report informs us of what happened to Adam and his wife and what they did after their disobedience to God's command (cf. 2.16-17). It shows the emotional situation that confronted Adam and his wife shortly after the Fall: for the first time they felt shame about their naked bodies. In their original nakedness they felt no shame (Gen. 2.25), but now in their fallen nakedness they feel overwhelming shame, resulting in their veiling themselves with makeshift coverings.

As the clause of וַיֵּדְעוּ כִּי עֵירֻמִּם הֵם ('they knew that they were naked') refers to the reason why Adam and his wife made coverings, their physical nakedness must have given them a feeling of shame. Yet, instead of their physical nakedness, a spiritual reason for their shame is perhaps operative in the story. G. Anderson affirms that 'the "opening of the eyes" does not signify any change in one's *physical* nature; rather it is a sign which points to an internal transformation'.[56] The schematic similarity between Gen. 3.5 and 3.7 suggests that Adam and his wife's recognition of their nakedness was related to their knowledge of good and evil.[57] The fact that fallen man came to possess the knowledge of good and evil is significantly emphasized in Gen. 3.22 (cf. 2.9, 17).

By putting the tree of the knowledge of good and evil in the garden of Eden and forbidding Adam to eat its fruit, God entered into a covenantal relationship with him. But Adam with his wife broke God's commandment, resulting in their obtaining the knowledge that good is to be faithful to God's commandment and evil is to be unfaithful to it.[58] Obedience would have brought them good; but disobedience brought them evil. The good and evil consequences of good and evil they now knew and experienced. Such a knowledge of good and evil made Adam and his wife see the reality of their fallen naked bodies. They saw that instead of life, death prevailed in their bodies (cf. Gen. 2.7).[59] Their fallen bodies no longer radiated the splendour of life. Adam and his wife would have remembered God's covenant of life and death: 'in the day that you eat of it you shall die' (Gen. 2.17). Their knowledge of good and evil made them perceive that God's life had left their bodies, and consequently made them feel shame.

Gen. 3.10 suggests that Adam's shame was followed by his fear: 'I was afraid, because I was naked; and I hid myself'. Adam felt fear toward God, so he avoided God and hid from him. Adam does not merely mean that his physical nakedness gave him fear, but he means that he realized that the glory of the divine life had disappeared from his body and so he felt fear. His rejection of God's commandment and so of the destruction of his covenantal relationship with God evoked a sense of panic in the presence of God.

---

56. Anderson, 'Garments of Skin', p. 6.

57. In fact, Gen. 3.7 is a combination of phrases from 2.25 and 3.5 (see G. J. Wenham, *Genesis 1-15* [WBC, 1; Dallas: Word Books, 1987], p. 76). Yet, it has also to be noted that 3.7, by following the same scheme as in 3.5, brings into close relationship the statement about realization of nakedness (3.7) and the statement about the knowledge of good and evil (3.5).

58. Cf. D.S. Briscoe, *Genesis* (ComC; Waco: Word Books, 1987 [1979]), p. 59.

59. At the Fall Adam experiences not only spiritual but also physical death; his physical body starts dying at that very moment, because he then becomes a mortal being.

Accordingly, God's clothing Adam and his wife with garments of skin (Gen. 3.21) probably signifies his veiling of their fallen, shameful nakedness and his banishing their fear; more positively, it can be thought of as his restoring them from death to life and from fear to peace. While fallen nakedness connotes man being deprived of life, plunging him into an abyss of shame and fear, God's covering of this fatal nakedness signifies man being restored by him to life, with glory and peace with God.

Insofar as the clothing imagery in Gen. 3.21 signals Adam and Eve's restoration to their original state, it can be said that the Genesis text itself implies their pre-lapsarian clothing. Before the Fall they had been dressed in life and glory which were reflections of the image of God, but afterwards they were stripped of these divine elements. E. Peterson argues that

> Diese 'Aufdeckung' des Leibes, die die 'nackte Körperlichkeit' sichtbar werden lässt, diese schonungslose Entblössung des Leibes mit allen Kennzeichen seiner Geschlechtlichkeit, die als Folge der ersten Sünde für die jetzt 'aufgetanen Augen' sichtbar wird, lässt sich nur unter der Annahme begreifen, dass vor dem Sünden-fall 'bedeckt' war, was jetzt 'aufgedeckt' wird, dass vorher verhüllt und bekleidet war, was jetzt enthüllt und entkleidet wird.[60]

> this 'unclothing' of the body, which reveals the 'naked bodiliness', that is, this unsparing exposure of the body with all the genital organs of sexuality, which has come to be visible for 'opened eyes', as the result of the first sin, can only be understood under the assumption that what was clothed before the fall is now 'unclothed', and that what is now uncovered and undressed was veiled and clothed before.

2.4. *Conclusion: A Sign of Restoration to Life, Glory, Peace and Dominion*
Both Gen. 1.26-27; 2.7, 25 and 3.7, 10-11 suggest that the clothing image in Gen. 3.21 signals a restoration from death and shame to life and glory. This restoration points to the restoration of God's image, because such a life and glory can be detected only in that image which was originally implanted in man. Adam's restoration to God's image particularly denotes the restoration of his royal status. The garment of skin also connotes reconciliation with God. When Adam wore his own fig-leaves apron, he was afraid of God, but when he was clothed with a garment of skin provided by God, he did not panic before him. In short, the clothing image in Gen. 3.21 signifies that Adam's restoration to his original life and glory, to peace with God, and to kingship over the other creatures has started. It also implies that the first human couple had been previously clothed with divine features, although this concept of pre-Fall clothing does not directly occur. The Pauline imagery of clothing with Christ or the new man (Gal. 3.27; Rom. 3.14; Col. 3.10; Eph. 4.24) and with the resurrection body (1 Cor. 15.49, 50-54; 2 Cor. 5.1-4), behind which the Adam–Christ metaphor predominates, seems to bear in mind the above-mentioned passages in Genesis.

---

60. E. Peterson, 'Theologie des Kleides', *BM* 16 (1934), pp. 347-56 (348).

3. *Priestly Garments*

3.1. *Introduction*

One of the most obvious features of the priestly garment is its social function of
distinguishing the wearer as a priest. But when the claim is made that it is 'sacred'
with glory and beauty (Exod. 28.2), it seems to claim a much greater role than that.
In this sub-chapter, I aim to examine what is meant by the priest's being attired in it.
With this concern, we will first look into the items of the priestly garment (Exod. 28,
etc.), then we will examine the ritual of putting on/off the priestly garment (Exod.
29.4-9 [par. 40.12-15]; Lev. 6.10-11; 16.3-4; Ezek. 42.13-14; 44.19). Finally, we
will attempt to explicate the meaning of the antithesis between Joshua's filthy garments and the new garments which appear in Zechariah's vision (Zech. 3.3-5).

3.2. *Priestly Garments—Sacredness, Glory and Beauty*

The apparel of the priest is impressively presented in the OT. Exodus 28, 29, 39,
Lev. 8, 16, etc. give detailed information concerning it.[61] God commands Moses to
let Aaron and his sons serve him as priests dressed in distinguished garments,
namely 'sacred garments' (Exod. 28.2, 40; 39.41; 40.13; Lev. 16.32). The items of
Aaron's garments consisted of an ephod (with a breastpiece in which the Urim
[הָאוּרִים] and the Thummim [הַתֻּמִּים] are put), a blue robe, a linen-woven tunic,
linen undergarments, a linen turban with the holy crown thereupon, and a linen
sash (Exod. 28.4, 39-40; 29.5-6, 8-9; 39.1-31; Lev. 8.7-9; 16.4).

The outermost garment, the ephod, is made of gold, and of blue, purple and
scarlet yarn, and of finely twisted linen (Exod. 28.6). D.R. Edwards imagines that
the threads of four kinds of colour are probably woollen[62] and suggests that a
mixture of four coloured woollen threads and fine linen signifies the importance of
the priest's status.[63] However, this argument cannot be sustained, because (1) God
prohibits Israel from wearing clothing made of a mixed fabric of wool and linen
(Deut. 22.11; cf. Lev. 19.19), and this would surely be applied to the priesthood
too; (2) this prohibition is involved in the symbolic significance of keeping pure
(see Lev. 19.19; Deut. 22.11) and of refraining from infringing Israel's dignity; (3)
no clue is given to indicate that the coloured threads are woollen; and (4) no passage
mentions that a garment, which is composed of a mixture of coloured yarn and
linen, signifies dignity. The dignity of priestly garments depends on their sacredness
and not on the mixture of the material. What kind of material the coloured yarn is
made from is not important. What is crucial is the fact that the splendour of the
priest's garments (due to its coloured threads woven with white linen) demonstrates divinity, glory and beauty (cf. Exod. 28.2, 40).

At two corners of the ephod are attached two shoulder pieces, on each of which
an onyx stone is fastened. Two onyx stones are engraved with the names of the
sons of Israel in the order of their birth, viz. six names on each (Exod. 28.9-10).

---

61. Exod. 28.1-4 is a root-passage concerning the Mosaic institution of priestship. See also its
parallels: Exod. 29.9, 44; Num. 3.10; 18.7; 1 Chron. 23.13.
62. Edwards, 'Dress', p. 233.
63. Edwards, 'Dress', p. 232.

Their names are borne before God upon the priest's shoulders, to remind him of his people (Exod. 28.12). Over the ephod is put a breastpiece of judgment which is made like the ephod, that is, of gold, and of blue, purple and scarlet yarn and of finely twined linen (Exod. 28.15). In turn, on the breastpiece of judgment are mounted four rows of precious stones, each of which has three different stones (Exod. 28.17-20). These twelve stones represent the names of the sons of Israel, and each is engraved like a seal with the name of one of the twelve tribes (Exod. 28.21). All these features imply that the priest functions as a representative figure in relation to all the Israelites.[64]

Whenever the priest enters the Holy Place, he should bear this breastpiece of judgment (Exod. 28.29), in which are put the Urim (הָאוּרִים) and the Thummim (הַתֻּמִּים), so as to be over the priest's heart, and by means of them he is to discern the will of God for the Israelites (Exod. 28.30 [LXX 28.26]). The breastpiece symbolizes God's judicial power; it seems to have been a simple purse containing the Urim (הָאוּרִים) and the Thummim (הַתֻּמִּים), in other words the sacred lots.[65] These were dice or sticks, one of which signified 'yes' and the other 'no' in relation to a question asked. This device belonged to the pre-Israelite sanctuaries of Palestine, and was adopted by the Israelites and used by them until the time of the early monarchy.[66] By operating the lots, the priest played the role of a deliverer of God's will to his people. This oracular function of the priest seems to have been grounded in his union with God by his being clothed with the sacred priestly garment.

Apart from this, we need to briefly consider the meaning of the Urim (הָאוּרִים)[67] and the Thummim (הַתֻּמִּים), in order to explain the character of the priestly garments. אוּרִים probably originates from אוֹר 'light'.[68] If so, הָאוּרִים can be thought of as indicating 'lights'. תֻּמִּים is rooted in תָּמַם 'to be complete'; it is the plural form of one of תָּמַם's derivatives, תֹּם, one of the major meanings of which is 'perfection'. תֻּמִּים, therefore, signifies 'perfections'.[69] Probably the Urim and the Thummim in the sense of lights and perfections are symbolic objects to indicate that the Israelites (represented by the twelve precious stones described in the preceding verses [Exod. 28.17-21]) are supported by God's supreme guidance. The priest's part of donning the breastpiece of judgment in which the Urim and the Thummim are set signifies that he is enveloped in 'lights and perfections'.

A blue robe is worn under the ephod. Around its hem are pomegranates of blue, purple and scarlet[70] yarn, and finely twisted linen alternates with gold bells

---

64. Cf. D.M.G. Stalker, 'Exodus', in M. Black and H.H. Rowley (eds.), *PCB* (London: Nelson, 1975 [1962]), pp. 208-40 (236).

65. Stalker, 'Exodus', p. 236.

66. P. Zerafa, 'Exodus', in *NCCHS* (London: Nelson, 1969), pp. 173-92 (225).

67. This term is found seven times in the OT, only in the plural: Exod. 28.30; Lev. 8.8; Num. 27.21; Deut. 33.8; 1 Sam. 28.6; Ezra 2.63; Neh. 7.65. In all but two cases (Num. 27.21 and 1 Sam. 28.6) the Urim is always combined with the Thummim.

68. H. Wolf, 'אוֹר', in R.L. Harris *et al.* (eds.), *TWOT*, I (Chicago: Moody Press, 1980), p. 26.

69. J.B. Payne, 'תָּמַם', in R.L. Harris *et al.* (eds.), *TWOT*, II (Chicago: Moody Press, 1980), pp. 973-74; J.A. Motyer, 'Urim and Thummim', in J.D. Douglas (ed.), *NBD* (Grand Rapids: Eerdmans, 1973 [1962]), p. 1306; A.H. McNeile, *The Book of Exodus* (London: Methuen, 1908), p. 183.

70. These colours altogether seem to symbolize the high priest's royal status in relation to the

(Exod. 28.33-34; par. 39.24-26). Under the blue robe is a woven tunic of fine linen (Exod. 28.4, 39),[71] under which are linen undergarments, worn in order to cover nakedness (Exod. 28.42; 39.28; Lev. 16.4; Ezek. 44.18). Both the turban, upon which the holy crown is put, and the sash are also to be made of fine linen (Exod. 28.39; 29.6; Lev. 16.4).

All these garments seem to constitute the formal apparel of Aaron the [high] priest.[72] No doubt, whenever he entered the Holy Place[73] for the performance of his ministry, he had to wear them (cf. Exod. 28.29, 35-43; 29.29-30). Yet, when he entered the most holy place, he might wear only the linen tunic, linen undergarments, the linen sash and the linen turban, and not the ephod and the blue robe (cf. Lev. 16.2-4; Ezek. 44.17-19). The author of the Pentateuch does not provide any explanation concerning this difference. But as the whiteness of the four linen items can represent divine holiness,[74] the difference probably means that when the high priest entered the most holy place, he had to endue himself with a holiness which was suited to the supreme sacredness of the place. On the other hand, these four items seem to have been Aaron's basic and regular apparel which he had to always wear not only inside the holy places (i.e. the holy place and the most holy place) but also in the outer court (cf. Exod. 28.40-43; 29.8-9).[75] The high priest was obliged to keep himself constantly holy.

In sum, the priest's being clothed with the priestly garment signifies that he is identified with its sacredness, glory and beauty (Exod. 28.2, 40). As clothes typify their wearer's appearance, these elements will characterize the priest. Specifically,

---

people of Israel; cf. Est. 8.15, where a purple robe of fine linen indicates a royal status; see A. Brenner, *Colour Terms in the Old Testament* (JSOTSup, 21; Sheffield: JSOT Press, 1982), p. 146. Philo, *Vita Mos.* ii.133, who imparts cosmological significance to the high-priestly garments, specifically speaks of the scarlet in pomegranates as signifying fire. Josephus, *Ant.* iii.184-87, who also endows the high priest's garments with cosmic implications, holds that the blue of the ephod denotes the sky; the blue of pomegranates, lightning; and the blue of the mitre, heaven. But Philo's and Josephus' description of other items also seem to include perception of their colour, although this is not explicitly referred to.

71. According to Josephus, this linen tunic extended to the ankles and had long sleeves; see *Ant.* 3.153.

72. Although the title of 'the high priest' is not applied to Aaron, his function is identified with that of the high priest. The status of Aaron as the priest is superior to that of his sons, who are also called as priests to serve God. 'The high priest' as a formal title appears after the institution of the office (Lev. 21.10-15; Num. 3.32).

73. The tent of meeting (cf. Exod. 30.18-20; 40.30) included both the Holy Place and the Most Holy Place (Exod. 26.33).

74. Cf. Dan. 7.9 and *1 Enoch* 14.20, which describe God's holiness by the symbolism of his garment's whiteness.

75. In particular, of four items of a tunic, a sash, a headband and linen undergarments in Exod. 28.40-42, the 'headband' in v. 40 (also 29.9; 39.28) is rendered from מִגְבָּעוֹת ('the mitre of the common priests'), while the linen turban in v. 39 (also 28.4) is called מִצְנֶפֶת ('the mitre of the high priest'); see S.P. Tregelles (trans.), *Gesenius' Hebrew and Chaldee Lexicon* (Milford: Mott Media, 1979), p. 447. The former was also made of fine linen (Exod. 39.9). The difference between מִגְבָּעוֹת and מִצְנֶפֶת might be that a gold plate having the words 'Holy to the Lord' engraved on it was attached to the front part of the מִצְנֶפֶת (vv. 36-37).

as the Urim and the Thummim symbolize God's light and perfection (Exod. 28.30), the priest who retains them in his breast would be considered as a figure identified with such divine features. Accordingly, it may be said that clothing with the priestly garment divinized its wearer. Further, the symbolism of two onyx stones (on each of which six names of the sons of Israel are engraved) or twelve precious stones for all the Israelites (Exod. 28.12, 17-20) signifies that the priest becomes a representative figure of God's sacred people.

3.3. *The Ritual of Putting On/Off the Priestly Garments*

3.3.1. *Washing with Water*
3.3.1.1. At Ordination (Exodus 29.4-9 [par. 40.12-15]). In Exod. 29.4-9 (par. 40.12-15) God teaches Moses how Aaron and his sons should be clothed with priestly garments, when they are ordained as priests. Because of the holy nature of the priestly garments, the priest must be cleansed with water before wearing them. Washing gives a purity which befits the sacredness of the clothing. It obviously presupposes the putting off of clothes which have been previously worn. But what our texts emphasize is that by means of consecration, attirement with priestly garments and ordination, Aaron and his sons become specifically holy people for leading the worship of God. Their being clothed with the sacred garments means that they become more than ordinary Israelites.

3.3.1.2. At the Entry into the Sanctuary Area (Leviticus 16.3-4). Lev. 16.3-4 presents another example of the priest's washing. The passage reads,

> 3 But thus shall Aaron come into the holy place: with a young bull for a sin offering and a ram for a burnt offering. 4 He shall put on the holy linen coat, and shall have the linen breeches on his body, be girded with the linen girdle, and wear the linen turban; these are the holy garments. He shall bathe his body in water, and then put them on.

This passage speaks of how the priest is to be attired when he enters the holy area on the day of atonement for a sin offering and a burnt offering. As Aaron comes into the holy area (which covers both the holy place and the most holy place) for such offerings, he has first to bathe himself in water. The bath is to prepare the purified body for the sacred priestly garments, before entering the holy place. Only a consecrated body is qualified to wear holy garments. The bath symbolizes, in a word, purification. Obviously it presupposes putting off the priest's previous clothes. When Aaron is dressed in the sacred priestly garments for presenting offerings in the holy area, he intends to participate in God's holiness. His being clothed with priestly garments denotes that he becomes holy in harmony with God's sacredness.

3.3.2. *Linen Garments at the Holy Place Only*
3.3.2.1. At the Exit from the Sanctuary Area (Leviticus 16.23-24; Ezekiel 42.13-14; 44.19). Lev. 16.23-24 is concerned with what the priest has to do in relation to his apparel when he comes out from the holy area. The passage reads,

> 23 Then Aaron shall come into the tent of meeting, and shall put off the linen garments which he put on when he went into the holy place, and shall leave them

there; 24 and he shall bathe his body in water in a holy place and put on his
garments, and come forth, and offer his burnt offering of the people, and make
atonement for himself and for the people.[76]

When Aaron comes out from the tabernacle of witness, (1) he has to put off the
linen garments in which he was dressed when he went into the holy area, (2) then
leave them in a holy place (perhaps the Most Holy Place),[77] then take a bath, (3)
then put on his regular sacred garments. The text does not explain why the priest
should change garments. We may, however, imagine that the linen garments in
which the priest has ministered are so holy that they cannot consistently be worn
when he goes into other less sacred places.[78] The sacredness of those particular
linen garments which have been worn in a specific priestly rite does not allow him
to keep on wearing them when he goes outside the holy area (cf. Lev. 6.10-11;
Ezek. 42.14; 44.19). The priestly garments that have been used in a sacred ministry
have to be kept in the holy area, i.e. in an appropriate place which conforms to their
degree of sacredness.

One interesting aspect is that the priest takes a bath before coming out of the
sanctuary area. What is the reason for this bath? It cannot be because his regular
garments are holier than the sacred linen ones which have been worn in his ministry. There are perhaps two reasons. Firstly, it is conceivable that the priest might
be defiled in the process of performing an offering, in particular, a sin offering. On
the Day of Atonement, washings and cleansings (symbolizing getting rid of all
taint of sin) are significantly performed in various situations (Lev. 16.26, 28). R. E.
Clements holds that 'contact with the sin-bearing animal could lead to the rubbing
off of sin onto the person touching it'.[79] The sacrificial blood of the animal is holy,
but this holiness, paradoxically, defiles the high priest; a garment which is stained
with the blood should be washed in a holy place (cf. Lev. 6.27). Secondly, he may
need to consecrate himself as a proper precaution for his subsequent ministry, i.e.
the burnt offering. Aaron as the priest who would offer the burnt offering for himself and for the people, should first consecrate himself through the bath in water.

Another example of changing garments when the priest comes out of holy pre-
cincts is found in Ezek. 42.14; 44.19, which is part of Ezekiel's vision of the new,
restored temple.[80] Once he had entered this sanctuary area, he should not come out
to the outer court without first putting off and leaving his clothes in the rooms

76. Ezek. 42.14 echoes this passage, although it neither includes a direct reference to 'putting
off', nor refers to a bath or to burnt offerings. But the passage from Ezekiel does make an obvious
distinction between the holy area and the outer court, the places for the people, and it maintains the
idea of 'different area, different garments'.
77. The RSV renders הַקֹּדֶשׁ 'the Most Holy Place'.
78. The distinction between the most holy place, the holy place, the outer court, the camp, and
the outside of the camp implies a hierarchy of degrees of holiness. Concerning the Jewish concept
of 'ten degrees of holiness', see *Kelim* 1.6-9 (H. Danby, *The Mishnah* [Oxford: Oxford University
Press, 1933], pp. 605-606).
79. R.E. Clements, 'Leviticus', in *Leviticus-Ruth* (BBC, 2; London: Marshall, Morgan & Scott,
1971), pp. 1-74 (46).
80. R.A. Wilson, 'Ezekiel', in *HBC* (San Francisco: Harper, 1988), pp. 652-94 (693); L. Boadt,
'Ezekiel', in *NJBC* (London: Geoffrey Chapman, 1993), pp. 305-28 (326).

reserved for this purpose,[81] then putting on other clothes. The reason for this is that the clothes are holy (Ezek. 42.14). The author of Ezekiel seems to consider that the garments in which the priest has performed a sacred ministry in the holy area are more sacred than other priestly garments (cf. Lev. 6.10-11; 16.23-24). The holiness of the clothes may not be contaminated by contact with people or things of a profane character. Another reason why the priestly garments may not be carried to the outer court is to protect them from the touch of ordinary worshippers, lest they be inappropriately consecrated by chance contact with the sacred garments (Ezek. 44.19).[82] The common people must be consecrated by other rituals, not by this particular means (cf. Exod. 29.37; 30.29; Lev. 6.27). As the priest wears the sacred garments, enters the holy places and performs sacred rites, he becomes identified with the sacredness of the garments and the places, so as to be holier than other people outside the area.[83]

3.3.2.2. *At the Exit from the Camp (Leviticus 6.10-11)*. Another instance of how the priestly linen garments have to be treated when the priest goes outside the Israelite camp is found in Lev. 6.10-11:

> 10 And the priest shall put on his linen garment, and put his linen breeches upon his body, and he shall take up the ashes to (*sic*) which the fire has consumed the burnt offering on the altar, and put them beside the altar. 11 Then he shall put off his garments, and put on other garments, and carry forth the ashes outside the camp to a clean place.

As part of the regulations regarding the burnt offering, this passage deals with the attire of the priest who has the morning duty of clearing away the overnight fat and ashes. The priest has to remove the fat and ashes which have been smouldering on the altar overnight. The procedure for doing this is as follows: (1) he has first to collect the fat and ashes of the burnt offering from the altar, (2) then to place them beside the altar, (3) then to put off the linen garments[84] and put on other garments,[85] (4) and finally to carry the fat and ashes outside the camp to a clean place. Here again, a similar idea to that in Lev. 16.23-24 is found. The clothes in which the priest has ministered for a sacred ritual are so holy that he must not continue to wear them as he goes outside the camp, that is, into a less sacred place (cf. Ezek. 42.14; 44.19). The principle of 'sacred garments, sacred place' is consistently

---

81. In the rooms to the north and south, the priests ate, stored offerings in excess of their immediate requirements, and robed themselves for the service of the altar (Ezek. 42.13-14).

82. J.W. Wevers (ed.), *Ezekiel* (CBNS; London: Nelson, 1969), p. 322 affirms that 'in post-exilic times holiness was considered to be almost a material thing, and like a communicable disease could infect people simply by touch'; K.W. Carley, *Ezekiel* (Cambridge: Cambridge University Press, 1974), p. 283, holds that in Ezek. 42.13-14; 44.19 holiness is described 'as a semi-physical substance'.

83. Cf. Isa. 65.5: 'come not near to me; for I am holier than thou' (KJV).

84. The text refers to the linen tunic and linen undergarments only, but the linen sash and the linen turban might have been put on also (cf. Lev. 16.4).

85. Probably these point to the priest's regular sacred garments; see N.H. Snaith, 'Leviticus', in M. Black and H.H. Rowley (eds.), *PCB* (London: Nelson, 1962), pp. 241-53 (244). Similar words are also found in Lev. 16.23; Ezek. 42.14; 44.19.

applied to every ritual activity. In any case, the quoted passage implies that the priest, who adorns himself with the linen garments for the offering, is identified with the garments' sacredness.

3.4. *Filthy Garments/New Garments (Zechariah 3.3-5)*

In Zech. 3.3-5 we encounter a remarkable reference to the priest's filthy garments and to their being changed. The passage is part of Zechariah's vision regarding Joshua the high priest. It reads,

> 3 Now Joshua was standing before the angel, clothed with filthy garments. 4 And the angel said to those who were standing before him, 'Remove the filthy garments from him'. And to him he said, 'Behold, I have taken your iniquity away from you, and I will clothe you with rich apparel'. 5 And I [Zechariah] said, 'Let them put a clean turban on his head'. So they put a clean turban on his head and clothed him with garments; and the angel of the Lord was standing by.

In this passage the focus is on the antithesis between Joshua's filthy garments and the new garments that God's angel puts on him. The filthiness of Joshua's clothes necessitates such a change. Since the current garments are dirty, they have to be taken away. They have to be replaced by proper clean garments.

One peculiar aspect of this passage needs to be noted. A moral statement is inserted between God's angel's command to remove the filthy garments and his disclosing of his intention to clothe Joshua with pure garments. The insertion is that he has removed Joshua's iniquities. This moral statement immediately after the command to take off the dirty garments indicates that God's angel links their filthiness with moral iniquities. S. Bullough rightly argues that 'the "filthy garments" here represent the sins of the people which brought the afflictions of exile (cf. vv. 4 and 9)'.[86] As Joshua, the high priest, represents the whole of Israel, the passage symbolizes that as a garment clothes its wearer, so sins have covered the Israelites, but the dirty sins will be taken away from them as their garments are stripped off. At that time, God's people will be transformed into sacred people who are in harmony with God's holiness. As a garment dominates its wearer's appearance, sacredness (which is suggested by Joshua's new garments) will be their dominant characteristic. To be sure, a garment is not the same thing as its wearer. So sacredness may not be equated with Israel, since it is extrinsic to them. But since a garment is in such close contact with its wearer, sacredness may be almost identified with them.

3.5. *Summary and Conclusion*

The outstanding characteristic of the priestly garment is its sacredness. When the priest puts it on, he is symbolically divinized. Because of the priestly garment's sacredness, the priests are required to consecrate themselves before being attired in it at their ordination or at their entry into the sanctuary area, and to leave the linen

---

86. S. Bullough, 'Zechariah', in R.C. Fuller *et al.* (ed.), *NCCHS* (London: Nelson, 1969 [1953]), pp. 726-27; cf. H.G. Mitchell, 'Haggai, Zechariah', in *A Critical and Exegetical Commentary on Haggai, Zechariah, Malachi and Jonah* (ICC; Edinburgh: T. & T. Clark, 1937 [1912]), p. 150; C.L. Meyers, *Haggai, Zechariah 1-8* (AB; Grand Rapids: Doubleday, 1987), pp. 218-19.

garment at the holy place when they leave the sanctuary area or the camp. When they wear such a sacred garment, they are identified with its sacredness, and they share in its characteristics of glory and beauty, which dominate their appearance. This thought is reflected in the way in which Pauline clothing imagery refers to a change in a human being's nature through union with Christ (Gal. 3.27; Rom. 13.14; Col. 3.9-10; Eph. 4.22-24). Further, as the priestly garment denotes the divine light and perfection, the priests are typified by these features. In particular, the changing of Joshua's filthy garments into new clean garments in Zechariah's vision symbolizes that the Israelites will eventually be renewed by the removal of their sins, and will be immaculate like the new sacred garments. Although their future holiness will be provided from outside, like a garment, it will become a dominating part of their nature. This ethical significance in connection with the priestly garment is perhaps echoed in the emphasis on righteous conduct in the Pauline clothing passages referred to above.

4. *God's Garment: Clothing with a Man*
(Judges 6.34; 1 Chronicles 12.18; 2 Chronicles 24.20)

As I pointed out,[87] the concept of God's clothing occurs in a number of Old Testament passages. Of these, passages which refer to God's taking as his clothing a particular individual are relevant for the Pauline clothing passages. In this sub-chapter we will concentrate on Judg. 6.34; 1 Chron. 12.18 and 2 Chron. 24.20. These three passages all speak of God's Spirit's dressing himself with a human being.

The passages can be translated as follows: Judg. 6.34, 'the Spirit of the Lord put on Gideon'; 1 Chron. 12.18, 'the Spirit put on Amasai, a captain of the thirty'; 2 Chron. 24.20, 'the Spirit of God put on Azarias the son of Jodae the priest'.[88] The qal form of לבשׁ in the Hebrew text common to these verses support this rendering.[89] The LXX also supports our translation of the verses, as in all three cases it uses the same verb, ἐνδύειν, which means 'to put on': Judg. 6.34, Καὶ πνεῦμα Κυρίου ἐνέδυσε τὸν Γεδεών; 1 Chron. 12.18, Καὶ πνεῦμα ἐνέδυσε τὸν Ἀμασαὶ ἄρχοντα τῶν τριάκοντα; 2 Chron. 24.20, Καὶ πνεῦμα Θεοῦ ἐνέδυσε τὸν Ἀζαρίαν τὸν τοῦ Ἰωδαὲ τὸν ἱερέα.

There are three explicit points common to these verses: first, the person who is being clothed is God's Spirit; second, the clothing is a specific human being; third,

---

87. See Chapter 1, §1.
88. My literal translations from the Hebrew texts.
89. Many commentators render the word 'clothed itself with', e.g. G.F. Moore, *A Critical and Exegetical Commentary on Judges* (ICC; Edinburgh: T. & T. Clark, 1918 [1895]), p. 197; J.R. Dummelow, (ed.), 'Judges', in *CHB* (London: Macmillan, 1920 [1909]), pp. 155-72 (164); E.L. Curtis, *A Critical and Exegetical Commentary on the Books of Chronicles* (ICC; Edinburgh: T. & T. Clark, 1952 [1910]), p. 198; W.O.E. Oesterley, 'Judges', in F.C. Eiselen *et al.* (eds.), *ABC* (New York: Abingdon, 1929), pp. 357-76 (364); D. Jackman, *Judges, Ruth* (ed. L.J. Ogilvie; ComC; Dallas: Word Books, 1991), p. 116. Cf. other English translations: RSV, 'took possession of' (Judg. 6.34), 'came upon' (1 Chron. 12.18), 'took possession of' (2 Chron. 24.20); NIV, 'came upon' in all these three verses.

God's intention is to enable a man to have divine power in warfare. God's Spirit puts on a specific human being as his clothing in order to empower that person.

If so, what is meant by this strange metaphor of the Spirit of God putting on a human being? Perhaps it means that the Spirit of God identifies himself with the man,[90] so that he may exercise his power through that man. When such a union between God and man takes place, the man is dominated by God's Spirit, so that the man's being is under the Spirit of God's control. In the light of the context of the related passages, God's identification with the man indicates the man's being armed with God's power. When he is taken possession of by God, he demonstrates a tremendous power, becoming a war hero. He who displays the great power is a man, but he who makes it operate in the man is God. In this vein, we may say that God's putting on a man is in fact God's act of arming the man. If so, why is a human being not said to have put on the Spirit? Perhaps the passages intend to suggest that in the warfare God himself directly participates. He who initiates the warfare is not the man being empowered but God who is doing the empowering. In the warfare, human beings become like God's weapons. When he battles against human enemies,[91] he takes specific human beings as his equipment. When God identifies himself with a man, God becomes the man's actual owner, while the man becomes God-like. This divinization of a human being resembles the priest's becoming divine when he put on priestly garments. But whereas the former instance underlines a human being's identification with God's power, the latter emphasizes his identification with God's holiness. The concept of a man's demonstrating divine power through his being clothed by God (in other words, a man's union with God) seems to be borne in mind by Pauline clothing-with-a-person passages, especially Rom. 13.12-14, which combines the concept of clothing with the armour of light (v. 12) with clothing with Christ (v. 14).

In conclusion, in Judg. 6.34, 1 Chron. 12.18 and 2 Chron. 24.20 the metaphor of God's Spirit's being clothed with a particular human being describes how God identifies himself with that man. This metaphor is employed in order to describe what God can do when he is willing to fight against the foes of his people. By means of becoming one with a man, God empowers the man physically so that he may exercise a supernatural power. At that moment, the man is made to be at one with God, as a garment virtually becomes one with its wearer. But this does not mean that the man can be totally equated with God, because the raiment can never be equated with its wearer. This is similar to the fact that although God's people are divinized by being identified with God's holiness, they cannot be thoroughly equated with God's divinity itself (cf. Zech. 3.3-5).

90. Cf. J.M. Myers and P.P. Elliott, 'Judges', in *IB*, II (New York: Abingdon, 1956), pp. 677-825 (736), who asserts that 'The spirit of the Lord became incarnate in Gideon, who then became the extension of the Lord.' In *I Chronicles* (AB; New York: Doubleday, 1979 [1965]), p. 97, Myers holds that the Spirit of God's putting on of a person is a most significant concept of inspiration and revelation in the Old Testament and may be a forerunner of the idea of incarnation.

91. God is described as one who equips himself with divine attributes in order to combat the wicked in Isa. 59.17, although this passage does not suggest a human medium who is used as God's weapon.

5. *Cosmological Garment (Psalm 102.26; cf. Isaiah 51.6; Hebrews 1.11-12)*

In Ps. 102.26b we can find another analogy between the cosmos and a garment. The psalmist of the passage says,

> They [the earth and the heavens] will all wear out like a garment. Thou changest them like raiment, and they pass away.

This passage maintains an eschatological view of the cosmos. Its point is that in the future the cosmos will vanish; in order to describe this idea, the psalmist employs the theme of wearing out a garment and replacing it. As a garment wears out, so the cosmos will also wear out; as a worn-out garment is replaced by another, so the cosmos will also be replaced by a new one (cf. Isa. 65.17; 66.22). The psalmist is concerned with the fact that the garment is actually replaced, rather than with how it is related to its wearer. So our passage does not present who the wearer of the cosmological garment is or how that garment functions. Its only concern is with the eschatological change which will happen to the universe. The universe will come to an end and will be replaced by a new one, just as a worn-out raiment is replaced by a new one.

A similar analogy is used in Isa. 51.6, which reads,

> the heavens will vanish like smoke, the earth will wear out like a garment.

This passage also maintains an eschatological view of the universe. Although only the earth is analogized to a garment here, the concept of the universe's decomposition is exactly the same as that in Ps. 102.26b. Although our passage does not use the concept of 'replacement' of a garment as in Ps. 102.26b, its author seems to envisage such a thing when he makes use of the concept 'wearing out like a garment'. That is, as a worn-out garment is replaced by a new garment, so the present cosmos when it is dissolved will be exchanged with a new one (cf. Isa. 65.17; 66.22).

The author of Hebrews quotes both Ps. 102.26 and Isa. 34.4[92] to express a strongly eschatological view of the cosmos. Heb. 1.11b-12a writes,

> 11b they [the earth and the heavens] will all grow old like a garment, 12a like a mantle thou wilt roll them up, and they will be changed.

Verse 11b is quoted from Ps. 102.26b, while verse 12a is cited from Isa. 34.4a. In particular, verse 12a replaces the concept of a scroll (Isa. 34.4a) with the concept of

---

92.   Although it does not employ the concept of a garment, Isa. 34.4a also shares the same thought as that in Ps. 102.26b. It reads, 'All the host of heaven shall rot away, and the skies roll up like a scroll'. Here the concept of a garment in Ps. 102.26 is replaced by the concept of a scroll. Whereas Ps. 102 refers to the passing away of the earth and the heavens, the present passage speaks of the dissolving of the stars of the heavens and the skies. Despite these differences, what is clear in both passages is that they equally maintain an eschatological view of the cosmos. All the starry host will disintegrate, and the sky, which contains them, will be rolled up like a scroll. Here the concept of 'replacing', which is seen in Ps. 102.26b and implied in Isa. 51.6, does not occur. The concept of a scroll seems to have naturally required the use of its matching verb 'rolling up' instead of a clothing verb, which includes the idea of change as one of its important implications.

a mantle. Probably the author of Hebrews thinks that this alteration does not pervert the original meaning of Isa. 34.4a and matches rather well the concept of a garment in verse 11b. In any case, what the author wishes to highlight in Heb. 1.11b-12a is that the present cosmos will be changed into a new one (cf. Rev. 6.14; 20.11; 21.21). [93] As a garment wears out and is exchanged with a new one, so the cosmos will grow old and will be replaced by an indestructible one in keeping with God's eternal being (cf. Isa. 66.22). As a mantle is rolled up, so the present universe will be rolled up and instead a new one will come into existence.

Apart from its echo in Heb. 1.11b-12a, the idea of a cosmological garment in Ps. 102.26b and Isa. 51.6 (cf. 34.4a) seems also to be reflected in Philo's and Josephus' description of the Jewish high priest's garment. Philo believes that the Jewish high priest's garment symbolizes the universe, because of its imitation of all the pictures of the universe. When he adorns himself with the garment, the high priest becomes a microcosm and is identified with the universe. [94]

In brief, the imagery of a cosmological garment in Psalms and Isaiah (as well as their quotations in Hebrews) seems to indicate mainly the replaceable character of clothes. The writers of these books seem to have thought of this image of a garment as outstandingly apt for describing the eschatological change in the mode of existence of the cosmos.

6. Conclusion to Chapter 1

We have so far, then, investigated the significance of Old Testament clothing passages in four separate categories: Adam's garment, priestly garments, God's garment, and the cosmological garment. The involvement of the concept of the garment of skin (Gen. 3.21) not only with such positive concepts as the image of God (Gen. 1.26-27), life (Gen. 2.7), and lack of shame (Gen. 2.25) but also with the negative concept of shame at Adam's fallen nakedness (Gen. 3.7) suggests that clothing with the garment of skin signals man's restoration from death to life. The sequence of (1) man's original unashamed nakedness with the divine life in God's image, (2) his shameful nakedness in the state of death due to the Fall, and (3) God's clothing of Adam and Eve with garments of skin produced by the death of an animal, supports this interpretation.

The priest's attiring himself with the priestly garment symbolizes that he is identified both with God and with the people. The sacred character of the priestly garment implies that the priest's being clothed with it signifies that he is unified with its sacredness, which is typified by its glory and beauty (Exod. 28.2). In particular, the putting on of אוּרִים and תֻּמִּים signifies that the priest is symbolically identified with God's divinity. [95] When he dresses himself with the priestly garment, he becomes a man who is set apart from the ordinary people. Further, the

---

93. Cf. J. Jeremias, *The Parables of Jesus* (London: SCM Press, 1963), p. 118.

94. A further discussion on this issue will be performed in Chapter 2, §4.3.

95. In particular, the concept of 'light', which is embraced in the word אוּרִים, is frequently used in the OT as a term which designates God, e.g. Pss. 27.1; 43.3; 104.2; Isa. 2.5; 60.19; Dan. 2.22; Mic. 7.8.

symbolism of the priestly garment, as it includes various decorations (i.e. two onyx stones, on each of which six names of the sons of Israel are engraved, or twelve precious stones) which stand for the twelve tribes of Israel, suggests that the priest's donning of it connotes that he is identified with all the Israelites. As a garment tends to be identified with its wearer, so the priest, when he is dressed in such a garment which symbolizes the twelve patriarchs, is identified with the people of Israel. In particular, the dramatic scene of the high-priest Joshua's taking off the filthy garment and putting on the new garment symbolizes that God's people in their sinful nature will be changed into holy ones in their renewed nature (Zech. 3.3-5).

God's adorning himself with a human being signifies that God identifies himself with him, so as to take him into his personal possession (Judg. 6.34; 1 Chron. 12.18; 2 Chron. 24.20). This metaphor seems to have in mind a garment's closeness to, or oneness with, its wearer, rather than its prominence in manifesting his or her appearance or a tendency to express his or her character.

The cosmos' wearing out like a garment and its being replaced with a new one symbolizes that it will be radically changed into a new mode of existence (Ps. 102.26; Isa. 51.6; cf. Isa. 34.4; Heb. 1.11-12). The present cosmos will be transformed into an indestructible one in harmony with the eternal God. This metaphor seems to have in mind the exchangeable character of clothes.

Chapter 2

CLOTHING IMAGERY IN OTHER JEWISH LITERATURE

1. *Introduction*

This chapter aims to discover the significance of clothing images which occur in a wide range of Jewish documents. For this task, we will look into clothing imagery in the following documents: *1* and *2 Enoch* (which are normally classified as apocalyptic literature), *The Life of Adam and Eve* (which is a haggadic document), Philo, and the rabbinic literature.[1] All these documents contain significant references to 'clothing', which may throw light on the meaning of the clothing imagery in the Pauline corpus.

2. *1 and 2 Enoch*

2.1. *Introduction*

A cycle of Jewish legends about Enoch which, on the basis of Gen. 5.24, ascribes superhuman knowledge to him, finds literary expression in three pseudepigrapha attributed to Enoch: *1, 2* and *3 Enoch*. Of these, our concern in this sub-chapter is with *1 Enoch* (the so-called 'Ethiopic Enoch') and *2 Enoch* (the so-called 'Slavonic Enoch'),[2] because these documents refer to the garments of God (*1 Enoch* 14.20), of the righteous (*1 Enoch* 62.15-16), and of Enoch (*2 Enoch* 22.8-10).

1 Enoch 1.9, which is the only apocryphal book cited in the New Testament (Jude 14), is 'the best typical example of an apocalypse' on account of the great extent and the variety of its material.[3] The evidence of the Qumran fragments suggests that the book was originally written in Aramaic, with the possible exception of chapters 37–71, which could have been in Hebrew.[4] The book is in fact a collection of several previously independent works from different periods stretching from the

---

1. *Joseph and Aseneth* could have been included in the present chapter. But since four kinds of clothing images significantly penetrate the whole story of *Joseph and Aseneth*, a separate chapter will be assigned to this document (see Chapter 3).

2. *3 Enoch* is the so-called 'Hebrew Enoch', which dates from the fifth to sixth century AD.

3. C.C. Torrey, *The Apocryphal Literature: A Brief Introduction* (New Haven: Yale University Press, 1953 [1945]), p. 110; cf. E. Littmann, 'Enoch, Books Of (Ethiopic and Slavonic)', in I.K. Funk *et al.* (eds.), *JE*, V (New York and London: Funk and Wagnalls, 1903), pp. 179-82 (181).

4. L. Rost, *Judaism Outside the Hebrew Canon* (Nashville: Abingdon, 1976), p. 139; E. Isaac, '1 (Ethiopic Apocalypse of) Enoch', in J.H. Charlesworth (ed.), *OTP*, I (London: Darton, Longman & Todd, 1983), pp. 5-89 (6).

second century BC to the first century AD.[5] *1 Enoch* can be divided into five basic books: the 'book of the Watchers', which describes Enoch's journey (chapters 1–36), the similitudes (chapters 37–71), an astronomical section (chapters 72–82), dream visions (chapters 83–90) and the admonitions of Enoch (chapters 91–105). 'Chapters 106-108 are an addendum taken from a book of Noah (cf. Jub 10.13; 21.10).'[6] The provenance of *1 Enoch* is not certain, but 'it is clear that the work originated in Judea and was in use at Qumran before the beginning of the Christian period'.[7]

2 Enoch, which is also called 'The Book of the Secrets of Enoch', has been preserved only in two Slavonic versions.[8] This book is 'a free revision' of *1 Enoch*.[9] It is a midrashic amplification of Gen. 5.21-32, 'covering the life of Enoch and his posterity until the flood'.[10] As with *1 Enoch*, the first and main part of *2 Enoch* (chapters 1–68) can be divided into five parts: Enoch's notification about his imminent ascension (chapters 1–2), his ascent to the Lord through the seven heavens (chapters 3–21), his meeting with the Lord and his recording his revelation (chapters 22–38), his return to the earth (chapters 39–66), and his rapture into the highest heaven (chapter 67; the long version adds chapter 68).[11] The second part, chapters 69–73, briefly speak of the life of Enoch's successors. The original language of the main part of the book might be Greek; but certain portions of it were based on Hebrew originals.[12] The former may date to the period AD 1–50; the latter is at

---

5.   Isaac, '1 (Ethiopic Apocalypse of) Enoch', pp. vi, 6-7; cf. W.O.E. Oesterley, *The Books of the Apocrypha* (London: Roxburghe House, 1914), pp. 202-203; E. Schürer, *The History of the Jewish People in the Age of Jesus Christ* (175 BC-AD 135) III/1 (Edinburgh: T. & T. Clark, 1986 [1885]), p. 250.

6.   J.H. Charlesworth, *The Pseudepigrapha and Modern Research with a Supplement* (SBLSCSS, 7S; Michigan: Scholars, 1981), p. 99; cf. Rost, *Judaism Outside the Hebrew Canon*, pp. 134-36; Schürer, *The History of the Jewish People*, III/1, pp. 252-54; M.A. Knibb, '*1 Enoch*', in H.F.D. Sparks (ed.), *AOT* (Oxford: Clarendon, 1984), pp. 169-320 (especially, pp. 173-77).

7.   Isaac, '1 (Ethiopic Apocalypse of) Enoch', pp. 7-8; cf. Charlesworth, *The Pseudepigrapha and Modern Research*, p. 98; Rost, *Judaism Outside the Hebrew Canon*, pp. 134-35, 139-40; M.A. Knibb, 'The Date of the Parables of Enoch: A Critical Review', *NTS* 25 (1979), pp. 345-59; C.L. Mearns, 'Dating the Similitudes of Enoch', *NTS* 25 (1979), pp. 360-69; D.W. Suter, *Translation and Composition in the Parables of Enoch* (SBLDS, 47; Missoula: Scholars, 1979), pp. 11-33.

8.   Rost, *Judaism Outside the Hebrew Canon*, p. 111: 'a longer South Russian version in a manuscript from the second half of the seventeenth cenntury, published in 1880 by A. Popov, and a shorter version, itself incomplete, in a Serbian manuscript belonging to the public library in Belgrade, published in 1884 by S. Novakovic.' Cf. J.H. Charlesworth, 'Seminar Report: The SNTS Pseudepigrapha Seminars at Tübingen and Paris on the Books of Enoch', *NTS* 25 (1979), pp. 315-23 (especially pp. 316-18); E. Schürer, *The History of the Jewish People* (175 BC-AD 135) III/2 (Edinburgh: T. & T. Clark, 1987 [1885]), p. 746.

9.   Schürer, *The History of the Jewish People*, III/2, p. 746.

10.   Schürer, *The History of the Jewish People*, III/2, p. 746; F.I. Andersen, '2 (Slavonic Apocalypse of) Enoch', in J.H. Charlesworth (ed.), *OTP*, I (London: Darton, Longman & Todd, 1983), pp. 91-213 (91).

11.   Cf. Charlesworth, *The Pseudepigrapha and Modern Research*, p. 104.

12.   R.H. Charles, 'Enoch, Book of the Secrets of', in J. Hastings (ed.), *DB*, I (Peabody: Hendrickson, 1988 [Edinburgh: T. & T. Clark, 1898]), p. 709; Littmann, 'Enoch', p. 182; Oesterley, *The Books of the Apocrypha*, p. 221; W.R. Morfill, *The Book of the Secrets of Enoch* (Oxford:

latest pre-Christian.[13] The writer of *2 Enoch* was a 'Hellenistic Jew who lived in Egypt'.[14]

We turn now to a detailed investigation of the garment passages in *1* and *2 Enoch*, for the purpose of unfolding the significance of the imagery.

2.2. *A Garment of God (1 Enoch 14.20)*

1 Enoch 14.8-25 recounts Enoch's experience of ascending to heaven in a vision. In heaven he sees the throne of God. God is dressed in a splendid garment, which is described in verses 18-21.

> 18 And I observed and saw inside it a lofty throne—its appearance was like crystal and its wheels like the shining sun; and (I heard?) the voice of the cherubim; 19 and from beneath the throne were issuing streams of flaming fire. It was difficult to look at it. 20 And the Great Glory was sitting upon it—as for his gown, which was shining more brightly than the sun, it was whiter than any snow. 21 None of the angels was able to come in and see the face of the Excellent and the Glorious One; and no one of the flesh can see him.[15]

'The Great Glory' in verse 20a undoubtedly refers to God. 'The Excellent [One]' and 'the Glorious One' in verse 21 are its equivalents. God's characteristics are directly used as his titles. Verse 20b is an explanation of God's identity as 'the Great Glory'. He is so glorious that neither angels nor human beings can see him face to face (v. 21; cf. *Asc. Isa.* 10.2).[16] For the author, God's being 'Glory' can be described in terms of the pre-eminent radiance and whiteness[17] of his raiment. Out of this observation, two significant questions may be raised: (1) why is the clothing idea used to elaborate the idea of God as glory? and (2) what is the meaning of his garment's radiance and whiteness?

Clarendon, 1896), pp. xvi-xvii; cf. Andersen, '2 (Slavonic Apocalypse of) Enoch', p. 94; Schürer, *The History of the Jewish People*, III/2, p. 748.

13. Charles, 'Enoch, Book of the Secrets of', pp. 709-10; cf. Littmann, 'Enoch', p. 182, who imagines that *2 Enoch* was probably written between 50 BC and AD 70 on the ground that it makes use of *1 Enoch*, Ecclesiasticus, and Wisdom of Solomon; Charlesworth, *The Pseudepigrapha and Modern Research*, p. 104; Morfill, *The Book of the Secrets of Enoch*, p. xxv; A. Pennington, '2 Enoch', in H.F.D. Sparks (ed.), *AOT* (Oxford: Clarendon, 1984), pp. 321-62 (323-25).

14. Charles, 'Enoch, Book of the Secrets of', p. 710; cf. Andersen, '2 (Slavonic Apocalypse of) Enoch', pp. 95-97; Charlesworth, *The Pseudepigrapha and Modern Research*, p. 104; Rost, *Judaism Outside the Hebrew Canon*, p. 113; Oesterley, *The Books of the Apocrypha*, p. 221; Morfill, *The Book of the Secrets of Enoch*, p. xvii.

15. Translation from Isaac, '1 (Ethiopic Apocalypse of) Enoch', p. 21.

16. Cf. Exod. 34.29-35, which informs that God's glory, which was revealed in Moses' face after his having been in the presence of God at the top of Mt Sinai, was so radiant that the Israelites could not tolerate the sight of Moses, resulting in his putting a veil on his own face. In a sense, the veil can be thought of as God's covering which hides his sublime glory.

17. On the splendour of God's throne, cf. Ps. 104.1-2; on the whiteness of God's raiment, cf. Dan. 7.9. M. Black, *The Book of Enoch or 1 Enoch* (Leiden: Brill, 1985), p. 150 affirms that the literary relationship between LXX Dan. 7.9 and *1 Enoch* 14.20 in the Gizeh Papyrus text cannot be denied.

In relation to question (1), we posit that the author's wish to clarify his description of God as Glory[18] results in his using the imagery of God's being dressed in a sunlight-like gown. He wants to symbolize God's gloriousness by this clothing imagery.[19] He perhaps has in mind various aspects of the relationship between a garment and its wearer. The raiment and its wearer always go together, acting as one so that the raiment almost becomes part of its wearer. Further, the raiment defines and dominates the appearance of its wearer, since it wraps the whole body. Its physical colour, design and quality bespeak his individual character or status. Nevertheless, the raiment cannot be equated with its wearer, even though the one is closely linked with the other. Whatever God's garment is like, he never fails to remain a being who transcends it. The splendid glory of God's garment is always there with him, determining his appearance and disclosing his character, although this cannot be completely equated with the being of God himself.

We turn to question (2): what is meant by the notion of God's garment's being radiant and white? The author speaks of God donning the garment of glory, and so this notion can be regarded as a description of his glorious appearance. In Judaism glory is often associated with light.[20] The concept of whiteness seems to be influenced by the whiteness of the high priest's linen garments, which he wore when he entered the most holy place once a year (cf. Lev. 16.4). In the Book of the Watchers (*1 Enoch* 1–36) which includes 14.20, heaven is pictured as a temple, so the heavenly temple is considered as corresponding to the earthly temple. According to this scheme, God's throne is thought of as the heavenly holy of holies; angels, as heavenly priests; and Enoch, as the heavenly high priest. The whole picture of heaven as a temple might remind the author of the white linen garments of the high priest and further encourage him to apply the whiteness to God's gown, as God's throne was considered the most holy place of the heavenly temple. As the high priest's white linen garments are called 'sacred garments' (cf. Lev. 16.4, 32), it is probable that the whiteness of God's garment stands for his holiness.[21] Further, as

18. In many other places in *1 Enoch*, the concept 'God' (or the 'Lord') is called or modified by 'Glory', e.g. 14.19; 22.14; 25.7; 27.3; 36.4; 40.3; 63.2; 75.3; 83.8; 91.13; 102.3. Many other Jewish writings also recognize God as glory; see *Apoc. El.* 1.3; *3 Bar.* 6.12; 7.2; 11.2; 16.4 (Slavonic only); *3 Enoch* 24.22; *4 Ezra* 7.91; 8.21; *Gk. Apoc. Ezra* 6.8; *Quest. Ezra* Recension A, 21, 29; *Test. Levi* 3.4; *Ladd. Jacob* 2.22; *Pss. David* 154 (11 QPs[a] 154), 9; 154 (*5 Apocry. Syr. Pss.* 2), 1-2; *Pss. Sol.* 18.10; *Asc. Isa.* 9.37; 10.2. This theme of God-as-Glory seems to succeed to the same motif in OT; see Exod. 16.10; 24.16; 40.34; Num. 14.21; Deut. 5.24; 1 Chron. 29.11; Pss. 19.1; 29.1; 57.5; 72.19; 108.5; Isa. 6.1-3; Ezek. 1.28; 10.4; 43.2; 44.4; Hab. 2.14; 3.3; Zech. 2.5, among which Ezek. 10.4, in particular, applies the combined concept 'the brightness of the glory' to God.

19. Cf. Isa. 6.1-3, where the motif of God's robe is combined with his glory: '… the train of his [God's] robe filled the temple…the whole earth is full of his glory'. R.P. Spittler, 'Testament of Job', in J.H. Charlesworth (ed.), *OTP*, I (London: Darton, Longman & Todd, 1983), pp. 829-68 (especially, p. 866, fn. 48h) notes that Hekhalot Rabbati 24 describes God as 'glorified with embroideries of songs'; he also quotes Hekhalot Rabbati 3.4 which speaks of God's garment as 'And it is every part engraved from within and from without JHWH JHWH'.

20. Cf. *Gen. Rab.* 12.6; *HPrl* 64-66, 75, 83, 86; *JA* 20.6; 21.5. See also relevant OT passages, e.g. Exod. 28.2 ('glory'), 30 ('Urim', i.e. lights); Ps. 104.1-2. Apuleius, *Metam.* XI.24 describes Lucius' glorious attirement of himself with twelve garments as being sun-like.

21. As we shall see in section 2.4, a description of Enoch's garment (*2 Enoch* 22.8-10) entirely

Pauline clothing-with-a-person passages (especially Rom. 13.14; Col. 3.9-10; Eph. 4.22-24) emphasize a believer's righteous conduct and imply his attainment of a glorious state like that of the prelapsarian Adam,[22] they seem to envisage the believer's being identified with God's glory and holiness.

2.3. *Garments of the Righteous (1 Enoch 62.15-16)*

The author of the Similitudes (*1 Enoch* 37–71) expresses a serious concern for the fate of souls after death. The central theme of the book is that the righteous will be redeemed and the wicked will be condemned. In particular, chapter 62 stresses the curse on the wicked ruling class and the blessedness of the righteous ones. This implies that the author of the Similitudes takes a defiant attitude toward the 'haves', the powerful.

The place where the idea of the righteous' garments appears is in *1 Enoch* 62.15-16, which reads,

> 15 The righteous and elect ones shall rise from the earth and shall cease being of downcast face. They shall wear the garments of glory. 16 These garments of yours shall become the garments of life from the Lord of the Spirits. Neither shall your garments wear out, nor your glory come to an end before the Lord of the Spirits.[23]

R.H. Charles argues that verse 15 'does not refer to the resurrection but signifies that all the humiliations of the righteous are at an end'.[24] Yet, considering that the Similitudes highlight Enoch's ascent to heaven and his eventual transformation (71.11), it is likely that the phrase 'rise from the earth' (v. 15b) signifies not merely an escape from earthly conditions but also an entrance into heavenly conditions. This may be supported by the following statement (vv. 15b-16), which refers to the same point in time as 15a, and to what the state of the righteous' existence will be like in heaven. In fact, as was pointed out, chapter 62 as a whole refers to future affairs which will take place on the day of God's judgment. Verse 13, moreover, states that 'the righteous and elect ones shall be saved on that day', which is recounted in our passage in a different fashion. Accordingly, we conclude that verses 15b-16 refer to the heavenly body which will be owned by the righteous after their earthly lives.[25]

depends on the description of God's garment here in *1 Enoch* 14.20. This suggests that in the author's mind (at least in *2 Enoch* 22) the picture of the heavenly temple is the model of that of the earthly temple. But inasmuch as the concept of the whiteness of God's garment (*1 Enoch* 14) is concerned, as has been argued, the earthly priestly linen garments could be seen as its background.

22. See Chapters 8 and 9.

23. Quoted from Isaac, '1 (Ethiopic Apocalypse of) Enoch', p. 44.

24. R.H. Charles, *The Book of Enoch* (Oxford: Clarendon, 1893), p. 166; *The Book of Enoch or 1 Enoch* (Oxford: Clarendon, 1912), p. 125.

25. C.M. Pate, *Adam Christology as the Exegetical & Theological Substructure of 2 Corinthians 4.7-5.21* (New York: University Press of America, 1991), pp. 46-50; Oesterley, *The Books of the Apocrypha*, p. 208. Charles, *The Book of Enoch or 1 Enoch*, p. 125 believes that 'the garments of glory' can be compared with various garments which are seen in 2 Cor. 5.3-4; Rev. 3.4-5, 18; 4.4; 6.11; 7.9, 13-14; *4 Ezra* 2.39, 45; *Herm. Sim.* 8.2. He contends that the garments of glory are 'spiritual bodies that await the righteous' (cf. 2 Cor. 5.2-5).

If so, what kind of heavenly body do the phrases about garments suggest? 'The garments of glory' (15b)[26] implies that the future body of the righteous will be similar to the existence of God as Glory. It seems that the author of the Similitudes models our passage on *1 Enoch* 14.20, in which God's garment can be called the garment of glory. If this is acceptable, 'the garments of glory' can be considered as referring to the body of glory. As a garment envelops its wearer, so glory will encompass the future body of the righteous.

We also pay attention to the identification of 'the garments of glory' with the words 'the garments of life'. For the author, the terms are interchangeable. Our passage makes it clear that the body of glory, which will be the reality of the existence of the righteous after their death, will be the body of life. The future body of the righteous will be characterized by immortality.[27] As a garment prevails over the appearance of its wearer, so life will dominate the appearance of the future body of the righteous. In order to reinforce this idea, the author highlights the everlasting character of this body: the statement 'neither shall your garments wear out,[28] nor your glory come to an end' undoubtedly underlines its immortal nature. These implications in *1 Enoch* 62.15-16 look forward to the Pauline resurrection clothing imagery, which stresses that immortality will be dominant in the believer's resurrection body (1 Cor. 15.49, 50-54; 2 Cor. 5.1-4).

2.4. *Enoch's Change of Garments (2 Enoch 22.8-10)*
The story in *2 Enoch* of Enoch's changing his garments belongs to his report as to what happened to him at the seventh heaven: as he was brought before the face of the Lord, who sat on his throne and before whom the ten great orders of angels were standing.

> 8 And the Lord said to Michael, 'Go, and extract Enoch from his earthly clothing. And anoint him with my delightful oil, and put him into the clothes of my glory'. 9 And so Michael did, just as the Lord had said to him. He anointed me and he clothed me. And the appearance of that oil is greater than the greatest light, and its ointment is like sweet dew, and its fragrance myrrh; and it is like the rays of the glittering sun. 10 And I looked at myself, and I had become like one of the glorious ones, and there was no observable difference.[29]

This passage describes Enoch's experience of transformation from an earthly to a heavenly mode of existence. 'The clothes of my [God's] glory' could be interpreted as the garment which is 'composed of God's glory'.[30] It is likely that

---

26. Charles, *The Book of Enoch or 1 Enoch*, p. 125 also follows this reading, though he recognizes that some other documents describe it as 'garments of life'. M.A. Knibb, *The Ethiopic Book of Enoch*, II (Oxford: Clarendon, 1978), p. 152 renders *2 Enoch* 22.15b 'the garment of life' on the basis of Rylands Ethiopic MS. 23, though he recognizes that in many other texts the phrase is written as 'the garment of glory'.

27. Black, *The Book of Enoch or 1 Enoch*, p. 237 insists that 'the further description of these garments in v. 16 as "garments of (eternal) life" points unequivocally to the idea of "garments of immortality"'.

28. This concept echoes Deut. 8.4; 29.5.

29. Quoted from Andersen, '2 (Slavonic Apocalypse of) Enoch', p. 138.

30. Charles, *The Book of Enoch or 1 Enoch*, p. 272.

Enoch's earthly clothing signifies his earthly body, and the clothes of God's glory symbolize his glorious heavenly body. This view can be supported by the fact that the 'clothes of my glory' corresponds with 'the garments of glory' (*1 Enoch* 62.15), identified as 'the garments of life' (*1 Enoch* 62.16), which indicates the immortal body of the righteous after their death.[31] In fact, Enoch's discovery of an angelic appearance in himself after his threestep investiture (that is, his being divested from his earthly garments, his anointing with the divine oil, and his being dressed in the clothes of God's glory) clearly suggests that he has been transfigured into a heavenly being.[32]

Enoch's being adorned with the clothes of God's glory signifies that his existence has been transformed into a radiant and holy one. This interpretation can be supported by the fact that our passage closely parallels *1 Enoch* 14.20, which includes such concepts as God's throne, sun, radiance and glory. This implies that Enoch's clothes being made up of God's glory (*2 Enoch* 22.8) can be compared with God's extremely splendid and white gown (*1 Enoch* 14.20), in which 'splendour' highlights his glory, while 'whiteness' denotes his holiness. It is probable that behind the statement that Enoch has been transformed into an angelic being, there lies the idea that his existence has become radiant and holy like that of God.[33]

Apart from this parallelism, our passage also proves that Enoch's transformed appearance is full of glory. The anointing serves to heighten Enoch's splendour to the maximum; the anointing oil is extremely brilliant and its radiance is like the glittering sun. Enoch's explanation as to his own appearance after transformation also proves that he has become splendid, that is, he 'became like one of glorious ones'. It is true that our text does not overtly refer to his being holy. But, as we have already discerned, the parallelism of our passage with *1 Enoch* 14.20 implicitly indicates this. And as the language of anointing and clothing suggests our passage to be 'a heavenly version of priestly investiture',[34] it can be concluded that the holiness of his transformed body is implied.

2.5. *Conclusion*

God's garment of brightness and whiteness (*1 Enoch* 14.20) describes his appearance as the Great Glory. As a garment reflects its wearer's character, so God's gloriousness and holiness characterize his existence. His glory is so supreme that neither human nor angelic beings can directly face him.

31. Cf. Charles, *The Book of Enoch or 1 Enoch*, p. 272; Morfill, *The Book of the Secrets of Enoch*, p. 28.

32. M. Himmelfarb, *Ascent to Heaven* (Oxford: Oxford University Press, 1993), p. 4 points out that an important element common to apocalyptic literature is 'the belief that human beings can become the equals of angels.'

33. This identification of Enoch with God is in line with one of *2 Enoch*'s central ideas: that as the image of God, man is the facsimile of God, God's visible face.

34. Himmelfarb, *Ascent to Heaven*, p. 40; see also pp. 38-39 and 41-44: in *2 Enoch* the angelic liturgy is prominent most explicitly in the sixth and seventh heavens. Enoch is regarded as a priest: in other words, he is God's chosen who carries away men's sins. The closing chapters of *2 Enoch* refer to the succession of the priestly office after Enoch's translation into heaven. Ascent to heaven would indicate entering into a temple and becoming an angel would signify becoming a heavenly priest.

The garments of glory or life, which the righteous will wear (*1 Enoch* 62.15-16), symbolize the heavenly body which they will possess from the day of judgment onwards. It will be a glorious body, which will resemble the appearance of God the Great Glory, and its outstanding characteristic will be immortality. As a garment epitomizes the nature of its wearer, so glory and life will be decisive elements in the future body of the godly. The combination of these two elements seems to originate in Gen. 2–3, which links life with being free of shame (cf. Gen. 2.7, 17, 25; 3.7, 10-11).

Enoch's change of earthly garments for the garments of God's glory (*2 Enoch* 22.8) symbolizes that his earthly body is replaced by a heavenly body. The transformation from the one to the other means that he becomes an angelic being. In the light of the passage's parallelism with *1 Enoch* 14.20 and 62.15-16, it is implied that he has become a glorious being who is characterized by life and holiness.

3. *The Books of Adam and Eve*

3.1. *Introduction*
L.S.A. Wells says that the 'The Book, or rather Books, which bear the name of Adam belong to a cycle of legendary matter, of which the Jews were fond, and which the Christians took, and developed, from them'.[35] Of the books which belong here, the most important are the Greek text *Apocalypse of Moses* (hereafter *Apoc. Mos.*), which is misnamed,[36] and the Latin text *Vita Adae et Evae* (hereafter *Vita*).[37] The former was published by von Tischendorf in 1866[38] on the basis of four manuscripts (A1 B C D);[39] the latter was edited by W. Meyer in 1878.[40] The original texts of *Apoc. Mos.* and *Vita* are much earlier than these times, and they

---

35. L.S.A. Wells, 'The Books of Adam and Eve', in R.H. Charles (ed.), *APOT*, II (Oxford: Clarendon, 1913), pp. 123-54 (123); cf. J.T. Marshall, 'Adam, Books Of', in J. Hastings (ed.), *DB*, I (Peabody: Hendrickson, 1988 [Edinburgh: T. & T. Clark, 1898]), pp. 37-38.

36. O. Eissfeldt, *The Old Testament: An Introduction* (Oxford: Basil Blackwell, 1965), p. 637; Schürer, *The History of the Jewish People*, III/2, p. 757; Wells, 'The Books of Adam and Eve', p. 124.

37. J.R. Levison, 'Adam and Eve, Life Of', in *ABD*, I (New York: Doubleday, 1992), p. 64. Both *Apoc. Mos.* and *Vita* provide a midrashic narrative of the story of the first man and woman described in the first chapters of Genesis, after their expulsion from Paradise, especially of their deathbed retrospections and instructions. Although these two texts show different plots, they overlap in about half their material (*Apoc. Mos.* is shorter than *Vita*). This overlap implies that there is a literary relationship between them.

38. Torrey, *The Apocryphal Literature*, p. 131; M.D. Johnson, 'Life of Adam and Eve', in J.H. Charlesworth (ed.), *OTP*, II (New York: Doubleday, 1985), pp. 249-95 (249); L.S.A. Wells (trans.) and M. Whittaker (rev.), 'The Life of Adam and Eve', in H.F.D. Sparks (ed.), *AOT* (Oxford: Clarendon, 1984), pp. 141-68 (especially pp. 141-42).

39. Concerning the classification of the manuscripts, see Johnson, 'Life of Adam and Eve', p. 250.

40. J.H. Mozley, 'Documents: the "Vita Adae"', *JTS* 30 (1929), pp. 121-49; Charlesworth, *The Pseudepigrapha and Modern Research*, p. 74; Wells (trans.) and Whittaker (rev.), 'The Life of Adam and Eve', pp. 142-43.

pre-date the Armenian[41] and Slavonic texts which are renderings from the Greek text, and to the other Adam literature.[42]

There is a wide consensus that the original text, from which the Greek and Latin texts derive, was composed in Hebrew or Aramaic,[43] and that *Apoc. Mos.* is probably earlier than *Vita*.[44] If so, what are the dates of the Semitic original and of *Apoc. Mos.* and *Vita*? It needs to be noted that *Apoc. Mos.* and *Vita* have many parallels with early rabbinic traditions,[45] with the Dead Sea Scrolls, with pseudepigraphical works (e.g. *Jubilees, 4 Ezra* and *2 Baruch*,[46] *1* and *2 Enoch*[47] [especially *2 Enoch*[48]], *Testament of Job*[49]), and with Josephus.[50] Although the range of the dates of these documents is wide, some parallels imply that the Greek and Latin recensions came into existence at a time near the early stages of Christianity. Johnson asserts that 'the original [Hebrew] composition would be between 100 BC and AD 200, more probably toward the end of the first Christian century. The Greek and Latin texts were produced between that time and AD 400'.[51]

41.   For an English translation of the Armenian text, see F.C. Conybeare, 'On the Apocalypse of Moses', *JQR* 7 (1895), pp. 216-35; also M. Stone, 'The Death of Adam: An Armenian Adam Book', *HTR* 59 (1966), pp. 283-91, which includes a short translation of an Armenian text and a brief commentary on it.

42.   E.g. *The Cave of Treasures* preserved in Syriac, Arabic and Ethiopic; all of *The Combat of Adam and Eve, The Testament of Adam* and *The Apocalypse of Adam*, which are among the gnostic works found in Nag Hammadi; these documents show that there was 'continued interest among Christian writers in speculating upon the life of the protoplasts Adam and Eve' (Johnson, 'Life of Adam and Eve', pp. 250-51); cf. Wells, 'The Books of Adam and Eve', pp. 125-26. Yet, Levison, 'Adam and Eve, Life Of', pp. 64-65 points out that such Adam documents 'have no direct literary relationship with the *Apocalypse of Moses* and *Vita Adae et Evae*'.

43.   Johnson, 'Life of Adam and Eve', p. 251. He imagines that *Apoc. Mos.* was translated directly from a Hebrew text; *Vita*, either directly from the Hebrew or from the Greek. Cf. J.M. Evans, *Paradise Lost and the Genesis Tradition* (Oxford: Clarendon, 1968), p. 55.

44.   Johnson, 'Life of Adam and Eve', p. 251; cf. Wells, 'The Books of Adam and Eve', pp. 128-29; see also Schürer, *The History of the Jewish People*, III/2, pp. 757-58 who says that 'the *Life* (= *Vita*) was unknown to the editor of the *Apocalypse* (= *Apoc. Mos.*) but that, by contrast, the *Apocalypse* is presupposed by the arrangement of the *Life*'. In contrast, Meyer regards the *Vita* as earlier (Levison, 'Adam and Eve, Life Of', p. 65). But as Torrey, *The Apocryphal Literature*, p. 131 argues, since all the versions of the Adam story go back to 'a single Greek translation made from the Jewish (and Semitic) archetype', Meyer's opinion would scarcely be supportable.

45.   Johnson, 'Life of Adam and Eve', p. 252.

46.   Levison, 'Adam and Eve, Life Of', pp. 65-66; *idem, Portraits of Adam in Early Judaism: From Sirach to 2 Baruch* (JSPSS, 1; Sheffield: JSOT Press, 1988), pp. 189-90.

47.   Concerning the parallels between *Vita* 25-29; 49-50 and *1 Enoch*, see G.W.E. Nickelsburg, 'Some Related Traditions in the Apocalypse of Adam, The Books of Adam and Eve, and *1 Enoch*', in B. Layton (ed.), *The Rediscovery of Gnosticism* II: *Sethian Gnosticism* (SHR, 41; Leiden: Brill, 1981), pp. 526-33.

48.   Johnson, 'Life of Adam and Eve', p. 255; Wells, 'The Books of Adam and Eve', p. 132; J.J. Collins, *Between Athens and Jerusalem: Jewish Identity in the Hellenistic Diaspora* (New York: Crossroad, 1983), p. 225.

49.   Collins, *Between Athens and Jerusalem*, pp. 224-25.

50.   Cf. Josephus, *Ant.* i.2.3 with *Vita* 50.

51.   Johnson, 'Life of Adam and Eve', p. 252; cf. Schürer, *The History of the Jewish People*, III/2, p. 759; Eissfeldt, *The Old Testament*, p. 637; Wells, 'The Books of Adam and Eve', p. 127.

The provenance and author of the original document are far from clear. Yet, several elements which are included in the Greek and Latin texts suggest that it was written by a Jew in Palestine. The Adam texts manifest the midrashic or haggadic character[52] which is 'so typical of Qumran and the Rabbis'.[53] Considering that the documents show no traces of Philonic interpretation of biblical passages, the author of the main traditions was probably 'a Jew who had not absorbed much of Greek piety or the Philonian exegetic methods'.[54]

The occurrence of several parallels between these two texts and the New Testament, especially the Pauline writings,[55] suggests that the former are worthwhile investigating. In the following section, we will concentrate on an examination of the ideas of Adam and Eve's pre-Fall clothing as seen in *Apoc. Mos.*, of the nature of their original garments, and of the symbolism of the heavenly linen and silken cloths which were put on Adam's dead body. We will then draw a conclusion about the clothing imagery of *Apoc. Mos.*

3.2. *Adam and Eve's Pre-Fall Clothing: Righteousness and Glory (Apoc. Mos. 20–21)*

The clothing image occurs in *Apoc. Mos.* 20–21 in a most striking manner, which results from a haggadic interpretation of Gen. 3.7. *Apoc. Mos.* 20–21 belong to the context of the account of what Adam and Eve recognized about their nakedness, immediately after their Fall.[56] Direct reference to clothing occurs only twice in *Apoc. Mos.* 20, but these allusions are of great importance, because they purport to convey what happened to the first couple's nature in the transition from the pre-Fall to the post-Fall period. In *Apoc. Mos.* 20.1-5 Eve confesses:

> And at that very moment my eyes were opened and I knew that I was naked of the righteousness with which I had been clothed. And I wept saying, 'Why have you done this to me, that I have been estranged from my glory with which I was clothed?'... And I took its [the fig tree's] leaves and made for myself skirts.[57]

This passage apparently shows that the author of *Apoc. Mos.* maintains Adam and Eve's prelapsarian clothing. This is made clear by the expressions, 'the

---

52. Cf. Torrey, *The Apocryphal Literature*, p. 132, who argues that 'The book [of Adam and Eve] is mainly pure haggada; incidents in the life of Adam and Eve not furnished by the Biblical narrative are here supplied'; cf. Eissfeldt, *The Old Testament*, p. 636; Charlesworth, *The Pseudepigrapha and Modern Research*, p. 74; Levison, *Portraits of Adam*, pp. 164-65.

53. Johnson, 'Life of Adam and Eve', p. 252.

54. Johnson, 'Life of Adam and Eve', p. 252; cf. Schürer, *The History of the Jewish People*, III/2, pp. 758-59; Wells, 'The Books of Adam and Eve', p. 129; Collins, *Between Athens and Jerusalem*, p. 225.

55. E.g. [*Apoc. Mos.* 14.2//2 Cor. 11.3; Rom. 5.12-21; 1 Tim. 2.4], [*Vita* 9.1; *Apoc. Mos.* 17.1// 2 Cor. 11.14], [*Apoc. Mos.* 37.5//2 Cor. 12.2], [*Apoc. Mos.* 19.3//Rom. 7.7]. However, as Johnson points out, these parallels cannot be a proof that our texts are involved with the NT ('Life of Adam and Eve', p. 255); cf. Wells (trans.) and Whittaker (rev.), 'The Life of Adam and Eve', p. 142.

56. *Apoc. Mos.* 20–21 belong to a larger unit, chapters 15–30, which cover Eve's account of the Fall and its consequences. The story of the Fall is concentrated in chapters 15–23.

57. Johnson, 'Life of Adam and Eve', p. 281; text quotations below will be from Johnson. Cf. *Gen. Rab.* 19.6; *Pirqe R. El.* 14.

righteousness with which I had been clothed'[58] and 'my glory with which I was clothed'. For the author, Adam and Eve were originally dressed in 'righteousness' and 'glory', but at the Fall they were stripped of these characteristics. If so, what is meant by their pre-Fall investiture with these characteristics? J.L. Sharpe holds that

> when Eve ate the fruit, her first realization was that she had been stripped of the *righteousness* and the *glory* which she had at the beginning. The righteous and glorious nature of God's creatures may be described as their unblemished inner quality and spiritual endowment, which was a reflection of their Creator in them.[59]

Eve's statement of her having been clothed with righteousness as well as with glory reveals that righteousness and glory have a close relationship with one another. The author of *Apocalypse of Moses* seems to think that these character-istics are interdependent. When there is righteousness, there is also glory; when there is glory, there is also righteousness. As righteousness is maintained, glory continues. Thus it seems that they are conditional upon one another.[60]

Yet we need to analyse what is meant by each item of the pre-Fall clothing: righteousness and glory. Concerning the concept of clothing with righteousness, we note that Eve's recognition of being denuded of righteousness results from her betrayal of God's commandment. This implies that righteousness indicates an ethical perfection which can be established by obedience to God's covenantal command-ment.[61] In *Apoc. Mos.* 23.3, God says that Adam's recognition of his nakedness has been caused by his neglect of his command. Without ethical loyalty[62] in relation-ship to God, there can be no righteousness. But how can ethical faithfulness to God's commandment be designated by the concept of righteousness? An answer may be deduced from the statement of *Apoc. Mos.* 27.5a, 'You are righteous, Lord.' Inasmuch as God is righteous, his commandment is also righteous. As one keeps the righteous commandment, he becomes righteous. One who observes God's righteous commandment can exist as a person of righteousness. Hence Eve's original investi-ture with righteousness denotes that she was endued with ethical perfection. Her loss of righteousness results from her ethical failure in her relationship with God. The Fall has caused an 'evil heart' in men (*Apoc. Mos.* 13.15), which cannot produce good conduct.

---

58. Cf. *Šabb.* 14a; *Meg.* 32a; *Gen. Rab.* 19.6; *Pirqe R. El.* 14.

59. J.L. Sharpe, 'The Second Adam in the Apocalypse of Moses', *CBQ* 35 (1973), pp. 35-41 (37).

60. Sharpe asserts that 'the writer of the *Apoc. Mos.* treats the terms "righteousness" and "glory" as synonymous and inseparable correlatives, and, since both are the visible splendor which symbolize divine perfection, they are "the majesty or goodness of God manifested to men"' (Sharpe, 'The Second Adam', p. 37). In this statement the word 'inseparable' is acceptable, but the word 'synonymous' is not; this exaggeration seems to cause Sharpe to fail to see each concept's peculiar force.

61. God speaks of Adam's having eaten the forbidden fruit as his having forsaken his 'covenant' (*Apoc. Mos.* 7.1 and 8.2; cf. 23.3; 24.1, 4; 25.1).

62. L. Ginzberg, *The Legends of the Jews*, V (Philadelpha: The Jewish Publication Society of America, 1954), pp. 121-22, fn. 120, notices that 'the haggadic interpretation of עֵירֻמִּם (Gen. 3.7, 10) is: "And they became aware that they were bare of good deeds"'.

What does the pre-Fall investiture with glory then signify? It is clear that 'my glory' in *Apoc. Mos.* 20.2 does not mean that Eve's glory is derived from herself. The words may be rendered 'God's glory in me'. As Adam speaks of his loss of 'the glory of God' (*Apoc. Mos.* 21.6), beyond doubt 'my [Eve's] glory' connotes the glory which is given to her. If so, what is the substance of the divine glory granted to Adam and Eve? We note that the concept 'glory' is closely linked with the concept of the 'image of God' in the *Books of Adam and Eve.*[63] Like the glory, the image of God is derived from God and is bestowed on man (cf. *Vita* 13.3; *Apoc. Mos.* 31.4). C.M. Pate argues that *Vita* 12.1 and 13.2-3; 14.2 show that 'Adam was originally created in the image of God and that he possessed the glory of God, as well'.[64] As the glory is always with him like clothes, so the image of God constantly occupies his being, to the extent that he is called 'the image of God'. In fact, Eve calls herself and her son Seth 'the image of God' in *Apoc. Mos.* 10.3; 12.1 (cf. *Vita* 37.3[65]). The angel calls Adam 'your [God's] image' in *Apoc. Mos.* 33.5; 35.2 (cf. *Vita* 13.3; 14.1-2; 15.2);[66] in particular, in *Apoc. Mos.* 33.5 these words are juxtaposed with the phrase 'the work of your (holy) hands' (cf. *Vita* 27.2; *'Abot R. Nat.* i.). In 31.4, Adam calls himself 'his [God's] own vessel which he has formed'.

If the image of God thus parallels 'my [Eve's] glory' or 'the glory of God' (*Apoc. Mos.* 20.2; 21.6), what is its central idea? *Vita* 13-14 may provide certain insights into this issue. In chapter 13, the author of *Vita* speaks of God's creation of Adam in his image,[67] then of Michael's bringing forth Adam in order to make the devil worship him in the sight of God, and then of God's statement that he has made him in his image. In chapter 14, Michael instructs all the angels to 'worship the image of the Lord God, as the Lord God has instructed' (v. 1), then he himself worships Adam, and then urges the devil to worship 'the image of God' (v. 2). The worship of Adam is thus commanded by God. All the angelic beings should worship him. The reason for this, the author obviously implies, is because Adam is the image of God. This tells us that God's image in man is such as to merit being worshipped. Aside from Adam, only God is to be worshipped by the angels (*Apoc. Mos.* 17.1; 33.5). And God is full of glory (cf. *Apoc. Mos.* 33). A clear point is that Adam is worthy of being worshipped since in him the image of God is retained. Because of God's image in him, he is regarded as being almost as high as God;[68]

63. Cf. 1 Cor. 11.7, which includes the phrase, 'the image and glory of God'.

64. Pate, *Adam Christology*, p. 60.

65. See also *Vita* 39.2-3, in which Seth as the speaker calls himself 'the image of God' (cf. Gen. 5.1-3).

66. No doubt in significance the statement that Adam is the image of God (cf. *Apoc. Mos.* 33.5; 35.2) is stronger than the statement that he is created in the image of God (cf. *Vita* 13.3). While the former gives the nuance that Adam is an incarnation of God, the latter connotes that Adam is a reflection of God. It is interesting that 'the image of God' is made use of as Adam's actual title even after the Fall; it cannot be annihilated. Yet the Fall so seriously affects the image of God that its function has been minimized. When the divine image in Adam and Eve had been so gravely defaced (cf. *Apoc. Mos.* 21.6, 'destruction'), they could not be beings of glory any more.

67. See Levison, *Portraits of Adam*, p. 178.

68. G.A. Anderson, 'The Exaltation of Adam and the Fall of Satan', *JJTP* 6 (1997), pp. 105-34 (107).

because of it, he can share the supreme status of God. In short, the image of God can be designated as the reflection of God's supremacy. As Adam and Eve were clothed with glory, which is reflected in the image of God in them, they had royal rulership over the other creatures.[69] When Adam reproaches Eve after the Fall, saying, 'Why have you wrought destruction among us and brought upon us wrath, which is death gaining rule over all our race?' (*Apoc. Mos.* 14.2), he perhaps looks back to his rulership before the Fall.

Specifically, the notion of the garment of righteousness and glory in *Apoc. Mos.* 20–21 could be compared with the notions 'the garments of glory' and 'the garments of life' in *1 Enoch* 62.15-16, although these do not refer to men's pre-Fall garments.[70] If *Apoc. Mos.* 20–21 is modelled on the latter, the concept of the pre-Fall clothing with righteousness and glory probably means that before the Fall Adam and Eve were glorious like God, because the garment of glory or life in *1 Enoch* 62.15-15 resembles God's splendid garment in *1 Enoch* 14.20, which symbolizes his supreme glory.[71] Further, the image of Adam and Eve's pre-Fall clothing is not far from the rabbinic thought that they were clothed with garments of light before the Fall (cf. *Gen. Rab.* 20.12).[72] It also seems to correspond with Genesis' implication that the first human couple retained the image of God, the prominent features of which were divine life and unashamedness.[73]

To sum up, the clothing image *Apoc. Mos.* 20–21 seems to be intended to express some specific ideas involved in the wearing of clothes: that they cover, so as to become almost a part of their wearer and that they give expression to his character but remain distinct from him. Before the Fall, like a garment, righteousness and glory dominate the appearance of Adam and Eve. As long as they keep God's commandment that they must not eat from the forbidden tree, righteousness is the decisive ethical feature in their relationship with God, and glory is the dominant characteristic of their whole existence. But once they break the commandment of God, such qualities vanish from them. Now that they are fallen, their ethical aspects and their existence are no longer typified by righteousness and glory. The Fall deprives them not only of ethical perfection in their relationship with God, but also of the splendour of their being in the image of God. Like a garment which can be taken off, righteousness and glory are parted from them.[74]

---

69. It is probable that the author of *Apoc. Mos.* has in mind Gen. 1.26-28, which suggests that man's lordship over the other creatures depends upon God's image which is duplicated in him, and the early Jewish literature which maintains the idea of Adam's kingship, e.g. *Sir.* 17.4; *Jub.* 2.14; *Wisd. Sol.* 7.1; 9.1-3; Philo, *Op. Mun.* 66, 69, 83–84, 88, 148; *2 Enoch* 30.10-15; 31.3; 44.1-2; 58.1-3; *2 Bar.* 14.17-19.

70. See section 2.2.3.

71. See section 2.2.2.

72. See section 2.5.

73. See Chapter 1, §2.2.

74. In *Apoc. Mos.* 21.6 Adam blamed Eve for his having lost his glory: 'You have estranged me from the glory of God'.

3.3. *Covering with Cloths of Linen and Silk (Apocalypse of Moses 40.1-2)*
The last portion of *Apoc. Mos.* contains a reference to the death and burial of Adam
and Eve (chapters 31–43). In particular, *Apoc. Mos.* 37–40 shows that on the one
hand, Adam's soul is taken up to the heavenly Paradise in the presence of God
after being washed three times in 'the Lake of Acheron' (*Apoc. Mos.* 37.3), while
on the other hand, his dead body on the ground is covered with sacred heavenly
cloths and anointed with a special oil. The washing of his soul seems to symbolize
that his very self, which has been polluted in this worldly life, is cleansed in order
to be taken to the holy God in heaven. In light of *Apoc. Mos.* 20–21, divine cloths
of linen and silk may symbolize clothes of righteousness and glory in relation to
God's image. Yet, as the clothes come from 'Paradise in the third heaven' (*Apoc.
Mos.* 40.1), where God's throne is located, the fabrics seem to symbolize that
Adam will ultimately be resurrected as an immortal, royal being. With the 'linen'
the author probably thinks of incorruptibility and brilliance (cf. Philo, *Som.*
i.217).[75] *Apoc. Mos.* 28 and 41 state that Adam will eventually gain immortal life at
the time of resurrection. With the 'silk' he probably thinks of a royal status.[76] In
The Hymn of the Pearl, the prince's 'royal silken garment' (v. 66) symbolizes his
original royal self, the image of God from which he was estranged when he was
made to leave his Father's Kingdom (vv. 1-9).[77] If this is acceptable, the covering
of his corpse with the heavenly cloths and the anointing of it with 'oil from the oil
of fragrance' (*Apoc. Mos.* 40.1-3)[78] may be understood as symbolizing a promise
that he will be restored to an imperishable, royal existence by his restoration to the
image of God at the end. Adam will be established in his 'dominion on the throne
of his seducer' (*Apoc. Mos.* 39.2-3).

3.4. *Conclusion*
Apoc. Mos. 20–21 portrays man's prelapsarian clothing, a portrait which seems to
result from the author's interpretation of the story of Adam in Genesis in dependence on the Jewish thought of Adam's pre-Fall investiture with radiance, as later
found in rabbinic literature.[79] While Genesis 1–3 implies that Adam and his wife
were full of glory, when they were given life with the image of God (cf. Gen. 1.26-
27; 2.7, 25), *Apoc. Mos.* 20.12; 21.6 clearly suggests that before the Fall they were
clothed with 'righteousness' and 'glory'. Although Genesis does not directly use
the concept of pre-Fall clothing, its description of the appearance of the pre-Fall

75. See Chapter 2, §4.3.

76. *Theodosian Code* 10.21.3 includes a number of regulations limiting the use of murex dyes
as well as the wearing of silk. In the Graeco-Roman world, purple and silk usually symbolized the
high-class status of its wearer. See C. Vout, 'The Myth of the Toga: Understanding the History of
Roman Dress', in I. McAuslan and P. Walcot (eds.), *Greece & Rome* (Second Series, XLII;
Oxford: Oxford University Press, 1995), pp. 204-220 (especially pp. 214-15).

77. For a detailed explanation of the prince's royal robe, see Chapter 4.

78. In *Apoc. Mos.* and *Vita* there are both an earthly Paradise (Eden) and a heavenly Paradise
(which is located in the third heaven). The other places where the latter is mentioned are *Apoc.
Mos.* 37.5 (cf. Ḥagi, 12b), *Vita* 25.3 and 29.1. The remaining references to Paradise in *Apoc. Mos.*
and *Vita* point to the earthly Paradise.

79. See below, section 5.

Adam is very similar to that in *Apoc. Mos.* 20–21, which does refer to Adam and Eve's pre-Fall clothing. It can be said that the idea of prelapsarian clothing has already been implied in the first three chapters of Genesis. In their original state, righteousness represented Adam and Eve's ethical life; glory was the all-embracing characteristic of their existence, which depended upon God's image in them. Like clothes, these qualities always accompanied them, determined their appearance, typified their characters. The retention of these qualities signified that the God-given life was in them. As long as they kept God's command, life with righteousness and glory was maintained.

However, they failed to keep God's command, so that like garments being taken off, righteousness and glory were stripped from them. Their Fall brought about the loss of ethical perfection, of the honour that was bound up with the image of God, and of immortality. The nakedness which was recognized by Adam and Eve after the Fall symbolizes their forfeiture of these elements. However, 'three cloths of linen and silk' (with the oil of fragance), which cover Adam's dead body, symbolize God's promise that at the time of the resurrection (*Apoc. Mos.* 28.4) Adam will be restored to his original clothes, viz. those of righteousness and glory. In other words, these clothes signify God's promise of Adam's restoration to the original image of God, which is characterized by incorruptibility and kingship. As the Pauline metaphor of clothing with Christ or the new man (Gal. 3.27; Rom. 13.14; Col. 3.9-10; Eph. 4.22-24) implicitly underlines the believer's restoration to the pre-Fall Adamic supremacy in relation to God's image in him, the metaphor seems to echo not only the idea of Adam's pre-Fall clothing with righteousness and glory in *Apoc. Mos.* 20–21, but also the idea of linen and silken cloths being put over Adam's corpse in *Apoc. Mos.* 40.

4. Philo

4.1. Introduction

Philo, who lived between c. 20 BC–c. AD 50,[80] was a Jewish biblical commentator, apologist and philosopher.[81] He seems to have spent most of his time in Alexandria, Egypt. He was wealthy and belonged to a leading Jewish family in Alexandria.[82] His participation in an embassy to Rome in order to plead the religious rights of the Jews with the emperor Gaius Caligula[83] in AD 39[84] indicates that he was a leader

---

80. F.L. Cross, (ed.), 'Philo', in *ODCC* (London: Oxford University Press, 1963 [1957]), pp. 1065-66; W.D. Davies, *Invitation to the New Testament: A Guide to Its Main Witnesses* (London: Darton, Longman & Todd, 1967), p. 397; R.M. Berchman, 'Philo of Alexandria', in E. Ferguson *et al.* (eds.), *EEC* (New York: Garland, 1990), pp. 726-27; cf. C.K. Barrett, *The New Testament Background: Selected Documents* (London: SPCK, 1987 [1956]), p. 252 who suggests the approximate period of 20 BC–AD 45.

81. E. Ferguson, *Backgrounds of Early Christianity* (Grand Rapids: Eerdmans, 1993), p. 450; Collins, *Between Athens and Jerusalem*, p. 112.

82. W.A. Meeks, *The Moral World of the First Christians* (LEC, 6; Philadelphia: The Westminster Press, 1986), p. 81; Collins, *Between Athens and Jerusalem*, p. 112; Berchman, 'Philo of Alexandria', p. 726.

83. See Philo's works which include biographical details about himself, e.g. *Leg. Gai.* 148–51,

and respected figure in the Alexandrian Jewish community. Those specializing in Philo have viewed him from various perspectives,[85] but one major point that all agree on is that he was primarily a Jew invincibly loyal to Judaism.[86] C.K. Barrett affirms that 'unlike some Hellenistic Jews, he never ceased to be a Jew, and to maintain the strict observance of the national laws'.[87] His mixed background[88] is reflected in his prolific writings, which make him the most significant figure among the Hellenistic Jews of his age. In his philosophy are included both Greek wisdom and Hebrew religion; he sought to fuse and harmonize these two elements by means of allegory. Further, it is also probable that he adopted some other religious ideas, for example those of Hellenistic mystery religions, for the sake of his philosophical system.[89] As a religious leader he seems to stand 'in the tradition of the philosophical mystics'.[90]

Philo's works attract our interest, because the occurrences of the clothing concept in them are remarkably multifarious, appearing as they do in a wide range of his writings.[91] The verbs used for the image are diverse,[92] and the aspects to which it is

---

178–83; *Spec. Leg.* ii.1 and also Josephus, *Ant.* xviii.8, 1 (cf. xix.5, 1; xx.5, 2); cf. Collins, *Between Athens and Jerusalem*, pp. 112-17. Concerning the anti-Jewish feeling in Alexandria in Philo's day, see W.O.E. Oesterley, *A History of Israel*, II (Oxford: Clarendon, 1945 [1932]), pp. 402-12.

84. Josephus, *Ant.* xviii.257-58; Philo, *Flac.* 73–75.

85. For example, E.R. Goodenough sees Philo as a representative of a Hellenized Judaism in the diaspora (*An Introduction to Philo Judaeus* [Oxford: Blackwell, 1962]); H.A. Wolfson regards him as related more closely to a broader version of Pharisaic Judaism, emphasizing his philosophical importance and yet his essential Jewishness (*Philo: Foundations of Religious Philosophy in Judaism* [2 vols.; Cambridge: Harvard University Press, 1947]), and S. Sandmel regards him as in many ways unique in the context of a broadly Hellenistic Judaism (*Philo of Alexandria: An Introduction* [Oxford: Oxford University Press, 1979]).

86. D. Winston, *Philo of Alexandria: The Contemplative Life, the Giants, and Selections* (London: SPCK, 1981), p. xi; cf. O. Seyffert, *A Dictionary of Classical Antiquities: Mythology, Religion, Literature & Art* (London: Swan Sonnenschein, 1899), p. 479; Berchman, 'Philo of Alexandria', p. 726; J.M.G. Barclay, *Jews in the Mediterranean Diaspora: From Alexander to Trajan (323 BCE-117 CE)* (Edinburgh: T. & T. Clark, 1996), p. 159.

87. Barrett, *The New Testament Background*, p. 252; cf. Ferguson, *Backgrounds*, p. 450.

88. Cross (ed.), 'Philo', p. 1065 argues that 'in his religious outlook, Philo was essentially an eclectic. He reproduced a variety of doctrines, gathered from contemporary philosophical systems as well as from Jewish sources, without welding them into an harmonious whole.'

89. E.R. Goodenough, *By Light, Light: The Mystic Gospel of Hellenistic Judaism* (Amsterdam: Philo Press, 1969) emphasizes Philo's Hellenized character, even finding in him a Jewish version of a Hellenistic mystery religion.

90. Cross (ed.), 'Philo', p. 1066; cf. Collins, *Between Athens and Jerusalem*, pp. 111-12, who insists that 'There is no doubt that his [Philo's] own approach to Judaism was primarily philosophical and mystical.'

91. E.g. Philo, *Leg. Al.* ii.28, 53-54, 153-54; *Cher.* 9, 95; *Sacr.* 21; *Quod Det.* 42, 157; *Gig.* 17; *Quod Deus* 102; *Agr.* 66; *Ebr.* 7, 86; *Conf. Ling.* 31; *Mig. Abr.* 186; *Fuga* 110; *Som.* i.96, 101, 147, 214-16, 225; *Som.* ii.44; *Abr.* 243; *Ios.* 32; *Vita Mos.* ii.135; *Decal.* 31; *Spec. Leg.* i.82-84, 102, 315; ii.148; iii.41, 156; iv. 43, 93, 203; *Virt.* 18, 21, 196, 217; *Aet. Mun.* 41; *Flac.* 30, 37–38; *Leg. Gai.* 79, 97, 101, 103.

92. For instance, ἀμπέχω in Philo, *Leg. Al.* ii.53, *Cher.* 95, *Sacr.* 21, *Som.* i.96, 101, iii.41, iv. 93, 203, *Virt.* 18; ἀναζώννυμι in *Leg. Al.* ii.28; ἀναλαμβάνω in *Ebr.* 86, *Abr.* 243, *Ios.* 32, *Spec. Leg.* i.82, 84, 216, *Virt.* 18, 21, *Flac.* 37, *Leg. Gai.* 79, 101; εἵλω in *Sacr.* 95; ἐνδύω in *Cher.* 9, *Ebr.* 86,

applied are also very many. It is, therefore, natural that the ideas in which the image is involved are numerous. For instance, when he establishes his doctrine of God,[93] anthropology[94] and ethics,[95] and when he attempts to elucidate the meaning of priestly garments,[96] Philo uses the imagery of clothing.

In subsequent sections, we will concentrate on two themes, 'Man's Garment' and 'Priestly Garments', which seem to be relevant to the Pauline clothing imagery.

4.2. *Man's Garment (cf. Quae. Gen. i.53; Leg. Al. ii.53, 64; Ebr. 7; Quod Det. 42)*
Regarding the anthropological use of clothing imagery in Philo, it would be reasonable to begin with an investigation of his view of man, which is pre-dominated by his understanding of those Genesis passages which include the story of man's creation and his Fall. The fundamental basis of his anthropology is his interpretation of 'Adam' in Gen. 1.26-27 and 2.7.

Philo finds different elements in these two passages. For him, Gen. 1.26-27 refers to 'man' who, as an idea or type or seal, is an object of thought only, incorporeal, neither male nor female, by nature incorruptible, while 2.7 speaks of 'man' who is an object of sense-perception, partaking of qualities, consisting of body and soul, male or female, by nature mortal (*Op. Mun.* 134). *Leg. Al.* ii.4 states that 'there are two races of men, the one made after the (Divine) Image, and the one moulded out of the earth'. The former man is designated as the heavenly mind and the latter, as the earthly mind.[97] While the former points to the genus man, male and female,[98] the latter indicates the species (*Leg. Al.* ii.13).

Philo appears to speak of two different kinds of beings. However, he does not seem to mean that God has created two different Adams, that is, one invisible and the other visible, so that they may exist as two independent beings. Rather he seems to ascribe two different explanations of 'man' to the one Adam. The two explanations are of two paradoxical elements of the same Adam. As a basis of this view, we note Philo states that the image of God planted in man is related to the Mind, viz. 'the sovereign element of the soul' (*Op. Mun.* 69)[99] and that man consists of body and soul. It can be said that in Philo man's soul is the seat of God's image,

---

Conf. Ling. 31, *Fuga* 110, *Som.* i.214, 215, 225, *Leg. Gai.* 97; κοσμέω in *Quod Det.* 5, 42, *Ebr.* 86; περιβάλλω in *Quod Det.* 157, *Vita Mos.* ii.6, *Decal.* 31, *Spec. Leg.* ii.148, *Flac.* 30; περιτίθημι in *Virt.* 217, *Aet. Mun.* 41; ὑποδύω in *Gig.* 17, *Agr.* 66, *Spec. Leg.* i.102, 315, iii.156, iv. 43, *Virt.* 196; φορέω in *Leg. Al.* ii.28, iii.153, *Leg. Gai.* 103.

93. Philo, *Fuga* 110; *Mig. Abr.* 186.
94. Philo, *Leg. Al.* ii.28, iii.153-54; *Som.* i.147; *Fuga* 110; *Virt.* 217; *Vita Mos.* ii.135.
95. Philo, *Ebr.* 7, 86; *Quod Det.* 42; *Abr.* 243; *Leg. Al.* ii.53-64; *Fuga* 110.
96. Philo, *Som.* i.214-18; *Vita Mos.* ii.135, 143; *Mut. Nom.* 43–44; *Spec. Leg.* i.84; *Leg. Al.* ii.56.
97. Philo, *Leg. Al.* i.31-32, 90; *Op. Mun.* 134; *Quae. Gen.* i.4. For detailed discussions of Philo's interpretation of Gen. 1.26-27 and 2.7, see Levison, *Portraits of Adam*, pp. 63-88; R.H. Fuller, *The Foundations of New Testament Christology* (London: Lutterworth, 1965), pp. 76-78.
98. When 'man' in Gen. 1.26-27 is neither male nor female (*Op. Mun.* 134), the term describes one who is male and female simultaneously.
99. That is to say, that man has been made after the image of God points to the fact that 'after the pattern of a single Mind, even the Mind of the Universe as an archetype, the mind in each of those who successively came into being was moulded' (*Op. Mun.* 69).

because the Mind,[100] which is the soul's ruler, is typified by the image of God. Thus 'man' in Gen. 1.26-27 is in an inseparable relationship with 'man' in 2.7. Adam's body is made from clay, that is, the earthly element, while his soul (ψυχή) originated from the Father and Ruler of all, as He breathed His divine breath into man.[101] It is probable that for Philo the soul (ψυχή), which has been breathed into man, is nothing other than the divine life of the Mind, which is in conjunction with the image of God. Philo holds that the 'mind' par excellence is the 'life-principle of the life-principle itself, like the pupil in the eye' (*Op. Mun.* 66).[102]

The following seems to be a summary of Philo's anthropology; he asserts that 'man is the border-land between mortal and immortal nature', partaking of each as far as it is necessary for him; he continues, 'he [man] was created at once mortal and immortal, mortal in respect of the body (σῶμα), but in respect of the mind (διάνοια) immortal'.[103] In brief, for Philo, man is a dialectical being of a dual nature, mortal in his body and immortal in his soul.

We turn now to an investigation of how his anthropology is reflected in his reference to man's being clothed. In *Quae. Gen.* i.53, which deals with Gen. 3.21, Philo, by concentrating on the concept of clothing with the garment of skin, attempts to explain the nature of man in Gen. 2.7.[104]

> the tunic of skin is symbolically the natural skin of the body. For when God formed the first mind, He called it Adam; then He formed the sense, which He called Life; in the third place, of necessity He made his body also, calling it symbolically a tunic of skin, for it was proper that the mind and sense should be clothed in the body as in a tunic of skin, in order that His handiwork might first appear worthy of the divine power (*Quae. Gen.* i.53).

For Philo, 'the garment of skin' is symbolic language, which is nothing other than the physical human body which wraps the mind and the sense. Yet Philo here distinguishes 'the first mind, Adam' from 'the sense, Life'. The former seems to indicate the man-of-dust, into whom the divine has yet to be breathed. The phrase 'the sense, Life' seems to be linked with Philo's comment on a living soul. The earthly mind would be really corruptible, if God did not breathe into it a power of real life.[105] It is with this action of God that the mind becomes a soul,[106] which is

100. The 'mind' par excellence is 'life-principle of the life-principle itself, like the pupil in the eye' (*Op. Mun.* 66).

101. Philo, *Op. Mun.* 135; cf. *Leg. Al.* iii.161; *Som.* i.34. In *Virt.* 217 Philo argues that 'the divine spirit which was breathed upon from on high made its lodging in his soul, and invested his body with singular beauty'.

102. For detailed discussions of Philo's interpretation of Gen. 1.26-27 and 2.7, see T.H. Tobin, *The Creation of Man: Philo and the History of Interpretation* (CBQMS, 14; Washington: CBAA, 1983); also see Levison, *Portraits of Adam*, pp. 63-88; Fuller, *Foundations of New Testament Christology*, pp. 76-78.

103. Philo, *Op. Mun.* 135; cf. *Leg. Al.* i.32.

104. Note that the concept of 'the first mind, Adam' in *Quae. Gen.* i.53 (on Gen. 3.21) corresponds to the concept of 'the moulded man, Adam' in *Quae. Gen.* i.4 (on Gen. 2.7), who is defined as the earthly and corruptible mind (Gen. 2.7).

105. Philo, *Leg. Al.* i.32.

106. Philo, *Leg. Al.* i.32.

'endowed with mind and actually alive', which is the reason why man is said to become a living soul.[107] Yet a living soul finds its residence in a body, becoming in effect the object of sense-perception.[108] It seems that, for Philo, the body is indispensible in order that the mind may become a living soul of genuine life. As a garment, the body encompasses the mind and sense. This thought is naturally expanded to the similar thought that the body plays the part of clothing the soul, which is the principle of physical life.[109] For Philo, the soul is still being tossed in the body as in a river, but God and His word gird it up with quickening deliverance (ψυχὴν σωτήριον πνέοντες ἀναζωῶσι).[110] This seems to be reminiscent of the metaphor of a priest being clothed with salvation in the Old Testament (cf. 2 Chron. 6.41; Ps. 132.16). While the thought of the soul's agony in the body is a traditional Greek one, God and his word's enclosure of it with deliverance is undoubtedly Jewish.

In his comment on Gen. 2.25, Philo, by using the concept of clothing, attempts to explain the original state of Adam and his wife. He says,

> The mind that is clothed neither in vice nor in virtue, but absolutely stripped of either, is naked, just as the soul of an infant, since it is without part in either good or evil, is bared and stripped of coverings: for these are the soul's clothes, by which it is sheltered and concealed. Goodness is the garment of the worthy soul, evil that of the worthless (*Leg. Al.* ii.53).[111]

What is clear here is that vice or virtue is thought of as the garment of the soul and that the first human couple are considered to have had neither of these. For Philo, their nakedness, then, typifies the nakedness of the neutral mind, clothed neither with vice nor with virtue (cf. *Leg. Al.* iii.55). He insists that in three ways the soul can obtain nakedness (whether good, bad or neutral). The first way, which produces good nakedness, is one in which the soul (ψυχή) continues in an unchangeable state and is entirely free from all vices, and estranges itself from all passions and casts them away (*Leg. Al.* ii.54). The second way, which yields a bad nakedness, is one in which the soul (ψυχή) changes its own condition in a negative direction by depriving itself of virtue, when it becomes foolish and goes astray (*Leg. Al.* ii.60). The third way, which brings about a neutral nakedness, is one in which the mind (νοῦς) is in an irrational state and has no part as yet either in virtue or in vice. This is the case of Adam and his wife's nakedness in Gen. 2.25: 'Neither mind nor sense was performing its functions, the one being bare and barren of mental action and the other of the activity of sense-perception' (*Leg. Al.* ii.64). At any rate, the point is that in Philo goodness or evil is regarded as the soul's garment.

---

107. Philo, *Leg. Al.* i.32.

108. Therefore, it is not surprising that Philo presents 'sense' and 'Life' as having the same meaning.

109. Philo, *Fuga* 110.

110. Philo, *Som.* i.147.

111. Quotation from F.H. Colson and G.H. Whitaker (trans.), *Philo* (LCL; 10 vols. of major works and 2 vols. of supplement; London: William Heinemann, 1962). All the quotations below will also be from this edition, unless otherwise noted.

In connection with his interpretation of Gen. 2.25, Philo further advances his ethical clothing thought with his statement that a human being after the Fall is either clad with virtue or with vice.[112] These ethical realities are inevitable human conditions. In *Ebr.* 7 he affirms that no one can possibly take off both at the same moment; if somebody removes one, he necessarily wears the other. Further, in *Quod Det.* 42 Philo teaches that if someone, who has adorned (κεκόσμηται) his soul with all the virtues, does not use them in speech and instead keeps silent, he will procure safety, a prize worn without risk. Here the word κοσμέω seems to mean 'to make beautiful or attractive spiritually, religiously, morally'.[113]

In sum, for Philo, God's clothing of Adam and Eve with garments of skins means that God wrapped their flesh and soul with physical skin, namely the body. In a sense this body is their soul's abode. If Philo thinks of the interchangeability of the concept of 'body' as a garment with the concept of 'body' as a residence, there would be a certain parallel to Paul's formation of the mixed metaphor of clothing with a heavenly house (2 Cor. 5.2-3). Philo's concept of a human being's being clothed with either vice or virtue connotes that he or she cannot help being characterized by one of these two aspects of morality, as a garment reveals its wearer's character. This thought also seems to be echoed in the concept of putting on Christian virtue in Col. 3.12.

4.3. *Priestly Garments (cf. Vita Mos. ii.131; Som. i.214, 215, 218; ii.133, 135)*

Philo's thoughts on the priest's clothing are expressed in his interpretation of some OT texts, for example Exod. 29, Lev. 6 and 16.[114] Philo distinguishes the priest's garments into two kinds, that is, the variegated garment and the linen robe.[115] The former indicates 'the long robe and the ephod in the shape of a breastplate',[116] which is also called the 'many-coloured one [robe] with the long skirt';[117] the latter, the white robe which is made of fine linen.[118] Philo believes that when the high priest performs his office dressed in these sacred garments, he becomes superior to all men, not only to all private individuals, but also to all kings (cf. *Vita Mos.* ii.131). Philo seems to implicitly portray the high priest as a royal figure.

Yet the most remarkable point in his interpretation of the high priest's vesture is that he discovers a cosmological significance in it. This can be confirmed directly by these passages.

---

112. This thought is in line with his anthropology which is described in *Leg. Al.* ii.28, iii.153-54, where he holds that man is clothed with passion (πάθος), which must be girded up by reason (λόγος). For Philo, reason overviews, equips and clothes passion properly; God desires that we gird up our passion and do not wear it loosely.

113. Cf. J.H. Moulton and G. Milligan, 'κοσμέω', in BAGD (Chicago and London: The University of Chicago, 2nd edn, 1979), p. 445.

114. Regarding the priest's garment in the OT, the texts that attracted our attention were Exod. 29, Lev. 6, 16, Ezek. 42 and Zech. 3. See Chapter 1, §3.

115. See Philo, *Som.* i.216; *Mut. Nom.* 43–44.

116. Philo, *Vita Mos.* ii.143.

117. Philo, *Mut. Nom.* 43–44.

118. Philo, *Spec. Leg.* i.84.

he has entitled the embroidered or variegated breastplate (Exod. 29.5), a representation and copy of the shining constellations (*Som.* i.214).

to put on the aforesaid tunic, the representation of the universal heaven, in order
that the world may join with the man in offering sacrifice, and that the man may
likewise co-operate with the universe (*Som.* i.215).

The former passage emphasizes that the high priest's apparel holds a heavenly
splendour, while the latter stresses the unity between man and the universe and
their mutual co-operation.

In *Vita Mos.* ii.133 Philo presents a detailed explanation of the high priest's
robe. The long robe symbolizes the air; the pomegranate, water; the flowery hem,
earth; the scarlet dye of his robe, fire; the ephod, heaven; the round emeralds on the
shoulder-blades with six engravings in each, the two hemispheres; the twelve
stones arranged on the breast in four rows of threes, the zodiac; the oracle-place,
namely the logeum, that Reason which holds together and administers the universe.[119] For Philo, that the high priest enters the temple dressed in the priestly garment denotes that the whole of the universe enters in with him, by means of this
cosmological symbolism.[120] His being attired with it indicates his being clothed with
the cosmos. In other words, it signifies that the priest is actually identified with the
universe.

This idea is clearly seen in Philo's argument that when the high priest adorns
himself with the priestly garment he becomes a microcosm.

ἴσως μέντοι καὶ προδιδάσκει τὸν τοῦ θεοῦ θεραπευτήν, εἰ καὶ μὴ τοῦ κοσμοποιοῦ
δυνατόν, ἀλλὰ τοῦ γε κόσμου διηνεκῶς ἄξιον εἶναι πειρᾶσθαι, οὗ τὸ μίμημα
ἐνδυόμενος ὀφείλει τῇ διανοίᾳ τὸ παράδειγμα εὐθὺς ἀγαλματοφορῶν αὐτὸς τρόπον
τινὰ πρὸς τὴν τοῦ κόσμου φύσιν ἐξ ἀνθρώπου μεθηρμόσθαι καὶ... βραχὺς κόσμος
εἶναι (*Vita Mos.* ii.135).

---

119. Cf. *Spec. Leg.* i.84; *Vita Mos.* ii.143 includes the following words: 'the vesture, woven with
its manifold workmanship to represent the universe, that is the long robe and the ephod in the shape
of a breastplate'. In particular, it is worth noticing that Josephus also postulates a cosmological
interpretation of the high priest's garments. In his *Ant.* iii.184-87, Josephus says that the vestment
(being made of linen) symbolizes the sky; its pomegranates are like lightning; the noise of the bells
resembles thunder; the ephod presents the universe of four elements; the gold interwoven stands
for the splendour by which all things are enlightened; the breastplate in the middle of the ephod
indicates the earth, which is located in the centre of the universe; the girdle points to the ocean;
each of the sardonyxes on the high priest's shoulders connote the sun and the moon; the twelve
stones symbolize the months or the like number of the signs of that circle, namely the Zodiac; the
mitre which is blue in colour stands for heaven. W. Whiston (trans.), *The Works of Josephus* (Peabody: Hendrickson, 1987), p. 91 asserts that Josephus' explication of Jewish high-priestly garments
'is taken out of Philo, and fitted to Gentile philosophical notions'. Probably Josephus' interpretation aims to describe the high priest (clothed in sacred garments) as a cosmological figure who has
been unified with the universe and incorporated into God. Cf. Lucius, who emerges immediately
after his initiation into the Isiac mystery also clothed in twelve splendid cosmological garments
(see Chapter 5, §2.2.3).

120. Concerning the analogy between the universe and a garment, cf. Ps. 102.26; Isa. 51.6 (Isa.
34.4; Heb. 1.11-12); see Chapter 1, §5. Cf. also Chapter 5, §2.2.3.

Probably, indeed, he [the Father's Son in *Vita Mos.* ii.134] gives to the servant of
God [the high priest] a pre-lesson that, even though he [the high priest] cannot be
worthy of the cosmos-Maker, he should, at least, persistently try to be worthy of
the cosmos, when he clothes himself with the imitation [of the cosmos] in a way
in which he is obliged to straightly carry about the pattern [of it] in his mind, so as
to be transformed from a man into the nature of the cosmos and..., be himself a
little cosmos.[121]

As the word μεθαρμόζω means 'to alert, dispose differently, correct, etc.', the high
priest's donning of the priestly garment seems to mean that he has been changed
into a God-like being. This understanding can be supported by Philo's identification of the universe with God (cf. *Leg. Al.* iii.29; *Op. Mun.* 67), although God
remains, at the same time, separate from the universe.

Philo believes that the linen robe also has a symbolic meaning. He affirms that it
is an emblem of strong fibre, incorruptibility and the most brilliant light; 'for fine
linen is hard to tear, and is made from no mortal creature, and moreover when carefully cleaned has a very brilliant and luminous colour'.[122] He applies this figurative
meaning of the linen robe, in particular, to the worshipper, saying:

> among those who worship Him that is with guileless purity, there is not one that
> does not, in the first place, exercise strength of will and judgment by a contempt
> for human interests which ensnare and hurt and enfeeble us; and, in the second
> place, laugh to scorn all the unsubstantial aims of mortal men, and set his heart on
> immortality; and, last of all, live irradiated by the cloudless splendour of truth, no
> longer entertaining any of the creations of false opinion so dear to darkness (*Som.*
> i.218).

Further, Philo sees that the two varieties of priestly garments symbolize two
aspects of the soul. That is to say, while the linen robe signifies one aspect of the
soul which is undefiled towards God with respect to inward things, the many-
coloured robe with the long skirt indicates the other aspect of the soul which is
pure with respect to the world of our senses and human life in outward things.[123]

Yet the variegated garment may be called 'the garment of opinions and impres-
sions of the soul',[124] which should be laid aside, as the high priest enters into the
most holy place; he should leave it behind for those that love outward things and
value semblance above reality, 'then enter naked with no coloured borders or
sound of bells, to pour as a libation the blood of the soul and to offer as incense the
whole mind to God our Saviour and Benefactor'.[125] Here, nakedness undoubtedly
indicates purity of the soul and not physical nudity, since the high priest never

---

121. My free rendering. Colson and Whitaker (trans.), *Philo*, VI, p. 515 argues that 'The Son
here [*Vita Mos.* ii.134] is of course the World.' If this is correct, the first 'he' in *Vita Mos.* ii.135
should indicate 'the World'. But, when we read the passage with this view, it does not give proper
significance to the context. Therefore, the World and the Father's Son should be considered as
pointing to two different realities.

122. Philo, *Som.* i.217.

123. Philo, *Mut. Nom.* 43–44.

124. Philo, *Leg. Al.* ii.56.

125. Philo, *Leg. Al.* ii.56.

officiated in the nude. In brief, Philo underscores that when the high priest adorns himself with priestly garments he becomes a different figure from others, that is, a God-like being. As far as Philo's emphasis is on the high priest's identification with God, this idea can be associated with the Pauline emphasis on the believer's change in his status or nature and his mode of existence through union with Christ (Gal. 3.27; Rom. 13.14; Col. 3.9-10; Eph. 4.22-24; 1 Cor. 15.49, 50-54; 2 Cor. 5.1-4).

4.4. *Conclusion*

I have so far focused on the theme of Adam's clothing and the priest's, in which Philo's philosophical thought is reflected. It seems that Philo sees biblical texts primarily from a Platonic point of view, and would deal with them by means of Stoic allegory.

Every human being is destined to be endued with vice or virtue, though Adam and Eve were originally clothed with neither vice nor virtue. Virtue functions as a panoply (παντευχία) of the human reason (λόγος).

Adam's being clothed in a garment of skin in Gen. 3.21 symbolizes that his mind and sense have been enclosed by the natural human body. His earthly mind, the so-called man-of-dust, and his sense, namely the soul, are wrapped by the physical skin. This idea may be regarded as a clarification of the concept of the dust-plus-divine-breath man in Gen. 2.7, which is contrasted with the concept of the man in whom God's image is implanted. For the soul, the human body is residence and garment at the same time.

The priest's clothing himself with the white linen robe signifies that he equips himself with strength, incorruptibility and radiance, which can also be applied to the worshipper's strength of holy willpower, concentration on immortality, and living of a life illuminated by truth. On the other hand, his investiture with the coloured robe signifies that he is united with the universe, which is identified with the Mind (νοῦς) in the universe, that is, God.[126] When he adorns himself with the robe, he becomes a microcosm, which connotes that he has been identified with God.

5. *Rabbinic Literature*

We cannot afford to overlook rabbinic literature in connection with the imagery of clothing, if only because of its similarity to intertestamental literature. This similarity implies that there is also some similarity between the two bodies of literature, and that motifs in the theology of intertestamental Judaism were later developed in rabbinic theology.[127] In particular, Adamic motifs related to clothing occur repeatedly in rabbinic writings. It is likely that some clothing motifs in rabbinic literature

126. In *Leg. Al.* iii.29 he asserts that there are two kinds of minds, that is, the mind of the universe, i.e. God, and the separate mind of each individual; see also *Op. Mun.* 67. Cf. *Op. Mun.* 24, which equates the world (κόσμος) with God's word (λόγος).

127. R. Scroggs, *The Last Adam: A Study in Pauline Anthropology* (Oxford: Basil Blackwell, 1966), p. 32. Pate, *Adam Christology*, pp. 61-62 also argues that Adamic motifs, which are found in Qumran, *Wisdom of Solomon* and various apocalyptic and pseudepigraphical works, recur consistently in rabbinic discussions.

are developments of clothing motifs that were found in intertestamental Jewish theology but have not survived in the extant sources.

The clothing imagery in rabbinic documents has in the main to do with Adam's garments, which are related to haggadic interpretations of Gen. 3.21. On the basis of the way rabbinic writings interpret Gen. 3.21, they may be divided into two categories: ones which see Gen. 3.21 as a reference to the pre-Fall state of the first human pair (e.g. *Gen. Rab.* 20.12; cf. 18.6), and ones which see the passage as depicting the post-Fall state of the couple (e.g. *Pirqe R. El.* 14.20; *Tg. Yer.* Gen 3.21).[128] The former interpret the word עוֹר ('skin') in Gen. 3.21 as if it were written אוֹר ('light'), while the latter maintains a reading of עוֹר. In brief, the pre-lapsarian theory posits that the first human couple wore 'garments of light' before the Fall, while the post-lapsarian theory posits that they wore 'garments of skin' after the Fall.

In relation to the prelapsarian theory, it is worthwhile looking into *Gen. Rab.* 20.12,[129] which is introduced by a quotation from Gen. 3.21. That unit consists of several rabbinic dicta. G.A. Anderson analyses it as follows.[130]

And the lord God made for Adam and his wife, garments of skin and clothed them.

A. In the Torah of R. Meir, it is written: 'Garments of Light'.
B. These are the garments of Primal Man. For they were similar to a lantern being wider at the bottom and narrower at the top.
C. R. Yishaq Ravya said: 'They were smooth like fingernails and beautiful like precious stones'.
D. R. Yohanan said: 'They were like the fine flax of Bet-Shean'.
E. [They were called] coats of skin for they adhered closely to the skin.
F. R. Elazar said, 'They were cloaks of goat-skins'.
G. R. Yehoshua, b. Levi said, 'They were cloaks of rabbit-skins'.
H. R. Yossi, in the name of R. Hanina said, 'They were cloaks of goats-hair'.
I. Resh Laquish said, 'They were milky-white [in color] and in them the first-born sons [prior to Sinai] served [as priests]'.
J. R. Shmuel bar Nahman said, 'They were cloaks of wool from camels, wool from rabbits'.
K. They were called 'garments of skin' because they came from skin.

Anderson argues that sections A–D, in particular, presume that 'Adam and Eve were clothed with garments of glory *prior* to their eviction from the Garden'.[131] He points out that R. Meir's[132] dictum in section A is on the basis of the text in his

128. S.N. Lambden, 'From Fig Leaves to Fingernails: Some Notes on the Garments of Adam and Eve in the Hebrew Bible and Select Early Postbiblical Jewish Writings', in P. Morris and D. Sawyer (eds.), *A Walk in the Garden: Biblical, Iconographical and Literary Images of Eden* (JSOTSup, 136; Sheffield: JSOT Press, 1992), pp. 74-90 (87).

129. See H. Freedman and M. Simon (eds.), *Midrash Rabbah: Genesis*, I (trans. H. Freedman; London: Soncino Press, 1939), p. 171.

130. G.A. Anderson, 'Garments of Skin, Garments of Glory' (unpublished paper, n.d.), pp. 1-42 (16).

131. Anderson, 'Garments of Skin', p. 17.

132. According to H.L. Strack and G. Stemberger, *Introduction to the Talmud and Midrash*

version of the Torah which reads 'garments of light' (אוֹר) instead of 'garments of skin' (עוֹר).[133] He holds that sections B and C elucidate what garments of light are like; images of a bright effulgence and fingernails are of 'a piece with those Rabbinic traditions which understand Adam's likeness to God in bodily terms... As God's physical form was conceived to be that of a fiery effulgence, so was that of Adam's.'[134]

Citing the tradition in *b. B. Bat.* 58a, according to which 'the luminosity of the heel of Adam was so great that only the Shekinah could overcome it', Anderson holds that 'this *topos* recalls the mythopeic descriptions of the *kabod-YHWH* in the Bible, and suggests that Adam's garments are somehow akin to the covering of the deity'.[135] He also points out that so-called 'high anthropology', which sees the Fall from the perspective of the loss of original gifts, was very common in later kabbalistic thinking and was closely involved in 'an interest in recovering through halakhic observance [or its Christian correlate, ascetic practice] some semblance of this lost supernatural glory'.[136] Anderson rounds off his argument as follows.

> Several texts from *Gen. Rab.* make clear that Adam and Eve's glorious bodies were a part of their prelapsarian state... R. Meir uses Gen. 3.21 as a description of the pre-Fallen condition of Adam and Eve [when they wore garments of light] as opposed to the moment when they fell [and put on garments of skin]. R. Assi asserts that these garments were lost on the day they sinned...[137]

In short, the pre-Fall theory views that God originally clothed Adam and Eve with garments of light,[138] but on account of their sins, these garments were removed from them. In particular, they had been originally dressed in glory, but at the Fall they forfeited it.[139]

According to the post-lapsarian theory, God made, and clothed Adam and Eve with, garments of עוֹר ('skin') after the Fall. *Gen. Rab.* 12.6 includes Adam's 'lusture' and other five things, that is, 'his immortality [lit. 'life'], his height, the fruit of the earth, the fruit of trees, and the luminaries', in the six things which were taken away from him at the Fall. It is stated that God made garments for Adam and

(Edinburgh: T. & T. Clark, 1991), pp. 83-84, R. Meir was one of the third generation Tannaim (c. 130–160); cf. A.R.C. Leaney, *The Jewish & Christian World 200 BC to AD 200* (CCWJCW, 7; Cambridge: Cambridge University Press, 1989 [1984]), p. 194.

133. Anderson, 'Garments of Skin', p. 17; A.G. Gottstein, 'The Body as Image of God in Rabbinic Literature', *HTR* 87.2 (1994), pp. 171-95 (179); Lambden, 'From Fig Leaves to Fingernails', p. 87; S. Brock, 'Clothing Metaphors as a Means of Theological Expression in Syriac Tradition', in *Typus, Symbol, Allegorie bei den östlichen Vätern und ihren Parallelen im Mittelalter* (EB, 4: Abteilung Philosophie und Theologie; Regensburg: Verlag Friedrich Pustet, 1981), p. 14; *idem*, 'Jewish Traditions in Syriac Sources', *JJS* 30.2 (1979), pp. 212-32 (222); cf. Scroggs, *The Last Adam*, p. 49.

134. Anderson, 'Garments of Skin', p. 18.

135. Anderson, 'Garments of Skin', pp. 18-19.

136. Anderson, 'Garments of Skin', p. 19.

137. Anderson, 'Garments of Skin', p. 20.

138. Cf. *Lev. Rab.* 20.2, which portrays Adam as having possessed a body of light: 'Resh Lakish in the name of R. Simon ben Menasseya said: "the apple of Adam's heel outshone the globe of the sun; how much more so the brightness of his face"...'.

139. Gottstein, 'The Body as Image of God', pp. 178-83.

Eve after their fall, out of the skin which was stripped from the serpent (*Pirqe R. El.* 20; *Tg. Yer.* Gen. 3.21).[140] This view may be designed to express that even after the Fall Adam and Eve were connected with something like 'light', because the skin of the serpent is glossy. A similar view is found in much later rabbinic works, according to which the garments for Adam and Eve were made out of the skin of Leviathan, 'since the skin of Leviathan has a shining lustre'.[141] Other midrashim further support the view that the garments which Adam and Eve received from God after the Fall were of a superior and unusual kind.[142] Their garments 'were not only of extraordinary brilliance and splendor, but had also supernatural qualities'.[143] It is held that these garments belong to the primordial creation, because they were created by God at the twilight of the first Friday, 'on account of which both Adam and his descendants wore them as priestly garments at the time of the offering of the sacrifices'.[144] Identifying Adam's post-Fall priestly garments with the garment of light, Abkir in *Yal.* i.34 says that God made high-priestly garments for Adam which were like those of the angels, but when he fell, God removed them from him (cf. *'Abot R. Nat.* ii.42, 116).[145]

Above all, it should be remembered that the post-Fall theory also retains the legend about the light which shone on the first pair. That is, it is said that Adam and Eve before the Fall were overlaid with a horny skin, and wrapped with the cloud of glory,[146] but immediately after the Fall, the horny skin and the cloud of glory dropped from them and they stood in nudity and were ashamed (*Pirqe R. El.* 14; *Tg. Yer.* Gen. 3.7, 21). This seems to mean that Adam and Eve were originally clothed with a glossy skin which shone like a horn and with glory which shone like a bright cloud. *'Abot R. Nat.* ii.42, 116 states that 'Adam wore splendid garments, which were removed from him after the commission of the sin'.[147] On the basis of his survey of a number of midrashim, Ginzberg argues that 'twenty-two or twenty-four blessings are enumerated which God had bestowed on Adam, of which man was gradually deprived after the Fall of Adam and the sins of the following generations, and which mankind will receive again in Messianic times';[148] specifically in connection with Adam himself, he states that 'on account of his sins Adam forfeited the so-called image of God (i.e. the God-like splendour), tall stature, paradise and the tree of life'.[149]

140. Ginzberg, *Legends*, V, pp. 80, 103.

141. Ginzberg, *Legends*, V, p. 103 (cf. Ginzberg, *Legends*, I, pp. 27-28; V, p. 42); cf. Lambden, 'From Fig Leaves to Fingernails', pp. 87-88.

142. Ginzberg, *Legends*, V, p. 103.

143. Ginzberg, *Legend,* V, p. 103.

144. Ginzberg, *Legends*, V, pp. 103, 199.

145. See Ginzberg, *Legends*, V, p. 104.

146. Cf. *b. B. Bat.* 58a, which says that Adam's person was so handsome that the very sole of his foot obscured the splendour of the sun. For sources of referring to Adam and Eve's beauty, see Ginzberg, *Legends*, V, p. 80.

147. Ginzberg, *Legends*, V, p. 104.

148. *See* Ginzberg, *Legends*, V, p. 113.

149. Ginzberg, *Legends*, V, p. 113.

Thus whether rabbinic writings view Gen. 3.21 as speaking of man's pre-Fall situation or of his post-Fall situation, both interpretations commonly maintain that Adam and Eve were originally clothed with garments of supreme grandeur, which may be designated garments of light.[150] These clothes may also be called the garments of glory (cf. *Pirqe R. El.* 14; *Tg. Yer.* Gen. 3.21). In *Gen. Rab.* 12.6 the rabbis associate glory with light.

> He [Adam] passed the night [the eve of the Sabbath] in his glory, but at the termination of the Sabbath He [God] deprived him [Adam] of his splendour and expelled him from the Garden of Eden, as it is written, *'thou changest his countenance, and sendest him away'* (Job XIV, 20).

This view makes it clear that the Fall caused the loss of the first human couple's primeval glory. Therefore, we may say that the light which the first couple lost was their glory. *Targum Pseudo-Jonathan*, for example, adds to Gen. 2.25 the words, 'but they did not tarry in their glory'. *b. Ber.* 8, 20 also identify men's nakedness after the Fall with the forfeiture of their original glory.[151] A similar but indirect statement is found in *Cant. Rab.* 6: 'the original abode of the Shekinah was among men. When Adam sinned it ascended away to the first heaven' (cf. *Num. Rab.* 12.6). The idea of Adam's prelapsarian clothing seems to stand behind the Pauline metaphors of clothing with a person and with the resurrection body (Gal. 3.27; Rom. 13.14; Col. 3.9-10; Eph. 4.24; 1 Cor. 15.49, 50-54; 2 Cor. 5.1-4), which are concerned with believers' restoration to the Adamic pre-Fall state.

6. Conclusion to Chapter 2

1 Enoch underlines that after the model of God being dressed in glory and holiness (14.20), the future body of the righteous will be clothed with glory or life (62.15-16). This thought is reinforced by *2 Enoch* 22.8, which speaks of Enoch being stripped of the earthly garment and clothed with the heavenly garment (the symbolism of his transfiguration from the earthly body into the heavenly). As a garment can be exchanged with another garment, so the present human body is to be replaced by a future body. This idea seems to anticipate the imagery of clothing with a resurrection body in 1 Corinthians 15 and 2 Corinthians 5.

Apoc. Mos. 20–21 maintains the idea of Adam and Eve's pre-Fall clothing; they were clothed with righteousness and glory, but at the Fall they were stripped of these qualities. As a garment dominates its wearer's appearance, so righteousness and glory used to pervade the general appearance of the first human couple before the Fall. This prelapsarian clothing thought seems to be reflected in the Pauline

---

150. This understanding occurs also in other late documents; for instance, Origen, *Contra Cels.* 4.40 suggests that the garments of skin which were given to Adam and Eve after the Fall point to their bodies, because they existed as spiritual beings until the Fall (cf. Philo, *Quae. Gen.* i.53); see Ginzberg, *Legends*, V, p. 103.

151. This rabbinic thought that Adam and Eve had been originally clothed with glory but lost it after the Fall may be regarded as being in line with *Apoc. Mos.* 20–21, where Adam and Eve are said to have been stripped of righteousness or glory after the Fall.

clothing passages, prominently in Gal. 3.26-29, Rom. 13.14, Col. 3.9-10 and Eph. 4.22-24, which speak of clothing with Christ or the new man.

Philo uses the concept that human beings are clothed with either vice or virtue. This is probably reflected in the imagery of clothing with Christian virtues in Col. 3.12, which is linked with the imagery of clothing with the new man in Col. 3.10. As a garment reveals its wearer's character, so goodness or evil is to typify a human being. For Philo, the concept of the garment-of-skin's enclosing the soul (and the earthly mind, i.e. the man-of-dust) is perhaps interchangeable with the concept of its being the soul's abode. This sort of compatibility may be behind the mixed imagery in 2 Cor. 5.1-2, that is, clothing with the heavenly building. Philo also underlines the high priest's identification with God, when he attires himself with the sacred, priestly garment. This view is also similar to the Pauline clothing imagery, for example the imagery of clothing with Christ or the new man in Gal. 3.27, Rom. 13.14, Col. 3.10 and Eph. 4.24, and with the resurrection body in 1 Cor. 15.49-54 and 2 Cor. 5.1-4.

Rabbinic literature, whether it sees Gen. 3.21 as a reference to Adam and Eve's prelapsarian state or post-lapsarian state, maintains that they were originally clothed with a divine splendour. In particular, *Gen. Rab.* 12.6 links glory with light and 20.12 suggests that Adam and Eve wore light before the Fall. *'Abot R. Nat.* ii.42, 116 identifies the image of God with God-like splendour. As the wearer is closely in contact but cannot be equated with his or her garment, so was the relationship between the first human couple and their pre-Fall radiance. It seems that the idea of Adam and Eve's pre-Fall clothing lies at the back of the Pauline passages about clothing with Christ or the new man and the resurrection body (Gal. 3.27; Rom. 13.14; Col. 3.9-10; Eph. 4.24; 1 Cor. 15.49, 50-54; 2 Cor. 5.1-4).

Chapter 3

CLOTHING IMAGERY IN *JOSEPH AND ASENETH*

1. *Introduction*

Joseph and Aseneth (hereafter *JA*) is 'a romantic love story in which the author has put a midrashic elaboration of Genesis 41.45, 50-52 and 46.20 into the form of a Hellenistic romance'.[1] The biblical story of Joseph's marriage with the heathen woman Aseneth might have motivated the writer to compose *JA*, because exogamy was an offence against the patriarchal precepts and Mosaic regulations. The dating of *JA* is uncertain, but there seems to be a broad consensus that it was written some-time between the first century BCE and the first century CE.[2] The provenance of *JA* was probably Egypt, but the work itself was originally composed in Greek.[3] The Septuagintal character of its Greek and its emphasis on the superiority of Jewish religion to pagan religions imply that an anonymous Egyptian Jew has composed it. *JA* was so popular that it was circulated in a number of places and translated into several languages.[4]

---

1.   E. Schürer, *The History of the Jewish People in the Age of Jesus Christ* (175 BC-AD 135) III/1 (Edinburgh: T. & T. Clark, 1986 [1885]), p. 546; M. Philonenko, *Joseph et Aséneth: Introduction, Text Critique, Traduction et Notes* (Studia Post-Biblica, 13; Leiden: Brill, 1968), pp. 43-48; H.C. Kee, 'The Socio-Cultural Setting of Joseph and Aseneth', *NTS* 29 (1983), pp. 394-413 (398).

2.   J.M.G. Barclay, *Jews in the Mediterranean Diaspora: From Alexander to Trajan (323 BCE-117 CE)* (Edinburgh: T. & T. Clark, 1996), p. 204. G.D. Kilpatrick, 'Living Issues in Biblical Scholarship: The Last Supper', *ExpT* 64 (1952–53), pp. 4-8 suggests that *JA*'s lack of any reference to the Romans is in favour of a date before 30 BC. Yet C. Burchard, *Untersuchungen zu Joseph und Aseneth* (WUNT, 8; Tübingen: Mohr, 1965), pp. 133-51 would ascribe *JA* to c. 100 BC, though he admits the possibility of the earlier part of the first century AD. In contrast, Philonenko, *Joseph et Aséneth*, pp. 99-109 dates the book in AD 100–110, before the great Jewish Revolt (which broke out in AD 115) under Trajan's domain (AD 98–117). R.D. Chesnutt, *From Death to Life: Conversion in Joseph and Aseneth* (JSPSup, 16; Sheffield: Sheffield Academic Press, 1995), pp. 80-85 holds that 'the devastating Jewish revolt of 115-17CE provides a firm *terminus ante quem* for the writing of a document such as *Joseph and Aseneth* in Egypt' and that suggests a similar date, i.e. some time between 100 BCE and 115 CE.

3.   Philonenko, *Joseph et Aséneth*, pp. 27-29 observes that only about 40 words of *JA*'s 1042 words (including proper names) are not found in the LXX; compare some 30 words in John, which has about the same number of words as *JA*; G. Delling, 'Einwirkungen der Sprache der Septuaginta in "Joseph and Aseneth" ', *JSJ* 9 (1978), pp. 29-56; Chesnutt, *From Death to Life*, pp. 69-71.

4.   E.g. Greek, Latin, Syriac, Armenian and Slavonic; see Chesnutt, *From Death to Life*, pp. 20-22; C. Burchard, 'The Importance of Joseph and Aseneth for the Study of the New Testament: A General Survey and a Fresh Look at the Lord's Supper', *NTS* 33 (1987), pp. 102-34 (103); S. West, '*Joseph and Aseneth*: A Neglected Greek Romance', *CQNS* 24 (1974), pp. 70-81 (70).

JA consists of two parts: the first part (chapters 1–21) introduces a cast of characters, especially Aseneth the heroine; narrates the initial affair of her father's (Pentephres') attempt to give her to Joseph in marriage; and recounts Aseneth's conversion and marriage to Joseph. The second part (chapters 22–29) tells the story of Pharaoh's son's attempt to abduct Aseneth and to hold power in Egypt. *JA* takes the form of a Greek novel,[5] but it is overwhelmingly pre-occupied with the theme of Aseneth's conversion (chapters 10–17).[6] This aesthetic failure of *JA* as a romance[7] seems to be caused by the fact that its composition was motivated by the socio-religious milieu[8] in which the current pattern of exogamy was problematic in Jewish society.[9] The author of *JA* is apparently worried that exogamy may occur indiscriminately between nominal proselytes[10] and Jews.

In *JA* Aseneth's significant actions for conversion may be regarded as ritual-like actions, as she enters into the Jewish religion through them. Paradoxically, the author suggests the ritual-like elements in a totally non-ritual-like manner, that is, as a private and personal experience. But the abundant ritual-like actions in *JA* such as intercessory prayer (8.9), the rejection of idolatry (9.2), asceticism and prayer (chapters 10–13), enrolment in the book of the living (15.4), change of clothing (14.15–15.2), washing of the face and hands (14.12-15), change of name (15.7), formulaic bread-cup-ointment (16.16, etc.), physical transformation (18.10), and Joseph's kissing Aseneth three times (19.10-11),[11] all seem to reflect the rituals of specific religions,

5.   R.I. Pervo, 'Joseph and Aseneth and the Greek Novel', *SBLSPS* 10 (1976), pp. 171-81 (178, fn. 1): 'For ancient literature the terms "novel" and "romance" may be used interchangeably'.

6.   After the formidable statement in 8.5, the conversion motif dominates the following ten chapters, which are 'the heart of the work' (Barclay, *Jews in the Mediterranean Diaspora*, p. 206).

7.   Barclay, *Jews in the Mediterranean Diaspora*, p. 205.

8.   Chesnutt, *From Death to Life*, pp. 254-56.

9.   H.C. Kee, 'The Socio-Religious Setting and Aims of "Joseph and Aseneth"', *SBLSPS* 10 (1976), pp. 183-92 (187) argues that *JA* points to '(1) the problem of exogamy and (2) to the related issue of the admission of proselytes to the community as a central concern for the author and the community for which he is writing'; see also West, 'Joseph and Aseneth', pp. 76-78. On the other hand, that *JA* deals with the social issue of exogamy in Jewish society does not mean that its readership would be limited to Jews only; the author's emphasis on the thoroughness of Aseneth's penitence prior to her conversion to Judaism may imply that he also envisages a non-Jewish readership; see Chesnutt, *From Death to Life*, pp. 260-61.

10.   W.A. Oldfather (trans.), *Epictetus: The Discourses As Reported by Arrian, the Manual, and Fragments*, I (ed. E. Capps *et al.*; LCL; London: Heinemann, 1926), p. 273. Epictetus speaks of cases in which there is doubt as to whether people had really converted to Judaism: 'whenever we see a man halting between two faiths, we are in the habit of saying, "he is not a Jew, he is only acting the part". But when he adopts the attitude of mind of the man who has been baptized and has made his choice, then he both is a Jew in fact and is also called one. So we also are counterfeit "baptists", ostensibly Jews, but in reality something else, not in sympathy with our own reason, far from applying the principles which we profess, yet priding ourselves upon them as being men who know them' (Book II, 9.9-21). Schürer, *The History of the Jewish People*, III/1, p. 174 holds that 'the oft-quoted saying of Epictetus, as reported by Arrian, can best be understood of proselyte baptism'. Epictetus lived in c. 50–130 CE; see M. Stern (ed.), *Greek and Latin Authors on Jews and Judaism* I: *From Herodotus to Plutarch* (PIASH; Jerusalem: IASH, 1974), p. 541.

11.   See Chesnutt, *From Death to Life*, pp. 119-39.

for instance, Jewish proselyte baptism,[12] initiation into mystery religions (e.g. Isiac mysteries),[13] and so on. As I have argued, if *JA* has in mind exogamy between prose-lytes and Jews, it is probable that proselyte baptism stands behind this document.

JA's significance for our study is that, by using the concept of clothing, it describes diverse aspects of Aseneth's identity which undergo a meaningful trans-formation. Aseneth's abandoning her original, idolatrous garments and instead adorning herself with a new linen robe and a wedding garment seems to have particular relevance to the Pauline concept of putting off the old man and putting on the new man (Col. 3.9-10; Eph. 4.22-24; cf. Gal. 3.27; Rom. 13.14). In *JA* the description of Aseneth's conversion by clothing imagery constitutes the central part of the narrative. The frequency of occurrence of the clothing concept is very high; and places where it appears are widespread.[14] The author of *JA* describes Aseneth's attirement in four kinds of apparel in sequence: (1) idolatrous apparel, (2) a black tunic, (3) a new linen robe, and (4) a wedding garment. I will attempt to probe the significance of each of these clothing images.

12.   C. Burchard, 'Joseph and Aseneth', in J.H. Charlesworth (ed.), *OTP* II (New York: Double-day, 1985), pp. 177-247 (193) suggests the possibility of the ritual-like actions' connection with proselyte baptism, by saying that 'Ritual, however, or at least accepted custom, nevertheless, may be reflected in Joseph and Aseneth. Entry into Judaism may well have been performed by a period of fasting, praying, meditating, washing, a symbolical changing of clothes (and perhaps of name), and celebrating a festive meal. But corroborative evidence is needed before we can be certain.' Concerning the earliest references to proselyte baptism, see Chapter 7. Note also T. Holtz, 'Christ-liche Interpolationen in "Joseph und Aseneth" ', *NTS* 14 (1968), pp. 482-97, who suggests that the notion of rebirth and the exalted description of Joseph, as well as the terminology of sacred meals betrays Christian influence (cf. Burchard, 'The Importance of Joseph and Aseneth', pp. 102-34).

13.   Barclay, *Jews in the Mediterranean Diaspora*, pp. 206-220. For a comparison between the ritual elements of *JA* and features of Isiac initiation, see Chesnutt, *From Death to Life*, pp. 235-53, although he denies that they are related to each other; Barclay, *Jews in the Mediterrean Diaspora*, pp. 206-207.

14.   C. Burchard, 'Ein Vorlaufinger griechischer Text von Joseph und Aseneth', *DBAT* 14 (1979), pp. 1-53 shows that *JA* uses various clothing-verbs in a number of texts. Ἐνδύω is in the main used for the wearing of an outer garment, e.g. a linen robe (3.6; 14.12, 14; cf. 5.5), a white tunic (5.5), a mourning tunic (10.8, 10; 13.3), a wedding robe (15.10; 18.5; 20.6). Ζώννυμι is used for girding with a girdle, e.g. a golden girdle (3.6) or the twin girdle (14.12, 14). Περιζώννυμι is used for girding with other kinds of apparel, e.g. a rope and sackcloth (13.4; cf. 10.10, 14), a golden and royal girdle (18.6). Τίθημι is used in two cases, firstly, for adorning oneself with ornaments or ornamental apparel (3.6); secondly, for equipping oneself with armour (26.6). Ἐπιτίθημι, which is found once, expresses the putting on of an ornamental material on one's body (21.5). Similarly, περιτίθημι is also used for decorating one's body with diverse kinds of ornaments (3.6; 15.10; 18.6) or with ornamental apparel (18.6). No doubt κατακοσμέω is also used in the same sense of decking (15.10). Finally, κατακαλύπτω, which appears three times, means to cover the human head with a veil (3.6; 14.15; 18.6). Except for two passages, viz. 5.5 (which refers to the apparel of Joseph) and 26.6 (which speaks of the armament of Leah's sons, i.e. Levi and his brothers), all the above verses involve Aseneth's attire. This implies that the story of Aseneth's attire has a special significance.

2. *Symbolism of Four Scenes of Aseneth's Attire*

2.1. *Scene 1: Idolatrous Apparel*

In *JA* we encounter the first scene of Aseneth's attirement; she dresses herself in extravagant garments and adorns herself with various kinds of ornaments, most of which were conspicuously idolatrous. This is shown in 3.6,

> [Aseneth]… dressed in a (white) linen robe interwoven with violet and gold, and girded herself (with) a golden girdle and put bracelets on her hands and feet, and put golden buskins about her feet, and around her neck she put valuable ornaments and costly stones which hung around from all sides, and the names of the gods of the Egyptians were engraved everywhere on the bracelets and the stones, and the faces of all the idols were carved on them. And she put a tiara on her head and fastened a diadem around her temples, and covered her head with a veil.[15]

No doubt this corresponds to the explanation of Aseneth's idol-worship in 2.3-4. Within the first chamber of the ten chambers in her tower, Egyptian gods of gold and silver were fixed to the walls; she worships them all and fears them and performs sacrifices to them every day (2.3). The author of *JA* seems to pour scorn on her iconic worship and polytheism.[16] Within the second chamber there were her ornaments, chests, gold and silver, clothes interwoven with gold, precious stones, distinguished cloths, and all the ornaments of her virginity (2.4).

Considering that 3.6 is the climax of chapters 1–3 and that the author wishes her to express herself with what she wears, the verse reveals what her identity is. 'A (white) linen robe interwoven with violet and gold', which is later redescribed as her 'linen and gold woven royal robe' (10.10), implies that she belongs to the highest class in society. The precious jewels demonstrate her wealth. The veil may connote her virginity.[17] Above all, according to the writer's central emphasis on Aseneth's conversion from her pagan religion to the Jewish religion, we note that the statement that the names of the Egyptian gods were inscribed on her bracelets and the stones, and also that the faces of all the idols were carved on them, highlights the fact that she was a fervent worshipper of idols. She was so engrossed in idolatry that she could not help expressing it by actually wearing idols.

It would be appropriate to view her present state of idolatry in the light of Joseph's prayer for her conversion afterward in 8.9.

> Lord God of my father Israel, the Most High, the Powerful One of Jacob, who gave life to all (things) and called (them) from the darkness to the light, and from the error to the truth, and from the death to the life; you, Lord, bless this virgin, and renew her by your spirit, and form her anew by your hidden hand, and make her alive again by your life, and let her eat your bread of life, and drink your cup

---

15. Burchard, 'Joseph and Aseneth', pp. 205-206. Subsequent quotations of *JA* will also be from this translation.

16. Barclay, *Jews in the Mediterranean Diaspora*, pp. 207-208.

17. Cf. 14.15–15.2; see 1.4-5; 2.6-7. When Aseneth comes to marry Joseph afterwards, the 'veil', which she puts on, symbolizes her bridal character (again in 14.15–15.6). The clause, 'with a veil she covered her head like a bride' (18.6), clearly emphasizes the bridal connotation of a veil.

of blessing, and number her among your people that you have chosen before all
(things) came into being, and let her enter your rest which you have prepared for
your chosen ones, and live in your eternal life for ever (and) ever.

In his prayer Joseph first confesses who God is, then beseeches his blessing to
bring about Aseneth's conversion. Joseph underlines that God is he who called all
things 'from the darkness to the light, and from the error to the truth, and from
death to life' (8.9a). This anticipates the conversion which Aseneth is to experience.
Then, Joseph stresses three points (8.9b): Aseneth's renewal,[18] access to Jewish
table fellowship,[19] and acquirement of membership of God's chosen people.[20] In
short, Joseph's prayer implies that Aseneth's identity, which is symbolized by her
idolatrous attire, is characterized by darkness and death. It needs to be re-created
by God's spirit; it needs to be renewed by God's hands; it needs to be filled with
divine life. This interpretation can be further supported by the fact that, as preparation for repentance, she first takes off 'her linen and gold woven royal robe' (10.10).
We, accordingly, conclude that her pagan attire connotes an identity that is characterized by religious darkness and death.

In contrast to Aseneth's pagan apparel, the author describes how Joseph is
adorned with a garment of Jewish style. He states that

> Joseph was dressed in an exquisite white tunic, and the robe which he had thrown
> around him was purple, made of linen interwoven with gold, and a golden crown
> (was) on his head, and around the crown were twelve chosen stones, and on top of
> the twelve stones were twelve golden rays (5.5).

In brief, Joseph's attire is a royal one, which matches his status as the appointed
king of the whole land of Egypt (4.7). His royal attire resembles the priestly
garment in the Old Testament, although it is different in individual points.[21] The
exquisite white tunic can be compared with the linen tunic which was worn under
the blue robe (Exod. 28.4, 39). The purple robe can also be compared with the blue
robe which was worn under the ephod (Exod. 28.33-34; par. 39.24-26). Twelve
selected stones around a golden crown remind us of the twelve stones (which
symbolize the twelve tribes of Israel) on the breastpiece of judgment which is put
over the ephod (Exod. 28.17-20). For the author, though Aseneth's apparel is
idolatrous, Joseph's apparel is sacred like the priestly garment. 'Twelve golden
rays', which lend Joseph's image a solar connotation,[22] add to the splendour of his

---

18. For Joseph, the present state of her being is the same as the state of death. She needs to be
formed anew by God in order to be made alive.

19. This seems to be related to the previous topic. That is, Aseneth's spiritual renewal will be a
chance to gain the right to participate in the Jewish table. Joseph prays that Aseneth may be
authorized to gain access to the divine bread of life and cup of blessing. Without this authorization,
she may not participate in Jewish table fellowship. For Joseph, the bread and cup, which must be
blessed according to the customary table ritual, indicate a constant supply of sacred life and grace
to their partakers.

20. This is, in turn, an extension of the second point. That is, those who are entitled to join
Jewish meals are members of God's chosen people.

21. See Chapter 1, §3.2.

22. Note Aseneth's description of Joseph: 'Behold, the sun from heaven has come to us on its

apparel (cf. 18.5; 20.6). His apparel may be considered to symbolize the heavenly, royal, sacred radiance of his identity.

Looking at the splendour of Joseph, Aseneth's heart is broken (6.1); she bitterly regrets that she had poured out wicked words to insult Joseph (6.2-8). She now calls him 'the sun from heaven' (6.2), the 'son of God' (6.3, 5), which are titles similar to 'the Powerful One of God' (4.7). The author of *JA* portrays Joseph as almost a divine figure. Aseneth's marriage to Joseph, which will happen in the near future, will be her unity with a divinized being.

At any rate, by highlighting Aseneth's religious death, which is symbolized by her idolatrous garment, the author of *JA* emphasizes the superiority of Judaism to Hellenistic pagan religion. The tension between these two groups is further described not only by Joseph's action of not eating with the Egyptians (7.1)[23] but also by his refusal to be kissed by Aseneth. For Joseph, Aseneth is an alien woman (γυνὴ ἀλλοτρία).[24] When she attempts to kiss him, he physically keeps her away from him (8.2-5a), and says that

> it is not fitting for a man who worships God, who will bless with his mouth the living God and eat the blessed bread of life and drink a blessed cup of immortality and anoint himself with the blessed ointment of incorruptibility to kiss a strange woman who will bless with her mouth dead and dumb idols and eat from their table bread of strangulation and drink from their libation a cup of insidiousness and anoint herself with the ointment of destruction (8.5b).

In *JA*, the kiss theme occurs throughout the narrative[25] and signifies greeting, affection, loving union, a tender feeling, amicable relations, and so on. The reason for Joseph's refusal to be kissed is clear: without religious unity, he cannot accept any kiss. As a worshipper of the living God, he does not want to be defiled by being kissed by lips that are also kissing idols. The author seems to be inclined to show how great was the hostile feeling the Jewish religion had for other religions in the Graeco-Roman world.

Specifically, we note that in contrast to Joseph who blesses the living God, eats blessed bread, drinks a blessed cup, and anoints himself with blessed ointment, Aseneth is, for Joseph, a woman who blesses idols, eats from their table the bread of strangulation, drinks from their libation a cup of insidiousness, and anoints

---

chariot' (6.2), which can be compared with the sun-like face of Aseneth who is dressed in her wedding dress (18.9). Kee, 'The Socio-Cultural Setting of Joseph and Aseneth', p. 402 affirms that 'the use of solar imagery in Judaism of the post-temple period was a common feature' and 'it is regularly linked with the twelve signs of the zodiac'.

23. Barclay, *Jews in the Mediterranean Diaspora*, p. 208 says that 'our author subtly inverts an embarrassing text in Genesis, according to which the Egyptians would not eat with the Hebrews since to do so was an abomination to *them* (Gen. 43.32)'.

24. Here 'strange' (ἀλλότριος) does not simply mean 'unfamiliar' but 'alien' in terms of religion, not just of ethnic group or birth-land; cf. Gen. 24.3; 28.1, 6; Deut. 7.3-4; Neh. 13.13-29; for more examples, see Burchard, 'Joseph and Aseneth', p. 211, fn. k.; cf. esp. ἀπηλλοτριωμένοι in Eph. 2.12. At any rate, although the word 'strange' occurs in the context of the friendly meeting between Joseph and Aseneth, it clearly indicates that there is a religious conflict between them, which is to be actualized by Joseph's refusal of Aseneth's attempt to kiss him.

25. E.g. 4.1, 5; 8.5-7; 18.3; 19.10-11; 20.5; 21.7; 28.14-15.

herself with the ointment of destruction. The 'formulaic language' of blessing the living God, eating blessed bread, drinking a blessed cup and anointing with blessed ointment seems to be a summary of major items in the Jewish daily life rather than of rigorously fixed rituals. But considering the serious religious significance attached to them (which is shown by the modifying words 'living', 'of life', 'of immortality', and 'of incorruptibility'), they may be called 'Jewish semi-rituals', or 'ritual-like Jewish customs', or 'customary Jewish rituals' in daily life.[26] The same interpretation may be applied to the language of blessing, eating, drinking and anointing which are used of Aseneth. This language reflects the Egyptians' habitual rites of worshipping idols; the modifying words 'dead and dumb', 'of strangulation', 'of insidiousness', and 'of destruction' express the writer's opinion of such pagan rituals. The author's deliberate contrast between Jewish formulae and pagan ones is designed to underline the pagans' unworthiness and inferiority to the Jews. Further, it stresses that Aseneth's conversion to Judaism is not merely an affair with an individualistic dimension but also one with a socio-religious dimension.

Joseph's refusal to allow her to kiss him means that Aseneth is humiliated and frustrated. Joseph also feels some distress, so he prays for her conversion (8.9). His prayer results in her bitter regret of, in particular, her paganism (chapter 9); 'she wept with great and bitter weeping and repented of her (infatuation with the) gods whom she used to worship, and spurned all the idols'. Aseneth seems to recognize that her paganism is an obstacle to progress in their relationship.

2.2. *Scene 2: A Black Tunic*
We turn to the second scene of Aseneth's attirement, that is, her being dressed in a black tunic. After Joseph departs, Aseneth commits herself to exhaustive repentance as a sign of her conversion. Of many actions for remorse taken by Aseneth, our specific concern is with the point that she not only throws away all of her valuables (especially her idols), but also takes off her splendid clothing and puts on humble apparel. Chapter 10.8-15 states that

> 8 Aseneth...opened her coffer and took out a black and somber tunic. And this was her tunic of mourning when her younger brother died. In this Aseneth had dressed and mourned for her brother. 9 And she took her black tunic and carried it into her chamber... 10 And Aseneth...put off her linen and gold woven royal robe and dressed in the black tunic of mourning, and loosened her golden girdle and girded a rope around (her), and put off the tiara from her head, and the diadem and the bracelets from her hands and feet, and put everything on the floor. 11 And she took her chosen robe and the golden girdle and the headgear and the diadem, and threw everything through the window... 12 And Aseneth...took all her gods..., the ones of gold and silver who were without number, and ground them to pieces, and threw all the idols of the Egyptians through the window... 13 And Aseneth took her royal dinner and...all the sacrifices of her gods and the vessels of their wine of libation and threw everything through the window... 14 And after that Aseneth took the skin (full) of ashes and poured it on the floor. And she took a

---

26. J.J. Collins, *Between Athens and Jerusalem: Jewish Identity in the Hellenistic Diaspora* (New York: Crossroad, 1983), pp. 213-15. Burchard, 'The Importance of Joseph and Aseneth', p. 117 goes further, saying that Jews used food, drink and ointment as 'a special rite', i.e. '*sacramentalia*'.

piece of sackcloth and girded it around her waist. And she…sprinkled ashes upon her head. 15 And she scattered the ashes on the floor…

Beyond doubt the centrepiece here is Aseneth's denunciation of her past life. Her action is one which removed the obstacle laid on the road to love between a Jew and an alien. Aseneth thoroughly removes everything that she has formerly cherished. First of all, she throws away all her valuables and opulent royal apparel: the tiara, the bracelets, her chosen robe, the golden girdle, the headgear and the diadem, and so on. She also abandons her royal meals. All of this connotes that she renounces her lavish lifestyle. Secondly, she removes all her idols; she smashes all her gods into pieces, and throws out all her Egyptian idols and the food and drink which has been offered to them. This signifies that she refuses to continue to be an idol-worshipper. Thirdly, she girds a piece of sackcloth around her body, sprinkles ashes upon her head, and weeps upon the ashes, which are scattered on the floor, for seven days. This indicates that she humbles herself, renouncing her former arrogant character.

We, accordingly, argue that Aseneth's removal of her extravagance, idolatry and boastfulness signifies the burial of her previous existence characterized as it had been by her pagan religion and by her being spiritually dead (cf. 27.10). In particular, her taking off her pagan clothes connotes that she alienates paganism from herself. The author of *JA* symbolizes her inward change by the black mourning tunic 'symbolic of death'.[27] As the author emphasizes that the black tunic was the one in which she was dressed when her brother died, the wearing of it may signify that she puts to death her previous pagan identity.

In her mute prayer for repentance, Aseneth believes that everyone, including her parents, hate her, because she has abandoned their religion of idols, and that the God of the powerful Joseph also hates her, because she has not only worshipped strange gods and dead and dumb idols but has also eaten their sacrifices (11.1-18). This reflects that there was a social distinction and conflict between Jews and Gentiles in the author's context.[28] In her spoken prayer, Aseneth calls God the creator and confesses that she has committed the particular sin of worshipping idols (12.5; 13.11). Yet, she adds, she has destroyed and ground them into pieces, and because of this she has been abandoned by her parents, and become a desolate orphan (12.12-14). She confesses that she takes refuge in God, in sackcloth and ashes (13.1-2). She wishes to remind God of the fact that she has taken off her extravagant royal garments and has put on a black mourning tunic with other clothes of repentance (13.3-4). This confirms that her previous action of changing garments, that is, of replacing her idolatrous garment with the black tunic, symbolizes that her pagan identity has been mortified and instead a transformation into a Jewish identity has been inaugurated. In other words, the change of garments connotes that her idolatrous nature has been abandoned and the adoption of a new Jewish nature has been brought into existence.

27. Kee, 'The Socio-Cultural Setting of Joseph and Aseneth', p. 400.
28. R.D. Chesnutt, 'The Social Setting and Purpose of Joseph and Aseneth', *JSP* 2 (1988), pp. 21-48 (especially pp. 22-30).

2.3. *Scene 3: A New Linen Robe*

Then follows the third scene of Aseneth's attirement, that is, her being clothed with a new linen robe. When Aseneth's confession comes to an end, an angel comes to her from heaven (14.1-3). He calls himself 'the chief of the house of the Lord and commander of the whole host of the Most High' (14.8). His appearance and attire are almost the same as Joseph's (14.9). He says to Aseneth,

> put off your black tunic of mourning, and the sackcloth put off from your waist, and shake off those ashes from your head, and wash your face and your hands with living water, and dress in a new linen robe (as yet) untouched and distinguished and gird your waist (with) the new twin girdle of your virginity (14.12).

In this passage, taking off the clothes of repentance implies a break with the old identity; the washing with living water symbolizes purification from past sins and the obtaining of new life. In particular, the wearing of new apparel is a symbol of adopting a new nature, that is, an identity characterized by new life (cf. 15.2-5). Aseneth is to obtain a new nature in Judaism. The words, 'untouched' and 'distinguished', connote that the new robe is not defiled by her former idolatry. The symbolism of Aseneth's new linen robe for her new nature in her new Jewish identity could be compared with that of Lucius' linen garment (with which he is clothed after his transformation) and his new linen garment (with which he is dressed immediately before his initiation ceremony) in Apuleius' *Metamorphoses*,[29] which symbolize Lucius' new nature in his new life. There is, of course, a difference between the two; while *JA* speaks of the new life which is obtained by conversion from paganism to Judaism, *Metamorphoses* refers to the new life which is acquired by Lucius' ass-mask being stripped off. Despite this difference, the manner in which they are initiated into a specific religion, and the idea of their obtaining a new identity by this, is identical to both.

The new linen garment further symbolizes that Aseneth has been incorporated into Judaism. This is implied in the angel's words given to Aseneth. The angel says,

> Behold, from today, you will be renewed and formed anew and made alive again, and you will eat the blessed bread of life, and drink a blessed cup of immortality, and anoint yourself with the blessed ointment of incorruptibility (15.5).[30]

Here obtaining access to bread, cup and ointment, which seem to reflect the customary table rituals and anointing habits of the Jews, signifies that she will certainly be accepted into the Jewish community. Therefore, the new linen garment, with which Aseneth is clothed, symbolizes that she is to be a member of the Jewish community. R.C. Douglas believes that Aseneth's putting on new garments signifies 'her new status and her incorporation into the Jewish community'.[31]

The symbolism of the new linen garment for her acceptance into the Jewish community is further implied by the angel's feeding Aseneth with honeycomb. The

---

29. See Chapter 5, §§2.2.1; 2.2.2.
30. Burchard, 'Joseph and Aseneth', p. 226.
31. R.C. Douglas, 'Liminality and Conversion in Joseph and Aseneth', *JSP* 3 (1988), pp. 31-42 (37).

gift of participation in a miraculous honeycomb (15.13–17.3) is a crucial token of her having been accepted into the Jewish community. The angel connects the honeycomb with 'the bread of life, the cup of immortality and the ointment of incorruptibility' (16.16; cf. 8.5, 9; 15.5; 19.5). Barclay argues that this connection 'has led to suggestions that this text reflects the practice of a Jewish mystery cult, associated by some with the Therapeutae or Essenes, by others with groups not otherwise attested'.[32] At any rate, the combination of the honeycomb and the Jewish formulae seems to suggest that a mystical experience of Judaism is involved not merely in individualistic facets but also in socio-religious facets (cf. 11.4-5; 12.10-15).[33] It seems to be clear that *JA* is concerned with the social world of the Jewish community, not just with the world of Aseneth herself.

The new linen garment further stands for the whole company of Aseneth's imitators, and this is implied in the angel's continued blessings upon Aseneth. The angel declares that

> your name shall no longer be called Aseneth, but your name shall be City of Refuge, because in you many nations will take refuge with the Lord God, the Most High, and under your wings many peoples trusting in the Lord God will be sheltered, and behind your walls will be guarded those who attach themselves to the Most High God in the name of Repentance (15.7).

This statement emphasizes that Aseneth will be a 'City of Refuge' (cf. 16.15; 17.6; 19.5) for subsequent converts. She will be a prototype of those who will repent before God as she has done. She is to play a representative rôle for others, as an exemplary figure to those who take refuge with God.[34] This indicates that the new linen garment, with which she dresses herself, symbolizes the totality of her followers who will undergo conversion to Judaism. This is further clarified by the angel's repeated words, 'you shall be seven pillars of the City of Refuge, and all the fellow inhabitants of the chosen of that city will rest upon you for ever (and) ever' (17.6).

---

32. Barclay, *Jews in the Mediterranean Diaspora*, p. 211. He continues, 'In certain respects the text does invite comparison with mystery-initiations: besides the reference to "the ineffable mysteries of God" (16.14), the theme of rebirth and the accompanying visions, reclothing, sacred meals, and miraculous symbols all have parallels in Lucius' initiation in *Metamorphoses* 11' (Barclay, *Jews in the Mediterranean Diaspora*, pp. 211-12); but he adds, however, that 'these probably represent not a reflection of specific cultic activities but a literary effort to portray Judaism as a "mystery religion" with its secrets, sacred meals and promise of eternal life' (cf. Burchard, 'The Importance of Joseph and Aseneth', p. 112; Collins, *Between Athens and Jerusalem*, p. 218); see also Kee, 'The Socio-Cultural Setting of Joseph and Aseneth', pp. 400-403, 409-410. Chesnutt, *From Death to Life*, pp. 242-53 presents a detailed comparison between *JA* and Apuleius' *Metamorphoses*, although he denies that the account of Aseneth's initiation was shaped by that of Lucius. Kilpatrick, 'Living Issues', p. 6 imagines that as Aseneth's conversion to Judaism is shown as an initiation into a mystery, Hellenistic Judaism seems to be 'presented to the pagan world under the guise of a mystery'.

33. Barclay, *Jews in the Mediterranean Diaspora*, p. 212.

34. Cf. Burchard, 'Joseph and Aseneth', p. 189.

2.4. *Scene 4: A Wedding Garment*

Finally there is the fourth scene of Aseneth's attirement, that is, her being adorned with a wedding garment. The heavenly figure repeats that Joseph will be Aseneth's bridegroom and commands:

> dress in your wedding robe, the ancient and first robe which is laid up in your chamber since eternity, and put around you all your wedding ornaments, and adorn yourself as a good bride, and go meet Joseph (15.10).

As Aseneth's wedding garment is spoken of as having been kept since eternity and as it is about to be worn by Aseneth who has, in a sense, already obtained eternal life (cf. 15.5; 16.16), it seems to symbolize her new identity, to which she has been predestined from eternity. Hearing the heavenly man's command, Aseneth is full of joy and responds, 'Blessed be the Lord your God the Most High who sent you out to rescue me from the darkness and to bring me up from the foundations of the abyss' (15.12). This is her own understanding of her past life characterized by her idolatrous garments of paganism.

Eventually, when the wedding day comes, Aseneth adorns herself as a bride. Aseneth dresses in her wedding robe, puts on a golden and royal girdle, puts golden bracelets on her fingers and golden buskins on her feet, puts precious ornaments around her neck and a golden crown on her head, covers her head with a veil like a bride, and takes a sceptre in her hand (18.5-6). When Aseneth leans over a basin of water to wash her face, she finds that her face has already become like the sun (18.9). She is startled at the beauty of her transfigured appearance (18.10).

Joseph has been informed of her conversion in a vision, and when he comes to Aseneth for marriage, he hugs her and kisses her three times, giving her the spirit of life, wisdom and truth (19.10-11). Here Joseph's kissing means that the religious obstacle between paganism and Judaism has been removed. Aseneth's conversion to Judaism mean that she now deserves to be Joseph's bride. This does not merely mean that he has been accepted to the Jewish community but also connotes that she has obtained a royal status by being one with Joseph, the appointed king of Egypt (4.7) and also signifies that she has been, in a sense, identified with God through a marital unity with Joseph, who is a God-like person (cf. 4.7; 6.3, 5). This last point can be justified by Aseneth's appearance which is like 'light' (20.6; cf. 18.5, 'like lightning in appearance'); she radiates a heavenly beauty (20.6). The link between the concept of light and her wedding dress reminds us of the rabbinic theory that Adam was originally clothed with 'light'.[35] At any rate, Aseneth's bridal appearance resembles that of Joseph, 'the sun from heaven' (6.2), namely 'the son of God' (6.3, 5). We can, therefore, argue that Aseneth's being dressed in a wedding garment symbolizes her identification with God in Judaism. The wedding garment symbolizes that by being united with God, she has acquired a new identity, full of glory, privilege, honour, authority and power, which are eternal. It is probable that Aseneth's wedding garment finds its echo in Apuleius' *Metamorphoses*, where Lucius is eventually clothed with twelve-fold garments, which symbolize his

---

35. See Chapter 2, §5.

having been identified with Isis.[36] In addition, Aseneth's adorning herself with a wedding garment could also be compared with the prince's clothing himself with the royal garment (the symbolism for his original self, i.e. the image of God) in *The Hymn of the Pearl*, if this be understood as his recovery of the life which used to be his original self.[37]

3. *Conclusion: New Life out of Death*

In *JA* every step of Aseneth's life is symbolized by a clothing image; every step of her conversion is represented by her changing garments, which point to the transformation of her very being. (1) Aseneth's original apparel indicates her old identity in paganism, which is identified with death. That is, it connotes her spiritual death in the worship of idols. (2) Her black tunic signifies the burial of her old pagan identity. This is implied by the statement that it is the apparel which she wore when she mourned her brother's death. (3) Her new linen robe stands for her new identity in her conversion into Judaism,[38] which is identified with life. She comes to life spiritually and obtains full membership in God's people. (4) Her wedding garments symbolize her being identified with God through her marital unity with a God-like being, that is, Joseph, which result in a new fulfilled identity, which is full of glory. This glory is to be given to those who convert to the Jewish religion.

Aseneth's transformation can be designated by the following: the identity of death (the idolatrous apparel); the burial of the identity of death (the black tunic of mourning); the promise of the new life (the new linen robe); the fulfilment of the promise of new life by being identified with God through marital union with Joseph, the God-like figure (the wedding garments). We conclude that the gist of the clothing image in *JA*, which consists of four major garments, is the transformation of Aseneth's identity from one of death to one of life through conversion from paganism to Judaism. This change overlaps some parts of the story of Lucius' initiation into Isis in *Metamorphoses* as well as the story of the prince's reinvestiture with his original royal garment once disrobed, in *The Hymn of the Pearl*. It also resembles the Pauline thought of the believer's transformation from the old nature to the new nature, which is described especially by the imagery of putting off/on (Col. 3.9-10; Eph. 4.22-24; cf. Gal. 3.27; Rom. 13.14).

---

36. See Chapter 5, §2.2.3.
37. See Chapter 4, §3.4.
38. Douglas, 'Liminality and Conversion in Joseph and Aseneth', p. 31 affirms that 'This new identity establishes her as a prototypical figure for the Judaism represented by Joseph and Aseneth'.

Chapter 4

CLOTHING IMAGERY IN *THE HYMN OF THE PEARL*

1. *Introduction*

The Hymn of the Pearl (hereafter *HPrl*), which is also called *The Hymn of the Soul*,[1] is found in the apocryphal *Acts of Thomas*, which was probably written in Edessa, AD c. 200–225.[2] Most scholars agree that *HPrl* 'was in existence prior to its incorporation in the Acts [of Thomas]'.[3] Its date is presumably sometime during the Parthian dynasty of Persia (247 BC–AD 224), as Parthia is mentioned by name in verse 38.[4] The writer of *HPrl* is unknown. Its original language is a matter of controversy: Greek, Syriac, or a simultaneous publication in both, but the opinion that favours a Syriac original is strong.[5] The milieu, geography and language of *HPrl* suggests that it may have its 'origin in Christian East Syria'.[6] Its narrative structure is similar to 'a classic folktale or fairy tale'.[7]

---

1.   *The Hymn of the Pearl* and *The Hymn of the Soul* are titles that have been attributed to chapters 108–13 of *The Acts of Thomas* by modern scholarship (see B. Layton, *The Gnostic Scriptures* [London: SCM Press, 1987], p. 366; H. Jonas, *The Gnostic Religion* [London: Routledge, 1958], p. 112; J.K. Elliott [ed.], *The Apocryphal New Testament: A Collection of Apocryphal Christian Literature in an English Translation Based on M.R. James* [Oxford: Clarendon, 1993], p. 441; H. Kruse, 'The Return of the Prodigal, Fortunes of a Parable on Its Way to the Far East', in *Orientalia* [Nova Series, 47; Roma: Pontificium Institutum Biblica, 1978], pp. 163-214 [185]).

2.   Layton, *The Gnostic Scriptures*, p. 367.

3.   Elliott (ed.), *The Apocryphal New Testament*, p. 441.

4.   Layton, *The Gnostic Scriptures*, p. 369; he also says that 'if the work was composed in Edessa, it would have been composed during the Parthian control of that city, which ended in AD 165'; G. Quispel, 'Gnosticism and the New Testament', in J.P. Hyatt (ed.), *The Bible in Modern Scholarship* (Nashville and New York: Abingdon, 1965), pp. 252-71 (258) puts the date of *HPrl* at the end of the first century AD, when Christianity was introduced into Edessa by Jewish Christians.

5.   Elliott, (ed.), *The Apocryphal New Testament*, p. 441; Jonas, *The Gnostic Religion*, p. 112 (cf. F.C. Burkitt, *Early Eastern Christianity* [London: Murray, 1904], p. 212; V. Burch, 'Notes and Studies: A Commentary on the *Syriac Hymn of the Soul*', *JTS* 19 [1918], pp. 145-61 [145]); Kruse, 'The Return of the Prodigal', p. 178. These are other versions that are secondary in character: Arabic, Armenian, Latin, Coptic and Ethiopic (E.M. Yamauchi, *Pre-Christian Gnosticism: A Survey of the Proposed Evidences* [London: Tyndale, 1973], p. 95).

6.   J.W. Drijvers, 'The Acts of Thomas', in W. Schneemelcher (ed.), *New Testament Apocrypha*, II (Cambridge: Clarke, 1992 [Tübingen: Mohr, 1989]), pp. 322-411 (332).

7.   Layton, *The Gnostic Scriptures*, p. 369; cf. Elliott (ed.), *The Apocryphal New Testament*, p. 441.

The most distinctive feature in *HPrl* is its use of symbolism. *HPrl* as a whole is a symbolic epic, which consists of numerous component symbols.[8] Yet, of the many allegorical figures in *HPrl*, the garment seems to be most crucial, because it occurs consistently throughout the work and plays the most important part in every division of the poem.[9] This suggests that the idea of the garment functions as the central symbol of the whole narrative. Accordingly it would not be unsuitable to call the document 'The Hymn of the Garments'.

HPrl uses the symbol of the garment every time a significant change in the prince's life takes place.[10] Four critical changes, which he undergoes, are all symbolized by the garment image: (1) the prince's divestiture of the royal garment at his departure from his father's palace to Egypt, (2) his investiture with the Egyptian garment at the time of his indulgence in Egypt, (3) his divestiture of the Egyptian garment at his escape from Egypt, and (4) his reinvestiture with the royal garment at his return to his homeland. Our task is to investigate the significance of these garment motifs and how they define the whole work. But before proceeding to this, we first need to look into the meaning of crucial symbols, without the knowledge of which the significance of the garment imagery could scarcely be understood.

2. *Interpretation of Various Symbols*

Of the many symbolic concepts in *HPrl*, the prince and the pearl are particularly important. The question of what the prince represents is of primary consequence, because the significance of the other symbolic concepts must be adapted to the choice of identity for the prince. The pearl is the absolute condition for the prince's reinvestiture with his royal garment, which is, in a sense, the climax of the whole story. H. Jonas, one of the authoritative commentators on *HPrl*, affirms that perhaps nowhere else is 'the basic gnostic experience expressed in terms more moving and more simple'.[11] He argues that the prince points to 'the Saviour, a definite divine figure', who has assimilated himself to the forms of cosmic existence and thereby subjected himself to its conditions, who is 'the personification of the human soul in general', and who himself has to be saved.[12] He insists that 'the pearl', as a concept

---

8.   Jonas, *The Gnostic Religion*, p. 116.

9.   See section 3.

10.   This is similar to *Joseph and Aseneth*, which explains Aseneth's conversion from paganism to Judaism by four kinds of garments (see Chapter 3, §2). As there is no direct connection between the two documents, probably the central theme common to both, that is, a change of a human nature, makes them similar. Yet this coincidence seems to reflect how clothing imagery was popular in the early Christian era for describing a change in human nature. That Lucius' transformation and initiation into Isis-worship is symbolized by the various kinds of clothing imagery would be understood in the same vein (see Chapter 5. §2.2).

11.   Jonas, *The Gnostic Religion*, p. 116.

12.   Jonas, *The Gnostic Religion*, p. 127; a similar thought is found in R. Reitzenstein, *Das iranische Erlösungsmysterium. Religionsgeschichtliche Untersuchungen* (Bonn, 1921), pp. 70-73, 117 who identifies the prince as a type of pre-Christian Redeemed Redeemer and the pearl as a symbol of the inclusive soul whom he gathers to himself.

interchangeable with 'the prince', stands for the prince's soul which 'is present in every human soul, exiled, captive, stunned'.[13]

However, Jonas's argument can scarcely be upheld; *HPrl* never identifies the prince with the pearl, which 'is in no way a personal being, or something to be "redeemed"'.[14] Rather the epic identifies the prince with his own royal garment (cf. vv. 75-77). The poem never suggests the prince as the divine saviour who redeems himself. It is the prince's Father with his subjects who redeem him from being engrossed in the secular life of Egypt. As Jonas argues, it is true that *HPrl* includes a number of concepts of gnostic style,[15] but this does not necessarily mean that the epic describes a gnostic Redeemer myth. If *HPrl* were indeed a document which reflected the thought of the gnostic Redeemer myth, it would require that the prince be Christ as the Redeemer.[16] But how could this interpretation explain the fact that the prince adopts Egyptian customs (vv. 32-35)? A.F.J. Klijn ventures to oppose this view of the gnostic nature.[17] G. Quispel strongly argues that *HPrl* 'is not gnostic at all, but rather an orthodox Christian hymn tinged with Judaistic colours'.[18] H. Kruse believes that this latter opinion on *HPrl* is basically right, because 'no specifically gnostic idea can be shown in it'.[19] Remembering that *HPrl* includes some words which have a gnostic feel,[20] it is likely that it has some gnostic undertones whilst basically being a Christian didactic narrative.

We note that *HPrl* combines the parable of the Prodigal Son (Lk. 15.11-32) with that of the Pearl (Mt. 13.45-46), and 'reinterprets them in a quite specific sense'.[21] It is probable that the prince is based on the Prodigal son. If this is true, there is no specific reason to see him as 'the soul'.[22] As *HPrl* is composed on the basis of these biblical stories, it is natural to imagine that the writer has a biblical figure in mind. If we thus consider a person instead of 'the soul' as the protagonist, we can reduce the difficulties caused by the other symbols in the poem. The identity of the person

---

13. Jonas, *The Gnostic Religion*, p. 128.

14. Kruse, 'The Return of the Prodigal', p. 186.

15. See Jonas, *The Gnostic Religion*, pp. 116-29; A. Adam, *Die Psalmen des Thomas und das Perlenlied als Zeugnisse vorchristlicher Gnosis* (BZNW, 24; Berlin: W. de Gruyter, 1959), pp. 68-70.

16. Elliott (ed.), *The Apocryphal New Testament*, p. 441.

17. A.F.J. Klijn, 'The So-called Hymn of the Pearl', *Vigiliae Christianae* 14 (1960), pp. 154-64.

18. Quispel, 'Gnosticism and the New Testament', p. 259.

19. Kruse, 'The Return of the Prodigal', p. 185; he attempts to prove that *HPrl* is in line with Christian and Jewish traditions (see Kruse, 'The Return of the Prodigal', pp. 190-214).

20. E.g. v. 77 refers to the prince's attainment to a perfect self-*gnosis*: 'I perceived in it my whole self as well, And through it I recognized and saw myself'. This is a quotation from a translation based on the Greek version by Elliott (ed.), *The Apocryphal New Testament*, pp. 488-91. Subsequent quotations will be from this book.

21. Drijvers, 'The Acts of Thomas', p. 331; Layton, *The Gnostic Scriptures*, p. 369: 'the allegorical motif of the pearl was widely used not only by Mesopotamian Christian authors, but also in ancient world literature in general'.

22. Kruse, 'The Return of the Prodigal', p. 187: 'In a Semitic context the word "soul" (*nepeš/napšâ*) often seems to mean just the same as "man," or what later was called πρόσωπον/*persona*. Only in this sense could the Prince be regarded as a "soul," but for us such terminology would be ambiguous'.

now becomes of paramount importance. It is highly probable that the writer has Adam in mind.[23] As J.W. Drijvers points out, 'Adam as a child is a familiar idea in the apocryphal Acts';[24] he argues that the poem symbolically portrays 'the life of Adam, the man who of his own free will left his Father's house, Paradise, with a part of his inheritance'.[25] The author's identification of the royal garment, which is later put on again by the prince, with the image of the King of kings (v. 86), suggests that he perhaps considers Adam's garment to be God's image in him,[26] which reflects his kingly status. When the prince is thus seen as Adam, he does not necessarily symbolize the individual Adam only, since Adam as the first man can be a symbolic figure representing all human beings. In this vein, we may conclude that *HPrl* is the story of the fate of man.

H. Jonas argues that the 'pearl' is the central theme of *HPrl*.[27] However, comparing the function of the 'garment' with that of the 'pearl', it becomes clear that the 'garment' is actually the principal subject matter.[28] The 'pearl' has only an auxiliary role in establishing the primary theme of the poem.[29] A.F.J. Klijn, after surveying the pearl passages in the work (i.e. vv. 12-15, 29-30, 45-46, 61, 105), rightly declares that

> the pearl does not play a very important part in the hymn. Line 12 shows that the pearl is only a medium… The hymn is dealing in the first place with the principal person, his adventures and his reward. Especially the part dealing with the robe covers a great part of the hymn (line 75-105).[30]

Klijn's view seems to do justice to the pearl's function in the poem. If so, what is meant by the symbol of the one pearl? Considering the parable of Mt. 13.45-46, which is one of the major sources of the poem, it is highly probable that it symbolizes a life which is lived according to the principles of the kingdom of God.[31]

On the basis of this understanding of the prince and the pearl, we would interpret other important symbols which seem to be specifically relevant in working out the

23. A.F.J. Klijn, *The Acts of Thomas: Introduction—Text—Commentary* (NovTSup, 5; Leiden: Brill, 1962), p. 278.

24. Drijvers, 'The Acts of Thomas', p. 332.

25. Drijvers, 'The Acts of Thomas', p. 331.

26. Cf. Drijvers, 'The Acts of Thomas', p. 332: 'The robe symbolizes the image of God, immortality, which man recovers when he is clothed with his heavenly second self, his twin brother Jesus'; J.H. Moulton, ' "It is His Angel" ', *JTS* 3 (1902), pp. 514-27 (519).

27. Jonas, *The Gnostic Religion*, pp. 116, 125-29.

28. Klijn, *The Acts of Thomas*, p. 276: 'The main theme of this hymn consists of the description of the glittering robe which was promised to the author and which was given to him after having fulfilled his work'. The principal theme of *HPrl* is to describe man's fate when he discards his royal garment as he leaves his Father's kingdom, and when he rerobes as he returns to the kingdom. This will be made clear in section 3, below.

29. Kruse, 'The Return of the Prodigal', pp. 185-86.

30. Klijn, 'The So-called Hymn of the Pearl', p. 158. See also Drijvers, 'The Acts of Thomas', p. 331: 'Contrary to what the usual title suggests, the pearl is not the principal theme of the Hymn'.

31. Klijn, 'The So-called Hymn of the Pearl', p. 158 affirms that the contrast between the one pearl and the other pearls in Mt. 13.45, a major background theme of *HPrl*, implies that 'to fetch the one pearl means partaking in the kingdom'; *The Acts of Thomas*, p. 277.

significance of the garment imagery in *HPrl*: (1) the prince's parents (vv. 3, 36, 41, 61) = God and the Holy Spirit,[32] (2) the father's palace in the East (vv. 1, 15-16) = the heavenly kingdom of God, namely Paradise,[33] (3) Egypt (vv. 20, 28, 30, 39, 57) = the earthly kingdom of darkness,[34] (4) the serpent (vv. 13, 30, 58) = the demonic power,[35] (5) the Egyptian food (v. 32) = worldly enjoyment, (6) a letter (vv. 40-48) = a message (or call), (7) snatching away the pearl from the serpent (v. 61) = attainment of a life lived according to the principles of God's kingdom by conquering demonic powers.

3. Symbolism of Four Scenes of Changing Garments

3.1. Scene 1: Divestiture of the Royal Garment (vv. 1-19)

HPrl starts by saying that a young royal prince leaves his father's kingdom in the East and goes to Egypt on a mission; it is his parents' will that sets events in motion.[36] Before he leaves, his parents equip him with precious stones,[37] which signify his spiritual riches.[38] Then they take away from him his well-fitting royal garment (v. 9); they make a covenant with him, which is engraved in his heart: if he goes to Egypt and fetches the one pearl guarded by the serpent, he will be reclothed with his royal garment and will be the heir in the kingdom, with his brother at the second rank (v. 15). He leaves his father's kingdom accompanied by two guardians and travels through Mesopotamia.

The prince's being divested of his royal garment seems to mean that he is stripped of his heavenly self. This interpretation is grounded in the fact that his eventual reinvestiture with it signifies his recovery of his original self. V. Burch calls this royal self '[the prince's] spiritual other-self and insignia of Overship or Princehood'.[39] Yet it seems to signify more than this. That is, since verse 86 presents the image of God as the essential constituent of the prince's royal garment, it must refer to God's image in him.[40] As a man who is sent to Egypt (the material

---

32.   Drijvers, 'The Acts of Thomas', p. 331; Kruse, 'The Return of the Prodigal', p. 190; Burkitt, *Early Eastern Christianity*, p. 214.

33.   Kruse, 'The Return of the Prodigal', p. 190.

34.   See Kruse, 'The Return of the Prodigal', p. 198; Jonas, *The Gnostic Religion*, p. 118; A.A. Bevan, 'The Hymn of the Soul', in *TS* 5.3 (Cambridge: Cambridge University Press, 1897), pp. 1-40 (2, fn. 3); Burch, 'A Commentary on the *Syriac Hymn of the Soul*', p. 146; Hippolytus, *The Refutation of All Heresies*, Book V, Chapters 2 and 5.

35.   Cf. Jonas, *The Gnostic Religion*, p. 116: 'the ruler or evil principle of this world'.

36.   The emphasis on the prince's youthfulness when he leaves the kingdom of his father may imply that the King's plan of sending his son to Egypt is intended to mature him (cf. v. 75). Layton, *The Gnostic Scriptures*, p. 367 translates v. 92 from a Greek version: 'And for my part, I took note of my mature age', of which the concept, 'mature age' is the opposite emphasis from youthfulness. To the concept he gives a footnote: 'Or "stature"'.

37.   'Gold from the land above, silver from great treasuries, | And Stones, chalcedonies of India and agates from Kushan... | steel' (vv. 6-8).

38.   Burch, 'A Commentary on the *Syriac Hymn of the Soul*', p. 145.

39.   Burch, 'A Commentary on the *Syriac Hymn of the Soul*', p. 146.

40.   Cf. Drijvers, 'The Acts of Thomas', pp. 331-32; Moulton, ' "It is His Angel" ', p. 519.

world), the prince is deprived of his royal garment (his heavenly self, namely the image of God), which is suitable only for a man in the heavenly kingdom. When he fetches the pearl guarded by the serpent (to attain a life founded on the principle of his father's kingdom by defeating the evil power), he is reclothed with his own royal garment (his heavenly self in the divine image). In brief, the prince's being divested of the royal garment pictures the change in his person: from a person in union with self (i.e. one who bears the image of God) to a person in disunion with self (i.e. one who has forfeited that image).

3.2. *Scene 2: Investiture with the Egyptian Garment (vv. 20-35)*

When the prince enters Egypt, the guardians leave him (v. 20). He rushes straight to the serpent and camps near its den, in order that he may take the pearl from it when it has fallen asleep (vv. 21-22). He also disguises himself so that he should seem a local person (v. 23). He meets a free-born man, an oriental, with whom he shares his merchandise (vv. 24-27). Next he clothes himself with a garment of Egyptian style, so that he will neither appear an alien nor provoke the Egyptians to arouse the serpent against him (v. 29). But all these actions can perhaps be considered as symbolical 'compromises with his faith'.[41] Despite his efforts, the Egyptians recognize that he is not their countryman and deal with him treacherously, making him eat their food. Finally the prince sinks into forgetfulness of his identity as the royal prince, and this is followed by his servitude to the Egyptians' king; he also forgets his mission to take the pearl. He is overwhelmed by deep sleep induced by the heaviness of the Egyptians' food (v. 35).

In this narrative, it is true that the prince wears the Egyptian-style garment with good intentions and his fall into worldly enjoyment is not a direct consequence of his putting on this garment. However, the fact that this change of dress eventually has a bad effect has a particular message. The author wishes to show that good intentions can be a path to compromise and in fact can have bad results. The prince's wearing of the Egyptian garment aims at concealing his identity from them, but this actually brings about a crisis in his own identity and he ends up becoming like them. Although his robing with the Egyptian garment does not immediately follow his divestiture of his royal robe, it cannot be denied that the Egyptian garment replaces the royal garment.[42] Accordingly, the Egyptian garment can be regarded as a substitute for his original self. Thinking of the later recovery of his royal garment, it could also be called a symbol for an intermediate or provisional person. But its negative image allows us to call it a symbol for a worldly self. In short, that he puts on the Egyptian-style garment signifies that he is united to a worldly self and becomes a worldly person.

41. Burch, 'A Commentary on the *Syriac Hymn of the Soul*', p. 154.

42. Jonas, *The Gnostic Religion*, p. 119 holds that 'if we look at our text closely, we realize that the King's Son has actually no choice but to put on the terrestrial garments, seeing that he has left his own in the upper realm'. But this view is not plausible, because the prince still has an eastern-style garment, which he replaces with the Egyptian garment, because he is worried that his appearance will reveal that he is a foreigner (vv. 23, 29).

3.3. *Scene 3: Divestiture of the Egyptian Garment (vv. 36-70)*

While the prince is sunk in a deep sleep because of the heaviness of the Egyptians' food (v. 35), his parents with a number of their court send a letter to him (vv. 41-50), demanding that he awake and rise out of his sleep. As a matter of fact, his parents have taken note of all his plight. The letter flies through the air like an eagle. The letter reminds him, in particular, of (1) his being a royal prince, who at present lives as a slave of the worldly kingdom, (2) his gold-spangled royal garment, (3) his mission to fetch the pearl, and (4) his status as an heir of the kingdom together with his brother,[43] the 'crown prince'.[44]

Eventually, the prince rises from sleep and reads the letter. What is written in it concerns his Father's covenant, which has been engraved in his heart (v. 55; cf. v. 11). He immediately recalls that he is a royal prince and that he has been sent to obtain the pearl guarded by the serpent. Then he subdues the serpent by calling out his father's name and snatches the pearl from it. Without hesitation he turns around to go to his parents, taking off the dirty garment and leaving it behind in Egypt. He then goes straight to the road leading to the light of his father's house in the East (cf. vv. 61-63). Verses 64-66[45] state that he is guided by a female being (= the letter)[46] to the light (= the original garment).[47] At times the royal silken garment appears in his sight (v. 66). Again he travels through Mesopotamia.

In this part of the tale, the dirty garment indicates the garment of the Egyptians which the prince has worn while staying in Egypt. There is little doubt that it symbolizes his former assimilation to a worldly lifestyle. Therefore, his disrobing would mean that he disengages himself from his worldly self. His person at this stage may be equated with the one that existed when he first took off his royal garment. It is natural that when he is disengaged from the worldly self (the dirty garment), he is clothed with his heavenly self (his original royal garment).

3.4. *Scene 4: Reinvestiture with the Royal Garment (vv. 75-105)*

The story of the prince's rediscovery of himself in his royal garment constitutes the climax of the narrative of his returning home. The following verses describe the prince's restoration.

> 75 But I could not recall my splendour, For it had been when I was still a child and quite young that I had left it behind in my father's palace. 76 But, when

---

43. See the Syriac version of v. 48 and compare it with v. 15, which states that the pilgrim together with his brother, the next in rank, will inherit the kingdom.

44. See the Syriac version of v. 48.

45. In these verses 'motifs borrowed from the Exodus story' seem to be at work (cf. Exod. 13.21-22); Drijvers, 'The Acts of Thomas', p. 332.

46. See a translation of v. 64 from the Greek version by Layton, *The Gnostic Scriptures*, p. 374, who points out that in Greek the word 'letter' is grammatically feminine. In the Syriac version, 'a letter' is read instead of 'a female being', and indicates the royal message.

47. See the translation of vv. 65-66 from the Greek version by Layton, *The Gnostic Scriptures*, p. 374, who identifies 'the light' with 'the royal garment of silk'. This seems to be reasonable not only as the prince calls his original royal robe 'my splendour' (v. 75), but also as this regal robe is spoken of as having been sent to him as he returns home (v. 99).

suddenly I saw my garment reflected as in a mirror, 77 I perceived in it my whole self as well, And through it I knew and saw myself. 78 For though we originated from the one and the same we were partially divided, Then again we were one, with a single form.[48]

This passage, above all, makes us sure that the prince's original royal garment symbolizes his own self in its radiance.[49] This is unmistakably implied by the statement that the prince perceives his whole self in his royal garment and sees himself through it (v. 77). The robe functions like a mirror in which the prince recognizes himself. This signifies that 'the real likeness of man is found in heaven only'.[50] 'My splendour' in verse 75 is no doubt related to the prince's original royal garment, that is, his original self. The verse hereby implies that glory is the dominant characteristic of the prince's heavenly self.[51] Verse 78 summarizes the whole history of the prince's fate, that is, the state of his being in union with his self, then the state of his being in separation from his self, finally the state of his being in reunion with his self.

Some other features of the prince's royal garment, that is, his original self, are further referred to. Its glorious character is now overtly spoken of. The writer mentions its bright colours due to its being embroidered with gold, precious stones, and pearls (v. 83). It is also stressed that the royal garment is entirely covered with the image of the King of kings (v. 86), which in effect identifies the self with God's image.[52] This resembles the thought in Gen. 1–3, where the image of God in Adam (of which the centrepiece is the existence of the divine life in him), is implied to be full of glory. However, as Gen. 1–3 does not say that man was clothed before the Fall, *HPrl* probably interprets Gen. 1–3 by making use of the rabbinic thought that before the Fall man was adorned with a garment of 'light' (אור).[53] The writer of *HPrl* further refers to the garment's intellectual function[54] and linguistic ability.[55]

48. As v. 75 starts talking about the prince's recovery of his royal garment, it would be reasonable to include it within the category of his return to the father's kingdom. Cf. Jonas, *The Gnostic Religion*, p. 121 who asserts that the prince's ascent (cf. v. 98, my note) starts with his removal of his filthy garment. The Syriac version includes vv. 71-74: 'And my splendid robe which I had taken off | And my toga with which it was wrapped about | From the heights of Hyrcania | My parents sent there | By the hand of their treasures, | Who for their faithfulness were so entrusted' (Elliot [ed.], *The Apocryphal New Testament*, p. 490, fn. 58; cf. Drijvers, 'The Acts of Thomas', p. 383; Bevan, 'The Hymn of the Soul', p. 25).

49. Bevan, 'The Hymn of the Soul', p. 27 renders v. 77 from the Syriac text 'I saw it all in my whole self, | Moreover I faced my whole self in (facing) it'.

50. Klijn, *The Acts of Thomas*, p. 281.

51. Note that verses 65-66 connect light with the prince's royal garment, and verses 82-83 refer to the fine garment of glorious colours.

52. Cf. the Syriac version of v. 86 which is rendered by Kruse, 'The Return of the Prodigal', p. 183: 'And the full image of the King of kings was depicted all over it in embroidery.'

53. Kruse, 'The Return of the Prodigal', p. 192. See Chapter 2, §5.

54. Layton, *The Gnostic Scripture*, p. 374 translates verse 88 from the Greek version: 'And I saw, in turn, that impulses of acquaintance (*gnosis*) were rippling throughout it'.

55. See verse 91: 'Then I heard it speak: "It is I who belong to the one who is stronger than all men and for whose sake I was written about by the father himself"'.

The author makes three more points about the prince's restoration. First, the prince recovers his 'royal impulses' as the garment's energy increases (v. 93). This may mean that when the prince's self works properly according to its own capability, he becomes conscious of his original status as a royal prince. Second, the prince completely recovers his original royal robe (v. 97): 'And I covered myself completely with my royal robe over it'. This signifies that he achieves complete reunion with his heavenly self, which results not only in his ascent to the land of peace and homage (v. 98) but also in his access to the king himself (vv. 104-105). He has truly become the heir of the kingdom.

4. *Conclusion: Recovery of Self in God's Image once Lost*

HPrl as a whole is the story of the forfeiture of the heavenly self and its eventual recovery. Four stages of changing garments pervade the entire tale of *HPrl*. First, the prince's divestiture of the royal garment symbolizes his separation from his heavenly royal self. Second, his robing with the Egyptian-style garment connotes that he is united with a strange worldly self. Third, his disrobing of the Egyptian-style garment conveys the sense of his disengagement from this alien self. Fourth, his reinvestiture implies that he is reunited with his own original heavenly self. In this progress a dualism of the heavenly and earthly kingdoms functions as a fundamental element.

In particular, splendour is one of the most prominent characteristics of the heavenly self, which is identified with the image of God, to which linguistic and intellectual capability is specifically attributed. This is similar not only to the rabbinic concept of man's prelapsarian clothing but also to Gen. 1–3, which implies that the glory of life is to be retained in so far as God's image is preserved by being faithful to God's command. When man is reunited with his original heavenly self, that is, the image of God, his being will be full of brilliance. In short, *HPrl* can be called a story of how the prince has been reunited with his royal self, that is, the image of God (which was once lost), resulting in his perfect self-knowledge, namely, salvation. A similar thought seems to operate in the Pauline metaphor of clothing with Christ (Gal. 3.27; Rom. 13.14), the new man (Col. 3.9-10; Eph. 4.22-24), and clothing with the resurrection body (1 Cor. 15.49, 50-54; 2 Cor. 5.1-4), behind all of which the Adam–Christ typology is in evidence.

Chapter 5

CLOTHING IMAGERY IN MYSTERY RELIGIONS

1. *Introduction*

'Mystery religions' is a general term for a variety of ancient secret religious cults. These are 'some of great antiquity, which flourished in Greece and Asia Minor',[1] during the first to the third centuries. Their ritual activities frequently contained an important rite of changing garments. So the mystery religions must also be carefully investigated. These *mysteries* (μυστήρια) were 'societies with secret rites and doctrines, admission to which was through instruction, discipline, and initiation (τελετή literally "a making perfect")'.[2] The word 'mystery' is the rendering of μυστήριον, which derives from μυέω, meaning 'to initiate into'.[3] The mystery religions involved the worship of many kinds of deity from various lands. The mysteries of Demeter the 'Grain Mother' and her daughter Persephone (= Kore = Lat. Core) which were celebrated at Eleusis;[4] the mysteries of 'Demeter, Hermes, Apollo Karneios, Hagna [Hagne], and the great gods' which were celebrated at Andania in the southwestern Peloponnesus;[5] and the mysteries of Dionysos (or Bacchos = Lat. Bacchus)[6] which were 'the only new mysteries of Greek origin' and widespread in the Graeco-

1.   E. Ferguson, *Backgrounds of Early Christianity* (Grand Rapids: Eerdmans, 1993), p. 236.
2.   J. Finegan, *Myth & Mystery* (Grand Rapids: Baker, 1989), p. 172.
3.   Cf. D.E. Aune, 'Religions, Greco-Roman', in *DPL* (Leicester: IVP, 1993), pp. 786-96 (792); M.W. Meyer, 'Mystery Religions', in *ABD*, IV (New York: Doubleday, 1992), pp. 941-45 (especially pp. 941-42).
4.   F.R. Walton, 'Athens, Eleusis, and the Homeric Hymn to Demeter', *HTR* 45 (1952), pp. 105-114 argues that the earliest literary evidence for the Eleusinian mysteries is found in the Homeric *Hymn to Demeter*, which originated c. 550 BC. The Eleusinian cult started as the property of one family at Eleusis as early as the fifteenth century BC and was gradually made known to the town's people (Ferguson, *Backgrounds*, p. 238). Yet, with the increase of its fame, it spread to Attica, to all the Greek-speaking world in the late sixth and fifth centuries BC, and to the Roman empire after the conquests of Alexander. Initiation at Eleusis had a great attraction from the first century BC to the second century AD. An inscription at Eleusis' sanctuary, 'All the Greeks to the goddesses and the Emperor', implies how predominant this cult was. It continued to flourish until the *Telesterion*, the large temple at Eleusis where the cultic service (especially the initiation ceremony) was maintained, was destroyed by the Goths in AD 395 under Theodosius' command (cf. Aune, 'Religions, Greco-Roman', p. 792; O. Seyffert, *A Dictionary of Classical Antiquities: Mythology, Religion, Literature & Art* [London: Swan Sonnenschein, 1899], p. 212).
5.   Meyer, 'Mystery Religions', p. 942.
6.   J. Ferguson, *The Religions of the Roman Empire* (London: Thames & Hudson, 1970), pp. 101-104; A.J.M. Wedderburn, 'The Soteriology of the Mysteries', *NovT* 29 (1987), pp. 53-72 (especially pp. 64-67).

Roman world, all belong to Greece.[7] The mysteries of Isis and her husband Osiris originate from Egypt;[8] the mysteries of Astarte and Adonis come from Phoenicia;[9] the mysteries of Atargatis and Hadad are from Syria; the mysteries of Cybele and Attis are from Phrygia;[10] the mysteries of Mithras have their origin in Persia.[11]

In particular, the Eleusinian mysteries profoundly affected many of the mystery religions in the Greek world,[12] as the most popular and oldest of all mystery cults.[13] The mysteries of Eleusis were, as a matter of fact, rooted in the Egyptian mysteries of Isis and Osiris. Osiris was the vegetation god and king who ruled the netherworld; Isis was his sister and wife, and the mother of Horus.[14] When these deities were introduced into the Greek world, Osiris' name was replaced by that of Sarapis (Lat. Serapis),[15] and Isis was identified with Demeter (later with Aphrodite), which linked her with the most important goddess in the Greek world.[16] She was thought of as the all-embracing cosmopolitan deity, while the other goddesses were thought of only as her manifestations. In external appearance, for example, the statues, temples and language, the Egyptian mysteries of Isis and Osiris were totally Hellenized, but they never lost their original character.

It is misleading to stereotype the mysteries, not only because there is such diversity in their geographical origins, but also due to the 'heterogeneity in their patterns of historical development and theological orientation'.[17] Moreover, the evidence of these religions is for the most part fragmentary and very difficult to decipher. Most of it consists of single lines, passing allusions to ancient authors, inscriptions, artistic and other objects discovered by archaeologists.[18]

7. Ferguson, *Backgrounds*, p. 243.

8. During the first and second centuries AD, of the non-Greek mysteries, those of Egypt were the most popular and widespread. They were the first eastern mysteries to become famous in the Greek world. They were based on the myth of, and involved in the worship of, Isis and Osiris. This myth is found in Plutarch, *Is. Osiris* 12-19. See R.T.R. Clark, *Myth and Symbol in Ancient Egypt* (London: Thames & Hudson, 1959), pp. 103-123; Wedderburn, 'The Soteriology of the Mysteries', pp. 57-62.

9. Ferguson, *Backgrounds*, pp. 260-61.

10. E. Ferguson, *Backgrounds*, pp. 264-69; J. Ferguson, *The Religions of the Roman Empire*, pp. 104-106; Wedderburn, 'The Soteriology of the Mysteries', pp. 67-72.

11. Ferguson, *Backgrounds*, pp. 270-78.

12. Wedderburn, 'The Soteriology of the Mysteries', p. 55.

13. Aune, 'Religions, Greco-Roman', p. 792.

14. For the system of Heliopolis, see Clark, *Myth and Symbol in Ancient Egypt*, p. 18.

15. A.D. Nock, *Conversion: The Old and the New in Religion from Alexander the Great to Augustine of Hippo* (Oxford: Clarendon, 1933), pp. 51-54 holds that Sarapis inscriptions of Delos may indicate that it was when an Egyptian priest, Apollonis, came to Delos in the early third century BC and conducted worship to Sarapis that this cult started to be spread in the Greek world. See also Finegan, *Myth & Mystery*, p. 177.

16. Cf. R.M. Grant, *Gods and the One God* (LEC, 1; Philadelphia: The Westminster Press, 1986), pp. 34-39, 69-71, 121-22.

17. Meyer, 'Mystery Religions', p. 941; cf. A.J.M. Wedderburn, *Baptism and Resurrection: Studies in Pauline Theology against Its Graeco-Roman Background* (Tübingen: Mohr, 1987), pp. 90-113; Ferguson, *Backgrounds*, pp. 235-78.

18. C.K. Barrett, *The New Testament Background: Selected Documents* (London: SPCK, 1987 [1956]), p. 120.

Nevertheless, there are some features common to most of the mystery cults.[19] They were closely linked with myths, which were often ritually represented in a symbolic fashion. They commonly originated from 'tribal and even fertility rituals' of antiquity.[20] Many of them were linked with the agricultural cycle of the year. They manifested a private character, while the traditional cults of the Greek city-states showed a public character; that is, they emphasized salvation for those individuals whose own decision it was to be initiated into the mysteries.[21] Salvation meant escape from Fate, liberation from depravity, and a renewed moral life. It was effected by participating not only in public festivals, for example parades and processions with music and dancing, after preliminary rituals of bathing and sacrifice, but also in abstinence from food and the secret initiation ceremony which was the core of the whole affair. Usually a sacred meal was shared by the initiated. In particular, those who participated in the initiation ceremony 'underwent an extraordinary experience that could be described as death and rebirth'.[22] Through this experience, they became united with a god or goddess, could enjoy worldly success under his or her protection as well as mystical communication with him or her, and further were assured of safety in the afterlife in the underworld. The mysteries were strict in preserving the secrecy of their initiation ceremony, which is the chief reason why they remain largely unknown.

In the mystery religions the clothing motif seems to have been made use of quite frequently in different ways. But clear evidence is found only in Apuleius' *Metamorphoses*, where the wearing of a new linen garment was crucial at the climactic ritual of initiation into Isis. In this chapter we will concentrate on *Metamorphoses* XI.

2. Metamorphoses *of Lucius Apuleius*

2.1. *Introductory Remarks*
Apuleius' *Metamorphoses* (hereafter *Metam.*) is of great importance in two ways. First, it provides the most substantial account of the mystery religions, especially of the Isis cult. Second, it portrays some important events which happened in Lucius'[23] religious experiences by means of the clothing image. Apuleius' description of the

---

19. Ferguson, *The Religions of the Roman Empire*, p. 99 insists that there are three essential features common to all the mystery religions: (i) 'a ritual of purification through which the initiate has to pass'; (ii) 'communion with some god or goddess'; (iii) a 'promise to the purified and faithful of a life of bliss beyond the grave'. See also Wedderburn, 'The Soteriology of the Mysteries', p. 55.

20. Cf. Meyer, 'Mystery Religions', p. 941.

21. Cf. Ferguson, *The Religions of the Roman Empire*, p. 99; Barrett, *The New Testament Background*, p. 120.

22. Meyer, 'Mystery Religions', p. 941.

23. The protagonist's name in *Metam.*, which is the same as its writer Apuleius' first name. G. Luck, *ARCANA MUNDI: Magic and the Occult in the Greek and Roman Worlds* (Baltimore: John Hopkins University Press, 1985), p. 113 holds that as Lucius travelled to Thessaly, 'the country of witches', in order to study witchcraft, and as 'Apuleius was attracted to magic and got into trouble because of that', *Metam.* seems to be 'partly autobiographical'; Wedderburn, 'The Soteriology of the Mysteries', p. 57.

mysteries of Isis must be a reflection of his experience of the Greek world of the second century AD, but this cannot mean that all of what is spoken of in this book is limited only to that period. For, as was argued earlier, the Isiac mysteries to which Lucius, the protagonist of the novel, was initiated, had originated in ancient times and were prevalent in the first century in the Graeco-Roman world.[24]

Metam. consists of 'three main sections and a pendant, or sequel'.[25] In the first section, Lucius is changed into an ass, becoming an ass-man, 'a human soul enclosed in an animal body, an emblem of what is often portrayed as the human condition'.[26] Under the guise of an ass, without being detected, Lucius has abundant opportunities to observe outrageous human behaviour. In a sequel (XI), which completes the structure of the whole story, the ass-man Lucius is transformed into his original human shape at the festival of Isis. By being liberated from the asinine form of Seth, the enemy of Isis, he recovers his original human shape.[27] This sequel specifically attracts our attention, because it is rife with the image of clothing. Our particular concern is with its use when applied to Lucius. Apuleius uses a different clothing image for every important change in identity that Lucius experiences at an Isiac festival. Lucius clothes himself with ritual garments three times at three different stages of the Isaic spring festival in Corinth:[28] (1) a white linen garment which Lucius wears shortly after his restoration to human form from the shape of an ass, (2) a new linen garment which he wears prior to entering the innermost initiation chamber, and (3) 'a complicated twelve-fold garment'[29] which he wears

---

24. Wedderburn, *Baptism and Resurrection*, p. 393 points out that 'the mysteries were indeed alive and well and flourishing' in the time of Paul and his Christian predecessors. P.G. Walsh, *The Roman Novel: The 'Satyricon' of Petronius and the 'Metamorphoses' of Apuleius* (Cambridge: Cambridge University Press, 1970), pp. 186-89 tries to discover what significance *Metam.* had in relation to various religions, especially to Christianity, in the second century AD; he believes that when Christianity grew so rapidly as to became very powerful in the latter part of the century in Africa, Apuleius, who was a serious devotee of the Isiac cult, expressed a full commitment to it by means of *Metam.* According to him, *Metam.* contains a message that Christians, considered in Africa to worship an ass's head, would find their deliverance in Isiac belief (Walsh, *The Roman Novel*, pp. 86-87). He concludes that '*The Golden Ass* is a complex creation, masking behind its comic exterior an artful but sincere evangelism' (Walsh, *The Roman Novel*, p. 189). Considering that *Metam.* upholds Isis as the supreme god who can transform asinine man, giving him new life and salvation, Walsh's interpretation sounds persuasive. But in the present study our concern is with how the clothing image is used in the Isiac mysteries (which are described in *Metam.* XI and which have their origin in antiquity and seem to have been current in the first century AD).

25. C.C. Schlam, *The Metamorphoses of Apuleius* (London: Duckworth, 1992), p. 123.

26. Schlam, *The Metamorphoses of Apuleius*, p. 123.

27. According to what happened to Lucius, the appendix may be reasonably divided into six parts. Lucius appeals to the Isiac Moon-goddess, beseeching that his ass-mask be removed (XI.1-2). He sees a vision of Isis who teaches him what he should do in order to be transformed back into a human being (XI.3-6). When he performs what Isis has directed, he is transformed into a man (XI.7-15). He participates in the ritual activity of procession (XI.16-18). He receives an initiation into the mysteries of Isis (XI.19-24). Finally, he receives two more initiations into Osiris (XI.25-30).

28. See R.D. Chesnutt, *From Death to Life: Conversion in Joseph and Aseneth* (JSPSSup, 16; Sheffield: Sheffield Academic Press, 1995), p. 247.

29. W. Burkert, *Ancient Mystery Cults* (Cambridge: Harvard University Press, 1987), p. 97.

for public view after the completion of the initiation ritual. Each garment has a symbolic significance.[30]

2.2. *Symbolism of Three Scenes of Lucius' Attire*

2.2.1. *Scene 1: A Linen Garment.* In *Metam.* we can first see that Lucius is clothed with a linen garment immediately after he has experienced a most dramatic event, that is, transformation from an ass-man into a real man. Lucius explains how this transformation happens to him and what takes place in the next moment.

> Then I in my agitation, with my heart throbbing widely, took up with greedy mouth the crown which was bright with the bloom of lovely interwoven roses, and eagerly hoping for fulfilment of the promise, I most eagerly munched through it all. Nor was I disappointed in the heavenly promise: at once my ugly animal form left me (XI.13).[31]

Lucius' animal features have disappeared and he has been restored to a proper human shape. His shame has vanished away altogether; yet he is naked. His shame at being an ass is replaced by the shame of being a naked human being. So when he tries to veil his private parts with his hands as any naked man would do, the High Priest, who has been informed of all of Lucius' misfortunes, and has been surprised at the miracle, orders with a meaningful nod that a linen garment should be lent to cover him. Lucius explains how his nakedness is veiled.

> Then one of the band of devotees smartly took off his outer cloak and quickly put it over it (XI.14).

Undoubtedly this linen garment symbolizes significant changes that have happened at Lucius' transformation, as Isis' high priest encourages Lucius with the following words,

> Show, then a happier face in keeping with the white cloak you have assumed (XI.15).

For the high priest, having a happy face matches well the symbolism of the linen garment in which Lucius is now dressed. The white cloak stands for the reality in Lucius' change from an ass-man to a normal man. If so, what is the essence of the change?

(1) Before Lucius' transformation, Apuleius on several occasions implies what its centrepiece is. (i) One day, when Lucius is still in the form of a beast, he awakes in sudden terror, and sees a dazzling full moon rising from the sea. For him, the Moon-goddess is the sole sovereign of mankind; she invigorates not only all creatures but also all inanimate things (XI.1). So Lucius resolves to appeal to this visible image of the goddess regarding his sufferings. He goes to the sea and

---

30. Cf. R. Reitzenstein, *Hellenistic Mystery-Religions: Their Basic Ideas and Significance* (trans. J.E. Steely; Pittsburgh: Pickwick, 1978), p. 334 who argues that 'the outward symbol of this *transfiguratio* in every cult is the garment'.

31. Quotation from J.G. Griffiths (ed.), *Apuleius of Madauros the Isis-Book.Metamorphoses, Book* XI (Leiden: Brill, 1975). Other citations will also be from this book.

washes himself by dipping his head under the waves seven times. This seems to be a ritual bath, as it is performed as a preparation for going before a goddess. Lucius offers a silent prayer to the supreme goddess,[32] asking liberation from all his distresses, miseries and suffering, and asking for the removal of his ass-disguise. The last part of Lucius' prayer provides crucial information as to the meaning of his change.

> And if some deity is angered so as to pursue me with implacable cruelty, at least allow me to die, if I am not allowed really to live (XI.2).[33]

For Lucius, having the ass-mask is a situation in which he would prefer to die rather than live. His statement suggests that his change from an ass-form to a proper human signifies his restoration from death to life. If so, it is legitimate to argue that the white linen garment, which symbolizes Lucius' transfiguration, denotes his restoration to life out of death.

(ii) The equation of Lucius' restoration with renewed life is also traceable in Isis' response to Lucius' prayer (XI.3-4). After prayer, Lucius once more falls asleep, and in his sleep he sees a vision of a goddess emerging from the middle of the sea. Lucius attempts to describe the goddess' appearance in as much detail as possible. Her body is shining and she wears a many-coloured robe of finest linen. In particular, what catches and holds his sight more than anything else is the cloak of deepest black, which is worn slung across her body from the right hip to the left shoulder. Along the embroidered hem and elsewhere on the cloak, stars glitter here and there, and in their midst a half-moon exhales fiery flames.[34] For Lucius, the Moon-goddess is a cosmological deity who is pre-eminent over all other gods and goddesses. She introduces herself to him as the mother of the universe. She says that she knows she is called by a number of titles, and asks him to call her by her true name, 'Queen Isis'. She continues,

> I am here taking pity on your ills; I am here to give aid and solace. Cease then from tears and wailings, set aside your sadness; there is now dawning for you, through my providence, the day of salvation (XI.5).

This shows that the Moon-goddess Isis sees Lucius' impending restoration as salvation.

(iii) In accordance with Isis' promise of salvation, Lucius, when the time of his transformation comes, cries,

> And behold! here come to me the promised blessings of the most helpful goddess and a priest approaches bringing with him my destiny and my very salvation (XI.12).

---

32. XI.2 shows that the object of Lucius' prayer is also called the 'Queen of Heaven', who can be regarded as Ceres (the primal harvest mother), Venus (the unifier of the difference of the sexes), the sister of Phoebus, Proserpine, etc.

33. Griffiths, *The Isis-Book*, p. 73.

34. Cf. Philo's description of Jewish high priest's garment, which he thinks of as symbolizing the whole universe (*Som.* i.214 and 216; *Vita Mos.* ii.133, 135, 143; *Spec. Leg.* i.84); also Josephus, *Ant.* iii.184-87.

This makes it clear that Lucius' imminent restoration is to be understood in terms of salvation. Accordingly, we conclude that salvation as restoration described in XI.5 and 12 is equivalent to life as restoration in XI.2. If so, what is meant by this salvation (or life)? The answer is found in Isis' promise to Lucius:

> You shall live indeed a happy man, you shall live full of glory in my protection, and when you have completed the span of your lifetime, you will pass down to the nether world, but there also, in the very midst of the subterranean hemisphere, you shall often worship me… (XI.6).

Here we can observe that the salvation of which the goddess previously spoke indicates not only a happy life with fulness of glory under her protection during his lifetime but also a continuous fellowship with her through worship in the afterlife.

What becomes clear by implication presented before Lucius' actual transformation is that its essence is his acquisition of salvation bestowed by Isis, in other words, his obtainment of life-out-of-death, and this is to be symbolized by the linen garment with which he has been clothed immediately after his transfiguration.

(2) Also after Lucius' transformation, Apuleius implies the meaning of the symbolism of the white linen garment, which is worn by Lucius. After Lucius has been transfigured from a beast-man to a normal human being, Isis' high priest admonishes Lucius to be her devotee and says that blind Fortune has no power to harm those whose lives are committed to her majesty. He declares that Lucius is already under the protection of true Fortune. Further, he urges Lucius to enrol his name in the lifetime service of Isis, and to dedicate himself to the ministry of her religion. Probably with an intention to dedicate himself to Isis, Lucius joins the sacred procession, and people recognize him and cry,

> This is the man who has today been restored to human shape through the splendid divinity of the all-powerful goddess. Happy is he…to have clearly deserved…such a wondrous favour from heaven that he is, as it were, born again [*renatus quodam modo*] and has at once pledged himself to service in the sacred rite (XI.16).

This statement makes it clear that Lucius' restoration signifies his rebirth, a regained life. This idea of rebirth recurs throughout *Metam.*[35] The people's exclamation, 'he is born again', sounds most appropriate to Lucius, who looked on his previous life with the ass-mask as not worth living (XI.2). J.G. Griffiths argues that *renatus* conveys a double meaning here, that is, 'Lucius has been born again in the sense that he has been restored to human shape; he has also been born again spiritually in his acceptance of the protection and favour of Isis'.[36] The happy life with glory and security in the underworld after death (cf. XI.6) results from his being born again, that is, his transformation from the beast-man into a proper human and his dedication of himself to the mysteries of Isis. On the basis of all the

---

35. XI.21: *quodam modo renatos*; although these words refer to 'the recovery of health, by Isis' mediation, of those initiated on their (supposed) deathbeds' (K.E. Kirk, *The Vision of God: The Christian Doctrine of the Summum Bonum* [London: Longmans, 1932], p. 32), they are in affinity to the words *renatus quodam modo* in XI.16 in that the major theme of both is death and life. See also XI.24: *celebravi natalem sacrorum*, which speaks of a spiritual rebirth through initiation.

36. Griffiths, *The Isis-Book*, p. 258.

above observations, I conclude that the linen garment in which Lucius is dressed immediately after his transfiguration symbolizes that he has obtained a life-from-death.

2.2.2. Scene 2: A New Linen Garment. In *Metam.* we encounter the second scene of Lucius' attire when he is dressed in a new linen garment. Lucius says,

> when all the uninitiated had been far removed, I was dressed in a hitherto unworn linen garment and the priest, taking my hand, led me to the very heart of the holy shrine (XI.23).

Apuleius does not explains what this brand-new linen garment connotes, but by looking into what happens to Lucius (in the secret initiation-chamber) whilst dressed in it, we can unfold the symbolism of the garment. Lucius hesitates to recount what took place in the room, but within the scope of, he thinks, legal permission, he divulges a little about it, stating,

> accessi confinium mortis et calcato Proserpinae limine per omnia vectus elementa remeavi, nocte media vidi solem candido coruscantem lumine, deos inferos et deos superos accessi coram et adoravi de proxumo.

> I approached the boundary of death and treading on Proserpine's threshold, I was carried through all the elements, after which I returned. At dead of night I saw the sun flashing with bright effulgence. I approached close to the gods above and the gods below and worshipped them face to face (XI.23).

   In the first sentence of the Latin text, the word *accessi* points to the beginning of Lucius' mystical experience and the word *remeavi* speaks of his return from it. This suggests that what is mentioned between these two words describes what happened to Lucius. The second sentence seems to be a further explanation as to what Lucius experienced in his initiation, and the third sentence seems to sum up what was previously depicted.[37] If this analysis is acceptable, the strange sequence of *inferi* and *superi*[38] in the third sentence does not seem to be so unnatural, and we should reject Griffiths's inversion of the order, instead insisting on the translation 'the gods below and the gods above'. It is likely that Lucius first encountered the *inferi* in the underworld of Proserpine, then the *superi* in the region where he saw the brilliance of the sun, that is, a vision of the goddess Isis (cf. XI.6).[39] On this understanding of the structure, we may reconstruct Lucius' experience as follows: entrance into the realm of death, vision of the gods below, a journey through all the elements, an epiphany of the dazzling light of the sun-Isis followed by a vision of the gods above, and his happy return.[40] As this experience takes place whilst

   37. M. Dibelius, 'The Isis Initiation in Apuleius and Related Initiatory Rites', in F.O. Francis and W.A. Meeks (eds.), *Conflict at Colossae: A Problem in the Interpretation of Early Christianity Illustrated by Selected Modern Studies* (SBS, 4; Missoula: SBL & Scholars, 1975), pp. 61-121 (64).
   38. This order is striking, as they occur in a reverse order in *Metam.* XI.25 (*te superi colunt, observant inferi,* 'Thee do the gods above honour, and thou art worshipped by those below').
   39. Dibelius, 'The Isis Initiation in Apuleius', p. 64.
   40. Cf. Dibelius, 'The Isis Initiation in Apuleius', pp. 64, 77.

Lucius is clothed with a new initiation garment, this clothing can be thought of as symbolizing his being united to deistic beings, especially Isis. His journey through deistic realms suggests that he has been united to her.

Apuleius underlines that Lucius' unity with Isis is achieved through his death-like experience. Lucius' experience proceeds in a state of ecstasy,[41] which may be called a state of quasi-death.[42] He enters the region of death and even the gates of Proserpine (the netherworld), where he approaches the gods below and worships them close at hand, which involves 'communion with the gods'.[43] Perhaps he then journeys through 'all the elements'. Apuleius does not elucidate what is meant by these words. As XI.25 states that *serviunt elementa*, they seem to refer to cosmic deistic beings or 'elemental spirits'[44] who serve Isis. Apart from the gods below and the gods above, the cosmic deistic servants seem to function by performing what she commands. They 'represent the world that lies between below and above'.[45] Apuleius, therefore, seems to mean that when Lucius returns from the area of Proserpine, he goes past the way *per omnia elementa*, that is, through 'altars or pictures of the elemental gods or through rooms which are consecrated to them'.[46] As this event of being united with Isis takes place through an experience of quasi-death and whilst being dressed in the initiation garment, this garment symbolizes an ecstatic death resulting in union with Isis.

Further, the garment points to life with brilliance at the same time, because Lucius returns to a new life after he has experienced being united with Isis' radiance. The word *remeavi* suggests that he eventually comes back to a new state of life after all his experience in the ecstasy of quasi-death. His experience in initiation as a whole is a happy one. A.J.M. Wedderburn asserts that Lucius has experienced 'a proleptic entry into the realm of death and a subsequent demonstration of the privileges and powers that he would enjoy in that realm'.[47]

At midnight Lucius sees the bright light of Isis,[48] to whom he has devoted himself. He realizes then that both the realm of 'below' and the realm of 'above' and everything within them are under the rule of Isis (XI.2, 5, 25).[49] He learns that Isis has in her hands the keys of the netherworld and the power to save. With the vision of Isis, he also sees the gods above face to face, and perhaps has communion with them. In sum, Lucius' initiation garment symbolizes his voluntary death (XI.21) and life which has been acquired through his experience of being united with Isis.

41. See the Latin words *nocturnis orgiis* in XI.28.
42. Cf. the words 'voluntary death' (XI.21).
43. Wedderburn, 'The Soteriology of the Mysteries', p. 59.
44. Dibelius, 'The Isis Initiation in Apuleius', pp. 78-79. He also calls the elements 'the elemental gods' (p. 78), 'cosmic deities' (p. 79), or 'the cosmic powers' (pp. 81-82).
45. Dibelius, 'The Isis Initiation in Apuleius', p. 79.
46. Dibelius, 'The Isis Initiation in Apuleius', p. 78.
47. Wedderburn, 'The Soteriology of the Mysteries', p. 59.
48. Dibelius, 'The Isis Initiation in Apuleius', pp. 79-80 imagines that 'thus something like this must have occured [*sic*]: the initiate enters a room which displays the *dii superi* and whose brilliant illumination—perhaps kindled suddenly—appeared to him all the more dazzling as previously his eyes were accustomed to darkness'.
49. Cf. Ferguson, *Backgrounds*, p. 258.

M. Dibelius argues that

> he [Lucius] may cross the threshold of her [Isis'] realm and behold unharmed
> *inferi, elementa,* and *superi.* Thus, penetrating all the cosmic spheres, he becomes
> like the cosmic, all-ruling Isis; he becomes deified.[50]

His experience of being in the presence of Isis means that he becomes like her.
Lucius has experienced contact with cosmic deities under the protection of Isis. It
seems to be more appropriate to say that he has been on the way to being
mystically initiated into Isis.

In brief, Lucius' initiation can be regarded as an experience of death-and-life,
which may be symbolized by his initiation linen garment. His life at his happy
return may be thought of as life-out-of-death. It should be remembered that his
being clothed with the new linen garment is itself followed by an experience of
life, after one of death. This suggests that the new garment symbolizes the life-out-
of-death which is obtained by means of being initiated into Isis.

This interpretation is in harmony with the high priest's oration which was given
when Lucius decided to be initiated into Isis. The oration concerned how grave the
rite of initiation would be.

> For the gates of hell and the guarantee of life were alike in the power of the god-
> dess, and the very rite of dedication itself was performed in the manner of a volun-
> tary death and of a life obtained by grace. Indeed the goddess was accustomed to
> elect people who stood near the close of their life-span, on the very threshold of
> the end of light, but who could be safely entrusted, nevertheless, with the mighty
> mysteries of the faith. By her providence she caused them in some way to be born
> again and placed them once more on the course of a new life (XI.21).

This implies that initiation will be an experience of life-out-of-death. The ceremony
is intended to declare figuratively that the initiated are those who are saved from
death. They may have to pass through the realm of hell (cf. XI.23); they will be
initiated into Isis in their 'voluntary death'. But they will be under the protection of
Isis who rules over life and death. Although people who are near the end of their
lives are the initiates, they will be born again by Isis' providence. My point is that
this section also supports my opinion that the motif of life-after-death is at the heart
of the initiation ceremony, and is suggested by the new linen initiation garment.

2.2.3. *Scene 3: Twelve Garments.* As the solemn rites end at dawn, Lucius emerges
into public view wearing twelve robes which evidently represent 'his symbolic
journey through the heavenly elements before his return to earth'.[51] These robes
may point to the 'twelve zones' of the sky into which Lucius arrived 'only after his
journey through the elements'.[52] It is highly probable that Lucius' twelve-fold
garment portrays him as a priestly figure who is identified with cosmic gods.[53]

---

50. Dibelius, 'The Isis Initiation in Apuleius', p. 78.
51. Ferguson, *Backgrounds*, p. 258.
52. Dibelius, 'The Isis Initiation in Apuleius', p. 79.
53. Cf. Philo's cosmological interpretation of the high priest's garment, which is followed by
Josephus, *Ant.* iii.184-87; see Chapter 2, §4.3.

Specifically Lucius states that he has dressed himself in an outer garment of fine linen extravagantly embroidered, and a precious cloak which hung down his back from the shoulders to the heels. This attire seems to signify that he has become an Isis-like being, as it resembles her apparel when she first appeared to him in a vision before his transformation (*Metam.* XI.3-4). This argument can be reinforced by Lucius' further explanation of how he looked as a whole.

> Wherever you looked, I was adorned by beasts embroidered round about my garments in varied colours. Here were Indian dragons, there were griffons from the far north, animals created in the form of a winged bird by a world other than ours. The initiates call this the Olympian robe. But in my right hand I carried a torch with rearing flames and my head was garlanded gracefully by a crown of gleaming palm whose leaves stood out like rays (XI.24).

All these garments, above all, signify Lucius' being identified with Isis through his spiritual change. Wedderburn imagines that Lucius' apparel 'suggests a divine status, perhaps the rank of a son of Isis, for Horus could be represented as a solar deity'.[54] He insists that Lucius' identification with Isis signifies a change of his status and not a transformation of his nature.[55] However, Wedderburn's two points do not seem to be reconcilable, because a deistic status without a deistic nature is scarcely conceivable. Apuleius' emphasis on the resemblance of Lucius' apparel with that of Isis, who is dressed in a garment of finest linen of many colours (XI.3-4), suggests that Lucius has come to be identified with her, the key idea of which seems to be a change in his nature. When a vision appears to Lucius afterwards and orders him to receive the third initiation in Rome, it calls the twelve robes 'the garments of the goddess' (XI.29).[56] Lucius states that 'I had thus been adorned like the sun and set up in the manner of a divine statue' (XI.24); this statement doubtless indicates that by his experience of getting to the twelve zones of Isis' heavenly realm, he has become a being in union with Isis, having a deistic nature. J. Ferguson argues that 'this [Lucius' revelation, being dressed in twelve garments, to the people] is an epiphany; the initiate is one with the divine'.[57]

Furthermore, Lucius' splendid garments seem to symbolize the glory of his restored life from death, obtained by his initiation into the Isiac mysteries. This view can be supported by Lucius' statement that he carried a torch with rearing flames and wore a crown of gleaming palm whose leaves stood out like rays (XI.24). This description undoubtedly reinforces the idea that Lucius has acquired effulgent glory. Lucius' attire 'like the sun', in other words, 'in the manner of a divine statue', suggests that he has come to be radiant. Through his experience of cosmic migration from the underworld to the upperworld,[58] which has resulted in his acquiring a new life-out-of-death, Lucius has become identified with the goddess Isis. It is, therefore, natural that he is spoken of as having become as splendid as Isis. Yet, in fact,

---

54. Wedderburn, 'The Soteriology of the Mysteries', p. 59.
55. Wedderburn, 'The Soteriology of the Mysteries', p. 59.
56. See Griffiths, *The Isis-Book*, p. 339.
57. Ferguson, *The Religions of the Roman Empire*, p. 108.
58. Dibelius, 'The Isis Initiation in Apuleius', p. 81.

the initiation is a final ceremony which fulfils his transformation from an ass-man into a real human. In other words, it is a celebration of regaining life from death.

This view can be supported by Lucius' statement that

> exhinc festissimum celebravi natalem sacrorum, et suaves epulae et faceta convivia.

> Then I celebrated the most happy birthday of my initiation, and there were welcome feasts and merry banquets (XI.24).

He regards the day of his being initiated into Isis as the day of his sacred birth (cf. the words *celebravi natalem sacrorum*). The day is the day when he has been newly born in a spiritual sense. For him, the previous days are days of death, while the days from that day on will be days of life. Dibelius holds that the 'newly bestowed life is of divine character' and that 'the whole event is an ἀπαθανατισμός [immortalization]'.[59] The first point is in harmony with our earlier argument that the change in Lucius' nature is the central theme of his identification with Isis (symbolized by his twelve garments). However, the second point does not seem to be supportable, because in *Metam.* Apuleius does not concentrate on the motif of immortality; though he includes it in the motif of salvation, which can be summed up as a glorious life in this world and a secure existence in the afterlife, he does not lay greater stress on the second element than on the first. Apuleius' primary concern is with Lucius' salvation present and future, which results from his being unified with Isis.

2.3. *Concluding Remarks: New Life out of Death*

In *Metam.* we have found that the whole process of Lucius' initiation into the mystery religions signifies his experience of transformation from death to life, and this is symbolized by three kinds of specific ritual garments.

A white linen garment, in which Lucius is dressed at his participation in the festival procession immediately after his transformation from ass-man to true human being, symbolizes his re-gained life from two points of view: retrospective and prospective. It retrospectively carries the life of glory caused by restoration from death to life. For Lucius, transformation from beast-man to real human being is identified with restoration from death to life. Upon experiencing transformation into human form, Lucius takes part in a procession of worshippers as a devotee to the Isiac religion, and this emphasizes salvation. Perhaps the idea of life in salvation is dominant in the procession. As a devotee, Lucius has a strong aspiration for salvation. The white linen garment prospectively connotes the splendour of the future life, even of his afterlife.

A new linen garment, which Lucius wears at the secret initiation ceremony, symbolizes the new life-out-of-death, which is obtained by being in union with Isis. In the initiation ceremony, Lucius experiences an entrance into the netherworld of death and a journey through all the cosmological elements, he sees the sun-Isis's glittering epiphany with a vision of heavenly gods and returns to a new

---

59. Dibelius, 'The Isis Initiation in Apuleius', p. 63.

life. As Lucius wears the new linen garment and participates in the initiation ceremony, namely, the ritual of life-out-of-death, this garment stands for the new life
which is gained through the experience of mystical death at union with the Isiac
mystery.

Twelve religious robes (XI.24), with which Lucius is adorned at the public show
after his initiation, symbolizes the radiance of restored life accomplished through
his identification with the gods. These garments manifest the glory of life from a
cosmological perspective, as they represent Lucius' symbolic journey through the
heavenly elements. As was pointed out earlier, they seem to connote the 'twelve
zones' of the sky into which he has journeyed. In particular, the outer fine linen
garments that are extravagantly embroidered signify not only Lucius' identification
with Isis but also the glory of his achievement of life-out-of-death. As Lucius'
apparel resembles Isis' garments, it symbolizes that Lucius has acquired a divine
nature and status by means of his initiation-union with her. Furthermore, they
signify that he has obtained salvation, that is, bliss and security for the present and
for the future.

3. *Conclusion*

In the mystery religions there were no fixed-form festival events, and so no uniform style of clothing-rite. However, it seems that on some occasions probably
common to many of the mysteries, clothing had a significant meaning. For instance, the festive costume in processions (which included the initiates' white linen
garments), the initiates' attire worn shortly before the initiation ceremony, and the
new garments (with extra religious apparel) given to the initiated, all seem to have
had symbolical significance. We have obtained the most obvious evidence for this
from Apuleius' *Metamorphoses*. As this document, by using the clothing imagery,
describes a change in an initiate's existence (that is, from death to life) and at the
same time his identification with Isis, the use of clothing imagery overlaps with
that in Pauline passages. A change of garment at initiation seen in *Metamorphoses*
perhaps reflects the ritual of initiation in the earliest mystery religions, which is
probably borne in mind by the Pauline imagery of a change of garment related to
baptism (Gal. 3.27; Rom. 13.14; Col. 3.9-10; Eph. 4.22-24).

Chapter 6

ROMAN APPAREL: *TOGA VIRILIS*

The Romans dressed themselves in different kinds of *togae*[1] according to their social status or rôle, gender, age, and so on. This is therefore something worth careful study. From ancient times the toga was worn by the Romans; it was originally their national outdoor garment.[2] It was worn not only by men but also by women.[3] But in later times, for example by the time of Augustus (the first emperor at Rome, 63 BC-AD 14), if an adult female wore the toga, she was thought of as a prostitute or a dishonourable woman.[4] Young Roman girls, however, seem to have continued to wear the toga at least until about the beginning of the imperial period.[5] However, the toga survived into the Roman empire as a universal garment and was regarded as a ceremonial costume throughout the empire, although by the close of the third century AD,[6] at least for Roman girls, putting aside the garment (called the *toga praetexta*) at their marriage as a ceremonial act became an obsolete custom.[7]

1.   C. Vout, 'The Myth of the Toga: Understanding the History of Roman Dress', in I. McAuslan and P. Walcot (eds.), *Greece & Rome* (Second Series, 42; Oxford: Oxford University Press, 1995), pp. 204-220 (215) presumes that the verb 'to cover', *tegere*, was probably the origin of the word toga.

2.   S. Stone, 'The Toga: From National to Ceremonial Costume', in J.L. Sebesta and L. Bonfante (eds.), *The World of Roman Costume* (Wisconsin: The University of Wisconsin, 1994), pp. 13-39 (13).

3.   L.M. Wilson, *The Roman Toga* (ed. D.M. Robinson; JHUSA, 1; Baltimore: Johns Hopkins University Press, 1924), p. 27; Stone, 'The Toga', p. 13. Concerning the form of the toga, its size, and the method of wearing it, see O. Seyffert, *A Dictionary of Classical Antiquities: Mythology, Religion, Literature & Art* (London: Swan Sonnenschein, 1899), p. 639; J.E. Sandys (ed.), *A Companion to Latin Studies* (Cambridge: Cambridge University Press, 1943 [1910]), p. 191; H.B. Walters, *A Guide to the Exhibition Illustrating Greek and Roman Life* (London: Clowes, 1929), pp. 120-22; H. G.-Taylor, 'Toga', in S. Hornblower and A. Spawforth (eds.), *The Oxford Classical Dictionary* (Oxford: Oxford University Press, 1996), p. 1533.

4.   Wilson, *The Roman Toga*, p. 27; Seyffert, *A Dictionary of Classical Antiquities*, p. 640.

5.   Stone, 'The Toga', p. 13; L.M. Wilson, *The Clothing of the Ancient Romans* (ed. D.M. Robinson; JHUSA, 24; Baltimore: Johns Hopkins University Press, 1938), p. 136; *The Roman Toga*, pp. 27, 51.

6.   This date suggests that Aseneth's lavish pagan garment (in *Joseph and Aseneth*), with which she has been dressed before her conversion to Judaism in order to marry Joseph, may be a kind of a local toga.

7.   Wilson, *The Clothing of the Ancient Romans*, p. 136.

For males, the toga was considered to be the garment of their free-born status.[8] To wear the toga was a statement: 'I am Roman'; it was thus strongly linked with Roman citizenship.[9] Since it was the distinctive garment of a Roman citizen, the toga was not allowed to be worn by exiles and foreigners.[10] The Roman male's wearing of the toga continued throughout the period of the Empire. Although its popularity declined by the time of Augustus, it was always thought of as the garment to be worn by the Roman man conducting public business.[11] To be *togatus* was to be actively involved in the workings of the state, whether as a priest, an orator, a magistrate, a client or even as the emperor himself.[12] The toga was used both in time of peace and in time of war, but after the *sagum* had become popular as a military garment, the toga served as the exclusive garb and symbol of peace.[13] With Roman conquests the toga became widespread throughout the Empire, especially in the western provinces,[14] and came to be universally adopted as a garment.[15] In particular, its being used as a ceremonial garment for Roman men continued until the fourth century.[16]

In early times the toga was usually made of undyed (and so white) thick coarse woollen cloth,[17] 'hence, was well suited to a people whose early economy was heavily based on the herding of sheep'.[18] Yet, with the passage of time, it is likely that variations on the original garment appeared. A dark-coloured toga (brown or black, *toga pulla* or *sordida*) was used by the lower classes, or accused persons or for mourning.[19] A decorated toga was also developed during the Etruscan period.[20] Generals in their victory processions wore a special toga (which was made of purple wool and gold thread),[21] namely the *toga trabea* (or *picta*), which had a

8. G.-Taylor, 'Toga', p. 1533.

9. Vout, 'The Myth of the Toga', pp. 213-14.

10. Seyffert, *A Dictionary of Classical Antiquities*, p. 639. But people in the East (particularly those who were in royal or high official status) also wore the toga, although this apparel 'to the Oriental was a scarlet cloak or wrap'; see F.C. Burkitt, 'Notes and Studies: *Toga* in the East', *JTS* 23 (1922), pp. 281-82; C.L. Feltoe, 'Notes and Studies: *Toga* and *Togatus* in the Books of the Mozarabic Rite', *JTS* 23 (1922), pp. 57-59 (57). Note that the Syriac version of *The Hymn of the Pearl* recognizes the prince's original garment as a toga (vv. 10, 14, 72); see A.A. Bevan, 'The Hymn of the Soul', *TS* 5.3 (Cambridge: Cambridge University Press, 1897), pp. 1-40 (especially pp. 10-31).

11. Stone, 'The Toga', p. 13.

12. Vout, 'The Myth of the Toga', p. 214.

13. Seyffert, *A Dictionary of Classical Antiquities*, p. 639; Cicero, *Orat.* 3.42 states that the toga was used metaphorically by the Romans to symbolize peace (cf. Cicero, *Pis.* 29.72 and 30.73).

14. It is said that the toga never replaced the Greek *himation* (Lat. *pallium*) in the east (G.-Taylor, 'Toga', p. 1533). Whereas the Roman toga was always in the shape of a semi-circle with its characteristic curve, the Greek *himation* was rectangular (Stone, 'The Toga', p. 13).

15. Vout, 'The Myth of the Toga', p. 214.

16. Stone, 'The Toga', p. 13, 38.

17. Sandys (ed.), *A Companion to Latin Studies*, p. 191; G.-Taylor, 'Toga', p. 1533.

18. Wilson, *The Roman Toga*, p. 27; Stone, 'The Toga', p. 13.

19. Seyffert, *A Dictionary of Classical Antiquities*, p. 640; Sandys (ed.), *A Companion to Latin Studies*, p. 193.

20. Stone, 'The Toga', p. 13.

21. G.-Taylor, 'Toga', p. 1533.

decoration of coloured stripes along its edge. It is said that the *toga trabea* was the dress of the early kings and afterwards of the emperors,[22] the *equites*[23] and the priests.[24] Other people of high status also wore a specific toga, called the *toga praetexta*; the most important part of this garment was the *clavus* or purple stripe along the border which was 'the distinctive mark of the curule magistrates and censors, of the State priests (but only when performing their functions), and afterwards of the emperors'.[25]

The *toga praetexta* was also worn by high-born young Romans, that is, the garment was worn by young girls until marriage and by young boys until the age of sixteen years, when they attained manhood.[26] It seems that after their marriage women wore another kind of garment, called the *stola*, the lady's garment of honour; 'to be a Roman woman was to be *stolata*'.[27] O. Seyffert informs us that disgraced wives were forbidden to wear the *stola*.[28] A young Roman boy, when he came to be sixteen years of age, was permitted to wear the *toga virilis*,[29] which was also called the *toga liberior* since it indicated that he was free of parental control.[30] It was sometimes referred to as the *toga pura*, because it was white.[31] Changing out of the old garment, the *toga praetexta*, into the new, the *toga virilis*, was performed at a special ceremony[32] on an appointed day.[33] For the young Roman, being dressed

22. Stone, 'The Toga', p. 13. He argues that 'Until the time of the emperor Gordian (late 230s AD), emperors wore a state *toga picta* on ceremonial occasions' (Stone, 'The Toga', p. 39).

23. The members of the equestrian class, who were armed with lances and who rode their horses and who were allowed to wear narrow stripes on their tunics, were called *angustus clavus*; see Stone, 'The Toga', p. 15.

24. Sandys, (ed.), *A Companion to Latin Studies*, p. 191; cf. Wilson, *The Clothing of the Ancient Romans*, p. 64. Stone, 'The Toga', p. 13.

25. Seyffert, *A Dictionary of Classical Antiquities*, p. 640. According to social or political rank, the width of the purple stripe was different (cf. Pliny, *Epis.* 2.9.2); see Wilson, *The Clothing of the Ancient Romans*, pp. 63-64; Vout, 'The Myth of the Toga', p. 214; Stone, 'The Toga', p. 13. Further, the toga's colour was also indicative of status; the emperor enjoyed the privilege of wearing an all-purple toga and of granting others the same privilege.

26. Wilson, *The Roman Toga*, pp. 51-52; *The Clothing of the Ancient Romans*, p. 135 argues that the girls laid aside the *toga praetexta* on the eve of marriage; Seyffert, *A Dictionary of Classical Antiquities*, p. 640; Stone, 'The Toga', p. 13 suggests 'the age of fourteen to sixteen'.

27. Vout, 'The Myth of the Toga', p. 215.

28. Seyffert, *A Dictionary of Classical Antiquities*, p. 640.

29. Vout, 'The Myth of the Toga', p. 215 quotes from Quintilian 11.3.137, who advises orators: 'their [women's] style of dress (*cultus*) should be distinguished and masculine (*virilis*), as it should be with all respectable gentleman'.

30. Stone, 'The Toga', p. 39.

31. Wilson, *The Roman Toga*, p. 52; Seyffert, *A Dictionary of Classical Antiquities*, p. 640; Stone, 'The Toga', p. 15: 'Besides the toga praetexta, the Romans created other forms of the toga to indicate precisely the status or the nature of the wearer. The normal toga of the average male citizen was called *pura* to describe its natural color (likely an off-white or grayish hue).'

32. Wilson, *The Roman Toga*, p. 52; F. Rendall, 'The Epistle to the Galatians', in W.R. Nicoll (ed.), *EGT* III (London: Hodder & Stoughton, 1903), pp. 123-200 (174): Greeks and Romans made much of this occasion and celebrated the investment of a youth with an adult man's dress by family gatherings and religious rites.

33. That is, at the Liberalia on March 17, which has been evidenced by a number of documents,

in the *toga virilis* meant that he had passed into the rank of a citizen,[34] acquired the right to wear a purple border or a coloured toga depending upon his official position,[35] and acquired the right to take a place beside his father at the councils of the family.[36] L.M. Wilson is, therefore, quite right when he designates the *toga virilis* as 'the toga of manhood and the badge of Roman citizenship'.[37] When the boy was dressed in the *toga praetexta*, he was still an immature child under the control of all the rules and regulations of his father's house, but when dressed in the *toga virilis* as a full-grown man, he became enfranchised and independent. The replacement of the *toga praetexta* with the *toga virilis* thus symbolized the important transition from boyhood to manhood. Entering into manhood emancipated him from his earlier bondage to boyhood regulations.

This symbolic significance of the *toga virilis* seems to have particular relevance to the Pauline metaphor of clothing with Christ in Gal. 3.26-29, where the concept of clothing is in conjunction with the concept of a believer's acquiring sonship of God, so as to be the heir of his kingdom. Other Pauline metaphors about clothing with a person (Rom. 13.12; Col. 3.9-10; Eph. 4.22-24) may also echo the symbolism of the Roman apparel.

e.g. Ovid, *Fasti* 3.713; Cicero, *Philipp.* 2.18.44, *Amic.* 1.1, *Sest.* 69.144, *Epis. Att.* 5.20.9 and 6.1; Livy 26.19.5, 42.34.4; Suetonius, *Claud.* 2.2; Seneca, *Epis.* 4.2; see Stone, 'The Toga', p. 39.

34. Here the *toga virilis* is connected with political and civic responsibility.

35. Wilson, *The Roman Toga*, p. 52. Rendall, 'The Epistle to the Galatians': the youth, hitherto subject to domestic rule, was then admitted to the rights and responsibilities of a citizen; cf. Vout, 'The Myth of the Toga', p. 215.

36. Rendall, 'The Epistle to the Galatians', p. 174.

37. Wilson, *The Roman Toga*, p. 52; Vout, 'The Myth of the Toga', p. 214: 'The toga defined the wearer as a peaceful, civilized, male, Roman' (cf. Livy 3.26.9).

Chapter 7

BAPTISMAL PRACTICES IN THE EARLY CHURCH

In the present study, it is very important to perceive how the rite of baptism was practised and what its meaning was in the early church, because baptism seems to play a significant background rôle in the Pauline passages, which refer to being clothed with Christ or the new man (i.e. Gal. 3.27; Rom. 13.14; Col. 3.9-10; Eph. 4.22-24). The syntactical structure of Gal. 3.27 shows that the concept of βαπτίσ-θῆναι εἰς Χριστόν (27a) is equated with the concept of ἐνδύσασθαι εἰς Χριστόν (v. 27b).[1] The expression ἐνδύσασθε τὸν κύριον Ἰησοῦν Χριστόν in Rom. 13.14 not only belongs to the baptismal passage (Rom. 13.11-14),[2] but also has a connection, in an indirect manner, with Rom. 6.1-11, which is also a baptismal pericope and includes the words ἐβαπτίσθημεν εἰς Χριστὸν Ἰησοῦν (v. 3). The metaphors of putting off and putting on in Col. 3.9-10 and Eph. 4.22-24 seem to be a description of a significant part of the current mode of the rite of baptism.

Before looking into some ancient documents that refer to Christian baptism, a brief investigation of Jewish proselyte baptism will be profitable. Although the time when proselyte baptism originated is contested,[3] its probable influence on baptismal practice in the primitive church[4] suggests that an understanding of proselyte

---

1. Lit.: 'with Christ you did clothe yourself' (Χριστὸν ἐνεδύσασθε).
2. See Chapter 8, §3.3.2.
3. A. Edersheim, *The Life and Times of Jesus the Messiah*, II (London: Longmans, 1883), p. 744 asserts that 'at the time (previous to Christ) the baptism of proselytes was customary'; C. Burchard, 'Joseph and Aseneth', in J.H. Charlesworth (ed.), *OTP*, II (New York: Doubleday, 1985), pp. 177-247 (193); J. Jeremias, *Jerusalem in the Time of Jesus* (London: SCM Press, 1969), p. 320 argues that proselytes' baptism in the pool of Siloam in Jerusalem in the first century AD was not a rare occurrence; *idem*, *Infant Baptism in the First Four Centuries* (London: SCM Press, 1960), pp. 24-29. On the other hand, J.K. Howard, *New Testament Baptism* (London: Pickering & Inglis, 1970), pp. 14-18, points out that baptism (*tebilah*), circumcision (*milah*) and sacrifice constituted 'three essentials for the admission of the Gentiles into the fold of Judaism and the covenant community' (14); see E. Schürer, *The History of the Jewish People in the Age of Jesus Christ (175 BC-AD 135)* III/1 (Edinburgh: T. & T. Clark, 1986 [1885]), pp. 173-74; G.F. Moore, *Judaism in the First Centuries of the Christian Era: The Age of the Tannaim*, I (Cambridge: Harvard University Press, 1927), pp. 331-32; D. Daube, *The New Testament and Rabbinic Judaism* (Peabody: Hendrickson, 1956), pp. 106-107; W.G. Braude, *Jewish Proselyting: In the First Five Centuries of the Common Era the Age of the Tannaim and Amoraim* (Providence: Brown University, 1940), pp. 74-78.
4. D.E.H. Whiteley, *The Theology of St. Paul* (Oxford: Blackwell, 1974), p. 166 argues that Jewish Proselyte Baptism undoubtedly gave some influence to the Baptism of John, which was, in turn, in line with the baptism of the earliest church; P.W. Evans, *Sacraments in the New Testament* (London: Tyndale, 1946), p. 10; Jeremias, *Infant Baptism in the First Four Centuries*, pp. 29-30.

baptism would help in imagining how baptism was performed in the first-century church. Epictetus of c. 50–130 CE.[5] describes people about whom there is some doubt as to whether they are really converted to Judaism or not.[6] For Epictetus, baptism should have been a distinctive feature of the real convert to Judaism. The fourth book of the Sibylline Oracle, dated about the second half of the first century,[7] also seems to include a passage on proselyte baptism.[8] The Mishnah includes a discussion of a debate between R. Eliezer, a Shammaite, and R. Jehoshua, a Hillelite, in the first centuries BC and AD,[9] as to the relative importance of circumcision and baptism (see *b. Yebam.* 46a, 47ab); here baptism undoubtedly alludes to proselyte baptism.[10] Mishnah, *Pesahim* and *'Eduyyot* also contain a debate between the schools of Hillel and Shammai on the issue of the immersion of proselytes,[11] probably in the first century AD.[12]

If so, how was the actual rite of Jewish proselyte baptism performed? Probably it was a baptism of total immersion in water; it could be reconstructed as follows: the baptisand stripped off his clothes, then made a fresh confession of his sins and faith in front of three witnesses called the 'fathers of Baptism', that is, 'three Rabbis who constituted a court' and who assisted the baptisand.[13] Then he thoroughly

5.   M. Stern (ed.), *Greek and Latin Authors on Jews and Judaism I: From Herodotus to Plutarch* (PIASH; Jerusalem: IASH, 1974), p. 541; cf. D.S. Sharp, *Epictetus and the New Testament* (London: Kelly, 1914), pp. 132-37, who sees that Epictetus was born about AD 60, when the New Testament was in the process of formation.

6.   W.A. Oldfather (trans.), *Epictetus: The Discourses as Reported by Arrian, the Manual, and Fragments*, I (ed. E. Capps *et al.*; LCL; London: Heinemann, 1926), pp. 272-73 (Book II, IX.20-21).

7.   W.O.E. Oesterley, *The Books of the Apocrypha* (London: Roxburghe House, 1914), p. 209; G.R. Beasley-Murray, *Baptism in the New Testament* (Grand Rapids: Eerdmans, 1990 [1962]), p. 23 imagines 'about AD 80'.

8.   Jeremias, *Infant Baptism in the First Four Centuries*, pp. 33-35. See *Sibylline Oracles*, Book 4, lines 165-66: 'and wash your whole bodies in perennial rivers. Stretch out your hands to heaven and ask forgiveness for your previous deeds and make propitiation for bitter impiety with words of praise; God will grant repentance and will not destroy. He will stop his wrath again if you all practice honorable piety in your hearts' (see J.J. Collins, 'Sibylline Oracles', in J.H. Charlesworth [ed.], *OTP*, I [London: Darton, Longman & Todd, 1983], p. 388). Collins thinks that the washing here refers to a baptism and contends that it differs from the repetitive ritual cleansings of the Essenes. Apart from the Essenes, the Sibylline Oracle itself also includes the concept of repetitive ritual cleansings (see 3.191-93).

9.   Howard, *New Testament Baptism*, p. 14 sees that the first century BC is more likely; Jeremias, *Jerusalem in the Time of Jesus*, p. 321 insists 'before AD 30'; Beasley-Murray, *Baptism in the New Testament*, p. 24 argues for 'about AD 90'.

10.   Beasley-Murray, *Baptism in the New Testament*, pp. 28-30; Howard, *New Testament Baptism*, p. 14; Schürer, *The History of the Jewish People*, III/1, pp. 173-74.

11.   *Pesah.* 8.8 and *'Ed.* 5.2 include exactly the same words: 'the School of Shammai say: If a man became a proselyte on the day before Passover he may immerse himself and consume his Passover-offering in the evening. And the School of Hillel say: He that separates himself from his uncircumcision is as one that separates himself from a grave' (H. Danby, *The Mishnah* [Oxford: Oxford University Press, 1933], pp. 148 and 431).

12.   S. McKnight, *A Light Among the Gentiles: Jewish Missionary Activity in the Second Temple Period* (Minneapolis: Fortress, 1991), pp. 82-85; cf. H.L. Strack and P. Billerbeck, *Kommentar zum Neuen Testament aus Talmud und Midrasch*, I (Munich: Beck'sche, 1926), pp. 102-113.

13.   Edersheim, *The Life and Times of Jesus the Messiah*, II, pp. 742-44; I. Abrahams, 'How

immersed himself in the water,[14] while two 'disciples of the wise' stood by and recited some of the 'light' and some of the 'heavy' commandments, to the observance of which the newly baptized proselyte had now committed himself.[15] After baptism he wore new clothes. The whole of this baptismal ritual was thought of as bringing a completely new nature to him; he was regarded as one who had been born anew in baptism: the proselyte in his conversion was as 'a little child just born'.[16] He was no longer an unclean Gentile and his sins were forgiven.[17] It is probable that the clothes he had taken off symbolized that the whole of his heathen life was erased, while the new clothes indicated that he had obtained a new identity in Judaism.[18] This symbolism is perhaps linked with the Pauline metaphor of putting off/on in Col. 3.9-10 and Eph. 4.22-24 (cf. Gal. 3.27; Rom. 13.14), which symbolizes the change in a believer's nature which has taken place in baptism.

We turn now to an investigation of documents which are thought of as referring to Christian baptism. There has been an opinion that Logion 37 of *The Gospel of Thomas* contains an allusion to Christian baptismal praxis.[19] The Logion reads,[20]

> His disciples said 'When will you be revealed to us and when shall we see you?' Jesus said, 'When you undress without being ashamed, and you take your clothes and put them under your feet like little children do and trample on them, then you will see the Son of the Living One and you will not fear' (*Coptic* 37).

> His disciples say to him, 'When will you be revealed to us and when shall we see you?' He says, 'When you undress and are not ashamed...' (*P. Oxy.* 655).

If this Logion really describes the rite of baptism of the early church, it would be the earliest evidence suggesting the concrete form that Christian baptism assumed. The text is possibly from the first half of the second century.[21] It is of course true that this Logion cannot be the decisive clue to the praxis of first-century baptism, but, if 'the traditions within *the Gospel [of Thomas]* do not represent new creations

---

Did the Jews Baptize?', *JTS* 12 (1911), pp. 609-612; T.F. Torrance, 'Proselyte Baptism', *NTS* 1.2 (1954), pp. 150-54 (especially pp. 151-52). As a purifying washing proselyte baptism was self-administered and a baptismal candidate needed to be guided; see B.S. Easton, 'Critical Notes: Self-Baptism', *AJT* 24 (1920), pp. 513-18; D.A. Oepke, 'βάπτω κτλ', *TDNT*, I (1964), pp. 529-46 (especially pp. 545-46); cf. Isa. 1.16; *Sib. Ora.* 3.592-93; Titus 3.5.

14. Edersheim, *The Life and Times of Jesus the Messiah*, II, pp. 742-44; Abrahams, 'How Did the Jews Baptize?', pp. 609-612.

15. J.Z. Smith, *Map Is Not Territory: Studies in the History of Religions* (ed. J. Neusner; SJLA, 23; Leiden: Brill, 1978), p. 6 asserts that the immersion was performed naked, and in the case of a woman proselyte, the two learned men stood outside while she dipped herself in the water (*b. Yebam.* 47b); Edersheim, *The Life and Times of Jesus the Messiah*, II, p. 743.

16. *b. Yebam.* 22a; 48b; 97b; see Moore, *Judaism*, I, p. 332; Torrance, 'Proselyte Baptism', p. 152.

17. *Sib. Ora.* 4.165-67.

18. Cf. Moore, *Judaism*, I, p. 332; cf. Chapter 3, §§2.2 and 2.3.

19. Smith, *Map Is Not Territory*, pp. 1-23. cf. B. Layton, *The Gnostic Scriptures* (London: SCM Press, 1987), p. 377.

20. J.K. Elliott, (ed.), *The Apocryphal New Testament: A Collection of Apocryphal Christian Literature in an English Translation Based on M.R. James* (Oxford: Clarendon, 1993), pp. 140-41.

21. Cf. Layton, *The Gnostic Scriptures*, p. 377.

but, rather, reflect a varied history',[22] the Logion can be held to be a reflection of first-century baptism. The Logion implies that a candidate would undress himself and receive baptism naked,[23] afterwards reclothing himself. As the divested clothes are spoken of as ones which are to be trampled under foot, it is probable that they indicated the baptisand's old nature, which should be mortified. If this is true, the clothes that were worn after baptism symbolized his new nature. This view can be supported by the concept of lack of shame at being undressed. As the concept of seeing 'the Son of the living One' connotes the baptisand's union with him, the author seems to envisage an unashamedness which is restored by means of baptismal identification with him. This concept of lack of shame unmistakably envisages the statement in Gen. 2.25.[24] The concept of lack of fear also seems to allude to Adam's restoration from being afraid of being naked in the presence of God after the Fall (Gen. 3.11). The Logion thus implies that baptism signifies restoration to the original state of the first human couple.

In Hippolytus' *Apostolic Tradition* (hereafter *Apos. Trad.*), which reflects Roman practice at the end of the second century,[25] we can glance at how the early church exercised baptism. In column 21, Hippolytus speaks of the procedure of the baptismal ceremony. According to him, when the baptismal water[26] is ready, the baptismal candidates remove their clothing (*Apos. Trad.* 21.3). Then they are anointed with 'the oil of exorcism', which is a ritual of evil spirits being renounced (21.9-10). After being anointed, they enter into the water for baptism. Hippolytus continues:

> Then, after these things, let him give him over to the presbyter who baptizes, and let the candidates stand in the water, naked, a deacon going with them likewise. And when he who is being baptized goes down into the water, he who baptizes him, putting his hand on him, shall say thus… (21.11-12).[27]

After being baptized three times with the candidate's confession of belief in God, Christ Jesus, and the Holy Ghost, he comes up from the water, when 'he is anointed by the presbyter with the oil of thanksgiving' (21.19). Then each of the

22. Smith, *Map Is Not Territory*, p. 1; see O. Cullmann, 'The Gospel of Thomas and the Problem of the Age of the Tradition Contained Therein: A Survey', *Int* 16 (1962), pp. 418-38 (especially pp. 426-33, 437).

23. Smith, *Map Is Not Territory*, p. 2. Concerning the case of the female baptisand, see the same book, 6-7.

24. Smith, *Map Is Not Territory*, pp. 2, 7.

25. W.A. Meeks, *The First Urban Christians: The Social World of the Apostle Paul* (New Haven: Yale University Press, 1983), p. 150. See also Cyril of Jerusalem's *Mystagogical Catechesis* II (dated c. 350 CE), which contains a reference to baptismal practice (Beasley-Murray, *Baptism in the New Testament*, pp. 148-49).

26. Water of 'the baptismal tank' (if there is not scarcity of water), or of whatever water (if there is scarcity of water); see *Apos. Trad.* 21.1-2.

27. Quoted from B.S. Easton (trans.), *The Apostolic Tradition of Hippolytus* (Cambridge: Cambridge University Press, 1934), p. 46. In the text, as Easton points out, 'the pronouns are ambiguous and confusing' (Easton [trans.], *The Apostolic Tradition of Hippolytus*, p. 91). The first 'him' seems to points to the presbyter who has administered the ritual of anointment, the second 'him', to the individual baptisand of many baptismal candidates (cf. *Apos. Trad.* 21.9). 'The presbyter' here seems to point to him who performs the actual baptism.

baptized, 'after drying himself, is immediately clothed, and then is brought into the church' (21.20).

In all these rituals, baptism includes the rite of taking off and putting on clothes. When Hippolytus highlights that those who have been baptized are accepted by the church, he implies that the baptisand has undergone a change in his or her identity and entered into the community of Christian fellowship. Such a significant change can be further suggested by the rituals of being anointed with 'the oil of exorcism' and 'the oil of thanksgiving' shortly before and immediately after baptism. If this opinion is acceptable, it is probable that taking off and putting on symbolize that the baptisand's old identity has been removed and a new identity created.

Furthermore, we can see a clearer reference to putting off/on of clothes in connection with baptism in *Gos. Phil.* 101, which seems to date between the latter part of the second century and the latter half of the third.[28]

> The living water is corporal. It is fitting that (in it) we should put on the living man, because (it holds good): when he goes down to the water, he unclothes himself, that he may put this one on.[29]

It is true that this passage does not speak of literal clothes which are divested or invested, but the words 'unclothe' and 'put on' seem undoubtedly to have in mind a baptismal scene where the candidate takes off or puts on clothes. It is likely that the baptismal sequence was of the divestiture of normal clothes, immersion in the water, and investiture with baptismal robes.[30]

In this passage baptism is regarded as replacing the baptisand 'himself' with 'the living man'. It is likely that for the writer of *Gos. Phil.*, clothes being taken off before baptism connote the baptisand's old nature, and clothes being worn after baptism point to his new nature. This implies that the concept of putting off the old man and putting on the new man in Col. 3.9-10 and Eph. 4.22-24 (and also Rom. 13.14; Gal. 3.27) is drawn from early baptismal practice, although the rite of baptism is not directly referred to in these passages.

Evidence of undressing and redressing in baptism is abundant in later Patristic documents. For example, Jerome, *Epistle to Fabiola* 19, says,

> And when ready for the garment of Christ, we have taken off the tunics of skin, then we shall be clothed with a garment of linen which has nothing of death in it,

---

28. See also Hippolytus, *Apos. Trad.*, which reflects Roman practice at the end of the second century (Meeks, *The First Urban Christians*, p. 150) and Cyril (of Jerusalem), *Cate. Myst.* II (dated c. 350 CE), which contains a reference to the baptismal practice (Beasley-Murray, *Baptism in the New Testament*, pp. 148-49).

29. See H.-M. Schenke, 'The Gospel of Philip', in W. Schneemelcher (ed.), *New Testament Apocrypha* I: *Gospels and Related Writings* (trans. R.McL. Wilson; Cambridge: Clarke, 1991), pp. 179-208 (201); cf. W.W. Isenberg, 'The Gospel of Philip (II, 3)', in J.M. Robinson (ed.), *The Nag Hammadi Library in English* (San Francisco: Harper, 1990 [1978]), p. 154, where translation and numbering are different.

30. E. Segelberg, 'The Baptismal Rite according to Some of the Coptic Gnostic Texts of Nag-Hammadi', in *Studia Patristica*, V (TUGAL, 80; Berlin: Akademie-Verlag, 1962), pp. 117-28 (especially pp. 125-26).

but is wholly white so that, rising from baptism, we may gird our loins in truth and
the entire shame of our past sins may be covered.[31]

Jerome seems to endow the putting off/on at baptism with spiritual significance
in the light of his understanding of the story of Adam in Genesis. For him, the
putting off before baptism is to remove 'the tunics of skin', which must be
reminiscent of Gen. 3.21. He perhaps thinks that כָּתְנוֹת עוֹר in Gen. 3.21 symbolizes the death and shame of the Fall.[32] For him, to be baptized signifies being
stripped of this death and fall, which has been inherited from Adam. There is little
doubt that the concept of 'shame' bears in mind that which Adam felt after the Fall
(Gen. 3.7-10). The most important part of baptism is to put on 'the garment of
Christ', which is symbolized by the baptismal garment of pure white linen. To
wear this garment after baptism connotes that the shame of the baptisand's past
iniquities is covered over. When he is clothed with Christ, he is freed from the
shame of fallenness. In brief, for Jerome, the garment which is removed before
baptism stands for the Adamic tunic-of-skin signifying death and shame, while the
garment which is worn after baptism connotes Christ who covers the shame of sins.

It is not clear whether or not the first-century baptisand wore a *white linen
garment* after baptism; it is likely that this custom was only established formally at
a relatively late date. However, it is highly probable that even before the introduction of such a formal ritual, the general practice of undressing before baptism and
reclothing after baptism was prevalent in the earliest church and that it played a
very important part in the rite of baptism, signifying the removal of the old identity
which had been controlled by evil and the adoption of the new identity produced
by union with Christ.[33] C.F.D. Moule attempts to reconstruct the procedure of the
first-century baptism rite. The principal items which he suggests are: the removal
of the clothes, the formal declaration of faith, the creed, the water (probably total
immersion) then coming out from the water and re-clothing.[34]

---

31. Quoted from Smith, *Map Is Not Territory*, p. 17; also cited by R. Scroggs and K. Groff,
'Baptism in Mark', *JBL* 92 (1973), pp. 531-48 (537).

32. Cf. Philo, *Quae. Gen.* i.53 (on Gen. 3.21); also *Quae. Gen.* i.4 (on Gen. 2.7).

33. C.F.D. Moule, *Worship in the New Testament* (London: Lutterworth, 1961), pp. 52-53.

34. Moule, *Worship in the New Testament*, pp. 52-53; also see R.P. Martin, *Worship in the
Early Church* (Grand Rapids: Eerdmans, 1964), p. 101.

CONCLUSION TO PART I

We have so far concentrated on seeking the significance of clothing imagery which occurs in the Old Testament, other Jewish literature, *Joseph and Aseneth*, *The Hymn of the Pearl*, *Mystery Religions* (particularly Apuleius' *Metamorphoses*), Roman apparel (especially *toga virilis*), and the baptismal practices in the early church.

1. In the Old Testament, (i) Adam's being clothed in the garment of skin (Gen. 3.21) symbolizes that he is to be restored to his original state, that is, the image of God which is typified by his dominance over the other creatures, life, unashamedness, glory and peace with God; (ii) the [high] priest's being clothed with priestly garments connotes that he is unified with God, resulting in his status differing from that of others and so his being a very holy man (Exod. 29.4-9; Lev. 6.10-11; 16.3-4, 23-24; Ezek. 42.13-14; 44.19; cf. Zech. 3.3-5); (iii) God's clothing himself with a specific person (Judg. 6.34; 1 Chron. 12.18; 2 Chron. 24.20) signifies that he identifies himself with the man so that he may exercise his power through him.

2. In other Jewish literature, we have found a variety of uses for clothing imagery. The idea of Adam's prelapsarian clothing was quite prevalent in ancient times. Adam and Eve's clothing with righteousness and glory before the Fall (*Apoc. Mos.* 20–21) indicates that they were characterized not only by a right ethical attitude in relation to God but also by a radiance in their appearance, and this was related to their possession of God's image. This in turn was linked to their rulership over the created world. Linen and silken cloths which were put on over Adam's corpse symbolizes that his kingship will eventually be restored at the time of resurrection (*Apoc. Mos.* 41). An allusion to Adam's being clothed with light (*Gen. Rab.* 20.12) connotes that his body was endued with splendour. Many other rabbinic writings[1] also maintain that the first couple were typified by glory or brilliance, which is often linked to God's image in them.

Philo's assertion that human beings are destined to be clothed with either vice or virtue (*Ebr.* 7) signifies that they are to be characterized by evil or goodness. As a garment reveals its wearer's character, so either vice or virtue manifests people's character. For Philo, the soul's being clothed with the garment of skin is an equivalent to its residing in the body. Philo also underlines that the high priest's dressing himself in the priestly garment symbolizes his being identified with God, and so his being exalted to a kingly status.

1 and *2 Enoch* emphasize that the righteous will be clothed with the garment of life or glory. This connotes that they will enter into the heavenly condition of existence, that is, obtain a glorious body at the time of resurrection (*1 Enoch* 62.15-16),

---

1. E.g. *Pirqe R. El.* 14.20; *Tg. Yer.* Gen 3.7, 21; *'Abot R. Nat.* ii.42, 116.

which resembles the appearance of God who is himself endued with glory and holiness (*1 Enoch* 14.20). The replacement of Enoch's earthly garment with a heavenly garment symbolizes that his present body is to be transformed into a glorious resurrection body (*2 Enoch* 22.8-10).

3. In *Joseph and Aseneth*, the whole process of Aseneth's conversion from paganism to Judaism is symbolized by various kinds of clothing imagery. Her investiture with an extravagant idolatrous garment denotes that in her paganism she is dead religiously. Her divestiture of this apparel and investiture with a black mourning tunic indicates that she leaves paganism. Her investiture with a new linen garment connotes that she obtains new life in Judaism. Her investiture with a wedding garment symbolizes that she is unified with Judaism, and so acquires a new identity of life in it.

4. In *The Hymn of the Pearl*, similarly, the whole process of the protagonist's life is symbolized by various kinds of clothing imagery. His divestiture of his original royal garment connotes that he is separated from his heavenly self. His investiture with the Egyptian garment signifies that he has taken on a worldly self. His divestiture of this apparel denotes that he disengages himself from this worldly self. His reinvestiture with his original garment indicates that he is reunited with his heavenly, royal self, that is, the image of God.

5. Apuleius' *Metamorphoses* describes the whole process of Lucius' transformation from an ass-man to a real man by several kinds of clothing imagery: i.e. a linen garment worn immediately after his transformation, a new linen garment worn before the initiation ritual, and twelve extravagant garment worn after the initiation ceremony. Yet the central idea of all this garment imagery is Lucius' obtainment of a new life out of this death-like state. Emphasis is placed on the idea that Lucius is restored to a normal human state, that is, a re-born life, in his initiation into Isis. In particular, his investiture with the twelve robes symbolizes that he has been identified with Isis through his ecstatic experience of arriving at the zodiac region (XI.28).

6. The *toga virilis*, which was worn by a Roman boy instead of his previous apparel, the *toga praetexta*, when he reached the age of sixteen, symbolizes his transition from boyhood to manhood. This means that his status is changed not only from a slave-like to a free-man's position, but also from the status of being unqualified for official duty to that of being qualified for it. In other words, the apparel symbolizes that he has acquired not only heirship of his father's possessions but also full citizenship of the Roman Empire.

7. Materials such as *Gos. Thom.* 37, Hippolytus' *Apostolic Tradition*, *Gos. Phil.* 101, and Jerome, *Epistle to Fabiola* 19 suggest that putting off/on of clothes before and after baptism in the early church symbolizes the baptisand's experience of a spiritual change in his character from old to new. This seems to correspond to the Pauline putting off/on metaphor (Col. 3.9-10; Eph. 4.22-24) and clothing-with-Christ metaphor (Gal. 3.26-29; Rom. 13.14).

Part II

THE CLOTHING IMAGERY IN THE PAULINE CORPUS

Introduction to Part II

The purpose of this Part is to unfold the meaning of the clothing metaphor in the Pauline corpus, bearing in mind the history-of-religions background[1] already considered in Part I. In doing this, how relevant ancient clothing documents to Pauline clothing passages are will be ascertained. As each clothing text in the Pauline epistles is dealt with, specific features included in it will, of course, be carefully considered.

Pauline clothing passages refer to several kinds of clothing, that is, putting on a person (Christ [Gal. 3.26-29; Rom. 13.14], the new man [Col. 3.9-10; Eph. 4.22-24]), godly virtues (Col. 3.12), and the resurrection body (1 Cor. 15.49-54; 2 Cor. 5.1-4). It seems that all these ideas together constitute a significant part of Pauline theology.[2]

Gal. 3.26-29, Rom. 13.14, Col. 3.9-10 and Eph. 4.22-24 evidently draw on a common bank of ideas. The concept of putting on the new man in Eph. 4.24 closely parallels the same concept in Col. 3.10, which is the sister concept of putting on Christ in Gal. 3.27 and Rom. 13.14.[3] The primary concern of these passages is with a change in the Christian's nature from the old personality to the new one through union with Christ. Specifically, Col. 3.12 seems to be an extension of the preceding passage (vv. 9-11); a change in Christian personality will hopefully be accompanied by a change to Christian morals.

---

1. A metaphor is normally tied up with its background, from which a specific reality is described. It may be said that a metaphor forms a triangular relationship with this reality and with its background. S.J. Kraftchick, 'Seeing a More Fluid Model', in D.M. Hay (ed.), *Pauline Theology* II: *1 & 2 Corinthians* (Minneapolis: Fortress, 1993), pp. 18-34 (30-32) argues that 'as much as the contingent situation affects the expression of Paul's gospel, there is an equal, perhaps greater, effect which *his conception* of the gospel has on *his understanding* of the contingent situation', that 'we should distinguish between the rhetorical situation that is presented by Paul in the letter and the actual situation that gave rise to it', and that 'there are occasions when Paul uses a stock-in-trade formulation, derived from rabbinic forms of exegesis, Hellenistic philosophy, or rhetorical techniques, as part of his overall argument' (italics in original).

2. The concept of clothing with spiritual armour (1 Thess. 5.4-8; Rom. 13.12; Eph. 6.11-17) could also, in a wide sense, belong to the category of Pauline clothing imagery in that it uses the concept of 'clothing'. But when its fundamental concern is with Christians' spiritual armour, it seems to be different from other clothing, which speaks of a change in Christians' natures (followed by a change in their ethical conduct) and in their mode of existence.

3. See C.H. Dodd, 'Colossians', in F.C. Eiselen *et al.* (eds.), *ABC* (New York: Abingdon, 1929), pp. 1250-262 (1259); F.F. Bruce, *Paul: Apostle of the Free Spirit* (Carlisle: Paternoster, 1980 [1977]), p. 112; J.A. Beet, *A Commentary on St. Paul's Epistle to the Romans* (London: Hodder & Stoughton, 1887), p. 347.

1 Cor. 15.49-54 and 2 Cor. 5.1-5 are also in an inseparable relationship with one another, as they include in common the metaphor of being clothed with the resurrection body; the former passage refers to being clothed with incorruptibility/immortality, while the latter, with a heavenly building. In both passages, clothing imagery underlines a change in the Christian existence from the present to the future mode. At the parousia the believer's earthly body will be transformed into a heavenly body.

In this Part, I will treat the imagery of clothing with a person (Christ or the new man) in two separate chapters, and with the resurrection body in a further chapter. The imagery of clothing with Christian virtues in Col. 3.12 will be considered when the imagery of clothing with the new man (Col. 3.9-10) is dealt with, since both occur in the same context.

Chapter 8

CLOTHING WITH A PERSON (I): 'CHRIST'

1. *Introduction*

The task of this chapter is to clarify the significance of the putting-on-Christ metaphor in Gal. 3.27 and Rom. 13.14. We will first consider the former passage and then the latter. When we deal with each passage, we will first investigate not only the circumstances of the audience of the epistle to which the passage belongs but also the context to which it belongs. We will then concentrate on what is meant by the concept of being clothed with Christ; in particular, its relation to baptism, its involvement in the Adam–Christ analogy, its ecclesial tenor, and so on, will be highlighted. We will also consider contextual emphases and their relevance to the imagery of clothing-with-Christ; in particular, how theological features, for example soteriological, eschatological or ethical, disclose the significance of this metaphor. In covering all of these features, the way in which the ancient clothing traditions in Part I throw light on our quest for the significance of the imagery will be considered. Finally we will draw a comprehensive conclusion.

2. *Clothing with Christ in Galatians 3.27*

2.1. *The Situation of Galatians' Readers*
Galatians is a document which belongs to the so-called undisputed Pauline letters.[1] It was written to 'the churches in Galatia' (Gal. 1.2; cf. 3.1)[2] and perhaps dated around

---

1.   W.G. Kümmel, *Introduction to the New Testament* (Nashville: Abingdon, 1975), p. 304.

2.   It is not easy to identify who the addressees really were. The South Galatian Theory believes that they are Christians in the province of southern Galatia, while the North Galatian Theory believes that they indicate Christians in the region of northern Galatia. To reopen this old debate would not be relevant to the present study. Inasmuch as 'the churches in Galatia' in Gal. 1.2 and 'Galatians' in 3.1 refer to the congregation which came into existence by virtue of Paul's missionary journey, a 'South' Galatian destination seems to be more supportable, because Acts, which speaks of Paul's three missionary journeys, does not include an explicit reference to his visiting north Galatia. Frequently Acts 16.6 and 18.23 are used as texts which support the 'North' Galatian thesis. However, as D.A. Carson, D.J. Moo and L. Morris, *An Introduction to the New Testament* (Grand Rapids: Zondervan, 1992), pp. 290-91 argue, it is highly probable that the phrase τὴν Φρυγίαν καὶ Γαλατικὴν χώραν in Acts 16.6 points to 'the Phrygio-Galatic territory' and the similar phrase τὴν Γαλατικὴν χώραν καὶ Φρυγίαν in 18.23 seems to signify much the same. In particular, the words πάντας τοὺς μαθητάς in the latter verse seem to envisage Christians in the area through which Paul passed after leaving Lystra and Iconium (Acts 16.2).

AD 50,[3] probably between the end of Paul's first missionary journey and the Jerusalem Council.[4] The Galatian church was made up of Gentile Christians in the main (Gal. 4.8; 5.2-10; 6.12-13).[5] The Galatian church was faced with a crisis, because so-called 'Judaizers' had infiltrated the Galatian church from outside (cf. Gal. 1.6-9) and spread Judaizing teaching; Paul calls them 'false brothers'[6] (Gal. 2.4). They perhaps appealed in their teachings to the authority of James (cf. Gal. 2.12).[7]

These Judaizers insisted that every Christian ought to observe the law and believed that it is by the works of the Law that one can be righteous, gain life, and receive the inheritance which God promised to Abraham (cf. Gal. 2.16, 21; 3.6-9, 14-18, 24-29). This campaign seriously affected the Galatian believers. For Paul, it was a great agony that the Galatians had positively responded to the Judaizing propaganda (Gal. 4.9-11). So he severely blamed those who had been influenced by the Judaizing teaching (Gal. 3.1-4); he strongly expressed his wish to preserve his gospel (Gal. 1.6-9); he did not conceal his hostile feelings against the Judaizers (Gal. 5.10-12). Against the Judaizers' emphasis on the Law, Paul argues that it is by being identified with Christ through faith and not through the Law[8] that believers become

3. D.B. Knox, 'The Date of the Epistle to the Galatians', *EQ* XIII (1941), pp. 262-68; see also C.H. Buck, 'The Date of Galatians', *JBL* 70 (1951), pp. 113-22.

4. Carson *et al.*, *Introduction to the New Testament*, pp. 293-94.

5. It is not clear whether there were Jewish Christians in the church; considering that in the first century there were Jewish settlements in the province of Galatia (H. Conzelmann and A. Lindemann, *Interpreting the New Testament* [trans. S.S. Schatzmann; Peabody: Hendrickson, 1988], p. 171), such a possibility cannot be excluded.

6. W. Schmithals, *Paul and the Gnostics* (New York: Abingdon, 1972), pp. 13-64, imagines that as Paul's opponents urge the Galatians to observe special days, months, seasons and years (Gal. 4.10) and especially admonish them to be subject to 'the elemental spirits of the universe' (Gal. 4.3, 9), they are Jewish-Christian Gnostics who have something to do with a gnostic teaching such as a doctrine of the redeemer's embodiment in the cosmic elements. Against this view, R. McL. Wilson, 'Gnostics—in Galatia?' (*SE*, 4, TUGAL 102; Berlin: Akademie-Verlag, 1968), pp. 358-67 (367) argues that in Galatians there are no 'clear signs of anything that can really be called Gnostics'. J.L. Martyn, 'A Law-Observant Mission to Gentiles: The Background of Galatians', *SJT* 38 (1985), pp. 307-324 suggests that those whom Paul calls 'false brothers' might be the teachers who pursued their own Law-observant mission among Gentiles, a mission inaugurated not many years after the death of Jesus. R.H. Gundry, *A Survey of the New Testament* (Grand Rapids: Zondervan, 1994), p. 344 points out that 'Galatians has to do with the Judaizing controversy about which the Jerusalem Council met (Acts 15)'; 'many of the first Christians, being Jewish, continued in large measure their Jewish mode of life, including attendance at the synagogue and temple, offering of sacrifices, observance of Mosaic rituals and dietary taboos, and social aloofness from Gentiles'. In this atmosphere, the existence of Gentile Christians could not help raising a number of critical questions: whether they should receive circumcision, whether they should follow the Jewish mode of life, and whether they should believe in Christ only or believe in Christ and Judaism, in order to be true Christians. For a further discussion on Paul's opponents, see J.B. Tyson, 'Paul's Opponents in Galatia', *NovT* 10 (1968), pp. 241-54; T.D. Gordon, 'The Problem at Galatia', *Int* 41 (1987), pp. 32-43; J.D.G. Dunn, 'Echoes of Intra-Jewish Polemic in Paul's Letter to the Galatians', *JBL* 112.3 (1993), pp. 459-77; J.M.G. Barclay, 'Mirror-Reading a Polemical Letter: Galatians as a Test Case', *JSNT* 31 (1987), pp. 73-93.

7. The exact character of their linkage with James is unknown; it is only clear that there is no evidence of his supporting them.

8. There is little doubt that in Galatians Paul concentrates on the issue of Law and faith. In

heirs to the inheritance which God promised to give Abraham (cf. Gal. 3.7, 18, 29). For this very point, Paul employs the two-fold metaphor, that is, he says that those who were baptized into Christ have put on Christ (Gal. 3.27). For Paul, it is on the basis of union with Christ in baptism, and not observance of the Law, that people become God's children who are then entitled to inherit his kingdom.

2.2. *The Context of Galatians 3.27*

Gal. 3.27 belongs to a small unit, Gal. 3.26-29, which constitutes a concluding part[9] of Paul's long discussion on believers becoming the heirs of 'the blessing that was promised, the kingdom of God'[10] (3.1-29), and which is expanded to a supplementary repetition of the theme that they have obtained the full inheritance of God by means of their divine sonship,[11] and to an admonition not to return to their old status (4.1-11). This implies that Gal. 3.27 should be understood within the wider context. R.B. Hays rightly sees Gal. 3.1–4.11 as a unit.[12]

Appealing to the testimony of the Galatians' experience (Gal. 3.1-5) and of the OT (especially Gal. 3.6-9), Paul tries to vindicate his position that Christians have obtained the rights of Abraham's children on the basis of justification by faith so that they may become participants in his blessings.[13] For Paul, Abraham himself was justified by faith in what God promised to him and was entitled to the heirship; those who are of the same faith can share Abraham's blessing in Christ, who was cursed on the cross in order that they might receive the promise of the Spirit through faith (Gal. 3.6-14). Paul stresses that the covenant of promise, through which Abraham entered into this adoptive relationship with God, would not be nullified by the Law, and that God in his grace gave the inheritance to faithful Abraham according to his promise (Gal. 3.15-25). Believers are those who have received the promise that when they believed in Christ, they would become the heirs of the inheritance derived from God's covenant with Abraham (cf. Gal. 3.22). Their belief in Christ gives them justification (Gal. 3.21, 24).

Paul concludes that justification by faith in Christ, that is, baptism into Christ, which in turn means putting on Christ, makes them participate in Christ's status,

---

Gal. 2.16-21 he emphasizes the superiority of faith to the Law. Gal. 3 and 4, which are remarkably argumentative, focuses on the theme of Law and faith.

9.   Cf. H.D. Betz, *Galatians* (Philadelphia: Fortress, 1979), p. 181: Gal. 3.26-28 is 'the goal towards which Paul has been driving all along'; p. 186: 'In the formal composition of 3.26-28, v. 27 stands out as an explanatory insertion of great significance'.

10.   J. Dow, 'Galatians', in F.C. Eiselen *et al.* (eds.), *ABC* (New York: Abingdon, 1929), pp. 1207-221 (1215); cf. J. Bligh, *Galatians: A Discussion of St. Paul's Epistle* (HC, 1; London: St. Paul Publications, 1969), p. 322.

11.   R.N. Longenecker, *Galatians* (WBC, 41; Dallas: Word Books, 1990), p. 151 holds that 'the postpositive γάρ here [Gal. 3.26] has both explanatory and continuative functions'.

12.   R.B. Hays, *The Faith of Jesus Christ: An Investigation of the Narrative Substructure of Galatians 3.1-4.11* (SBLDS, 56; Chico: Scholars, 1983), p. 233.

13.   In Galatians Paul frequently uses the term *gospel* in 1.6-9, 11, 16, 23; 2.2, 5, 7, 14; 3.8; and 4.13. The gist of the term is evidently justification by faith apart from Law-works (2.16, 21; 3.9, 11; 4.2-6; 5.2-6; 6.14-16).

that is, sonship of God in Christ, resulting in their becoming the heirs of the inheritance (Gal. 3.26-29).[14] For Paul, God fulfilled his promises to Abraham and his seed by making the Law play a part as a custodian to lead both Jew and Gentile to Christ, so that they might be justified on equal terms, that is, by faith; by belonging to Christ they become Abraham's seed, in other words, the heirs of the inheritance according to the promise. Therefore, Christians are no longer children and slaves but sons and heirs (Gal. 4.1-7); they should overcome the desire to revert to their former status (Gal. 4.8-11).

With this understanding, we can recognize some significant ideas which are of importance in seeking the meaning of the clothing-with-a-person metaphor (Gal. 3.27b). First of all, we note the concept of 'through faith, in Christ' (NIV)[15] in Gal. 3.26. The affinity of this verse to 3.27 is evident, as the conjunction γάρ[16] and the phrase εἰς Χριστόν are used in 3.27. This suggests that a specific theological perspective in Gal. 3.1-25 can be thought of as operating even in Gal. 3.27, because Gal. 3.26 belongs to the initial part of the conclusion of what has been discussed in Gal. 3.1-25. Gal. 3.26 would thus be regarded as the bridge where vv. 1-25 and v. 27 meet. Secondly, we also note that Paul uses time-bound concepts which obviously affect the significance of the two-fold concept in Gal. 3.27: baptism into Christ and putting on Christ. He refers to 'till the offspring should come' (Gal. 3.19), 'before faith came' (Gal. 3.23), 'until faith should be revealed' (Gal. 3.23), 'now that faith has come' (Gal. 3.25) and 'when the time had fully come' (Gal. 4.4). It is clear, then, that when Paul speaks of faith as an essential element in gaining sonship of God in Christ (Gal. 3.1-29) and refers to believers' having received this qualification (Gal. 4.1-7), his point of view is eschatological. For him, the receiving of God's sonship and the right of the inheritance is an eschatological event which happens at a specific time in the history of salvation.[17] Thirdly, we can also note Paul's use of concepts such as 'all one in Christ' (Gal. 3.28) and 'Christ's [possession]'(Gal. 3.29) which cannot be irrelevant to the double concept in Gal. 3.27. Fourthly, we further note that Paul's emphasis on the Spirit's dwelling in believers must be involved in the two-fold clause of Gal. 3.27. Paul underlines that the Galatians received the Spirit as a result of their faith in what they heard (Gal. 3.1-5), the promise of the Spirit by faith (Gal. 3.14), and the Spirit of Jesus Christ the Son of God (Gal. 4.6).

---

14. Regarding the structure of Gal. 3.26-29, see Longenecker, *Galatians*, pp. 150-52.

15. My comma between phrases.

16. In effect, the γάρ-clause (v. 27) functions as a confirmative supplement to v. 26; see Longenecker, *Galatians*, p. 154: 'In Koine Greek... γάρ is sometimes repeated either "to introduce several arguments for the same assertion" (so 1 Cor. 16.7; 2 Cor. 11.19-20; see also *Sir.* 37.13-14; 38.1-2; *Wisd. Sol.* 7.16-17; Jn. 8.42) or "to have one clause confirm the other" (so Rom. 6.14; 8.2-3; see also *Jud.* 5.23; 7.27; 1 *Mac.* 11.10; Mt. 10.19-20; Lk. 8.29; Jn. 5.21-22; Acts 2.15).' Note also the similarity of ὅσοι (m. pl., 'as many as') in v. 27 to πάντες (m. pl., 'all') in v. 26.

17. R. Bultmann, *Theology of the New Testament*, I (trans. K. Grobel; London: SCM Press, 1983 [1952]), p. 319; Betz, *Galatians*, p. 176.

2.3. *The Meaning of Clothing with Christ*

2.3.1. *Introductory Remarks.* In this section I will first argue that the clothing-with-Christ imagery in Gal. 3.27 probably envisages the actual scene of the rite of baptism, where the believer became one with Christ.[18] I will then attempt to prove that this baptismal unity with Christ has multiple implications. That is, the metaphor indicates the believer's participation in Christ's death and life. It also points to his union with Christ's Spirit, with his priestly righteousness, or with his sonship of God, and signifies the believer's identification with Christ as the new Adam. It further denotes his incorporation into Christ's ecclesial body.[19] Although these connotations are not always overt, their importance is not diminished.

2.3.2. *Baptismal Unity with Christ: 'Putting on Christ' as* Βαπτίσθῆναι εἰς Χριστόν. In seeking the significance of 'putting on Christ' in Gal. 3.27, it is necessary to note that Paul identifies it as βαπτίσθῆναι εἰς Χριστόν. What reality is then described by this phrase? Paul seems to use the verb 'βαπτίζω' deliberately in order to suggest that the phrase delineates the rite of water-baptism. When the Galatians heard the statement of Gal. 3.27, they must have recalled the baptism which they had received.[20] J.D.G. Dunn holds that 'Gal. 3.27 does describe the rite of water-baptism as a "putting on Christ" or state that in baptism we put on Christ'.[21] Dunn, however, contradictorily argues that by using the baptismal metaphor (inasmuch as 'the rite [of baptism] provides and lies behind the metaphor [i.e. baptism into Christ]'[22]) Paul describes conversion-change.[23] Dunn makes a further effort to wrest these words from the rite of baptism. He argues that

> it [the metaphor] no more refers to water-baptism as such than it does in Romans,
> Colossians and Ephesians. Ἐνδύσασθαι Χριστόν can be repeated; baptism is not—
> or was Paul requiring his Roman readers to be rebaptized? 'To put on Christ' is

---

18. See Chapter 8, §2.3.2.

19. The concept of 'all-one-in-Christ' or 'Christ's' in Gal. 3.28-29 suggests that the clothing-with-Christ imagery in v. 27 is not merely applied to an individual Christian but also to all Christians as a whole; see Chapter 8, §2.3.6.

20. G.W. Hansen, *Abraham in Galatians: Epistolary and Rhetorical Contexts* (JSNTSup, 29; Sheffield: Sheffield Academic Press, 1989), p. 136; F.F. Bruce, *The Epistle to the Galatians: A Commentary on the Greek Text* (NIGTC; Grand Rapids: Paternoster/Eerdmans, 1992 [1982]), p. 185; also see J.A. Fitzmyer, 'The Letter to the Galatians', in *NJBC* (London: Geoffrey Chapman, 1990 [1968]), pp. 780-90 (787); F.J. Matera, *Galatians* (SPS, 9; Collegeville: The Liturgical Press, 1992), p. 145; K.H. Rengstorf, 'ποταμός κτλ', *TDNT*, VI (1968), pp. 595-623 (619).

21. J.D.G. Dunn, *Baptism in the Holy Spirit* (London: SCM Press, 1970), p. 109 (see also pp. 111, 112). Cf. D.A. Oepke, 'βάπτω κτλ', *TDNT*, I (1964), pp. 529-46 (539) who considers Gal. 3.27b to be 'a heightened form' of Gal. 3.27a.

22. Dunn, *Baptism in the Holy Spirit*, p. 112.

23. Dunn, *Baptism in the Holy Spirit*, p. 110. In *The Epistle to the Galatians* (BNTC; Peabody: Hendrickson, 1993), p. 203, Dunn explains that the preposition εἰς of the phrase εἰς Χριστόν connotes 'the moment in which and action by means of which their lives and destinies and very identities became bound up with Christ'. Dunn seems to believe that conversion and baptism are two separate realities and βαπτίσθῆναι εἰς Χριστόν concerns conversion alone.

simply a figurative usage to describe more expressively the spiritual transformation which makes one a Christian.[24]

Dunn seems to have struggled with a logical dilemma; he probably thinks that insofar as he maintains that the reality figured in the expression 'baptism into Christ' and 'putting on Christ' is the same,[25] and the latter can be repeated, if he then admits the relationship between 'baptism into Christ' and the rite of baptism, he would have to say that the rite itself must be repeated. However, the repeatable character of 'putting on Christ' does not necessarily require the rite of water-baptism to be repeated, because βαπτίσθῆναι εἰς Χριστόν, which is in close relationship with 'putting on Christ', does not point to baptism itself. Baptism as a rite, which is not to be repeated,[26] must be distinguished from βαπτίσθῆναι εἰς Χριστόν in its sense of being united with Christ, which must be repeated over and over again. When Dunn cannot appropriately explain how βαπτίσθῆναι εἰς Χριστόν *is* associated with the rite of baptism, he is inevitably made to focus *only* on its spiritual significance.

Refuting Dunn's interpretation of βαπτίσθῆναι εἰς Χριστόν, we affirm that this figure is not only drawn from baptism, but also describes what is meant by it. E.D.W. Burton holds that 'by ἐβαπτίσθη the apostle undoubtedly refers to Christian baptism, immersion in water'.[27] R.P. Carlson also affirms that in Gal. 3.27-28 'Paul focuses attention on the common experience of baptism'.[28] However, the ritual

24. Dunn, *Baptism in the Holy Spirit*, p. 110.
25. Dunn, *Baptism in the Holy Spirit*, p. 111.
26. Moule, *Worship in the New Testament*, p. 59: 'St. Paul writes of it [baptism] as something so closely comparable to one's own death and burial, and so closely linked with Christ's death and burial, that any going back on it or repetition of it would have been unthinkable'. One may raise a question: is reference to baptism for the dead (1 Cor. 15.29) not a suggestion of the repeatability of baptism? In relation to this issue, Whiteley, *The Theology of St. Paul*, p. 174 speculates: 'It may be that they [the dead] were what would later have been termed catechumens, and that their baptism was posthumously completed on their behalf, just as a mother may receive a military award on behalf of a son killed in action. On the other hand, it may be that a number of those who were already members of the Christian church and died, and their friends and relations in Corinth who were still pagans accepted baptism in order to join them again after death'.
27. E.D. Burton, *A Critical and Exegetical Commentary on the Epistle to the Galatians* (ICC; Edinburgh: T. & T. Clark, 1921), p. 203. Longenecker, *Galatians*, p. 155, argues that ἐβαπτίσθητε 'undoubtedly refers to Christian baptism, i.e. immersion in water, for this is the uniform meaning of the term in Paul (cf. Rom. 6.3; 1 Cor. 1.13-17; 12.13; 15.29)'; C.B. Cousar, *Galatians, Interpretation: A Bible Commentary for Teaching and Preaching* (Louisville: John Knox Press, 1982), p. 84. Cf. K.S. Wuest, *Galatians in the Greek New Testament: For the English Readers* (Grand Rapids: Eerdmans, 3rd edn, 1948), p. 111.
28. R.P. Carlson, 'The Role of Baptism in Paul's Thought', *Int* 47 (1993), pp. 255-66 (259). Our view that βαπτίσθῆναι εἰς Χριστόν is involved in baptism can be further reinforced by a probability that the words in Gal. 3.27 were a regular part of Christian baptismal catechesis, because if this is true, the phrase would be associated with the real practice of baptism; see E.G. Selwyn, *The First Epistle of St. Peter* (London: Macmillan, 1952 [1946]), pp. 394-95; P. Carrington, *The Primitive Christian Catechism* (Cambridge: Cambridge University Press, 1940), pp. 46-49; R.P. Martin, *Colossians: The Church's Lord and the Christian's Liberty* (Exeter: Paternoster, 1972), p. 111; G. Cannon, *The Use of Traditional Materials in Colossians* (Macon: Mercer University Press, 1983), p. 73. See W. Robinson, 'Historical Survey of the Church's Treatment of New Converts with Reference to Pre- and Post-Baptismal Instruction', *JTS* 42 (1941), pp. 42-45.

action of baptism is not all that the figure describes,[29] as it is linked with the idea of Christians' obtaining sonship of God through faith in Christ Jesus. It refers to more than being baptized with water; it refers not only to the ritual aspect of baptism but also to the spiritual reality which baptism accomplishes,[30] that is, identification with Christ through faith (which happened in conversion-initiation), resulting in becoming God's sons, in other words, his heirs.[31]

Thus, the rite of baptism cannot be separated from what it spiritually signifies.[32] Baptism symbolizes what has already been attained in Christ; baptism is what is performed as 'the consequence of the act of faith'.[33] However, when the rite of baptism achieves incorporation into Christ by faith (which took place in conversion), it cannot be considered as a pure symbol. J.A. Fitzmyer in his comment on Gal. 3.27a appropriately argues that 'baptism is the sacramental complement of faith, the rite whereby a person achieves union with Christ and publicly manifests his commitment'.[34] Baptism is the visible sign which sacramentally ratifies the believer's incorporation into Christ by faith.[35] From the moment of conversion-experience, the Christian begins to live his life in union with Christ.[36] Through his conversion-change he attains 'a new kind of life'[37] in union with Christ, which is accomplished by baptism in public.[38] Paul perhaps wishes to see the achievement of the believer's identification with Christ in baptism.

I have so far argued that the reality which baptism into Christ describes is baptism which completes union with Christ. This suggests that the metaphor of putting on

29. Cf. Dunn, *The Epistle to the Galatians*, p. 203: 'the "into Christ" is more than simply an abbreviation of "into the name of" used in baptism (as implied in 1 Cor. i.13), although it probably included the significance of the latter'.

30. Considering that obtaining of God's sonship through faith in Christ Jesus (Gal. 3.26) is elaborated by baptism into Christ as putting on Christ (3.27) and that baptism into Christ describes the rite of baptism (3.27), Paul probably regards baptism as the accomplishment of incorporation into Christ.

31. S. Kim, *The Origin of Paul's Gospel* (WUNT, 2.4; Tübingen: Mohr, 1981), p. 316 presents a noteworthy argument: '[Gal. 3.23-29] explains how we actually appropriate the divine redemption and sonship. We become sons of God as by faith and baptism we put on Christ and are incorporated into Christ. It is Christ who is properly the Son of God. But Christ is the *Stammvater*, a "corporate personality", in whom the *Stamm*, the redeemed humanity, is incorporated. So, as we are by faith and baptism united with him and incorporated in him, we participate in his divine sonship'.

32. R.Y.K. Fung, *The Epistle to the Galatians* (ed. G.D. Fee; NICNT; Grand Rapids: Eerdmans, 1953), p. 172. Concerning the symbolic character of baptism, see G.W. Bromiley, 'Aspects of Luther's Doctrine of Baptism', *EQ* 17 (1945), pp. 281-95 (especially pp. 283-86).

33. D.B. Orchard, 'Galatians', in *NCCHS* (London: Nelson, 1969 [1953]), pp. 1173-180 (1179); cf. J.C. O'Neill, *The Recovery of Paul's Letter to the Galatians* (London: SPCK, 1972), p. 55.

34. J.A. Fitzmyer, 'The Letter to the Galatians', in *NJBC* (London: Geoffrey Chapman, 1990 [1968]), pp. 780-90 (787).

35. Fung, *The Epistle to the Galatians*, p. 174; J.N. Sanders, 'Galatians', in *PCB* (London: Nelson, 1963), pp. 973-79 (976); Bruce, *The Epistle to the Galatians*, p. 184; H. Vogel, 'The First Sacrament: Baptism', *SJT* 7 (1954), pp. 41-58 (49-50).

36. J. Ziesler, *The Epistle to the Galatians* (London: Epworth, 1992), p. 50.

37. D. Guthrie (ed.), *Galatians* (CBNS; London: Nelson, 1969), p. 115.

38. Cf. D. Lührmann, *Galatians: A Continental Commentary* (Minneapolis: Fortress, 1992), p. 75: Gal. 3.27 refers to 'baptism as the sign of entrance into the church'; K. Grayston, *The Epistles to the Galatians and to the Philippians* (London: Epworth, 1957), p. 48.

Christ[39] also refers to baptism in the same sense, that is, the baptismal identification with Christ. R.N. Longenecker holds that:

> the metaphorical sense of clothing one's self with Christ was suggested to early Christians by baptismal candidates divesting themselves of clothing before baptism and then being reclothed afterwards.[40]

In the light of the baptismal mode of the primitive church, this assertion seems to be supportable.[41] O.S. Brooks, however, insists that 'since a similar statement is made apart from any reference to baptism, "put on the Lord Jesus Christ" (Rom. 13.14), its basic meaning is not dependent upon its proximity to baptism in Galatians';[42] he affirms that Gal. 3.27a is 'obviously not a statement that seeks to explain the meaning of baptism, rather to support the basic meaning of the context'.[43] However, it is not proper to interpret Gal. 3.27b by depending upon Rom. 13.14. Further, although the concept of putting on Christ does not appear in a direct combination with the mention of baptism in Rom. 13.14, it is highly probable that baptism was in mind even there (cf. Rom. 6.1-11).[44] Moreover, the indissoluble relationship between 'being baptized into Christ' and 'putting on Christ' hardly supports Brooks's view. Inasmuch as βαπτίσθῆναι εἰς Χριστόν (Gal. 3.27a) is connected with the rite of baptism, it may well be that ἐνδύσασθαι Χριστόν (3.27b) is also associated with it. C.F.D. Moule holds that 'it is difficult not to associate this metaphor [putting on Christ] with the actual movements of the baptized'.[45] Perhaps Paul wishes to apply the metaphor to those who have received baptism as the achievement of having entered into the unity relationship with Christ.

If so, why does Paul designate the baptismal union with Christ by means of the metaphor of putting on Christ? Why does he use it without directly saying that Christians have been united with Christ? Probably he believes that it can most appropriately stand for the baptismal oneness between the baptisand and Christ. It is likely that Paul has in mind the various aspects of human beings' normal clothing. He probably thinks that the closeness between a garment and its wearer could explain the intimate relationship between Christ and Christians. In a sense, a garment can be thought of as being part of its wearer. A garment always accompanies its wearer; where he or she is, there the garment is also. It shares everything that he or she experiences. This unifying relationship between a garment and its wearer could be part of what Paul wishes to portray with the metaphor of clothing-with-Christ in Gal. 3.27. Further, he probably has in mind how a garment and its wearer differ from one another, despite their close relationship when the garment is worn.

39. Inasmuch as 'baptized into Christ' is a metaphor, 'putting on Christ' may also be regarded as a metaphor. Dunn, *Baptism in the Holy Spirit*, p. 111: 'The sense is disrupted if we take one as a metaphor and one as a literal description of a physical act'.

40. Longenecker, *Galatians*, p. 156.

41. See Chapter 7.

42. O.S. Brooks, 'A Contextual Interpretation of Galatians 3.27', *SB* III (1978), JSNTSup, 3 (Sheffield: Sheffield Academic Press, 1980), p. 52.

43. Brooks, 'A Contextual Interpretation of Galatians 3.27', p. 54.

44. For a detailed discussion, see Chapter 8, §§3.3.2 and 3.3.3.

45. Moule, *Worship in the New Testament*, p. 52.

A garment preserves its own identity separate from its wearer's, despite its tendency to be one with its wearer when put on. Similarly, Christ remains different from the baptisand, even though He is metaphorically worn by him or her.

Paul might also think that the clothing-with-Christ metaphor would be readily understood by his readers amongst whom the use of clothing language was not uncommon. Paul probably has in mind Christ and the baptisand's unity idea reflected in the primitive church's baptismal traditions similar to those found in *Gos. Thom.* 37, *Gos. Phil.* 101 and *Epis. Fab.* 19. As was examined in Chapter 7, *Gos. Thom.* 37 implies that a believer enters into the unity relationship with Christ ('the Son of the Living One') through baptism. *Gos. Phil.* 101 implies that the baptisand's robe worn after baptism stands for his having been united with Christ, 'the living man'.[46] In *Epis. Fab.* 19, the phrase 'the garment of Christ' implies that the garment worn by the baptisand after baptism symbolizes the baptisand's union with Christ.

Yet, this imagery also seems to echo the priestly ritual of clothing. In the Pentateuch, Aaron and his sons at their ordination must first take off their garments and wash themselves with water before wearing the priestly garments, and Aaron must perform the same ritual before entering into the sanctuary area, because investiture with the sacred priestly garments signified that the wearer of such garments was unified with a holy God (cf. Exod. 29.4-9 [par. 40.12-15]; Lev. 16.3-4).[47] Perhaps Paul was also familiar with the rituals which Jewish proselytes went through when they were converted to Judaism, which is reflected in *Joseph and Aseneth*. In this document Aseneth's actions for conversion from paganism to Judaism—that is, taking off her idolatrous garments, repenting by being dressed in a black tunic, putting off this black tunic, bathing herself with water, putting on a new linen garment and eventually attiring herself in a wedding garment—symbolize her being united with Judaism. In particular, her wedding garment symbolizes that she has been united with an almost divine figure, that is, Joseph, whom she calls the 'son of God' (6.3, 5). It is also possible that Paul was familiar with the pagan practice of initiation ritual reflected in Apuleius' *Metamorphoses*. In this document the twelve garments, which Lucius wears when he emerges in public after the ritual of initiation, signify that he has been identified with Isis. All these observations support our opinion that the putting-on-Christ imagery in Gal. 3.27 symbolizes a believer's baptismal union with Christ.

2.3.3. Baptismal Participation in Christ's Death-and-Life: Implication of Galatians 2.19-20. As baptism into Christ refers to the spiritual union between the believer and Christ which baptism achieves, an important question emerges: what is the essence of such an identification of the believer with Christ? It is highly probable that Paul has in mind a sort of death-and-life unification, as stated in Gal. 2.20.[48]

---

46. See the terms, 'the living water', 'the living man', and 'this one'.

47. See Chapter 1, §3.3.1.

48. Ziesler, *The Epistle to the Galatians*, p. 50; G. Duncan, *The Epistle of Paul to the Galatians* (London: Hodder & Stoughton, 1939 [1934]), p. 123; cf. M.D. Hooker, *Pauline Pieces* (London: Epworth, 1979), pp. 46-48; Bromiley, 'Aspects of Luther's Doctrine of Baptism', pp. 289-93;

There Paul accepts Christ's death as his own. He believes that he died when Christ died on the cross; his past self does not exist any more, so it is not himself but Christ who lives in him; his present corporeal life is maintained by faith in Christ the Son of God, who sacrificed himself for him; it will eventually be transformed into resurrection life. Paul believes that the relationship between the believer and Christ is characterized by his participation in Christ's death and resurrection. His existence is totally dependent upon Christ: the believer died with Christ, but he is now living with Christ.[49] This is the central thought of Paul's reference to baptism into Christ in Gal. 3.27a. L.E. Keck significantly says that 'baptism "into Christ" was a rite by which one becomes a participant in Christ, the inclusive man (person, not male!), the new Adam (a phrase Paul does not actually use)'.[50] Similarly, D. Lührmann says that 'baptism is…the giving up of one's old identity in death with Christ and acquiring a new one in Christ (cf. Gal. 2.19-20; Rom. 6.1-11)'.[51]

When thus the believer's death-and-life relationship with Christ is considered as the centrepiece of the metaphor 'baptism into Christ' (Gal. 3.27a), the expression 'putting on Christ' (Gal. 3.27b) can also be interpreted in the same vein, that is, the putting on of Christ connotes the entering into a death-and-life relationship with Christ. Yet, can the wearing of Christ match participation in Christ's death-and-life? To answer this question, we need to go back to the statement in Gal. 2.20. In this passage Paul confesses that because his own self has been mortified by his participation in Christ's death on the cross, the present owner of his body is not himself, but Christ who has been raised and at present dwells in him. It is Christ who dominates Paul. When Paul describes this reality with the metaphor of 'putting on

Vogel, 'The First Sacrament', pp. 44-45; H. Ridderbos, *Paul: An Outline of His Theology* (trans. J.R. de Witt; Grand Rapids: Eerdmann, 1975), pp. 207-208.

49. Cf. R.M. Hawkins, 'The Galatian Gospel', *JBL* 59 (1940), pp. 141-46 (144); G. Schneider, *The Epistle to the Galatians* (London: Burns & Oates, 1969), p. 75; R.C. Tannehill, *Dying and Rising with Christ* (Berlin: Verlag Alfred Töpelmann, 1967), pp. 55-61.

50. L.E. Keck, *Paul and His Letters, Proclamation Commentaries* (ed. G. Krodel; Philadelphia: Fortress, 1988), p. 56.

51. Lührmann, *Galatians*, p. 75. In contrast, W.B. Badke points out that there is no explicit reference to the link between baptism and a dying-rising with Christ, and argues that in Galatians there is no connection between them ('Baptism into Moses—Baptized into Christ: A Study in Doctrinal Development', *EQ* 88.1 [1988], pp. 23-29 [especially pp. 24-25]). This view, however, can hardly be supported. As far as faith-justification is concerned, Gal. 2.19-21 corresponds with 3.23-25, which is related to 3.26-27, which speaks of the concept of faith-sonship to God, in Christ and also of the concept of 'being baptized into Christ' as 'putting on Christ'. Clauses such as ἐγὼ... διὰ νόμῳ ἀπέθανον of Gal. 2.19 (which corresponds to Χριστὸς ἡμᾶς ἐξηγόρασεν ἐκ τῆς κατάρας τοῦ νόμου γενόμενος ὑπὲρ ἡμῶν κατά of Gal. 3.13) and Χριστῷ συνεσταύρωμαι of Gal. 2.20 (UBS and Nestle-Aland, *Greek-English New Testament*, includes this clause in v. 19), which is an expansion of ἐγὼ... ἀπέθανον of Gal. 2.19, show an affinity with the baptismal statement of Rom. 6.2-11 (see H. Schlier, *Der Brief an die Galater* [KEKNT, 7; Göttingen: Vandenhoeck & Ruprecht, 1971], pp. 98-101). The statement in Gal. 5.24 that 'those who belong to Christ Jesus have crucified the flesh with its passions and desires' is indicative of the Galatians' attitude of mind when they decided to be baptized (Schlier, *Der Brief an die Galater*, p. 263). The cry of αββα ὁ πατήρ in Gal. 4.6 (cf. Rom. 8.15) is an exclamation breaking out at the moment of being baptized (P.M. Taylor, ' "Abba, Father" and Baptism', *SJT* 11 [1958], pp. 62-71).

Christ', he thinks of a garment dominating its wearer's appearance. As a garment is dominant in expressing its wearer's appearance, so Christ is dominant in Christians' lives. As a garment tends to be identified with its wearer, so Christ becomes one with Christians. As a garment also reveals its wearer's character, so Christ reveals a Christian's character. Yet as a garment maintains a difference from its wearer, so Christ is not equated with Christians; although Christ like a garment clothes Christians, he remains himself and they remain themselves.

In the Old Testament, when the priest clothes himself with the priestly garments, he is not seen as a normal person but as a divine being because of his identification with God's holiness which expresses itself in the sacredness of the priestly garment.[52] In *1 Enoch* 14.20, God who is clothed with radiance and whiteness, namely a 'sunlit-like gown', is called 'the Great Glory'. In *Apoc. Mos.* 20–21 what has remained most impressively in Adam and Eve's memory about their original state is that they were dressed in righteousness and glory. In Philo, the high priest who wears the priestly garments, which are spoken of as being full of cosmological symbolism, is looked on as a microcosm rather than as an ordinary man.[53] Both in *Joseph and Aseneth* and in *The Hymn of the Pearl* every crucial aspect of the protagonist's appearance is symbolized by various kinds of garments.[54] In Apuleius' *Metamorphoses* the appearance of Lucius dressed in twelve lavish garments is not simply one of an ordinary human being but almost of a divine being because of the strong symbolism which tells that he has become one with Isis.[55] The Roman male who wears the *toga virilis* is seen as a mature man, who is entitled to possess an official status.[56] All these instances show how a garment tends to be identified with its wearer, governs its wearer's appearance, reveals its wearer's character, and at the same time continues its own identity without being equated with him or her. For Paul, when Christ is worn like a garment by Christians, his resurrection life thus pervades every aspect of their lives.

Yet, another question emerges: how can clothing be related to the concept of death or the concept of life? As was discussed in an earlier chapter,[57] in Gen. 3.21 Adam's wearing of the garment of skin signals the restoration of his life. In other OT passages (e.g. 2 Chron. 6.41; Ps. 132.16; Isa. 61.10), the expression 'wearing salvation' indicates obtaining life from God. In *Joseph and Aseneth*, Aseneth's wearing 'the black mourning tunic' (10.10a) symbolizes the death of her idolatrous identity, while her putting on 'a new linen robe' (14.12) and a splendid wedding garment afterwards (15.10) points to her having gained a new identity of life. And in *The Hymn of the Pearl*, as the protagonist's eventual investiture with his original self is considered to be the acquisition of salvation, his previous wearing of an Egyptian-style garment probably indicates his state of spiritual death. In Apuleius' *Metamorphoses*, similarly, Lucius the protagonist assesses his previous state, in

52. Cf. Exod. 29 and 40; Lev. 16; Philo, *Vita Mos.* ii.131.
53. Philo, *Vita Mos.* ii.135.
54. See Chapters 3 and 4.
55. See Chapter 5, §2.2.3.
56. See Chapter 6.
57. See Chapter 1, §2.

which he assumed an ass-mask, as death, while he sees his later state of having taken it off and of being in a new garment, as life. All these examples imply that the concept of clothing can be linked with the concept of death or life. That is, one can clothe oneself with a garment that symbolizes death or a garment that symbolizes life. It is likely that, for Paul's audience, the combination of the concept of death or life with the image of clothing would not sound strange. As Paul speaks of believers' union with Christ's death and life (cf. Gal. 2.20) and then refers to the baptized believers' having put on Christ (3.27), his audience probably understands this concept of clothing with Christ as indicating that they have been unified with Christ in his death and life. That is, they probably accept Paul's words as saying that by participating in Christ's death and life, their fallen humanity has been mortified and instead a new humanity has been generated in them.

2.3.4. *Baptismal Union with Christ's Spirit, Righteousness and Status*
2.3.4.1. *Baptismal Union with Christ's Spirit (cf. Galatians 3.1-5, 14; 4.6)*. We note that the believer is spoken of as having received the Spirit (Gal. 3.2, 5, 14; 4.6). As was argued in an earlier section, the concept 'faith' in Gal. 3.26 can be thought of as playing a part in linking Gal. 3.1-25 with 3.27, in that it has a relationship not only with the 'faith'-passages in verses 1–25 but also with verse 27. Of the many references to faith in verses 1–25, the believer's reception of the Spirit by faith (Gal. 3.2, 5; cf. 3.14) should be taken seriously into account when interpreting Gal. 3.27, because it is when the believer receives the Spirit of God's Son that he obtains sonship of God, viz. heirship of His inheritance (Gal. 4.5-7).[58] In fact, the statement about the believer's acquisition of sonship of God through faith in Christ Jesus (Gal. 3.26) and about his being baptized into Christ as putting on Christ (Gal. 3.27), is a reference as to how he has become the heir to God's promise (Gal. 3.29).[59] Furthermore, the thought that 'by faith the Galatian converts have already entered into the experience of the Spirit (Gal. 3.1-5), which is the fulfilment of the promise (Gal. 3.14)',[60] can be related to Gal. 3.26-27. Our point is that the putting on of Christ, which is identified with being baptized into Christ, is obviously associated with the receiving of the Spirit.

J. Bligh argues that 'since in Gal. 2.20–3.5 the indwelling of Christ is practically identified with the infusion of his Spirit, "you have put on Christ" in 3.27 is practically equivalent to "the Spirit of Christ has clothed you" '.[61] This interpretation is highly acceptable, because in Gal. 3.2, 5, 14; 4.6 Paul presents the reception of the Spirit as the most substantial experience of Christ which the believer can have.[62]

---

58. Of course, this presupposes that the Spirit in Gal. 3.2, 5, 14 is identified with the Spirit of God's Son in 4.4. It is worthwhile to note that Paul refers to Christ's dwelling in the believer (Gal. 2.20), then subsequently speaks of the believer's reception of the Spirit (Gal. 3.2, 5). Schneider, *The Epistle to the Galatians*, p. 76: 'the Spirit of God is the Spirit of Christ'.

59. Cf. R.B. Hays, 'Christology and Ethics in Galatians: The Law of Christ', *CBQ* 49 (1987), pp. 268-90 (282-83).

60. Hansen, *Abraham in Galatians*, p. 132; Duncan, *The Epistle of Paul to the Galatians*, p. 123; Hays, *The Faith of Jesus Christ*, p. 231.

61. Bligh, *Galatians*, pp. 325-26.

62. Similarly, J.D.G. Dunn holds that Paul 'would probably equate putting on Christ with

Receiving the Spirit is the essential part of the 'putting on Christ'. When Christ is put on, the Spirit of Christ enters into the believer and occupies his whole being, resulting in the completion of his unification with Christ (cf. Gal. 4.19). Paul seems to draw on the idea of the unity between the Spirit and a human being found in the Old Testament. As was investigated in Part I, in Judg. 6.34, 1 Chron. 12.18 and 2 Chron. 24.20, God's Spirit clothes himself with men, where men come to be instruments through which he demonstrates his tremendous power. As we have suggested, if the Spirit's dwelling in them (Gal. 3.1-4) can be identified with believers' being clothed with Christ (Gal. 3.27), the latter can be regarded as being in harmony with the idea in the above-mentioned OT passages, although the subject and the object of clothing are exchanged. Yet whether the Spirit clothes himself with a specific human being or the opposite, as both delineate the unification between the Divinity and a human being, they can be regarded as indicating the same reality. It is true that the OT passages highlight men's becoming mighty through their union with God's Spirit, while Gal. 3.27 emphasizes believers' obtaining sonship of God through their union with Christ who is the real son of God. In Gal. 3.27 Paul seems to consider that the believer acquires God's sonship by becoming Christ-like, so as to be an inheritor of God's kingdom.

When Paul thinks of Christ's dwelling in believers with his metaphor of clothing with Christ, it is also probable that he has in mind the tendency of a garment to be identified with its wearer. A garment becomes almost part of its wearer, because of its intimate relationship with him or her. As was spoken of in earlier sections, the sacredness of the priestly garment makes the priest who wears it holy. In short, it seems that in the concept of the indwelling of Christ's Spirit, Paul finds a concrete way in which believers are clothed with Christ, that is, united with him. It is also probable that Paul has in mind the character of a garment which cannot be completely equated with its wearer, despite its tendency to become one with him or her. Although Christ wraps believers like clothes (in other words, although Christ's Spirit dwells in them), both Christ and believers do not lose their own identity. There is a paradoxical element in the imagery of putting on Christ.

2.3.4.2. Baptismal Union with Christ's Righteousness (cf. Galatians 3.24-26). The rite of baptism that lies behind the metaphor of being baptized into Christ is a rite of immersion.[63] Washing is one of the cardinal elements in this rite. It signifies the spiritual cleansing of sins in the baptized. The washing is performed in the name of Christ Jesus. This means that the baptisand enters into a state of oneness with Christ. As Paul states that he obtains justification by faith in Christ Jesus (Gal. 3.24-26), the essence of the state of oneness is the baptisand's incorporation into Christ's righteousness. His wearing of a garment after being baptized stands for his incorporation into Christ's righteousness. It is, therefore, natural that the baptisand

---

receiving the Spirit of Christ' (Dunn, *Baptism in the Holy Spirit*, p. 110). Yet we need to remember that as a metaphor 'putting on Christ' cannot be totally synonymous with receiving the Spirit of Christ. When these two concepts are regarded as entirely the same, there is the danger of diminishing the significance of the metaphor, which may deviate from Paul's intention.

    63. See Chapter 7.

has been clothed with Christ. Paul probably has in mind the priestly garments in the Pentateuch. The scheme of the baptisand's washing-then-wearing of a new garment is similar to the priest's practice of washing-then-wearing of the priestly garments, which symbolizes sacredness (Exod. 29.4-9; 40.12-15; Lev. 16.3-4). To Christians, Christ is the priestly garment which is holy. To wear Christ is to be infused with his priestly sacredness, in other words, with his righteousness (cf. Ps. 132.9).

When Paul speaks of 'incorporation into Christ's righteousness' as 'clothing with Christ', he also seems to think of the high priest Joshua's filthy clothes being replaced with new garments (Zech. 3.3-5). Before he is clothed with these new garments, his sins are taken away. When he becomes pure, he can be invested with the sacred garments.

In addition, it is also probable that Paul has in mind the occasion when people change their clothes, that is, when their bodies are not clean, they cleanse themselves in water and then put on a clean new garment. A cleansed body corresponds to a new garment. To Christians, Christ is an immaculate new garment. Putting Christ on him indicates that they have obtained his priestly righteousness.

2.3.4.3. *Baptismal Union with Christ's Sonship of God (cf. Galatians 3.16, 26, 29; 4.1-7).* A consistent issue in Galatians 3 is the identity of the heir of God's inheritance. The metaphor of putting on Christ eventually becomes part of this issue. Paul insists that only those who belong to Christ, who is Abraham's seed, and who has received the covenant of promise (Gal. 3.16), can inherit God's kingdom (cf. Gal. 3.26, 29; 4.1-7). Belonging to Christ can be achieved by faith in Jesus Christ and not by the Law. Only faith in him can infuse a person with Christ's righteousness; only righteousness can make them partake in Christ's sonship of God (cf. Gal. 3.21-25). To obtain this sonship of God means acquiring heirship with him (cf. Gal. 3.26). In this thought, participation in Christ's sonship refers to attaining a status as God's child.

Why does Paul portray participation in Christ's sonship of God as 'putting on Christ'? Probably he bears in mind one of the attributes of a garment, that is, that it tends to reflect its wearer's social status. Of course, in modern society, if a person is not wearing a clearly recognizable uniform, discerning his or her social status by the clothing he or she wears is almost impossible. But in the society of Paul's day, it is likely that the differentiation between social classes was quite distinctive;[64] thereby, a garment reflected its wearer's social status.[65] For example, the wearing of the *toga virilis* indicated the significant transition from youth to manhood.[66] The *toga virilis* indicated full Roman citizenship, with the right to enter a social, political, military or religious office. For Paul, Christ is a kind of *toga virilis*; for

---

64. Cf. Gal. 3.28; 1 Cor. 7.20-24; 12.13; Col. 3.11. In particular, Paul in Philemon 1 speaks of Onesimus who used to be a slave in the family of Philemon.

65. See Chapter 6, where the custom of Roman apparel is explained. Cf. J.J. Meggitt, *Paul, Poverty and Survival* (ed. J. Barclay, J. Marcus and J. Riches; SNTIW; Edinburgh: T. & T. Clark, 1998), p. 61.

66. See Chapter 6.

believers, to clothe themselves with Christ means that they obtain God's sonship, namely his heirship, resulting from baptismal identification with Christ, which is a significant change similar to the change from boyhood to manhood.

2.3.5. Baptismal Identification with Christ as the New Adam: Implications of the Connection between Galatians 3.27-28 and 6.15. As the metaphor ἐνδύσασθαι Χριστόν (3.27b) plays the role of specifying the metaphor βαπτίσθῆναι εἰς Χριστόν (3.27a), the former could be called an 'exegetical expression' for the latter.[67] The expression ἐνδύσασθαι Χριστόν is peculiar in that it includes an idea that a person puts on another person. For Paul, baptismal union with Christ signifies that a believer puts on Christ as his or her garment. The baptisand becomes a totally new being in union with Christ; he shares in the being of Christ; he is a new creation.[68] As a garment envelops its wearer and 'identifies his appearance and his life',[69] so Christ wraps the believer's being and dominates his person. The metaphor does not merely picture the change in the believer's external appearance or something related to his own being; it pictures Christ himself becoming that person's own self (Gal. 2.20). That is to say, putting on Christ by being baptized into Christ indicates 'a transformation of personal status, a being put "into Christ" and a taking on the character of Christ'.[70] G. Ebeling rightly says that:

> Those who have put on Christ have put off their own selves, they are released and set free from themselves. They look upon themselves as being past and as being totally incorporated into the future that has already begun with being in Christ.[71]

If so, who is 'Christ' with whom the baptized has been clothed; in other words, with whom he has been united? To this question, the passage does not give any obvious explanation. Therefore, it would be reasonable to probe the issue by depending on parallel passages. Above all, Gal. 6.15 is likely to provide an important clue to our question.[72] 'For neither circumcision counts for anything, nor uncircumcision, but a new creation'. This echoes the statement of 3.28 in a roundabout manner; the contrast between Jew and Greek (3.28) must correspond with the contrast between circumcision and uncircumcision (6.15).[73] In fact, a statement similar to 6.15 is seen earlier in 5.6. When Paul declares that in Christ Jesus neither circumcision nor uncircumcision has any value (5.6), he probably has in mind the earlier triple contrasts (Jew/Greek, slave/free and male/female), especially the contrast between

67. H.N. Ridderbos, *The Epistle of Paul to the Churches of Galatia* (London: Marshall, Morgan & Scott, 1976 [3rd edn, 1967]), p. 148.
68. Cf. Schneider, *The Epistle to the Galatians*, p. 75.
69. Ridderbos, *The Epistle of Paul to the Churches of Galatia*, p. 148.
70. J.D.G. Dunn, *The New Testament Theology: The Theology of Paul's Letter to the Galatians* (Cambridge: Cambridge University Press, 1993), p. 119.
71. G. Ebeling, *The Truth of the Gospel: An Exposition of Galatians* (Philadelphia: Fortress, 1985 [1912]), pp. 212-13.
72. See J.A.D. Weima, 'Gal. 6.11-18: A Hermeneutical Key to the Galatian Letter', *CTJ* 28 (1993), pp. 90-107; Hays, *The Faith of Jesus Christ*, p. 232.
73. Concerning the contrast between circumcision and uncircumcision, see Weima, 'Gal. 6.11-18', pp. 100-101.

Jew and Greek, in 3.28. Paul looks on circumcision as a distinguishing mark of Jews who are obligated to obey the whole Law (cf. 5.3), that Law whose function as a pedagogue is considered to have ended with the coming of faith (cf. 3.23-25; 4.1-5).

In Gal. 6.15 (cf. 5.6), Paul argues for the importance of the fact that the Christian is a new creation who is re-shaped in Christ.[74] For the Christian, what is of crucial importance is not whether he is circumcised or uncircumcised, but the fact that he is re-created in Christ. If this idea is at work in 3.28,[75] it may operate also in 3.27, because both are closely associated with each other. The putting on of Christ by being baptized into Christ is unmistakably in line with the idea of the oneness of all in Christ, where there is a going beyond the distinctions between Jew and Greek, slave and free, and male and female.

When Paul refers to the believer's putting on of Christ on the grounds of baptism into Christ, he probably has in mind the idea of re-creation. That is to say, the believer's entry into the new life in union with Christ, which is described by the twin metaphors of baptism into Christ and putting on Christ in Gal. 3.27, indicates that he is re-formed as a new creation. R.P. Carlson argues that

> baptism…means that one is inaugurated into the new creation (cf. 6.14-15) whose boundaries are defined by Christ because, in baptism, Christians are incorporated into and put on Christ.[76]

This may be supported by the fact that Col. 3.9-11, which is in parallel with Gal. 3.26-29,[77] contains the metaphor of the putting on of the new man (which is probably associated with baptism),[78] who is defined as a figure who experiences an ongoing renewal in knowledge after the image of his Creator (cf. Gen. 1.26-27). Even in texts such as Gal. 2.20; 3.27; 4.6-7, in fact, 'the unspoken assumption is that the risen Christ is the image of God, that is, the pattern of what God intended for humankind'.[79] As we discussed previously, if *The Gospel of Thomas* 37 can indeed be regarded as containing baptismal connotations, it implies that the baptisand's taking off of his former garment before baptism and putting on of a new garment after baptism symbolizes that he has replaced his old identity with a new one, which is equivalent to Adam's original identity of being unashamed of his nakedness.

---

74. B.D. Chilton, 'Galatians 6.15: A Call to Freedom before God', *ExpT* 89 (1977–78), pp. 311-13. Cf. Weima, 'Gal. 6.11-18', pp. 101-102, who sees καινὴ κτίστις (v. 15) as carrying the sense of 'the new age'. He considers καινὴ κτίστις as being opposed to κόσμος (v. 14), which for him means 'the present evil age' (Gal. 1.4; cf. 4.3, 9), but Paul never treats them as antithetical concepts. Rather, καινὴ κτίστις seems to indicate a 'new humanity' which has been created in believers.

75. Chilton, 'Galatians 6.15', p. 313.

76. Carlson, 'The Role of Baptism in Paul's Thought', p. 259.

77. B. Witherington, 'Rite and Rights for Women—Galatians 3.28', *NTS* 27 (1981), pp. 593-604 (598); cf. Bligh, *Galatians*, p. 326; W.A. Meeks, 'The Image of the Androgyne: Some Uses of a Symbol in Earliest Christianity', *History of Religions* 13.3 (1974), pp. 165-208 (180-183) argues that Gal. 3.28; 1 Cor. 12.13; Col. 3.10-11 shows 'the consistency of the major motifs', i.e. baptism into Christ, garment imagery, pairs of opposites, and concluding statement of unity.

78. See Chapter 9, §2.3.2.

79. Dunn, *The New Testament Theology*, p. 120.

If it is thus obvious that the creation motif stands behind Gal. 3.26-29, it seems to be legitimate to assume that the metaphor of 'putting on Christ' is controlled by the Adamic Christ motif.[80] D.A. Oepke believes that the metaphor presupposes the eschatological idea of Christ as the second Adam.[81] G.E. Sterling also asserts that in Gal. 3.28 the departure from the οὐχ…οὐδέ pattern (in the first two clauses) to the οὐκ…καί pattern (in the third clause) is 'in order to echo the language of Gen. 1.27', which reads ἄρσεν καὶ θῆλυ ἐποίησεν αὐτούς (LXX).[82] Similarly N.A. Dahl argues that the removal of conflict between ἄρσεν and θῆλυ in Christ means that Christ, as the image of God, plays a part as 'the prototype of redeemed mankind'.[83]

In Gal. 6.14, when Paul speaks of a new creation resulting from the work of the cross of Jesus Christ and a person's being united with Christ (cf. Gal. 6.17), he probably has in mind the effect of Adam's fall, which has been passed on to every human being. Insofar as this is true, it is probable that the putting-on-Christ metaphor in Gal. 3.27 describes what the new creation has brought about in the believer,[84] that is, a radical change from the Adamic to the Christ-like. The believer used to resemble the fallen Adam, but he has been re-created in Christ. The old nature of the fallen Adam, which used to occupy his being, has now been replaced by the new nature of Christ.[85] He has put on Christ as his garment; he is now governed by a Christ-like character.

With the clothing-with-Christ metaphor, what Paul primarily wishes to describe is that every believer begins to belong to Christ as the counter-figure of Adam, by being incorporated into Him in baptism. All Christians are together included in Christ's corporate personality. As there exists one united body inside a garment if the body is clothed by it, so there is one united Christian community in Christ if it is endued with him. As a garment, Christ encloses all Christians and represents them. This thought can be compared with the priest's garment which symbolizes all Israelites. That garment, it will be remembered, includes two shoulder pieces with two onyx stones engraved with the names of the sons of Israel, that is, six names

80. R. Scroggs, *The Last Adam: A Study in Pauline Anthropology* (Oxford: Basil Blackwell, 1966), p. xxiv believes that Paul's 'Adamic Christology is primarily directed by his awareness and reinterpretation of Jewish Adamic myths'.

81. D.A. Oepke, *Der Brief des Paulus and die Galater* (THKNT; Leipzig: Deichertsche Verlagsbuchhandlung, 1937), p. 320.

82. G.E. Sterling, ' "Wisdom Among the Perfect": Creation Traditions in Alexandrian Judaism and Corinthian Christianity', *NovT* 37 (1995), pp. 355-84 (378-79); N.A. Dahl, *Studies in Paul: Theology for the Early Christian Mission* (Minneapolis: Augsburg, 1977), p. 133.

83. Dahl, *Studies in Paul*, p. 133. Witherington, 'Rite and Rights for Women', pp. 597-98 holds that 'the adjectives ἄρσεν and θῆλυ are not the ordinary terms used to speak of man and woman, but they are specifically used to emphasize the gender distinction, male and female'.

84. Dow, 'Galatians', p. 1215.

85. Remembering that Galatians presents Christ Jesus as a figure who enables all believers to become heirs of God's promise which was given to Abraham and his seed Jesus Christ, one may ask how the idea of an Adamic Christ can be in accordance with the idea of his being the issue of Abraham. To this we would answer by quoting Bligh, *Galatians*, p. 327: they can be easily combined, because 'the blessing promised to Abraham's issue in Gen. 12.3 takes away the curse pronounced upon Eve and her issue in Gen. 3'.

on each (Exod. 28.9-10), as well as a breastpiece of decision with four rows of three different precious stones which stand for the twelve tribes (Exod. 28.15-21). When the priest is dressed in the priestly garment, he is identified with the whole Israel. Here the garment functions as if it encompassed the whole of Israel.

Further, the concept of Christ as the believers' garment embracing them as a whole perhaps draws on the clothing traditions reflected in the Johannine image of ὁ χιτὼν ἄραφος,[86] which is not torn (Jn 19.23-24), since it symbolizes the 'unity among Jesus' followers'.[87] Further, it is also possible that Paul has in mind the idea of a garment in the mystery religions, which is reflected in such symbolism as that of the new linen garment which was worn by Aseneth after she repented; when she was dressed in it, the heavenly man declared that her name shall be 'the City of Refuge' (15.7), which signifies all those people who will follow the way of her conversion from paganism to Judaism.[88]

Accordingly, we can affirm that when Paul uses the metaphor of putting on Christ (Gal. 3.27), he bears in mind Christian unity as Christ's body and Christ as its representative. This signifies that the metaphor involves an ecclesiological significance; I will discuss this issue further in the following section.[89] All human beings are born with Adam's fallen nature, but this fallen nature is to be restored to Adam's original pure nature or even to something greater than that.[90] This happens when they put on Christ by being baptized into Christ. At baptism, which accomplishes union with Christ, the believer divests himself of the old Adamic identity and instead invests himself with the new Christ-like identity.

2.3.6. Baptismal Incorporation into Ecclesial Oneness in Christ: 'All One in Christ Jesus' and 'Christ's' (Galatians 3.28-29). In the preceding section,[91] I pointed out that the metaphor of putting-on-Christ in Gal. 3.27 indicates that the Adamic Christ represents all believers and that this connotes that the metaphor has ecclesiological significance. There is no doubt that the strands of thought in Gal. 3.28-29 are in line with Gal. 3.26-27. R.N. Longenecker contends,

> the main expression of this section [Gal. 3.26-29] is 'in Christ Jesus' (ἐν Χριστῶι Ἰησοῦ, vv. 26, 28) with 'baptized into Christ' (εἰς Χριστὸν ἐμαπτίσθητε, v. 27), 'clothed with Christ' (Χριστὸν ἐνεδύσασθε, v. 27) and '[being] of Christ' (Χριστοῦ, v. 29) used in synonymous fashion.[92]

---

86. This is identified with ἱατισμός in LXX Ps. 22.18 [19, HB]) and is different from Jesus' other 'clothes' (rendered ἱμάτια in Jn 19.23a), of which the soldiers made four parts; see R.E. Brown, *The Death of the Messiah: From Gethsemane to the Grave. A Commentary on the Passion Narratives in the Four Gospels*, II (ABRL; New York: Doubleday, 1994), p. 955.

87. See Brown, *The Death of the Messiah*, pp. 957-58.

88. See Chapter 3, §2.3.

89. See §2.3.6, below.

90. Cf. Ridderbos, *Paul*, p. 225.

91. See §2.3.5, above.

92. Longenecker, *Galatians*, p. 151; cf. Burton, *Galatians*, p. 208; Hansen, *Abraham in Galatians*, p. 136; C.B. Cousar, *Galatians, Interpretation: A Bible Commentary for Teaching and Preaching* (Louisville: John Knox Press, 1982), p. 84.

In the baptismal society, which is covered by the same garment, viz. Christ,[93] there can be no ethnic (Jew and Greek[94]), social (slave and free), or sexual (male and female) divisions (v. 28).[95] It does not seem to be an accident that these three pairs of contrasts follow the metaphors of baptismal language (v. 27). In 1 Cor. 12.13 the pairings follow the reference to the baptismal language,[96] and in Col. 3.11 pairings are in an indirect manner associated with the concept of baptism (cf. Col. 2.12; 3.8-9).[97] Longenecker affirms that the pattern of pairings might be fixed 'at least in Paul's mind and probably as well in the early church', since the same pairings frequently occur in a number of other Pauline passages in either abbreviated or expanded form (e.g. 1 Cor. 7.17-28; 12.13; Col. 3.11).[98] H.D. Betz believes that Gal. 3.27-28 was 'originally part of a baptismal confession of early Christians'.[99]

In particular, we note that Gal. 3.28-29 includes the concepts, πάντες γὰρ ὑμεῖς εἷς ἐστε ἐν Χριστῷ Ἰησοῦ (v. 28) and ὑμεῖς Χριστοῦ (v. 29). These concepts are linked not only with the thought of the believer's union with the Adamic Christ in baptism (v. 27), but also with the thought of the acquisition of God's sonship through faith in Christ Jesus (v. 26).[100] For Paul, those who are baptized into Christ

93. Cf. K. Kertelge, *'Rechtfertigung' bei Paulus* (Münster: Aschendorff, 1967), p. 239.

94. Regarding this ethnic discrimination, see C.D. Stanley, ' "Neither Jew Nor Greek": Ethnic Conflict in Graeco-Roman Society', *JSNT* 64 (1966), pp. 101-124.

95. Carlson, 'The Role of Baptism in Paul's Thought', p. 259; E.K. Simpson, *Commentary on the Epistles to the Ephesians and the Colossians* (ed. F.F. Bruce; NICNT; Grand Rapids: Eerdmans, 1972 [1957]), p. 275: 'in Gal. 3.28 the choice of antithesis is apparently made with a view to overthrowing the threefold privilege which a pious Jew recalls morning by morning when he thanks God that he did not make him a Gentile, a slave or a woman' (A.Z. Idelsohn, *Jewish Liturgy and Its Development* [New York: Henry Holst, 1932], pp. 75-76 holds that this Jewish morning prayer is taken from *b. Ber.* 60b; cf. *b. Menaḥ.* 43b and *y. Ber.* ix.2; see S. Singer [trans.], *The Authorized Daily Prayer Book* [London: Eyre and Spottiswoode, 1962], pp. 5-7; concerning how the first Jewish prayer-book evolved, see S.C. Reif, *Judaism and Hebrew Prayer: New Perspectives on Jewish Liturgical History* [Cambridge: Cambridge University Press, 1993], pp. 122-52); Martin Luther, *A Commentary on St. Paul's Epistle to the Galatians: A Revised and Completed Translation Based on the 'Middleton' Text Prepared by P.S. Watson* (Cambridge: Clarke, 1978 [1953]; first German edn, 1535), p. 341; also see Longenecker, *Galatians*, p. 157; Bligh, *Galatians*, p. 322; M. Boucher, 'Some Unexplored Parallels to 1 Cor. 11, 11-12 and Gal. 3, 28: The NT on the Role of Women', *CBQ* 31 (1969), pp. 50-58 (53); Witherington, 'Rite and Rights for Women', p. 594; A. Richardson, *An Introduction to the Theology of the New Testament* (London: SCM Press, 1979 [1958]), p. 246 believes that the Adam motif permeates the three-fold antitheses in Gal. 3.28: 'though in Gal. 3.28 the name of Adam is not mentioned, the Adam-typology is not far beneath the surface: "There can be neither Jew nor Greek (as Adam was neither), bond nor free (Adam was God's free man), male nor female ("Adam" is common gender): πάντες γὰρ ὑμεῖς εἷς ἐστε ἐν Χριστῷ Ἰησοῦ" '.

96. E. Best, *One Body in Christ: A Study in the Relationship of the Church to Christ in the Epistles of the Apostle Paul* (London: SPCK, 1955), p. 73: 'the baptism of 1 Cor. 12.13, by which we are added to the one Body, is not water baptism but baptism in the Spirit; water baptism is the sign and seal of this latter baptism—just as in Rom. 6.1-14 water baptism does not effect our death and resurrection with Christ, which took place upon the cross, but is the sign and seal of it to us'.

97. See Chapter 9, §2.3.2.

98. Longenecker, *Galatians*, pp. 154-55.

99. Betz, *Galatians*, pp. 184-85.

100. Hansen, *Abraham in Galatians*, p. 136. The parallelism between v. 26 and v. 28d is remarkable:

and so put on Christ are no other persons than those who are all one in Christ Jesus (v. 28, πάντες γὰρ ὑμεῖς εἷς ἐστε ἐν Χριστῷ Ἰησοῦ) or those who belong to Christ (v. 29, ὑμεῖς Χριστοῦ).[101] The believers, who are united with the one person, Christ Jesus, through baptism, become one corporate identity in him, and so belong to him.[102] All believers are included in one baptismal reality which is subject to Christ (cf. Eph. 4.4-5). They form one collective community which is represented by Christ.[103]

It is highly probable that this idea of inclusiveness in Christ has an ecclesial significance.[104] The putting-on-of-Christ does not merely point to an individual's unification with Christ but also to the whole group of believers' incorporation into Him. R.A. Cole argues that 'Paul is going to apply to the collective whole of the Christian Church that which he has previously predicated of Christ in person—the inheritance of the Abrahamic promise'.[105] In Gal. 1.22 Paul makes use of the expression ταῖς ἐκκλησίαις...ἐν Χριστῷ ('the churches...in Christ'). It is true that 'the churches' indicate a number of individual local churches. But this expression signifies that the Christian community collectively exists in Christ; all Christians are corporately dependent upon him, in solidarity with him.

In brief, in its closeness to 'all one in Christ' and 'Christ's' (Gal. 3.28, 29), the putting-on-Christ imagery indicates that in baptism believers enter into ecclesiological oneness in Christ, who is the corporate person as the new Adam. As a garment wraps the whole of its wearer's body, Christ envelops the church community as a whole,[106] which may be called a transcendental collective humanity free of discrimination.

---

26 πάντες γὰρ υἱοὶ θεοῦ ἐστε διὰ τῆς πίστεως ἐν Χριστῷ Ἰησοῦ
28d πάντες γὰρ ὑμεῖς εἷς ἐστε   ἐν Χριστῷ Ἰησοῦ

Betz, *Galatians*, p. 200 rightly points out that the former emphasizes inclusiveness, while the latter stresses oneness (cf. 1.1, 10-12, one apostle/1.6-9; 2.7-8; 5.14, one gospel/3.16, oneness of Christ/3.20, oneness of God).

101. In Gal. 3.29 Paul uses a singular noun, 'seed' (σπέρμα), as a complement of the verb, '[you] are' (ἐστέ). At first glance this seems strange, because the verb is plural. However, by using such a contradiction Paul seems to make the point that Galatians are collectively one in union with Christ. J. Barclay, *Obeying the Truth: A Study of Paul's Ethics in Galatians* (Edinburgh: T. & T. Clark, 1988), p. 90 says that 'it is only those who belong to Christ who can truly be called Abraham's seed in the corporate sense (3.29)'.

102. In his comment on Gal. 3.28, J.B. Lightfoot, *St. Paul's Epistle to the Galatians* (London: Macmillan, 10th edn, 1890 [1865]), p. 146 speaks dramatically: 'One heart beats in all; one mind guides all; one life is lived by all. Ye are all one man, for ye are members of Christ'.

103. Cf. Burton, *Galatians*, p. 207; Fung, *The Epistle to the Galatians*, p. 176; Sanders, 'Galatians', p. 976.

104. 'All' (πάντες, Gal. 3.26), 'as many of you as' (ὅσοι, Gal. 3.27), and 'all' (πάντες, Gal. 3.28) seem to be in a consistent vein and to convey an ecclesiological nuance; see Ridderbos, *The Epistle of Paul to the Churches of Galatia*, pp. 147, 149-50; Guthrie (ed.), *Galatians*, p. 115.

105. R.A. Cole, *The Epistle of Paul to the Galatians: An Introduction and Commentary* (Grand Rapids: Eerdmans, 1975 [1965]), p. 111; cf. Best, *One Body in Christ*, p. 69.

106. See end part of §2.3.5, above.

2.3.7. *Concluding Remarks.* In Gal. 3.26-29, the putting-on-Christ metaphor is involved in the actual picture of contemporary baptism. For Paul, being a Christian is to assume Christ through baptismal union with Him. Believers are in baptism identified with Christ's death and life. Yet, the analogy of Adam–Christ stands behind this concept. Therefore, to be united with Christ in baptism (in other words, to put on Christ) does not simply point to ritual initiation into Christ, but also to incorporation into Christ as the new Adam. This suggests that putting on Christ indicates restoration to the original Adamic nature; basically, the putting-on-Christ metaphor seems to presuppose Adam's pre-Fall clothing, which seems to have been prevalent in the Jewish Adam traditions similar to those found in, for example, *Apoc. Mos.* 20–21; *Gen. Rab.* 20.12; *The Hymn of the Pearl.* Yet it is highly probable that the metaphor is also influenced by Paul's recognition of other clothing images found in a number of Old Testament clothing passages; he seems to be influenced by his understanding of the priestly garments (cf. Exod. 28–29). As he uses the concept of a believer's (a person) being clothed with Christ (other person), he also appears to make use of the concept of God's clothing of a specific person for his own purpose (cf. Judg. 6.34; 1 Chron. 12.18; 2 Chron. 24.20). He also seems to have in mind a Roman male's replacement of the *toga praetexta* with the *toga virilis*, which signifies a change in his status. It is also possible that he has in mind various clothing rituals of mystery religions, which are reflected in Apuleius' *Metamorphoses.* Further, as the Adam–Christ typology operates behind the concept of baptismal unity, it is implied that putting-on-Christ does not simply refer to the unification between Christ and an individual but also to the one between Christ and all believers as a whole.

2.4. *Some Contextual Emphases*

2.4.1. *Introductory Remarks.* In the context to which Gal. 3.27 belongs, some specific theological emphases are outstanding, so they influence the significance of the imagery of clothing-with-Christ. Soteriological indications are explicit in Gal. 3; eschatological implications are prominent not only in the unit, Gal. 3.19-23, with which Gal. 3.27 is closely associated, but also in the passage which follows it, that is, Gal. 4.1-7. An understanding of these elements will help to interpret the metaphor of putting-on-Christ in Gal. 3.27.

2.4.2. *Soteriological Elements (Galatians 3).* The double imagery in Galatians 3.27, that is, baptism into Christ and investiture with Christ, seems to be controlled by a specific theological outlook. Soteriological indications are explicit in the whole of Gal. 3. Gal. 3.27 needs to be seen from its close relationship with the two-fold phrase διὰ τῆς πίστεως ἐν Χριστῷ Ἰησοῦ in Gal. 3.26. It is unlikely that these two phrases form a single idea; rather, it seems that each connotes a separate idea, that is, it is 'through faith' and 'in Christ'[107] that believers have become God's children.

---

107. H.A.W. Meyer, *Critical and Exegetical Handbook to the Epistle to the Galatians* (Edinburgh: T. & T. Clark, 1873), p. 206, who argues that ἐν Χριστῷ Ἰησοῦ belongs to πίστεως, so for him, ἡ πίστις ἐν Χριστῷ, as the phrase 'to form one idea', manifests the sense of 'the faith resting in Christ'. AV,

Of course, although this is the case, there is little doubt that the 'faith' of the first phrase points to 'faith in Jesus Christ (cf. Gal. 3.22f, 25)'.[108] Believers obtain justification by faith and come to be identified with Christ. Those who are ἐν Χριστῷ Ἰησοῦ 'are united with him, participate in him, are incorporated into him'.[109] In particular, we note the phrase διὰ τῆς πίστεως, because in Gal. 3.1-26 the concept of 'faith' is consistently emphasized. It is true that in Gal. 3.27 the concept does not occur, but it must be presupposed in the verse, as εἰς Χριστόν (v. 27) is in an inseparable relationship with ἐν Χριστῷ (v. 26)[110] which is closely connected with the concept of 'faith'.

The significance of faith in Gal. 3.26 can be properly understood by investigating 'faith' in Gal. 3.1-25. It is, of course, unlikely that every reference to 'faith' in Gal. 3.1-25 is directly involved in Gal. 3.27. However, at least the interpenetration between the ideas of faith and redemption[111] cannot be overlooked in terms of the passage's interpretation. As a matter of fact, when Paul emphasizes that it is from faith that believers receive justification, the Abrahamic promise, heirship, adoption

NASV, and NIV also take the two phrases as a combined unit. However, the phrase ἐν Χριστῷ Ἰησοῦ does not seem to present the object of the Christian's faith. This view is maintained by RV, RSV and NEB which take the two phrases as modifying 'you are all sons of God' independently of each other. In evidence, the rare employment of ἐν which immediately follows πίστεως (see, however, Col. 1.4; Eph. 1.15) and Paul's consistent use of the genitive in Galatians (Gal. 2.16, 20; 3.22) imply that ἐν Χριστῷ Ἰησοῦ does not limit πίστεως; furthermore, Gal. 3.27-28 'takes up and dwells upon the fact that the Galatians are in Christ Jesus' (Burton, *Galatians*, p. 202). In conclusion, we see ἐν Χριστῷ Ἰησοῦ in Gal. 3.26 as the characteristic Pauline formula which functions as adverbial words.

108. Fung, *The Epistle to the Galatians*, p. 171. Some see that τῆς πίστεως ἐν Χριστῷ Ἰησοῦ refers to 'faith of Christ', that is, 'faith (which resides) in Christ' (e.g. G. Howard, *Paul: Crisis in Galatia: A Study in Early Christian Theology* [SNTSMS, 35; Cambridge: Cambridge University Press, 1979], p. 97). However, the preposition ἐν would not fit the rendering of 'of'. Further, the context, to which Gal. 3.26 belongs, would not allow such a view, because it emphasizes that it is by faith in Christ Jesus and not by observance of the Law that the believer is to obtain salvation (cf. Gal. 3.2, 5, 8, 9, 11, 14). The interpretation of πίστεως ἐν Χριστῷ Ἰησοῦ as 'faith of Christ' breaks the contextual flow. Even verses which use such expressions as διὰ πίστεως Ἰησοῦ Χριστοῦ and ἐκ πίστεως Χριστοῦ (Gal. 2.16), ἐν πίστει ζῶ τῇ τοῦ υἱοῦ τοῦ θεοῦ (Gal. 2.20) and ἐκ πίστεως Ἰησοῦ Χριστοῦ (Gal. 3.22) are to be best understood from the viewpoint of 'faith of the believer'. Further advancing of this issue will be beyond the present study.

109. Bruce, *The Epistle to the Galatians*, p. 184; also see Cole, *The Epistle of Paul to the Galatians*, p. 109; Grayston, *The Epistles to the Galatians and to the Philippians*, p. 47. Longenecker considers that the eight occurrences of the 'in Christ' motif in Galatians can be divided into three groups (*Galatians*, p. 153): (1) Gal. 1.22—a corporate sense, (2) Gal. 2.17; 3.14; 5.10—an instrumental sense, and (3) Gal. 2.4; 3.26, 28; 5.6—a local sense. This classification seems to suggest that in each passage the formula manifests only a single meaning. But relevant texts would not support this. For instance, the 'in Christ' of Gal. 1.22 can be considered as manifesting a local sense as well, and the phrase not only of Gal. 3.26 (note emphatic πάντες) but also of 3.28 can be regarded as including a corporate sense. It is likely that in each text the 'in Christ' formula possesses a leading significance which is primarily manifested, and at the same time possesses the other significances together (cf. Burton, *Galatians*, pp. 202-203).

110. Cf. Dunn, *The Epistle to the Galatians*, p. 203: if 'in Christ' can be compared with an effect, 'into Christ' can be considered as a means which brings about the effect; the state of being 'in Christ' is achieved by entering 'into Christ'; Best, *One Body in Christ*, pp. 65-66, 70, 73.

111. Paul uses the word ἐξηγόρασεν in Gal. 3.13.

as children of God, and the Spirit, his fundamental concern is indeed with salvation itself. In Gal. 3.1-25 Paul significantly contrasts faith with the concept of 'law'. He consistently highlights that faith is superior to Law in salvific function. For him, it is faith in Christ and not the Law that enables one to become God's son, namely, an heir to his inheritance. The fundamental thought at the heart of this argument is one as to who is included in the covenantal genealogy from Abraham to Christ.[112] Paul's concentration on this problem seems to be natural, because according to his reading of Genesis God promised Abraham and his seed, that is, Christ (Gal. 3.16), that they would enjoy what he would bestow on them (cf. Gen. 13.14-17; 17.1-10; 22.18). Whether or not one can join the genealogy of Abraham–Christ determines whether one can join the main stream of the history of salvation.[113]

In a number of passages Paul evidently refers to the soteriological significance of faith. Paul states that the principle of life by faith does not allow anyone to be justified by the Law (v. 11). For him, the Law does not depend upon faith, for he who observes the Law's requirements shall live by them (v. 12). He also asserts that by suffering a curse on the cross for his people Christ redeemed them from the curse of the Law (v. 13). Here Christ's suffering obviously concerns the salvation of his people. All these points imply that Paul's discussion on faith (in comparison with Law) is controlled by his soteriological perspective. R.B. Hays rightly asserts that the argument in Gal. 3.1-14 is directed by the leading thought in Gal. 3.15-29, that is, 'participation in Christ', which is 'the controlling soteriological motif'.[114]

If so, it is legitimate to infer that in its relation to the words 'through faith in Christ Jesus' in Gal. 3.26, the imagery of baptismal investiture with Christ in 3.27 delineates an aspect of the realization of God's salvation. Christians are those who have joined the genealogy from Abraham to Christ, who stand at the centre of redemptive history. The concept of clothing with the soteriological Christ seems to echo several Old Testament passages. For instance, in 2 Chron. 6.41, after having

112. Brooks, 'A Contextual Interpretation of Galatians 3.27', pp. 47-50.

113. Hays, *The Faith of Jesus Christ*, p. 233 thinks Gal. 3.1–4.11 forms a unit in which Paul makes 'a unified attempt to think through the implications of a gospel story in which salvation hinges upon the faithfulness of Jesus Christ'; cf. Fung, *The Epistle to the Galatians*, pp. 177-78. On the other hand, J.L. Martyn, 'Events in Galatia: Modified Covenantal Nomism versus God's Invasion of the Cosmos in the Singular Gospel. A Response to J.D.G. Dunn and B.R. Gaventa', in J.M. Bassler (ed.), *Pauline Theology* I: *Thessalonians, Philippians, Galatians, Philemon* (Minneapolis: Fortress, 1991), pp. 160-79 (especially pp. 172-74) argues that the covenantal promise given to Abraham remained 'in a sort of docetic state' prior to the advent of Christ, i.e. Abraham's singular seed, so there is no 'Heilsgeschichte as a view that encompasses a linear history of a people of God prior to Christ', 'there is no affirmation of a salvific linearity prior to the advent of Christ'. However, this is hardly acceptable, because the singular σπέρμα does not mean that there is no people of God in the period between Abraham and Christ. Rather the word highlights that Christ is the only figure in whom God's promises, which were given to Abraham, are accomplished. If Gal. 3.23 calls those who are in Christ the singular σπέρμα of Abraham, the same word in v. 16 might refer to Christ who includes all of his people. By designating Abraham as 'distinctly a punctiliar figure rather than a linear one' (Martyn, 'Events in Galatia', p. 173), Martyn attempts to argue for discontinuity between Abraham and Christ. But Paul's Abraham–Christ analogy is designed to suggest that Abraham and Christ are linearly linked to each other, thereby forming a so-called Heilsgeschichte.

114. Hays, *The Faith of Jesus Christ*, p. 234.

built the Temple, Solomon prays that God's priests may be clothed with salvation; in Ps. 132.16 the Psalmist states that the Lord has desired to clothe the priests of Zion with salvation. In Isa. 61.10 the writer of Isaiah professes that he will greatly rejoice in God, because he has clothed him with the garments of salvation. All these parallels imply that Paul's use of the clothing-with-Christ imagery, which includes a soteriological nuance, takes the Old Testament idea of the priest being endued with divine salvation as its background. If this is true, the putting on of Christ in Gal. 3.27 indicates that in baptism believers are incorporated into Christ as the salvific agent. Like a garment, Christians assume Christ, who is their salvation. In baptism they are incorporated into the salvific Christ.

Another analogy could be detected in Apuleius' *Metamorphoses*, in which Lucius' investiture with twelve robes after his being initiated into Isis signifies that he has been given salvation by means of his union with the goddess.[115] By being united with Isis, Lucius has been guaranteed his salvation, which she bestows. Of course, the tenor of Isiac salvation as the securing of good fortune at present and in the future is different from the concept of God's salvation as the forgiveness of sins, resulting in the obtainment of righteousness in Christ and sonship of God so as to be his inheritor, in Galatians 3. Yet, despite this serious difference between the two, it cannot be totally ruled out that Paul's image of clothing with Christ, namely baptismal union with him (which connotes becoming one with the salvific Christ) could bear in mind the ancient mystery religions' thought of salvation which is reflected in the story of Lucius' obtainment of a bliss-like salvation through initiation into Isis, that is, identification with her.

2.4.3. *Eschatological Elements: The Arrival of Jesus Christ and Faith (Galatians 3.19, 23); The Fullness of Time (Galatians 4.2, 4-5).*

For Paul, to become God's sons (through faith, in Christ Jesus), in other words, his inheritors, is a significant event at a specific point in time within the history of salvation. In Gal. 3.23-25 Paul makes it explicit that he divides salvation-history into two parts, when he speaks of 'before faith's coming' and 'until faith's being revealed' (Gal. 3.23). The equivalence of the coming of faith to the coming of the seed who received God's promise, viz. Christ (3.19),[116] implies that faith is intimately involved in Christ, that is, it is 'faith in Jesus Christ'.[117] It is unlikely that by personifying faith Paul attempts to equate it with Christ; if 'faith' is replaced by 'Christ', the contrast between faith and the Law (which is prominent throughout Galatians 3) is broken in verse 23, and it is difficult to find a specific reason why 'faith' is distinguished from 'Christ' in verses 23-24. Perhaps the personifying of faith is for the purpose of personifying the Law in verse 24. Paul seems to mean that the opening of the eschatological era, which is characterized by faith-righteousness, has begun with the arrival of faith and of Christ as its object. In the time prior to the arrival of faith and Christ, human beings were imprisoned under the custody of the Law (which ruled as a

---

115. See Chapter 5, §2.2.3.

116. Greek, 'ἄχρις οὗ ἔλθῃ τὸ σπέρμα'.

117. C.J. Allen (ed.), *2 Corinthians-Philemon* (BBC, 11; Nashville: Broadman, 1971), pp. 102-103.

paedagogue[118] to lead them to Christ in order that they might be justified by faith), while in the time following the arrival of faith and Christ, they were entitled to sonship of God through faith in Christ, so as to become heirs of the promise given to Abraham (vv. 26, 29).[119]

To make it clear that the event of the believers' obtaining heirship of God takes place at the eschatological time, Paul further postulates that ὅτε δὲ ἦλθεν τὸ πλήρωμα τοῦ χρόνου, ἐξαπέστειλεν ὁ θεὸς τὸν υἱὸν αὐτοῦ…ἵνα τοὺς ὑπὸ νόμον ἐξαγοράσῃ, ἵνα τὴν υἱοθεσίαν ἀπολάβωμεν (Gal. 4.4-5). This is not only an equivalent of the concept of faith's coming (Gal. 3.23-25) but also an expansion of the concept of the time being appointed by the Father (Gal. 4.2). J.D.G. Dunn asserts,

> The imagery is of a container being steadily filled (the passage of time) until it is full… The implication is of a set purpose of God having been brought to fruition over a period and its eschatological climax enacted at the time appointed by him (cf. iv.2; 1 QpHab vii.2; Eph. i.10; Mk i.15; Heb i.2).[120]

Undoubtedly Paul refers to a specific 'point in history, when God's salvific intervention took place'.[121] When the time set by God had come (cf. Rom. 5.6; 1 Cor. 10.11), he sent forth Jesus Christ. The coming of Christ Jesus, the Son of God, is the decisive event which proclaims the opening of the new era. This implies that the fullness of time signifies that time has arrived at the end of its track and simultaneously entered a new track. This thought of the overlap of times between this age and the age to come is part of Paul's paradoxical eschatology of *already/ not yet*, which was prevalent in earliest Christian theology.[122]

As Paul makes use of the putting-on-Christ imagery in its eschatological significance, it is probable that he bears in mind the Old Testament clothing idea which also has an eschatological significance. Ps. 102.26 (cf. Ps. 51.6) states that the heavens will wear away like a garment and so will be discarded when the eschatological moment comes. This implies that the present universe will be exchanged for a new one like clothes being changed. Citing Ps. 102.26, the writer of Hebrews in 1.12 states that the heavens are to be rolled up like a garment, that is, like a garment they will be changed in the end. The inserted concept of rolling up

118. The Greek, παιδαγωγός: custodian, lit., a 'boy-leader'; the KJV renders it 'schoolmaster', but this does not seem to be proper, because παιδαγωγός did not teach the boy (Allen, [ed.], *2 Corinthians-Philemon*, p. 103). Dow, 'Galatians', p. 1215: 'The paidagogos (tutor) was a male slave who took general charge over growing boys between the ages of six and sixteen. He did not merely bring the boy to school but kept him from evil courses. He was the symbol of minority age and immaturity'; Josephus, *Ant*. 1.56: φύλαξ αὐτοῦ καὶ τῶν ὑπ' αὐτοῦ πραττομένων; Sanders, 'Galatians', p. 976; L.L. Belleville, ' "Under Law": Structural Analysis and the Pauline Concept of Law in Galatians 3.21-4.11', *JSNT* 26 (1986), pp. 53-78 (especially, pp. 59-63). Further controversy regarding the role of a paedagogue will be beyond our present study.

119. Dunn, *Baptism in the Holy Spirit*, p. 111 sees that sonship and inheritance are 'the twin themes' of Gal. 3.26-27.

120. Dunn, *The Epistle to the Galatians*, pp. 213-14.

121. Fitzmyer, 'The Letter to the Galatians', p. 787.

122. See J.D.G. Dunn, *Jesus and the Spirit* (London: SCM Press, 1975), pp. 308-318; O. Cullmann, *Salvation in History* (London: SCM Press, 1967), pp. 248-68.

seems to come from Isa. 34.4, which speaks of the sky being rolled up like a scroll. It is true that in both Ps. 102.26 and Heb. 1.12 the authors speak of a renewal of the universe in the eschatological time, while Gal. 3.27 refers to a human being's eschatological transformation in his nature through the rite of baptism. Despite this difference, as the former two passages contain the concept of eschatological clothing, which is applied to the cosmos, they may be the model for the concept of believers' being clothed with Christ in Gal. 3.27, which contains eschatological connotations. By being united with Christ as the bringer of the eschatological time and the centre of it, believers discard their old nature and instead adopt a new nature, as they replace their worn-out clothes with new clothes.

In sum, when the time had reached the end of the specific period according to God's plan for salvation (cf. Gal. 4.2), God sent his Son, Jesus Christ, and started enabling believers to obtain God's sonship through faith in Christ Jesus. For Paul, putting on Christ by being baptized into Christ is what occurs when the old era is conquered by the new era. Accordingly, we can argue that the putting-on-Christ metaphor in Gal. 3.27 indicates that in baptism the believers are united with Christ who is the bringer of the *eschaton*. At the level of the individual, it signifies that he or she experiences new life with the eschatological Christ.

2.4.4. Concluding Remarks. In Galatians 3 the emphasis on the acquisition of sonship of God through faith in Christ (and not through the Law), resulting in obtaining heirship of God, suggests that the imagery of putting-on-Christ (3.27) signifies believers' faith-union with the salvific Christ (who is the centre of salvation) in baptism. For Paul, this is the most remarkable event to occur with the coming of faith in Christ Jesus. This implies that the putting-on-Christ metaphor indicates the believers' baptismal union with the eschatological Christ as the inaugurator of the *eschaton*.

3. *Clothing with Christ in Romans 13.14*

3.1. The Situation of Romans' Readers

Romans, which includes two kinds of clothing metaphors in the same context (13.12, clothing with the armour of light; 13.14, clothing with Christ), seems to be written 'in Corinth in the house of Gaius (cf. 16.22f with Acts 20.3f)' probably in AD 56.[123] In a number of passages Paul suggests Gentile Christians as his main audience (Rom. 1.5-6, 13; 11.13, 28-31; 15.15-16). But it is highly probable that Jewish Christians were part of the Roman churches, as Paul stresses the importance of the Jewish nation (Rom. 9–11), appeals to Abraham as an example of faith, cites several passages of the OT, and critically refers to Jewish objections (Rom. 2.17–3.8; 3.21-31; 6.1–7.6; 14.1–15.3). The Jewish Christians in Romans seem to be

---

123. P. Stuhlmacher, *Paul's Letter to the Romans: A Commentary* (Louisville: Westminster/John Knox, 1994), p. 5. When Paul has just finished collecting an offering for the Jerusalem church during his third missionary journey (Rom. 15.25-26), Gaius the Corinthian provides accommodation for him (Rom. 16.23; cf. 1 Cor. 1.14).

those who had returned to Rome after the death of Claudius,[124] the Roman emperor who had expelled the Jews from Rome probably in AD 49.[125] At any rate, there is little doubt that Gentile believers were in the majority in the churches at Rome.[126]

Paul's suggestion in Rom. 13.11-14 seems to be related to the situation of the Christians at Rome. It seems that there was tension between these two groups in the Roman churches. As a matter of fact, Paul advises Gentile Christians not to be proud of their superiority in faith over Jewish Christians (Rom. 11.17-32) or to despise them for their ritual observances (Rom. 14.1-23). Rather Paul underlines the significance of Israel in God's plan of the Gentiles' salvation. For Paul, all Christians, whether Gentiles or Jews in ethnic origin, are the same people of God (Rom. 9.25-26; cf. 15.10-12), who have received justification on an equal basis, that is, by the grace of God through faith in Jesus Christ. There cannot be ethnic divisions in the one body of Christ (Rom. 12.5; cf. Gal. 3.28; Col. 3.11, 15).[127] For Paul, it was nonsensical that Gentile believers were not harmonized with Jewish Christians who had come back from their exile.

Above all, to be engaged in ethnic conflicts at the time when the milieu of persecution continued[128] was opposed to what the church should pursue. In such a situation, Christians should rather prepare themselves to meet it in unity. Recognizing that they are living in an eschatological time, they should equip themselves with the armour of light (Rom. 13.12). It has been argued that Paul believed that persecution would be 'the immediate precursor' of the Day of God's judgment.[129] The believers, who would soon meet the ultimate Day, should discard all evil conduct

124. He lived in 10 BC–AD 54 and ruled the Roman Empire from AD 41 to 54; see J.P. Balsdon and B.M. Levick, 'Claudius', in *The Oxford Classical Dictionary* (ed. S. Hornblower and A. Spawforth; Oxford: Oxford University Press, 1996), pp. 337-38; C.H. Guyot, 'The Chronology of St. Paul', *CBQ* 6 (1944), pp. 28-36 (30).

125. Suetonius, *Claud.* 25.4 insists that Claudius expelled Jews in Rome who had caused disturbance *impulsore Chresto*. See A. Momigliano, *Claudius* (Cambridge: Cambridge University Press, 1961), p. 30; F.F. Bruce, *Commentary on the Book of the Acts* (NICNT; Grand Rapids: Eerdmans, 1977), p. 368; *The Epistle of Paul to the Romans: An Introduction and Commentary* (TNTC; Leicester: IVP, 1983 [1863]), p. 14.

126. See H.W. Bartsch, 'Die historische Situation des Römerbriefes' (*SE*, 4, TUGAL, 102; Berlin: Akademie-Verlag, 1968), pp. 281-91.

127. Concerning the correspondence of Rom. 13.11-14 with the ecclesiological statement of 12.4-8, see section 3.3.5, below.

128. Bruce, *The Epistle of Paul to the Romans*, p. 241 argues that 'the events of AD 64 and 66— the beginning of imperial persecution of Christians and the outbreak of the Jewish revolt, which was to end with the collapse of the Second Jewish Commonwealth—were already casting their shadows before'. In relation to the event of AD 66, in particular, Bruce seems to bear in mind the first Jewish revolt against the Romans, which might well bring about distress also in the church in Rome. Most Romans at that time probably thought that Christianity was just a new form of Judaism, not that much different from its 'parent'.

129. Bruce, *The Epistle of Paul to the Romans*, p. 241. As in the Thessalonian epistles, Paul believes that the second Advent of Jesus Christ is imminent, although he dwells less on the nearness of the parousia, when he speaks about the destiny of Israelites (Rom. 11.25-27). But, at least in Rom. 13.11-12, Paul clearly maintains that Jesus' second coming is near at hand, as he says that the final salvation is nearer than it formerly was.

and live godly lives; they should equip themselves with spiritual armour, namely, solid Christian morality. It is worthy of note that Paul has taken up the issue of eschatology in Rom. 2.5-11, where he states that 'God's righteous judgment' will be revealed as God recompenses every human being 'according to his work' (citing from Prov. 24.12).

Yet, for Paul, equipment with spiritual armour, namely, the armour of light (Rom. 3.12), which is to bring about right Christian conduct, can be achieved only by putting on Christ Jesus (Rom. 3.14). For Paul, clothing with Christ is the total solution to ethical depravity. Only by being united with Christ Jesus can the believers arm themselves with spiritual weapons, that is to say, with moral perfection.

3.2. *The Context of Romans 13.14*

Paul again employs the metaphorical command, 'Put on the Lord Jesus Christ' (ἐνδύσασθε τὸν κύριον ᾿Ιησοῦν Χριστόν)[130] in Rom. 13.14. This verse belongs to a unit, Rom. 13.11-14,[131] which exhorts the Roman Christians to behave properly from the perspective of 'present eschatology and the imminent parousia'.[132] Paul declares that his readers have to be awake, because the time of salvation is impending (v. 11). For him, the approaching salvation is re-expressed in the imagery, 'The night is far gone, the day is at hand'; the recognition of this eschatological time must result in a casting off of the works of darkness and a putting on of the armour of light (v. 12). Here the image of night/day is in harmony with the image of darkness/ light, which is combined with the image of clothing.[133] The deeds of darkness should be taken off, and instead the armour of light should be put on. The works of darkness are further defined by the negative advice to abandon evil deeds (v. 13), which is then followed by the positive injunction, 'put on the Lord Jesus Christ' (v. 14) which, in turn, corresponds with 'put on the armour of light' (v. 12b). The instruction to put on Christ is followed by an admonition to overcome the desires of the sinful nature (v. 14).

As this brief survey shows, Paul abruptly uses the metaphor of putting on Christ without any explanation of what is meant by it. He seems to believe that his readers understand what he intends to express with the metaphor. They seem to be familiar with the metaphor, perhaps through their experience of church practices.[134] It is hard to pinpoint an exact situation which enabled Paul's audience to follow this metaphor. But the context provides some indications; insofar as verse 14 sums up the exhortation in verses 11-14,[135] the context must suggest something about the

---

130. I follow this reading of the majority of MSS.

131. P. Stuhlmacher, *Paul's Letter to the Romans: A Commentary* (Louisville: Westminster/John Knox, 1994), p. 212 sees that in its epistolary structure Rom. 13.11-14 'present the counterpart to the introduction in 12.1-2'; M. Thompson, *Clothed with Christ: The Example and Teaching of Jesus in Romans 12.1–15.13* (JSNTSup, 59; Sheffield: JSOT Press, 1991), pp. 151, 153.

132. Cf. R. Morgan, *Romans* (NTG; Sheffield: Sheffield Academic Press, 1995), p. 124.

133. The mixture of the putting-on-Christ metaphor with both night/day and darkness/light is intended to indicate that the metaphor denotes not only an eschatological but also an ethical significance; see §§3.4.2 and 3.4.3, below.

134. See Chapter 7.

135. J.D.G. Dunn, *Romans 9-16* (WBC, 38A; Dallas: Word Books, 1988), p. 785 believes that

metaphor. That is, as Paul appeals to the *eschaton* as being in progress, the context implies that the metaphor includes an eschatological significance. We also note a linguistical connection between Rom. 13.11-14 and 6.12-13. Rom. 6.12-13 belongs to a parenetic section, 6.12-14, which with 6.1-11 constitutes a larger discrete section of the epistle.[136] The statement in Rom. 6.12-14 is dependent upon the baptismal pericope in 6.1-11,[137] which is in turn tied up with an Adam–Christ discussion in 5.12-21.[138] My point is that the concept of clothing with Christ probably has something to do with both the baptismal and the Adamic motif.[139] In addition, it is likely that the ecclesiological implications in Romans 12 have something to do with putting on Christ, because the concept of one body in Christ (Rom. 12.5) seems, in some way, to correspond with the idea of a unity between believers and Christ in the putting-on-Christ metaphor. From this survey of the context, we come to notice that the metaphor of clothing with Christ in Rom. 13.14 is involved in Paul's eschatological, ethical, baptismal and ecclesiological point of view and with his Adam–Christ typology.

3.3. *The Meaning of Clothing with Christ*

3.3.1. *Introductory Remarks*. In this section I will first argue that the clothing-with-Christ imagery in Rom. 13.14 probably bears in mind the actual praxis of baptism, where the believer entered into a relationship of being one with Christ.[140] I will then attempt to verify that this baptismal unity with Christ has manifold implications. That is, the metaphor stands for the believer's participation in Christ's death and life. It also connotes his identification with Christ as the new Adam. It further points to his incorporation into ecclesial oneness with Christ.[141] Although all these connotations are implicitly manifested, their importance must not be overlooked.

3.3.2. *Baptismal Unity with Christ: The Baptismal Nuance of 'Putting on Christ'*. Rom. 13.11-14 is frequently considered to be set in the context of early Christian baptism, because in both content and language, this passage shows an affinity to 1 Thess. 5.1-11, Col. 3.1-11 and Eph. 5.8-20; 6.11-17, which may reflect early Christian baptismal instruction[142] in its conjunction with baptism. As a matter of fact, the

---

Rom. 13.14 'is obviously as deliberate as the summary of the Law in the love of neighbor command (vv. 8-10)'; A.M. Hunter, *The Epistle to the Romans* (London: SCM Press, 1970 [1955]), p. 116.

136. J. Marcus, ' "Let God Arise and End the Reign of Sin!" A Contribution to the Study of Pauline Parenesis', *Biblica* 69 (1988), pp. 386-95 (386, fn. 3).

137. Cf. Scroggs, *The Last Adam*, p. xxii; Ridderbos, *Paul*, pp. 253-54.

138. See §3.3.4.

139. See §§3.3.2 and 3.3.4.

140. See §3.3.2.

141. The echo of the imagery of clothing-with-Christ in Rom. 13.14 with the concept of one-body-in-Christ in Rom. 12 implies that this imagery has something to do with the concept of the Christian community as a corporate whole; see §3.3.5.

142. Stuhlmacher, *Paul's Letter to the Romans*, p. 212; cf. Selwyn, *The First Epistle of St. Peter*, pp. 393-400. According to the latter, the expressions 'put off' and 'put on' are derived from the early church's catechetical code, which may stand behind a number of New Testament passages: for the former expression he suggests 1 Pet. 2.1, 2; Jas. 1.21; Rom. 13.12; Col. 3.8; Eph. 4.22, 25; Heb. 12.1;

contrast of night/day and darkness/light in Rom. 13.11-14 is also seen in 1 Thess. 5.1-11; both passages in common appeal to the arrival of eschatological time and the imminence of its consummation. Further, both passages use a military image; while Rom. 13.12 admonishes believers to put on the armour of light, 1 Thess. 5.8 exhorts them to put on the weapons of faith, love and hope. The imagery of putting off/on in Rom. 13.11-14 occurs also in Col. 3.1-11, and both passages are set in the context of eschatology. In particular, the concept of clothing with Christ in Rom. 13.14 corresponds to the concept of clothing with the new man in Col. 3.10. The ethical exhortation with the use of the antithetical concept, darkness/light, in Rom. 13.11-14, resembles Eph. 5.8-20, which does something similar. And the concept of putting on the armour of light in Rom. 13.12 seems to find its full expression in Eph. 6.11-17.

Basing his argument on this closeness between Rom. 13.11-14 and the passages referred to, P. Stuhlmacher reasons that

> in this section [Rom. 13.11-14] Paul is taking up in part hymnically formulated elements of the baptismal liturgy (cf. Eph. 5.14) and traditional motifs from the early Christian speeches of exhortation which were delivered to the baptized members of the church of Christ.[143]

Since consistent occurrences of similar content and vocabulary suggest that they were used by the early church in a quite formal manner, Stuhlmacher's argument sounds persuasive. E. Käsemann also asserts that Rom. 13.11-14 is 'determined by a fixed tradition'; 'the verses are to be regarded as typical baptismal exhortation'.[144] It is likely that Rom. 13.11-14 belongs to a set of formulae which were associated with a baptismal liturgy of the primitive church.

Therefore, it seems to be legitimate to argue that the imagery of 'putting off' in Rom. 13.12 is drawn from the action of the divestiture of the baptismal candidate. And although the imagery of 'putting on' in 13.14 is not a direct counterpart of 'putting off' in 13.12, the former seems also to be suggested by the picture of donning a [white] baptismal garment, which symbolizes new life.[145] In fact, the command to put on spiritual armour, which is the counterpart of the command to put off the deeds of darkness, seems to be 'part of the fixed baptismal vocabulary',[146] because a similar exhortation is frequently found in other baptismal contexts (e.g. 1 Thess. 5.8; Eph. 6.11-17).

---

and for the latter expression Rom. 13.14; Col. 3.10, 12; Eph. 4.24; 1 Thess. 5.8; Gal. 3.27 (Selwyn, *The First Epistle of St. Peter*, pp. 394-95); cf. also Cannon, *The Use of Traditional Materials in Colossians*, pp. 73-82. Specifically, in Rom. 13.12 Paul uses the expression of 'cast off' (ἀποθώμεθα, 2nd aor. subjunctive of ἀποτίθεμαι) in combination with 'put on the armour of light', but he normally correlates it with 'putting on Christ' (e.g. Gal. 3.27) or 'putting on the new man' (Col. 3.9-10; Eph. 4.24).

143. Stuhlmacher, *Paul's Letter to the Romans*, p. 212; cf. P.W. Meyer, 'Romans', in *HBC* (San Francisco: Harper & Row, 1988), pp. 1130-167 (1164).

144. E. Käsemann, *Commentary on Romans* (trans. G.W. Bromiley; London: SCM Press, 1980 [1973]), p. 362.

145. See Chapter 7.

146. Käsemann, *Commentary on Romans*, p. 363.

The validity of seeing Rom. 13.11-14 from a baptismal viewpoint can be further supported by its connection with Rom. 6.1-11, which is caused by its parallelism with Rom. 6.12-13. J.D.G. Dunn rightly points out that the exhortation in Rom. 13.11-14 'recalls the earlier counsel in Rom. 6.12-13'.[147] The expression τῆς σαρκὸς πρόνοιαν μὴ ποιεῖσθε εἰς ἐπιθυμίας (Rom. 13.14b) seems to be an abridged form of Μὴ...βασιλευέτω ἡ ἁμαρτία ἐν τῷ θνητῷ ὑμῶν σώματι εἰς τὸ ὑπακούειν ταῖς ἐπι-θυμίαις αὐτοῦ (Rom. 6.12). Both Rom. 6.12-13 and 13.11-14 use a military idea for the purpose of an ethical exhortation. The words τὰ ὅπλα τοῦ φωτός (Rom. 13.12) seem to echo the words ὅπλα ἀδικίας or ὅπλα δικαιοσύνης (Rom. 6.13).

The link between the two passages naturally paves the way for the opinion that Rom. 13.11-14 should be interpreted in the light of the baptismal language in Rom. 6.1-11. The conjunction οὖν at the beginning of Rom. 6.12 implies that the admonition in Rom. 6.12-14 proceeds from the baptismal statement in Rom. 6.1-11. Furthermore, Rom. 6.11, which exhorts the recipients to perceive 'the new anthropological situation which obtains in Jesus Christ', is the concluding remark of the paragraph Rom. 6.1-11 and is followed by 'the more properly parenetic exhortation' of Rom. 6.12-14.[148]

Accordingly, as the rite of baptism lies behind the words in Rom. 6.1-11 (espe-cially 'baptism into Christ') and as this passage is contextually related to Rom. 13.11-14 through Rom. 6.12-13, it seems legitimate to argue that the exhortation of ἐνδύσασθε τὸν κύριον Ἰησοῦ Χριστόν (Rom. 13.14a) should be considered from the perspective of *baptism*. It is true that Paul's major purpose in Romans 6 is not to set forth a theology of Christian baptism.[149] Yet it is likely that those hearing Rom. 6.1-11 would have related it to the concept of baptism.[150] It becomes quite evident that this passage is one of the most prominent pericopes in the Pauline corpus, which shows what the profound meaning of baptism is.[151] J.P. Heil rightly argues that 'in accord with the hope that comes from our baptismal faith (see Rom. 6.1-11) we are to "clothe ourselves" with the Lord Jesus Christ (Rom. 13.14a)'.[152]

Therefore, we argue that the imperative, ἐνδύσασθε τὸν κύριον Ἰησοῦ Χριστόν, admonishes the Roman Christians to embody what was ratified by baptism, viz. the decisive union[153] with Jesus Christ. E. Lohse argues that 'This admonition [Rom. 13.14] demands of the Christian that he actualize what has already happened, that he accept what God has done for him, and that, in obedience, he enter into the new life given him in baptism'.[154] Paul probably means that as clothes, when put on,

---

147. Dunn, *Romans 9-16*, p. 784.

148. Marcus, 'Let God Arise and End the Reign of Sin!', p. 386 with fn. 3.

149. Tannehill, *Dying and Rising with Christ*, p. 7; J.L. Price, 'Romans 6.1-14', *Int* 34 (1980), pp. 65-69 (66).

150. Cf. J.L. Lilly, 'Exposition of the Missal Epistles from Romans', *CBQ* 3 (1941), pp. 349-55 (350).

151. Cf. R. Schnackenburg, *Das Heilsgeschehen bei der Taufe nach dem Apostel Paulus* (MThS1; München: K. Zink, 1950), p. 106.

152. J.P. Heil, *Romans-Paul's Letter of Hope* (AnB, 112; Rome: Biblical Institute, 1987), p. 89.

153. C.J. Vaughan, *St. Paul's Epistle to the Romans* (London: Macmillan, 1890), p. 237.

154. E. Lohse, *Colossians and Philemon* (trans. W.R. Poehlmann and R.J. Karris; Philadelphia: Fortress, 1971), p. 142; cf. C. Hodge, *Commentary on the Epistle to the Romans* (Grand Rapids: Eerd-mans, 1955), p. 413; J.A.T. Robinson, *Wrestling with Romans* (London: SCM Press, 1979), p. 140;

become a dominant part of ourselves, so Christ, when put on, becomes an essential part of the believer's nature, from which godly conduct is to spring. As with the same metaphor in Gal. 3.27, this putting-on-Christ metaphor in Rom. 13.14 also seems to be formed not only from Paul's insights into the practices of baptism in the early church, but also from his deep understanding of Old Testament clothing language (especially the priestly garments), his perception of various clothing images in contemporary writings, and his thoughtful observation of various aspects of the custom of clothing by human beings. The issue of how these elements are reflected in the putting-on-Christ metaphor will be further considered in the following sections.

3.3.3. Baptismal Participation in Christ's Death-and-Life: Implication of Romans 6.3-5. If the putting on of Christ indicates believers' baptismal unity with Christ, what is the centrepiece of this unity? Paul probably desires to emphasize that the redemption given to Jews and Gentiles on an equal basis is caused by their dying and rising with Christ[155] in baptism (cf. Eph. 4.5, ἐν βάπτισμα). He seems to have in mind the atmosphere of the Roman churches, which brings Jews and Gentiles into conflict with each other.[156] Therefore, we argue that 'put on the Lord Jesus Christ' as it is connected with baptismal language in Romans 6 describes an essential part of baptism. 'Baptism into Christ'[157] (Rom. 6.3) suggests that 'put on Christ'

Hunter, *The Epistle to the Romans*, p. 116; W. Sanday and A.C. Headlam, *Critical and Exegetical Commentary on the Epistle to the Romans* (ICC; Edinburgh: T. & T Clark, 1925 [1895]), p. 379; Ridderbos, *Paul*, p. 224; C.E.B. Cranfield, *Romans: A Shorter Commentary* (Grand Rapids: Eerdmans, 1992 [1985]), p. 335: the believer 'has already put on Christ in his submission to baptism and his reception through the sacrament of God's pledge that—in what is the fundamental sense—he has already been clothed in Christ by virtue of God's gracious decision to see him in Christ'.

155. J.D.G. Dunn, 'Salvation Proclaimed VI. Romans 6.1-11: Dead and Alive', *ExpT* 93 (1982), pp. 259-64 (263) argues that Paul avoids employing the image of rising with Christ, preferring instead to use the image of walking in newness of life; resurrection still remains a future event, as ἐσόμεθα in v. 5 takes the form of the future tense; believers are fully identified with Christ's death but not to the same extent with his resurrection. However, the suggestion that the believer's resurrection is a future affair does not detract from the idea that rising with Christ is indeed implied in Rom. 6. As Paul in v. 4 refers to ὥσπερ ἠγέρθη Χριστὸς ἐκ νεκρῶν, it cannot be doubted that the clause οὕτως καὶ ἡμεῖς ἐν καινότητι ζωῆς περιπατήσωμεν presupposes the believer's identification with Christ's resurrection from a viewpoint of 'already', viz. a realized eschatology. Further, Paul's intention is not to contrast death as a past event with resurrection as a future event. In fact, in a literal sense, Paul's recipients have not yet died; their death is also still future. It needs to be noted that Paul desires to underline that they are to live their lives by identifying themselves with Christ's death and resurrection. Inasmuch as they are united with Christ's death, they will be definitively raised in the final consummation; yet, by recognizing that even now they are already identified with his resurrection, they should live their lives in such a way as to realize it. See Tannehill, *Dying and Rising with Christ*, pp. 21-23; E. Schweizer, 'Dying and Rising with Christ', *NTS* 14 (1967), pp. 1-14.

156. See §3.1, above.

157. Cf. Lilly, 'Exposition of the Missal Epistles from Romans', p. 350, who believes that being baptized into Christ refers to being 'incorporated into Christ Jesus' in baptism. On the other hand, B.N. Kaye, 'Βαπτίζειν εἰς with Special Reference to Romans 6' (*SE*, 6; TUGAL, 112; Berlin: Akademie-Verlag, 1973), pp. 281-86 sees the concept as indicating 'with reference to or in relation to'.

refers to a spiritual transformation through an identification with Christ which is publicly achieved in baptism.[158]

However, J.D.G. Dunn in his comment on Rom. 13.14a contends that,

> of course, it [Rom. 13.14a] is not a description of baptism or of what baptism as such does; Paul is hardly calling for a further baptism... It is, rather, a way of describing the spiritual transformation which has a decisive beginning in conversion-initiation, but which is hardly completed or final.[159]

Dunn does not allow any baptismal significance in the clause ἐνδύσασθε τὸν κύριον Ἰησοῦ Χριστόν. He seems to infer that if baptism *is* alluded to in this metaphor, it would infer that baptism could be repeated, something Paul never taught. However, it is highly probable that the metaphor was intended to summon the hearers to realize their inner change over and over again, a change which has already taken place at their baptism-rebirth.[160] They should demonstrate their incorporation into Christ by living in conformity with his mind (cf. Phil. 2.5).

What is clear in Rom. 6.3-5 is that Paul designates baptism into Christ Jesus as baptism into his death, which must then proceed to resurrection. For Paul, the believer's unity with Christ (= putting on Christ) signifies his being identified with his death, which results in the renewal of his life since he is also identified with his resurrection. It is obvious that at the heart of the idea of baptism into Christ there lies an idea of dying and rising with Christ. F.F. Bruce states that 'in baptism they had been united with Christ in his death, to rise with him in the likeness of his resurrection and so "walk in newness of life" (Rom. 6.3-5)'.[161] Accordingly, we conclude that to put on Jesus Christ means to be identified with him in his death and resurrection. By being united with Christ's death, believers mortify their old personality and conduct; by being identified with his resurrection, they are regenerated with a new personality and conduct. Putting on Christ signifies that as a garment not only manifests its wearer's character but also pervades his or her appearance, so 'Christ' not only reveals his people's character but also dominates the appearance of their ethical lives.

3.3.4. *Baptismal Identification with Christ as the New Adam: Implications of the Connection between Romans 13.11-14 and 5.12-21.* In order to attain an appropriate understanding of the metaphor of clothing-with-Christ in Rom. 13.14, we need to identify 'Christ' in it. The parallel between Rom. 13.11-14 and Rom. 6.12-13 is likely to provide some information. 'Put on the Lord Jesus Christ' in Rom. 13.14 recalls 'put on the armour of light' in 13.12, which is in turn linked with 'instruments of righteousness' in 6.13. This parallel paves the way for seeing Rom. 13.11-14 from the perspective of the Adam–Christ motif in Rom. 5.12-21.[162] For the

158. Cf. F.J. Leenhardt, *The Epistle to the Romans: A Commentary* (London: Lutterworth, 1961), p. 342; Bruce, *The Epistle of Paul to the Romans*, pp. 242-43.

159. Dunn, *Romans 9-16*, pp. 791, 793.

160. Cf. E. Brunner, *The Letter to the Romans: A Commentary* (London: Lutterworth, 1959), p. 113; see §2.3.2, above.

161. F.F. Bruce, *Paul: Apostle of the Free Spirit* (Carlisle: Paternoster, 1980 [1977]), p. 433.

162. Cf. Cannon, *The Use of Traditional Materials in Colossians*, p. 72.

baptismal precepts in Rom. 6.1-11 (which are expanded to the exhortation in Rom. 6.12-14) are unmistakably associated with the Adam–Christ discussion in Rom. 5.12-21. J.L. Price, in his article on Rom. 6.1-14, argues that this passage is part of a larger whole which begins with Rom. 5.1 and concludes with Rom. 8.39; he holds that the meaning of Rom. 6.1-14 is partly to be derived from that which precedes it, especially Rom. 5.12-21.[163]

In Rom. 5.12-21 Paul portrays Adam as the inclusive representative of all human beings who have been subject to sin and death, and Christ as the inclusive representative of the new people of God who have received justification and life on the basis of Christ's one act of righteousness.[164] In particular, 'verse 14b says of Adam that he is a type of the one who was to come (τύπος τοῦ μέλλοντος)—the type of the last (ἔσχατος) or second (δεύτερος)'.[165] Rom. 5.12-21 (even also 6.1-23) seems to reflect a Christian version of a Jewish apocalyptic cosmology (e.g. 2 Esd. 3.21-22; 4.30, etc.),[166] which holds that believers are living in the eschatological overlap between this present age (in which sin and death reign because of Adam's destructive influence) and the age to come (in which righteousness and life reign because of Jesus Christ's salvific work).[167]

After presenting in general terms this theory of believers' solidarity with Christ from the perspective of the Adam–Christ analogy (Rom. 5.12-21), Paul moves on, in more specific terms, to elaborating, using baptismal language, how such a solidarity can be achieved (Rom. 6.1-11). The believers' unity with Christ can be worked out by their baptismal unity with him, the thrust of which is their identification with his death and resurrection. The discussion of the analogy between Adam and Christ and the subsequent reference to baptism do not seem to be accidental. Paul probably maintains that the life lost in Adam is recovered in baptism into Christ (Rom. 6.3), that is, an entry into the relationship of union with him.

163. Price, 'Romans 6.1-14', p. 66; cf. T. Barrosse, 'Death and Sin in Saint Paul's Epistle to the Romans', *CBQ* 15 (1953), pp. 438-59 (438).

164. Cf. C.H. Dodd, *The Epistle of Paul to the Romans* (MoffNTC; London: Hodder & Stoughton, 1947 [1932]), pp. 78-86; J.L. Segundo, *The Humanist Christology of Paul* (New York: Orbis Books, 1986), p. 84; Barrosse, 'Death and Sin in Saint Paul's Epistle to the Romans', pp. 440, 447-50, 454-58; J.D.G. Dunn, 'Paul's Understanding of the Death of Christ as Sacrifice', in S.W. Sykes (ed.), *Sacrifice and Redemption: Durham Essays in Theology* (Cambridge: Cambridge University Press, 1991), pp. 36-37; A.J.M. Wedderburn, 'Adam in Paul's Letter to the Romans', *SB* III (1978), JSNTSup, 3 (1980), pp. 413-30 (especially pp. 423-24). For a detailed discussion on Rom. 5.12-21, see K. Barth, *Christ and Adam: Man and Humanity in Romans 5* (trans. T.A. Smail; Edinburgh: Oliver & Boyd, 1963 [1956]), pp. 4-45; C.C. Caragounis, 'Romans 5. 15-16 in the Context of 5. 12-21: Contrast or Comparison?', *NTS* 31 (1985), pp. 142-48.

165. O. Cullmann, *The Christology of the New Testament* (London: SCM Press, 1959), pp. 171-72.

166. Cf. Dodd, *The Epistle of Paul to the Romans*, p. 79; Sanday and Headlam, *Critical and Exegetical Commentary on the Epistle to the Romans*, pp. 136-38; Cullmann, *The Christology of the New Testament*, p. 170; Price, 'Romans 6.1-14', pp. 67-69; N.T. Wright, 'Adam in Pauline Christology', *SBLSPS* 22 (Chico: Scholars, 1983), pp. 359-89 (especially pp. 370-73).

167. Segundo, *The Humanist Christology of Paul*, 81, 85-86; cf. S.E. Porter, 'The Argument of Romans 5: Can a Rhetorical Question Make a Difference?', *JBL* 110.4 (1991), pp. 655-77 (especially pp. 671-72, 674-76).

If Rom. 13.11-14 can thus be connected further back with 5.12-21, it can be inferred that the Adam–Christ motif operates in the metaphor of putting on the Lord Jesus Christ in 13.14a. Therefore, 'Christ' in this metaphor can be thought of as pointing to Christ as the new Adam.[168] Yet, what is meant by putting on Christ as the new Adam? For Paul, putting on Christ should lead to right Christian conduct. This implies that it indicates that believers are to obtain a Christ-like character by assuming Christ himself. Yet, as Christ is the counterpart of Adam, to assume Christ signifies to be restored to the original state of Adam, and so to assume what Adam originally wore. Paul probably sees the original state of Adam as having been clothed, perhaps as a result of his acquaintance with the idea of Adam's pre-lapsarian clothing which is maintained in Jewish clothing traditions reflected particularly in rabbinic literature. *Gen. Rab.* 20.12 sees the statement in Gen. 3.21 as referring to Adam's pre-Fall state and interprets עוֹר in it as אוֹר; in rabbinic writings 'light' is usually identified with 'glory' (e.g. *Gen. Rab.* 12.6) and related to the concept of the image of God (e.g. *'Abot R. Nath.* 42, 116). Even in the case of rabbinic documents which see Gen. 3.21 as speaking of the post-Fall state of Adam and interpret עוֹר as human skin, it is still maintained that Adam was originally clothed with splendid garments, which disappeared with the commission of sin (e.g. *'Abot R. Nath.* 42, 116). G.A. Anderson points out that the rabbinic interpretations of עוֹר כָּתְנוֹת (Gen. 3.21) as human skin presume that Adam was clothed with this skin at the moment of his transgression, thereby also presuming that Adam had been adorned with another type of clothing before the Fall, and out of this thought the rabbinic tradition of the garments of glory was derived.[169] A number of midrashim[170] blame the Fall for having caused the first human beings' forfeiture of God's image, that is, their God-like splendour.

The idea of Adam's pre-Fall clothing is also shared by the *Apocalypse of Moses*, where Adam and Eve profess that they were clothed with righteousness and glory before the Fall (chs. 20–21). A similar thought is also found in *The Hymn of the Pearl*; when the prince took off the Egyptian-style garment and turned toward his Father's kingdom, a 'light', which is nothing else than his original self, namely the image of God, guided him, and was eventually united with him (v. 77).[171] The point is that Paul shares the idea of Adam's pre-Fall clothing, which is postulated by these documents, and he with the putting-on-Christ metaphor in Rom. 13.14 wishes to express an idea that in baptism the baptisand is clothed with the pre-Fall Adamic nature which is characterized by the moral perfection that flows from the recovered image of God.

Considering that the putting-on-Christ metaphor indicates a baptismal change, it probably reflects other clothing traditions. It is probable that Paul has in mind the practice of the priest's ritual change of garments, because the central elements of baptism (i.e. divestiture, immersion and investiture) resemble the priest's taking off

---

168. Käsemann, *Commentary on Romans*, p. 363; Dunn, *Romans 9-16*, p. 790.

169. G.A. Anderson, 'Garments of Skin, Garments of Glory' (unpublished paper, n.d.), pp. 1-42 (especially pp. 9-24).

170. E.g. *Gen. Rab.* 12.6; see Ginzberg, *Legends*, V, p. 113; Chapter 2, §5.

171. See Chapter 4, §§3.3 and 3.4.

his previous garment, purification, and the putting on of the priestly garments (cf. Exod. 29.4-9; Lev. 16.3-4), which are spoken of as being garments of sacredness, glory and beauty (cf. Exod. 29.2, 40). When the priest wears the priestly garment and comes to be united with God's holiness, he becomes virtually a divine being.[172] In particular, his putting on the breastpiece which contains Urim and Thummim connotes that he becomes a man of 'lights' and 'perfections'.[173] In *Joseph and Aseneth*, moreover, when Aseneth adorned herself with a wedding garment at her marriage with Joseph, some time after her washing-and-investiture with a new linen garment, her appearance became like light.[174] In Apuleius' *Metamorphoses*, when Lucius wore twelve lavish garments after bathing-then-initiation, his appearance was like the sun, which was a token of his having been united with Isis (XI.24). A radical change of one's status is also suggested by the Roman custom of apparel. When a Roman male took off the *toga praetexta* and put on the *toga virilis* at the age of 16 in a family ceremony, this meant that his status was changed from that of a youth to that of an adult.[175] Further, remembering that the putting-on-Christ metaphor in Rom. 13.14 emphasizes the right ethical life, this metaphor also seems to be analogous to the event which appeared in Zechariah's vision when the filthy garments are taken away from the high priest Joshua and the new garments are put on him (Zech. 3.3-5), symbolizing God's people's moral restoration. Almost certainly Paul knew his readers would have been familiar with the concept of a symbolic change described by clothing imagery, which is shared by these writings.

In the light of our observations, it does not seem to be an accident that 'put on the Lord Jesus Christ' (13.14) occurs in the same context as 'put on the armour of light' (Rom. 13.12). 'The Lord Jesus Christ' further specifies the figurative term 'armour of light'. For Paul, the Christ who is the believer's garment is the new Adamic Christ, a being of light. The centrepiece of this putting-on-Christ metaphor is to restore the original Adamic glory, namely the image of God, through baptismal union with Christ as the new Adam. This means that the baptisand is to be restored to the original Adamic nature of godliness, i.e. to a Christ-like character, which will produce an upright life. M. Thompson, therefore, rightly argues that

> by donning the characteristics of the second Adam, Christians reflect the true image of God and are changed into his likeness from one degree of glory to another, in anticipation of the final glory of resurrection life (2 Cor. 3.18).[176]

However, what has been so far suggested would not be all of the Adamic significance of the putting-on-Christ metaphor. The representative character of the Adamic Christ, which was referred to in earlier paragraphs, seems to have its own function in identifying the significance of the clothing-with-Christ metaphor. When Christ as the new Adam is presented as the only avenue through which believers can be restored to the original Adamic glory reflecting the image of God, they

172. Cf. Philo, *Vita Mos.* ii.131.
173. See Chapter 1, §3.2.
174. See Chapter 3, §§2.3 and 2.4.
175. See Chapter 6.
176. Thompson, *Clothed with Christ*, p. 158.

naturally come to enter into a relationship of solidarity with Christ. That is, to put on Christ means that they are incorporated into the Adamic Christ as their inclusive humanity. R. Morgan properly asserts that ' "Putting on the Lord Jesus Christ" at Rom. 13.14 is another phrase suggestive of the corporate Christ'.[177] As a garment envelops its wearer's whole body, Christ comprises every single Christian as a whole and he becomes a collective person. In the preceding section, it was pointed out that the inclusive character of Christ as the believers' garment not only echoes the OT, where the priestly garment symbolizes the whole Israel (Exod. 28.9-10, 15-21) but also reflects the clothing traditions found in the Johannine concept of Jesus' untorn tunic, which stands for his people as a whole (Jn 19.23-24). Further, the nuance of inclusiveness in the clothing-with-Christ imagery could draw on Jewish clothing traditions reflected in *Joseph and Aseneth*, where the new linen garment symbolizes the inclusive humanity of Aseneth as 'the City of Refuge', encompassing the whole of her would-be imitators (*JA* 15.7). In any case, as the putting-on-Christ metaphor involves Adamic Christ's inclusiveness of his people, it probably refers to the relationship between Christ and the church as his body.[178] This is suggested by the fact that the concept of the 'one body in Christ' (Rom. 12.5) is to be associated with the present metaphor.

3.3.5. *Baptismal Incorporation into Ecclesial Oneness in Christ: 'Christ' as the Church Body (Romans 13.14)?* In the preceding section,[179] it was pointed out that the metaphor of putting-on-Christ in Rom. 13.14 connotes that all believers are represented by the Adamic Christ and that this involves an ecclesiological implication. C.H. Dodd holds that in Rom. 13.14 'Paul is urging his readers to live out all that is implied in being a "member" of Christ (cf. xii.5)'.[180] In Rom. 12.5 Paul calls the Christian community 'one body in Christ' that consists of many members. J.A.T. Robinson argues that 'chapters 12-15 are really only the moral consequences of what Paul says in 12.5: "So all of us, united with Christ, form one body, serving individually as limbs and organs to one another" '.[181] It is indisputable that 'one body' here indicates the church as an organic unity. Christians share their corporate life[182] in the church which is encompassed by Christ. The concept of 'one body in Christ' is interchangeable with the concept of the body of Christ (cf. 1 Cor. 12.27).

It is probable that, when Paul says 'put on the Lord Jesus Christ' in Rom. 13.14a, he has in mind the believer's incorporation into the body of Christ, that is, the church. In the primitive church, when believers confessed their faith in Jesus Christ, they were to acquire church membership through the sacrament of baptism.[183] P. Stuhlmacher asserts that Rom. 13.14 recalls that the Roman Christians became

177. Morgan, *Romans*, p. 120.
178. This theme will be further discussed in section 3.3.5, below.
179. See section 3.3.4, above.
180. Dodd, *The Epistle of Paul to the Romans*, p. 210.
181. Robinson, *Wrestling with Romans*, p. 140.
182. Bruce, *The Epistle of Paul to the Romans*, p. 228.
183. Dodd, *The Epistle of Paul to the Romans*, p. 86.

members of Christ's body as a result of having been baptized into the body of Christ, namely, 'the salvific community' (cf. 1 Cor. 12.12-13; Rom. 12.4-5); Paul is here arguing that they should 'now live with a special determination as the new persons whom Christ has made (cf. 1 Cor. 8.6; Col. 1.15-20; 3.9-10)'.[184] The concept 'baptism into Christ Jesus' in Rom. 6.3 corresponds to the term 'baptism into the body of Christ' in 1 Cor. 12.13. In the early church, the believer's incorporation into the body of Christ, namely the church, was inseparable from his unity with Christ.

In sum, the putting-on-Christ metaphor in Rom. 13.14a can be considered 'a variant on the theme of incorporation into the body of Christ'.[185] It does not merely refer to an individual Christian's unification with Christ, but also the collective Christian community's inclusion in Christ as a corporate personality. As a garment envelops the whole body of its wearer, Christ embraces the whole church as his body. As the body within the garment is an organic whole, the church is also an organic whole, which is corporately included in Christ. As has been seen, Christ as a garment could be analogous to the priest's garment in its symbolism of the whole Israel, the high priest's garment which is interpreted by Philo (and also Josephus) as connoting the whole universe, Jesus' untorn tunic as it symbolizes all his followers, and Aseneth's new linen garment, as it represents the whole body of her would-be followers.[186]

3.3.6. *Concluding Remarks.* In Romans 13.11-14, the putting-on-Christ metaphor has in mind the actual picture of the current baptismal practice. For Paul, being a Christian is to be united with Christ through baptism. In baptism believers participate in Christ's death and resurrection life. Yet the Christ and Adam typology lies behind this concept, so that to be united with Christ in baptism does not merely indicate ritual initiation into Christ, but also incorporation into Christ who is the new Adam. This suggests that putting on Christ connotes restoration to the original state of Adam; basically, the putting-on-Christ metaphor seems to maintain Adam's pre-Fall clothing, which echoes Jewish clothing traditions similar to those found in such documents as *Apoc. Mos.* 20–21; *Gen. Rab.* 20.12; *The Hymn of the Pearl.* Yet, it is likely that the metaphor is also a product of Paul's perception of other clothing images found in a number of Old Testament clothing passages. In particular, as he combines the clothing-with-Christ metaphor (Rom. 13.14) with the clothing-with-the-armour-of-light metaphor (13.12), he seems to be influenced by his understanding of God's garment (cf. Judg. 6.34; 1 Chron. 12.18; 2 Chron. 24.20). He also seems to be influenced by his recognition of the Roman custom of clothing, especially exchanging the *toga praetexta* with the *toga virilis*. It is also possible that he bears in mind the mystery religions' initiation which is reflected by Apuleius' *Metamorphoses*. Further, as the Adam–Christ typology pre-dominates the concept of baptismal unity, it implies that putting-on-Christ not only indicates an individual Christian's union with Christ but also the whole church's unity with him.

184. Stuhlmacher, *Paul's Letter to the Romans*, p. 214.

185. T.W. Manson, 'Romans', in *PCB* (London: Nelson, 1963), pp. 940-53 (950); also See Käsemann, *Commentary on Romans*, p. 363.

186. See again end part of section 2.3.5, above.

3.4. *Some Contextual Emphases*

3.4.1. *Introductory Remarks.* In the context to which Rom. 13.14 belongs, some specific theological emphases are apparent, so they affect the meaning of the imagery of clothing-with-Christ. Eschatological implications are clear in the text which includes the putting-on-Christ imagery of Rom. 13.14a. In particular, Rom. 13.12, 13, 14b makes it clear that this imagery has an ethical significance. For a proper interpretation of the metaphor of putting-on-Christ in Rom. 13.14a, we need to understand these elements.

3.4.2. *Eschatological Elements: Appeal to the Sense of the Eschaton (Romans 13.11-14).* The statement in Rom. 13.11-14 is eschatological in outlook. Prior to his exhorting the Romans to 'put on the Lord Jesus Christ', Paul appeals to the sense of the *eschaton* in Rom. 13.11. He claims that the time of salvation is near at hand. He draws attention to the fact that his readers are living in the *eschaton*.[187] While Paul in Galatians 3 underlines that the believer's nature has been changed in union with Christ as the bringer of the eschatological time, here in Romans 13 he emphasizes that his moral life should be changed with his recognition of the emergency of the time and on the basis of his identification with Christ. J.D.G. Dunn aptly points out that 'the opening phrase [of Rom. 13.11-14] recalls the recipients to the eschatological perspective basic to Christian self-understanding—not only a new but the final age of God's purpose (3.26; 8.18; 11.5)'.[188] Paul's reference to the world being at its close points to a paradoxical period where the present world order meets the future world order.[189] Paul's point is that recognition of the approaching parousia should cause believers to lead their lives in a proper manner; they should reject evil conduct and instead live moral lives. Paul wishes that the perception of the imminent parousia might play a rôle in stimulating Christian good deeds.

Paul, however, seems to believe that virtues do not automatically result from a merely intellectual recognition of the eschatological time.[190] He argues that the recipients should 'put on the armour of light'; in other words, they should 'put on the Lord Jesus Christ'.[191] Paul's identification of these two metaphors with each other, as was pointed out previously, seems to spring from his perception of the

187. The opening theme of salvation is found in Rom. 1.16.

188. Dunn, *Romans 9-16*, p. 784.

189. Manson, 'Romans', p. 950: '[Rom. 13.] 11-14 contain the reminder that Christians are already living in the overlap of two ages (1 Cor. 10.11). The old order is moving to its close, and the new order to its consummation'.

190. Dunn, *Romans 9-16*, p. 785: 'the summary climax of the exhortation in terms of the character of Christ'.

191. Cf. NEB: 'let Christ Jesus himself be the armour that you wear'; JB: 'Let your armour be the Lord Jesus Christ'. Thompson, *Clothed with Christ*, pp. 149-50 argues that the change from impersonal armour (specific ethical qualities) to the person, who embodies and enables those characteristics, suggests that 'to put on the Lord Jesus Christ' transcends 'to put on the armour of light'. However, Paul does not say that 'the armour of light' is 'specific ethical qualities'; rather, he perhaps insists that when the believer is equipped with the armour of light, he is enabled to be virtuous.

Jewish understanding of the pre-Fall state of Adam—that Adam was originally clothed with light, radiance or glory, which were dependent upon the image of God.[192] Insofar as the putting-on-Christ metaphor is involved in the analogy of Adam–Christ,[193] this metaphor seems to points to the restoration to Adam's pre-Fall glory which accompanies the image of God in him.

Paul's point is that in order to be virtuous, a believer's character must first be transformed by union with Christ as the new Adam, namely the eschatological Adam. The ultimate goal to which the Christian life is directed is salvation, that is, 'the completed transformation of the whole person into the image of Christ, in body as well (Rom. 8.11, 23)'.[194]

3.4.3. *Ethical Elements (Romans 13.12, 13, 14b)*. In dealing with the putting-on-Christ imagery in Rom. 13.14a, its ethical significance needs to be underlined. In Rom. 13.14b Paul exhorts his readers to mortify the desires of the fleshly nature: καὶ τῆς σαρκὸς πρόνοιαν μὴ ποιεῖσθε εἰς ἐπιθυμίας. As the term σάρξ here is used of corrupt human nature dominated by sin (cf. Rom. 8.13),[195] the term seems to echo God's declaration to refuse to dwell in men, when they heavily indulge in transgressions, especially sexual malpractice: διὰ τὸ εἶναι αὐτοὺς σάρκας (LXX Gen. 6.4). Here the σάρξ characterizes the sinful nature of Adam's descendants. Paul's command in Rom. 13.11-14 is that by being aware of having been united with Jesus Christ, the antitype of Adam, believers have to mortify the desires of the fallen Adamic nature. Paul seems to acknowledge that there still remains an Adamic 'not yet' element in their nature. The believers are those who live in eschatological tension between what has already been done and what has not yet been done.

At any rate, what Paul means is that the more the believers make an effort to realize their allegiance to the person of Christ, the better they can practise Christian virtues (Rom. 13.12b, 13, 14b). C.E.B. Cranfield asserts that

> [in Rom. 13.14 Paul] uses the imperative, since putting on Christ has here its moral sense... To put on the Lord Jesus Christ means here to embrace again and again, in faith and confidence, in grateful loyalty and obedience, Him to whom we already belong.[196]

Paul wishes that 'putting on the Lord Jesus Christ' should function as the mainspring of good works. As Paul contrasts 'the works of darkness' with the putting on of the armour of light (v. 12), he means that the metaphor of putting on the armour of light should be seen from an ethical perspective. J. Murray holds that

> 'the works of darkness' are the works belonging to and characteristic of darkness and darkness is to be understood in the ethical sense (cf. 1 Cor. 4.5; 6.14; Eph. 5.8, 11; Col. 1.13).[197]

192. See Chapter 2, §§3 and 5; Chapter 4, §3.4.
193. See section 3.3.4, above.
194. Dunn, *Romans 9-16*, p. 792.
195. For the usage of σάρξ in Galatians, see Barclay, *Obeying the Truth*, pp. 202-215.
196. Cranfield, *Romans: A Shorter Commentary*, p. 335.
197. J. Murray, *The Epistle to the Romans* II (ed. F.F. Bruce; NICNT; Grand Rapids: Eerdmans, 1965), p. 170.

The same outlook needs to be applied to the metaphor, 'put on the Lord Jesus Christ', which specifies the metaphor of putting on the armour of light. In fact, Paul contrasts 'ἐνδύσασθε τὸν κύριον 'Ιησοῦ Χριστόν' with moral vices in Rom. 13.13-14. Paul presents three pairs of vices (v. 13) which are opposed to 'put on the Lord Jesus Christ' (v. 14a). F. Godet argues that '[Paul] certainly speaks of Christ here not as our *righteousness*, but as our *sanctification*'.[198] Whereas the putting-on-Christ metaphor in Gal. 3.27 emphasizes baptismal union with Christ so as to be an inheritor of God's kingdom, here in Rom. 13.14 it highlights identification with him so as to be godly (cf. Eph. 4.24; Col. 3.10, 12).[199]

If so, does the metaphor itself directly describe a course of ethical action? Luther contends that to put on the Lord Jesus Christ is to 'follow the example and virtues of Christ' and to 'do that which he did, and suffer that which he suffered'.[200] Luther virtually equates 'putting on the Lord Jesus Christ' with putting Christian morals into practice. However, as a person cannot be equated with his outward behaviour, so putting on the Lord Jesus Christ cannot be equated with taking actions to imitate him. Although an individual and his behaviour are indissoluble from one another, they cannot be identified. A person obviously consists of far more than just what he does. That is, the kind of behaviour one expresses is dependent upon the kind of personality one possesses.

It becomes clear, therefore, that the placing of 'put on the Lord Jesus Christ' in contrast to these pairs of vices does not necessarily indicate that this metaphor directly points to following the example of Christ. Rather, the contrast indicates that right behaviour can *only* be derived from a personality in union with Christ. As one's identification with Christ becomes clearer, one withdraws more and more from vice. Paul seems to present 'to put on the Lord Jesus Christ' as the ultimate counter-plan against moral vices.

When Paul thus includes a moral significance in putting-on-Christ, that is, baptismal union with him, and when he thinks of Christ as the new Adam, it is highly probable that he envisages restoration to the sinless state of Adam before the Fall. Paul seems to believe that Adam was clothed with righteousness before the Fall. If this is true, it is probable that Paul has in mind the Jewish concept of pre-Fall Adam's moral state. For example, *Apoc. Mos.* 20 suggests that the first human couple were dressed with righteousness and glory; this document seems to think that their righteousness was the cause of their glory. Paul's metaphor may also be a

198. F. Godet, *Commentary on St. Paul's Epistle to the Romans* II (trans. A. Cusin; Edinburgh: T. & T. Clark, 1884), p. 323.

199. Of course, an ethical significance of the clothing-with-Christ imagery is not all it connotes; see §§3.3.2; 3.3.4; 3.3.5; and 3.4.2, above.

200. Luther, *Galatians*, p. 339; cf. Godet, *Commentary on St. Paul's Epistle to the Romans*, II, pp. 323-24: 'The toilet of the believer…consists solely in putting on Christ, in appropriating by habitual communion with Him all His sentiments and all His manner of acting'; P. Althaus, *Der Brief an die Römer* (Göttingen: NTD, 1966), p. 137; U. Wilckens, *Der Brief an die Römer*, III (EKKNT; 3 vols.; Zürich: Benziger/Neukirchen: Neukirchener Verlag, 1978, 1980, 1982), p. 78; C.E.B. Cranfield, *A Critical and Exegetical Commentary on the Epistle to the Romans*, II (ICC, 2 vols.; Edinburgh: T. & T. Clark, 1975–1979), pp. 688-89, following Chrysostom; C.K. Barrett, *A Commentary on the Epistle to the Romans* (BNTC; Peabody: Hendrickson, 1991 [1957]), p. 234.

reflection of his understanding of the significance of the priestly garment in the Old Testament. When the priest wears the priestly garment, this means that he is unified with God's holiness, because the garment is sacred (cf. Exod. 29.4-9; 40.12-15; Lev. 16.3-4); in a sense, this union indicates that the priest has acquired a divine nature, because God himself wears righteousness (Isa. 59.17; cf. 61.10). Paul's clothing-with-Christ metaphor in its ethical force may also echo the clothing image in Zech. 3.3-5, where the high priest Joshua was separated from the filthy garment and clothed with the new garment, which signifies that God's people Israel would be stripped of the old nature of immorality and instead covered with the new nature of morality.[201] Further, it is also probable that Paul's concept of ethical 'clothing' makes use of contemporary clothing imagery. For instance, in Philo, it is suggested that people are to be clothed with virtues or vices; virtues are the panoply ($\pi\alpha\nu$-$\tau\epsilon\upsilon\chi\acute{\iota}\alpha$) of reason, by which passion ($\pi\acute{\alpha}\theta\circ\varsigma$) with which people are dressed should be controlled.[202]

Perhaps Paul's discernment of the close relationship between people's nature and their behaviour encourages him to contrast the putting-on-Christ metaphor with the list of vices in Rom. 13.12-14. Probably Paul thinks of the way in which a garment influences its wearer emotionally. A uniform tends to stimulate its wearer to behave in keeping with whatever it represents; for instance, a soldier who wears a military uniform tries to manifest behaviour which is in harmony with his military status, and a cleric who puts on ecclesiastical vestments tries to act in accordance with his clerical status. In *Joseph and Aseneth*, when Aseneth is adorned with a pagan garment (3.6), she is boastful and arrogant (1.6-2.1), so she manifests 'the lawless deeds' (11.10, 17). Of course, her noble status and her pagan behaviour seem to have caused her to wear such a garment in the first place, but it seems also that the garment in turn makes her manifest this proud behaviour. It is noteworthy that when she decides to do away with her past pagan life, she first throws away every item of her garments (10.10-11). When she replaces her lavish garment with a black mourning tunic of remorse (10.8-9), she shows an attitude of humiliation (11.1–13.15). It is true that her decision to leave paganism results in this humble behaviour, but it cannot be excluded that the black tunic also influences her changed conduct. Specifically we note that in her prayer to God Aseneth confesses that she has put off her linen royal robe (13.3), loosened her golden girdle and thrown it off (13.4), and removed her diadem from her head (13.5). In *The Hymn of the Pearl*, when the prince, who leaves his Father's kingdom and comes to Egypt, clothes himself with an Egyptian-style garment (the purpose of which is in order to conceal his alien status), this results in his indulging in Egyptian foods, which symbolizes his depravity.

3.4.4. *Concluding Remarks*. Romans 13 stresses that believers' recognition of their living in the eschatological times should result in their putting on Christ (i.e. union with Christ in baptism) and function to stimulate right ethical conduct. This implies, on the one hand, that clothing with Christ indicates the believers'

201. See Chapter 1, §3.4.
202. See Chpter 2, §5.2.

eschatological change in their nature by being united with Christ as the inaugurator of eschatological times; and on the other hand, that the metaphor is virtually identified with the believers' renewed behaviour. For Paul, Christians' baptismal union with Christ as the bringer of eschatological times should be worked out through their godly conduct.

4. *Conclusion to Chapter 8*

In both Gal. 3.26-29 and Rom. 13.11-14, the metaphor of putting-on-Christ is probably involved in the rite of baptism as it was practised in the first-century church. For the early Christians, the language of baptism-into-Christ, which is designated as putting-on-Christ (Gal. 3.27), would have been perceived as referring to the rite of baptism. Some ancient documents[203] suggest that baptism in the early church might consist of the divestiture of a former garment followed by immersion and investiture with a new garment; the strands of these rituals seem to have signified that the old nature of the baptisand was removed and a new nature was adopted.

While Gal. 3.26-27, by equating baptism-into-Christ with putting-on-Christ, emphasizes a change in a believer's status, Rom. 13.11-14, by conforming putting-on-the-armour-of-light to putting-on-Christ, underlines the believer's restoration to Adam's pre-Fall sinless state. The former may be compared with a Roman boy's wearing of the *toga virilis* in a sort of ceremony at his transition from youth to adult and with Lucius' wearing of twelve garments (after the initiation ritual), which symbolize his having changed into a divine being by being united with Isis; the latter may be compared with the thought of Adam's being clothed before the Fall with light, or righteousness and glory (which are tied up with the image of God). Therefore, it is no accident that Gal. 3.26-27 emphasizes believers' acquisition of sonship of God (because of Christ's own sonship) through baptismal unity with Christ, resulting in their becoming God's inheritors, while Rom. 13.11-14 underlines the obtainment of ethical perfection through baptismal identification with Christ. Yet, despite this kind of difference in nuance, both passages in common seem to be controlled by Paul's view of baptism, which is closely related to his opinion of the Adam–Christ typology. With the putting-on-Christ metaphor, he seems to mean that the original state of man, which has been lost in Adam, is recovered in Christ by a person's being incorporated into Christ in baptism.

For Paul, putting-on-Christ in its significance of baptismal unity with Christ has many significances: participation in Christ's death-and-life; entry into the life of union with his Spirit; infusion with his priestly righteousness; participation in his sonship of God; identification with his new Adamic humanity; and incorporation into his ecclesial body, the church as a collective whole. Further, the contextual features of Gal. 3.26-29 and Rom. 13.11-14 suggest that the putting-on-Christ metaphor denotes believers' baptismal union with Christ who is the soteriological agent, the bringer of the *eschaton*, and the ethical model.[204]

---

203. As was presented in Chapter 7.
204. See §§2.4 and 3.4, above.

In addition, it is also probable that the putting-on-Christ metaphor is redolent of the normal way human beings are clothed. For Paul, as a garment is identified with its wearer, so Christ identifies himself with his people. As a garment reveals its wearer's character, so Christ should represent the believer's character; as the garment pervades its wearer's appearance, so features of Christ should dominate his appearance. As the garment covers its wearer as a whole, so Christ as a corporate person embraces the Christian church as a whole.

Chapter 9

CLOTHING WITH A PERSON (II): 'THE NEW MAN'

1. *Introduction*

This chapter aims to explicate the significance of the putting-on-the-new-man metaphor in Col. 3.9-10 and Eph. 4.22-24. These passages will be investigated in two separate sub-chapters. When we deal with each passage, we will first investigate the situation of the addressees of the relevant epistle and the context to which the passage belongs. We will then attempt to disclose the significance of the metaphor not only by examining the reality it delineates, but also by looking into the identity of 'the new man' in it, and by considering too what is meant by its link with ecclesiological concepts. We will note that an eschatological perspective in Col. 3.1-4 is important in the putting-on-the-new-man imagery in 3.9-10 and that in both Colossians and Ephesians ethical implications are outstanding in this metaphor. In particular, throughout all of our observations, we will take into account how the documents of antiquity suggested in Part I contribute to unfolding its significance. Finally we will suggest a conclusion concerning the meaning of the metaphor.

2. *Clothing with the New Man in Colossians 3.9-10*

2.1. *The Situation of Colossians' Readers*

Colossians claims Pauline authorship in its opening (1.1) and in other verses (1.23; 4.18). Scholarly views on this issue are not unanimous. On the grounds of language, style and theology in the main, many argue that Colossians is post-Pauline, so they classify it as 'deutro-Pauline'.[1] Some contend that the presence of a number of *hapax legomena* verifies that Colossians is un-Pauline,[2] but all Paul's epistles contain *hapax legomena*, whether they are numerous or not. Differences in vocabulary may be caused by Paul's argument against the so-called Colossian 'heresy'.[3] For the purpose

---

1. E.g. R. Bultmann, *Theology of the New Testament*, I (trans. K. Grobel; London: SCM Press, 1983 [1952]), pp. 74, 76.

2. See E. Lohse, *Colossians and Philemon* (trans. W.R. Poehlmann and R.J. Karris; Philadelphia: Fortress, 1971), pp. 84-89; he discovers 34 *hapax legomena* in Colossians.

3. M.D. Hooker, 'Were There False Teachers in Colossae?', in *Christ and Spirit in the New Testament* (Festschrift C.F.D. Moule; ed. B. Lindars and S.S. Smalley; Cambridge: Cambridge University Press, 1973), pp. 315-31 assumes that the object of Paul's criticism is not a specific 'heresy' but the contemporary syncreticism which was popular with first-century people. However, although the author does not present a formal explanation of the false teaching in Colossae, 'he appears to be quoting slogans or catch-words of the opponents' in several crucial passages (e.g. Col. 2.9. 18, 21, 23); he

of more positive argument against his opponents, he seems to boldly employ their 'favorite terms, such as "knowledge" and "fullness", and turns them against the false teaching by filling them with orthodox content'.[4] Some focus on stylistic features and again insist that Colossians is non-Pauline,[5] but 'change in an author's style is a fairly common phenomenon in antiquity'.[6] Others concentrate on theology and contend that the absence of central Pauline concepts is a proof of inauthenticity,[7] but Paul does not necessarily have to use all his concepts in every epistle. In any case, neither language nor style and theology seem to be as decisive in establishing an argument against authenticity as has been suggested. It is not so strange that many scholars continue to maintain a Pauline authorship of Colossians.[8] If Rome is the letter's provenance, it may be dated to the early 60s.[9]

Colossians revolves round the problem of false teaching in the Colossian church. Colossians does not clearly elucidate what this heresy really was. But from Paul's counter-statements its characteristics can be assumed. It devalues the person of Christ (1.15-19), stresses human philosophy, cosmic elemental spirits (2.8), Judaic ordinances (such as circumcision [2.11; 3.11], dietary ordinances, and festival, new moon, and Sabbath observances [2.16]), and urges the worship of angels (2.18). This suggests that the false teaching was a syncretistic one that combined Jewish and Hellenistic teachings.[10] Paul believes that the prevalence of such syncretism threatened the Christians in Colossae, so he decides to write to the Colossians to protect them from harm. In particular, in order to deal with the heresy's detraction from the person of Christ, Paul underlines that all created things, including angels,

---

seems to find 'some distinguishing marks of the "heresy" ' there (P.T. O'Brien, *Colossians, Philemon* [WBC, 44; Waco: Word Books, 1982], p. xxxii). Hooker's opinion is criticized also by A.J.M. Wedderburn in A. Lincoln and A.J.M. Wedderburn, *The Theology of the Later Pauline Letters* (NTT; Cambridge: Cambridge University Press, 1993), pp. 3-4.

4. R.H. Gundry, *A Survey of the New Testament* (Grand Rapids: Zondervan, 1994), p. 395.

5. E.g. E. Schweizer, *The Letter to the Colossians: A Commentary* (London: SPCK, 1982), pp. 18-20; see O'Brien, *Colossians, Philemon*, pp. xliii-xliv.

6. H. Conzelmann and A. Lindemann, *Interpreting the New Testament* (trans. S.S. Schatzmann; Peabody: Hendrickson, 1988), p. 201.

7. E.g. Lohse, *Colossians and Philemon*, pp. 89-91.

8. There has never been a lack of those who argue for the authenticity of Colossians; see, e.g. Kümmel, *Introduction to the New Testament*, pp. 340-46; C.F.D. Moule, *The Epistles of Paul the Apostle to the Colossians and to Philemon* (Cambridge: Cambridge University Press, 1962), pp. 13-14; F.F. Bruce, *The Epistles to the Colossians, to Philemon, and to the Ephesians* (NICNT; Grand Rapids: Eerdmans, 1984), pp. 28-33; O'Brien, *Colossians, Philemon*, pp. xli-xlix.

9. Cf. N.T. Wright, *Colossians and Philemon* (TNTC; Leicester: IVP, 1986), pp. 36-37 who is inclined to see that Colossians was written in Ephesus (cf. Acts 19.8-10) 'in the period between 52 and 55 (or possibly 53 and 56)'.

10. Concerning the issue of the Colossian heresy, see J. Lähnemann, *Der Kolosserbrief* (Gerd Mohn: Gütersloher Verlagshaus, 1971), pp. 100-107; F. Zeilinger, *Der Erstgeborene der Schöpfung: Untersuchungen zur Formalstruktur und Theologie des Kolosserbriefes* (Wien: Verlag Herder, 1974), pp. 25-27; J.B. Lightfoot, *Colossians and Philemon* (London: MacMillan, 1900), pp. 71-95; F.F. Bruce, *Paul: Apostle of the Free Spirit* (Carlisle: Paternoster, 1977), p. 413; R.P. Martin, *Reconciliation: A Study of Paul's Theology* (London: Morgan & Scott, 1981), pp. 112-14; Wright, *Colossians and Philemon*, pp. 23-30; R. Yates, 'Colossians and Gnosis', *JSNT* 27 (1986), pp. 49-68; R.A. Argall, 'The Source of a Religious Error in Colossae', *CTJ* 22.1 (1987), pp. 6-20.

owe their existence to Christ, in whom all God's 'fullness' dwells (1.19; 2.9); for
him, Christ is the image of the invisible God and God's agent in his creative work
(1.15-16). This very idea seems to correspond to the imagery of putting-on-the-
new-man in 3.10, because the 'man' in this imagery is spoken of as one who is
continuously renewed 'after the image of God'. As we shall see, this concept involves a Christological force.[11] In contrast to syncretistic teachings, Paul wishes to
present a high Christology, from which he desires to extract practical exhortations
on the Christian life. Christians for him are those who experience a constant renewal
in their innermost being after the model of God's absolute image, namely Christ.[12]

2.2. *The Context of Colossians 3.9-10*
Col. 3.9-10 belongs to a wider unit, verses 1-17, which refer to how the gospel of
the believer's dying and living with Christ (cf. 2.12-13) is worked out in his life.[13]
In verses 1-4 the author puts forward the underlying principle of his ethical teaching,
an argument that the Christian life should be lived from the perspective of having
been raised with Christ.[14] The recognition of eschatological redemption, which
depends on union with Christ (who has ascended and is seated at the right hand of
God), should be the foundation of Christian ethics.

The implications in Col. 3.1-4 are explicated in 3.5-17. This consists of two parts
of exhortation, firstly negative and then positive (vv. 5-11/12-14),[15] and of con-
clusive remarks (vv. 15-17). In verses 5-11 Paul describes what the Christian life
should *not* be. Christians must not keep whatever belongs to their earthly nature:
sexual immorality, impurity, lust, evil desires, greed (v. 5), anger, rage, malice,
slander, and filthy language (v. 8).[16] Nor should they lie, because they have put off
their old nature with their practices (v. 9) and have put on a new nature which is
being renewed in knowledge in the image of its Creator (v. 10). In God's re-
creation there cannot be ethnic, religious, cultural or social discrimination (v. 11).

In contrast, in verses 12-14 Paul makes homiletical exhortations as to what the
Christian life should be. In this passage the author suggests affirmative precepts and
rounds off this unit of ethical exhortation. Believers should clothe themselves with
compassion, kindness, humility, gentleness, patience, toleration and forgiveness

11. See Chapter 9, §2.3.4.
12. See Chapter 9, §2.3.4.
13. Col. 3.1-17 is the larger part of 3.1–4.1, which may be called 'Paraenesis for the New Life';
see P. Pokorný, *Colossians: A Commentary* (Peabody: Hendrickson, 1991), p. 157.
14. Cf. J.D.G. Dunn, *The Epistles to the Colossians and to Philemon* (NIGTC; Grand Rapids:
Eerdmans, 1996), p. 202.
15. G. Cannon, *The Use of Traditional Materials in Colossians* (Macon: Mercer University Press,
1983), Chapter 3 (especially pp. 51-52, 70-73, 79-82) argues that the lists of vices and virtues in Col.
3.5-12 are based on materials already existing and drawn from a standard type of baptismal instruction.
16. J.C. Beker, 'Colossians', in *HBC* (San Francisco: Harper & Row, 1988), pp. 1226-229 (1228)
contends that the first series of five vices point to 'pagan sins of the past', while the second series of
five vices indicate 'ecclesial sins as present temptations'; see also R. Yates, 'The Christian Way of Life:
The Paraenetic Material in Colossians 3.1-4.6', *EQ* 63.3 (1991), pp. 241-51 (243); cf. M.P. Horgan,
'The Letter to the Colossians', in *NJBC* (London: Geoffrey Chapman, 1990 [1968]), pp. 876-82 (882).

(vv. 12-13), and over all these virtues put on love, which binds them all together in perfect unity (v. 14).[17]

In verses 15-17 the author expresses his desire that as members of one body the believers should maintain the peace of Christ (v. 15), that they may be appropriate participants in worship (v. 16), and that whatever they do, whether in word or deed, they may do everything in the name of the Lord Jesus, giving thanks to God through him (v. 17).

A number of ideas in Col. 3.1-17 are involved in the putting-on-the-new-man metaphor. As the concept of dying and living with Christ (vv. 1-4) corresponds to the metaphor in verses 9-10, the metaphor may have a 'realized' eschatological significance; the recognition of eschatological salvation should be the foundation for the life of those who put off the old man and put on the new (vv. 9-10).[18] Two negative imperative verbs in verses 8, 9 and their connection with similar words in Col. 2.11-12, imply that the clothing-with-a-person metaphor is associated with the baptismal idea.[19] The words 'with its practice', which follow the concept of the old man, make it clear that the metaphor includes a moral concern (v. 9);[20] modifying words for the new man suggest that the metaphor involves the Adam–Christ motif (v. 10).[21] Further, another clothing idea again suggests that the metaphor is concerned with Christian ethics (v. 12);[22] the concept of equality of human beings in the new man (v. 11) and of being called into one body (v. 15) implies that the metaphor has an ecclesiological significance.[23]

2.3. *The Meaning of Clothing with the New Man*

2.3.1. *Introductory Remarks*. In this section we will, first of all, attempt to prove that the clothing-with-the-new-man imagery in Col. 3.9-10 probably has in mind the rite of baptism in the first-century Christian community, so as to connote Christians' baptismal union with Christ.[24] On the basis of this, we will try to verify that the metaphor comprises a variety of implications, namely baptismal identification with Christ who was dead and has been raised, adoption of a new personality in Christ who is the new Adam,[25] and incorporation into his ecclesial body.[26]

---

17. Here the idea of putting on Christian virtues (vv. 12-14) seems to be bound up with the idea of putting on the new man (vv. 9-10). For Paul, those who are dressed in the new man should be able to show themselves to be dressed in Christian virtues. That the believer has put on the new man is a statement of his identity; that he should put on virtues is a statement of his expected practice. For an investigation of the meaning of the idea of putting on virtues, consult section 2.4.3.2, below.

18. See §2.4.3, below.

19. See §2.3.2, below.

20. See §2.4.3.1, below.

21. See §2.3.4, below.

22. See §2.4.3.2, below.

23. See §2.3.5, below.

24. Baptismal traces in Col. 3.8-11 are detected in its use of baptismal language; in particular, the correspondence of this passage with Col. 2.11-12, where baptismal concepts are noticeable, magnifies the probability that behind the clothing-with-the-new-man metaphor in Col. 3.9-10 there stands the rite of baptism.

25. In order to attain a proper understanding of the metaphor of putting-on-the-new-man, it is

2.3.2. Baptismal Unity with Christ: Implications of Baptismal Language in Colossians 3.8-11. In Col. 3.5-11 the author exhorts the Colossians to actualize the decisive change which has already taken place since their conversion. The contrast between 'then' and 'now' in Col. 3.7-8 obviously refers to 'the readers' pre- and post-conversion days'.[27] Yet, this does not necessarily mean that the two participles in Col. 3.9-10, ἀπεκδυσάμενοι and ἐνδυσάμενοι, refer to the event of conversion only.[28] With these words the author wishes to speak of baptism, which in turn recalls conversion. Conversion and baptism appear to the author as if they were one event. It would, therefore, be more accurate to argue that the two participles describe baptism as the completion of a union with Christ that was started at conversion. Their vivid and illustrative character suggests that they describe the practice of baptism. R.P. Martin affirms in a somewhat exaggerated manner,

> All commentators agree that there is a baptismal motif in these verbs [3.8-11], taken from the activity of disrobing and re-clothing for the act of baptism when the new Christian entered the water.[29]

E. Lohse also asserts that both ἀπεκδυσάμενοι and ἐνδυσάμενοι 'describe the past event of baptism, which should be determinative of the present' (vv. 9, 10).[30] The author desires to spur believers to live a godly life by reminding them that they have been united with Christ. The Colossians have already experienced in baptism not only a divestiture of their old identity but also an investiture with their new. They are now required to put into practice what has already taken place in them.

It is not accidental that Col. 3.8-11 includes some verbs associated with baptism. Following P. Carrington,[31] Martin argues that the verb ἀποτίθημι in Col. 3.8 is 'common property in the New Testament vocabulary of catechetical instruction, especially applicable to recent converts who were being educated for their new way of life' (Rom. 13.12; Eph. 4.22, 25; 1 Pet. 2.1).[32] He also asserts that the verb

---

necessary to discern who 'the new man' in it is. In Col. 3.9-10 the decisive summons to put off the old man and put on the new man is controlled by the Adam–Christ typology and seems to echo the Jewish thought of Adam's pre-Fall investiture in the Jewish Adam traditions, which are reflected in various clothing documents of antiquity, especially *Apocalypse of Moses*, rabbinic literature and *The Hymn of the Pearl*.

26. The connection of the putting-on-the-new-man imagery with the concept of human equality in Christ (Col. 3.11), one body (Col. 3.15), 'one new man' (Eph. 2.15) and mutual membership (Eph. 4.25) implies that the imagery includes a significance of believers' ecclesiological unity with Christ; see section 2.3.5, below.

27. R.P. Martin, *Ephesians, Colossians, and Philemon, Interpretation: A Bible Commentary for Teaching and Preaching* (Atlanta: John Knox, 1991), p. 123: 'the contrast of "then... now" referring to the readers' pre- and post-conversion days lies at the heart of much Pauline ethical exhortation and is seen in vv. 7-8'.

28. *Contra* O'Brien, *Colossians, Philemon*, pp. 188-89.

29. R.P. Martin, *Colossians and Philemon* (NCBC; London: Oliphants, 1974), p. 106.

30. Lohse, *Colossians and Philemon*, p. 141.

31. P. Carrington, *The Primitive Christian Catechism* (Cambridge: Cambridge University Press, 1940), pp. 46-49.

32. R.P. Martin, *Colossians: The Church's Lord and the Christian's Liberty* (Exeter: Paternoster,

ἀπεκδυσάμενοι in 3.9 'belongs to the act of baptism, where the new disciple was instructed to regard taking off his garments for the ordinance as a pictorial renunciation of an old life-style'[33] (cf. Gal. 3.27; Rom. 6.4-7). Similarly, C.J. Allen contends that the terms ἀπόθεσθε, ἀπεκδυσάμενοι and ἐνδυσάμενοι are 'key words of the primitive catechesis' and that the baptismal allusion is clear, whether it is specially to new baptismal garments, or to the new robe given to initiates in the mystery religions, or simply to the unclothing and reclothing of those baptized by immersion.[34] It would accordingly be legitimate to assume that the paraenesis Col. 3.8-11 is 'based on the believer's experience of baptism',[35] although Paul's major concern is primarily with its spiritual reality, namely, unity with Christ.

However, J.D.G. Dunn argues that if one were to see Col. 2.20; 3.1, 3, 9-10 as referring to baptism, one would make the mistake of 'externalizing what is primarily a spiritual transaction'.[36] He contends that 'baptism may play a part in it, but baptism is not at all the focus of attention', and that Paul exhorts his readers to repeat 'what they [the Colossians] did once at the beginning of their Christian lives (ἐνδύσασθε, v. 12; ἐνδυσάμενοι, v. 10)'. He believes that if the suggested passages are considered as being connected with baptism, Paul means to admonish his audience to repeat their baptism.[37] Accordingly he concludes that 'the putting off and putting on at conversion-initiation was essentially a spiritual act of self-renunciation and commitment (cf. 3.5 with Rom. 8.13)', and that 'Paul's mind is wholly on the spiritual change which can be represented under the different figures of death and resurrection, disrobing and enclothing, not on baptism'.[38]

However, it is hard to accept every aspect of Dunn's view. He seems to avoid acknowledging that the aorist participles ἀπεκδυσάμενοι/ἐνδυσάμενοι are linked with baptism. He seems to think that, if he acknowledged it, he would have to assume that baptism was repeatable. Yet, although the terms are associated with

1972), p. 111; cf. C.J. Allen (ed.), *2 Corinthians-Philemon* (BBC, 11; Nashville: Broadman, 1971), p. 245; Lohse, *Colossians and Philemon*, p. 140.

33. Martin, *The Church's Lord and the Christian's Liberty*, p. 111; cf. C.F.D. Moule, 'Colossians and Philemon', in *PCB* (London: Nelson, 1963), pp. 990-95 (994): 'put off' in Col. 3.11 refers to 'the baptismal divesture (cf. 2.11), perhaps symbolised by the baptisand's undressing for descent into the water'.

34. Allen (ed.), *2 Corinthians-Philemon*, p. 245; cf. J. Jervell, *Imago Dei: Gen 1,26f. im Spätjudentum, in der Gnosis und in den paulinischen Briefen* (FRLANT, 76; Göttingen: Vandenhoeck & Ruprecht, 1960), pp. 231-56; Martin, *Ephesians, Colossians, and Philemon*, p. 125; E. Käsemann, *Leib und Leib Christi: Eine Untersuchung zur paulinischen Begrifflichkeit* (BHT, 9; Tübingen: Mohr [Paul Siebeck], 1933), pp. 147-50; Horgan, 'The Letter to the Colossians', p. 882; Pokorný, *Colossians*, p. 168.

35. Cannon, *The Use of Traditional Materials in Colossians*, p. 71.

36. J.D.G. Dunn, *Baptism in the Holy Spirit* (London: SCM Press, 1970), p. 158. Cf. also E.F. Scott, *The Epistles of Paul to the Colossians, to Philemon and to the Ephesians* (MoffNTC; London: Hodder & Stoughton, 1942 [1930]), p. 68; D. Daube, 'Appended Note: Participle and Imperative in 1 Peter', in E.G. Selwyn, *The First Epistle of St. Peter* (London: Macmillan, 1952 [1946]), pp. 467-88; Yates, 'The Christian Way of Life', p. 247.

37. Dunn, *Baptism in the Holy Spirit*, p. 158.

38. Dunn, *Baptism in the Holy Spirit*, p. 158.

baptism, this does not necessarily mean that baptism itself has to be repeated. What the author wishes to do is to exhort believers to actualize what baptism has accomplished, that is, their conversion change, the reality of which is union with Christ. When the Colossian Christians 'recall their baptism they are to allow its dynamic effect to release them and to act out their baptismal profession of being true to it'.[39] For Paul, believers leave behind the evil practices of the old way of life in baptism, but they are unceasingly tempted by them; they are dead to the world with Christ, but they are continuously influenced by it; they live under a tension between 'already' and 'not yet'. For this reason, Paul sometimes uses the indicative and sometimes uses the imperative, looking both backwards and forwards.

Out of all these observations, we can conclude that the clothing-with-the-new-man metaphor portrays baptismal union with Christ. For the writer of Colossians, the baptisand's redressing with a garment after baptism symbolizes that he has been united with Christ. This symbolism seems to be influenced by the idea that the priest's washing himself with water and clothing himself with priestly sacred garments make him a being who is in union with God (cf. Exod. 29.4-9; Lev. 16.3-4).[40] When we dealt with the metaphor of clothing with Christ in Gal. 3.27, we suggested that part of its significance is probably a believer's being identified with Christ's priestly righteousness.[41] As was examined in Part I, a similiar thought occurs in Philo.[42] He explains that when the priest puts on priestly garments, he becomes superior to all men (*Vita Mos.* ii.131), probably meaning that the priest becomes a quasi-divine being. Philo ascribes a cosmological significance to the high priest's garments; he writes that when the high priest wears them he is changed into a microcosm. This implies that he is identified with God (as well as with the world, i.e. the universe), because for Philo the world is to be identified with God (cf. *Leg. Al.* iii.29). A similiar idea is found in Apuleius' *Metamorphoses*, as this document implies that Lucius' twelve garments which he wears after his initiation ceremony symbolize his union with Isis (cf. *Metam.* XI.24).[43] As was referred to in Chapter 5, the document reflects mystery-religions ideas. Probably Paul is also familiar with these ideas.

Furthermore, when the author of Colossians places emphasis on the present realization of what has already been done, he probably considers that clothes are dominant in picturing a wearer's appearance. Like clothes, Christ (who is the believer's garment) should be the dominant representation of the believer.

2.3.3. Baptismal Participation in Christ's Death-and-Resurrection: Implications of Correspondence between Colossians 3.8-11 and 2.11-12. The connection of the clothing-with-the-new-man metaphor with baptism (Col. 3.10) can be further

39. Martin, *Ephesians, Colossians, and Philemon*, p. 123; *Colossians and Philemon*, p. 106.
40. See Chapter 1, §3.3.1.
41. See Chapter 8, §2.3.4.2.
42. See Chapter 2, §4.3.
43. See Chapter 5, §2.2.3. Of course, every aspect of the initiation ceremony in *Metam.* XI.22-24 neither matches the symbolism of the wearing of a priestly garment after the purification ritual nor conforms to the significance of the clothing-with-the-new-man metaphor in Col. 3.10.

reinforced by the fact that Col. 2.11-12, which parallels Col. 3.8-11,[44] includes not only the cognate noun ἀπέκδυσις but also the term βαπτισμός. This implies that baptism is part of the interpretation of the concept of putting off the old man and putting on the new man.[45] As the 'putting off the body of flesh' signifies elimination of the carnal nature in Col. 2.11, it must correspond to the concept of putting off the old man (Col. 3.9). F.F. Bruce rightly argues that the twin exhortation in Col. 3.9-10 seems to be the elaboration of Col. 2.11-12, 'where their baptism was said to be in effect the stripping off, not of an insignificant scrap of bodily tissue, as the old circumcision was, but of the whole "body of flesh"—the old nature in its entirety'.[46]

After identifying the spiritual circumcision with putting off the body of flesh (that is, eliminating the corrupted nature), the author of Colossians, in turn, identifies the latter with the circumcision of Christ (Col. 2.11). What is meant by this circumcision of Christ? J.P.W. Hunt argues that the phrase ἐν τῇ περιτομῇ τοῦ Χριστοῦ is 'not a periphrasis for baptism, but a reference to Christ's death which is viewed metaphorically as circumcision'.[47] However, this is not persuasive, because τῇ περιτομῇ τοῦ Χριστοῦ is in keeping with the concept of περιτομῇ ἀχειροποιήτῳ (v. 11a), which is a circumcision of the Colossians and not of Christ. It would, therefore, be correct to see the circumcision of Christ as the circumcision that belongs to Christ and not as the circumcision that he received. Christ is the author of the spiritual circumcision and the figure who makes it constantly effective.

The author once again identifies the circumcision of Christ as baptism (Col. 2.12). This means that he links the spiritual reality (which is described by a series of three concepts in Col. 2.11, that is, spiritual circumcision, the elimination of the sinful nature, and the circumcision of Christ) with a sacramental symbolism (i.e. baptism). Here in verse 12 baptism refers to water-baptism.[48] Even Dunn is forced to affirm that 'βάπτισμα can be nothing more than the rite of water-baptism...seen in its symbolical significance'.[49]

If so, what is the spiritual reality that 'baptism' in verse 12 refers to? In other words, what is the spiritual reality which is delineated by the series of the three concepts in Col. 2.11? For the author, baptism signifies the believer's death and

44. Lohse, *Colossians and Philemon*, p. 141.

45. The author of Colossians in 2.11-12 speaks of spiritual circumcision. The phrase 'without hands' indicates a divine instrumentality. The concept of 'putting off the body of flesh' connotes discarding the sinful nature. The Colossians received a spiritual circumcision when their corrupt nature was removed. The author probably refers to 'the circumcision of the heart' (Jer. 4.4; Deut. 10.16; 30.6). In his mind there is a contrast between physical and spiritual circumcision. While the circumcision of the law (i.e. of Moses or of the patriarchs) is characterized by cutting away only a part of the body, the spiritual circumcision is characterized by putting off the whole body, which is full of lusts.

46. Bruce, *The Epistles to the Colossians to Philemon and to the Ephesians*, p. 146; also see E.K. Simpson, *Commentary on the Epistles to the Ephesians and the Colossians* (ed. F.F. Bruce; NICNT; Grand Rapids: Eerdmans, 1972 [1957]), p. 272; G.W.H. Lampe, '*Baptisma* in the New Testament', *SJT* 5 (1952), pp. 163-74 (171).

47. J.P.W. Hunt, 'Colossians 2.11-12', *TB* 41.2 (1990), pp. 227-44 (242).

48. *Contra* Hunt, 'Colossians 2.11-12', p. 243.

49. Dunn, *Baptism in the Holy Spirit*, p. 154.

resurrection with Christ through faith in the power of God who raised him from the dead. In other words, baptism connotes being incorporated into Christ in his death and resurrection.[50] K. Grayston presumes that this thought is 'borrowed from Rom. 6.4 and adapted to suggest that rising with Christ, which is prospective in Romans, is immediate in Colossians'.[51] The burial metaphor describes the death the believer experiences when he participates in Christ's death, while the resurrection metaphor symbolizes his resurrection through his participation in Christ's resurrection (Col. 2.12).[52] J.B. Lightfoot holds that

> baptism is the grave of the old man, and the birth of the new. As he sinks beneath the baptismal waters, the believer buries there all his corrupt affections and past sins; as he emerges thence, he rises regenerate, quickened to new hopes and a new life... Thus baptism is an image of his participation both in the death and in the resurrection of Christ.[53]

In their union with Christ's death believers experience the death of their degenerate nature; in their union with Christ's resurrection they also experience the renovation of that nature. Baptism, the outward event, achieves this two-fold inward event. The believers should actualize over and over again what happened in baptism, an event of mortification of their fallen nature and conduct and of regeneration of their new nature and conduct through being united into the death and resurrection of Christ.

It becomes clear that the believer's death-and-resurrection union with Christ is the reality which the three concepts in Col. 2.11 (spiritual circumcision, the removal of the sinful nature, and the circumcision of Christ) commonly describe. In particular, the circumcision of Christ connotes putting off the depraved nature by being united with Christ, as the physical circumcision indicates the cutting of bodily tissue. This well matches the metaphor of putting off the old man and putting on the new man in Col. 3.9-10.

What becomes clear is that the metaphor of putting off the old man and putting on the new (Col. 3.9-10) refers to identification with Christ in baptism, the essence of which is participating in his death and resurrection.[54] By no means should the link between baptism and Col. 3.9-10 be minimized. Baptism is the visible form which contains the spiritual reality, viz. unity with Christ in his death and resurrection. Above all, the author of Colossians seems to draw on the Old Testament

---

50. Cf. H. Ridderbos, *Paul: An Outline of His Theology* (trans. J.R. de Witt; Grand Rapids: Eerdmans, 1975), pp. 403-404.

51. K. Grayston, *Dying, We Live: A New Enquiry into the Death of Christ in the New Testament* (New York and Oxford: Oxford University Press, 1990), p. 138.

52. Dunn, *Baptism in the Holy Spirit*, pp. 154-55 sees ἐν ᾧ at the beginning of Col. 2.12b as speaking not of baptism but of Christ. But this does not seem to be natural, because the word βαπτίσμῳ immediately before the relative pronoun ἐν ᾧ is naturally taken as its antecedent. Moreover, the fact that burial and resurrection are twin metaphors in sequence would refute Dunn's argument that baptism is in connection with burial but not with resurrection.

53. J.B. Lightfoot, *Colossians and Philemon* (London: MacMillan, 1900), p. 182.

54. Cf. Cannon, *The Use of Traditional Materials in Colossians*, pp. 72-73.

clothing idea which is implicitly or explicitly in association with the concept of death or life. As was investigated in Chapter 1, section 2, the image of Adam and his wife being clothed with garments of skins in Gen. 3.21 symbolizes the restoration to their original life out of their spiritual death, which had resulted from their Fall. In 2 Chron. 6.41, Ps. 132.16 and Isa. 61.10, the words 'putting on salvation' stand for acquiring divine life.

Further, it cannot be excluded that Paul perhaps makes use not only of the Jewish 'death-or-life' clothing traditions similar to those found in *Joseph and Aseneth* and *The Hymn of the Pearl*, but also of other 'death-or-life' clothing traditions, which are reflected in Apuleius' *Metamorphoses* XI. It is unlikely that as he uses the clothing imagery, he has never shared a dialogue with any source other than the Old Testament. He has not been deprived of the freedom to look into other documents and use them for his own purpose. The thought of death-and-life with the clothing imagery is shared by *Joseph and Aseneth*. In this work, the taking off of idolatrous apparel and the putting on of a black tunic (10.10a) symbolizes the death of Aseneth's pagan nature. Her putting off the black tunic, washing with water (= purification), and putting on a new linen garment (14.12) and putting on a splendid wedding garment afterwards (15.10) points to her having gained a new identity of life.[55] As the renewal of the believer's nature is achieved by his or her being united with Christ in his death and life in Col. 3.9-10, so the renewal of Aseneth's identity is fulfilled by her bridal union with the God-like Joseph by means of her from-death-to-life conversion to Judaism in *JA*. But the analogy between Christ and Adam operates behind the former, while such an analogy is not found in the latter.

Although *The Hymn of the Pearl* does not overtly use the concept of death or life, it can be thought of as being over-shadowed by the notion. In this document the prince's dressing himself in the Egyptian-style garment indicates the loss of his own self, while his returning to his father's kingdom and re-wearing his royal garment points to the recovery of his original self, namely the image of God, which is full of vitality and splendour. Inasmuch as the protagonist's eventual reinvestiture with his original self is considered to be the acquisition of salvation, namely life, his having been stripped of his original royal robe and clothed with an Egyptian-style garment probably indicates his state of spiritual death. As was argued in Chapter 4, since the prince symbolizes Adam in Genesis, *HPrl* could be thought of as sharing the same idea as is described by the imagery of putting off and putting on in Col. 3.9-10, where an Adamic theme is implicitly at work. But in *Hprl* there does not occur the typology between Christ and Adam as in Col. 3.9-10.

In Apuleius' *Metamorphoses* XI, Lucius's wearing of a beast-form symbolizes the state of death, while his being stripped of it and instead clad with a linen garment, with a new garment at the initiation ceremony afterward, and with the twelve-fold garments after the ritual of initiation, all indicate his having obtained life. This symbolism implies that the concept of clothing can stand for death or life. That is, one can dress himself/herself with a garment of death or one of life. In *Metam.* XI, the typology of Adam–Christ and the eschatological and ethical emphases, which

---

55. See Chapter 3, §§2.1; 2.2; 2.3.

are found in Col. 3.9-10, do not occur. Therefore, it is not strange that the tenor of clothing imagery in the document differs from that in Colossians 3. But both develop in common the concept of being identified with death or life by using the imagery of putting off or putting on.

It seems that Colossians' readers were familiar with the correlation of the concepts of death and life with the image of clothing. As the author of Colossians refers to believers' identification with Christ's death and life (cf. Col. 2.11-12) and speaks of their putting off the old man and putting on the new man in a baptismal significance (Col. 3.9-10), his audience probably understood this putting off/on imagery as signifying that they had been identified with Christ's death and resurrection life. In other words, they probably understood that the metaphor of putting off/on connotes that their fallen nature had been mortified and a new nature had been assumed by union with Christ's death and life.

2.3.4. Baptismal Adoption of a New Humanity in Christ the New Adam: Putting off the Old Man/Putting on the New Man (Colossians 3.9-10). The clothing-with-the-new man metaphor belongs to the contrast between 'putting off of the old man' and 'putting on of the new man'.[56] As was asserted, this contrast probably has a connection with baptism. R. Yates asserts that the old man and the new man in Col. 3.9-10, with their corporate associations, are

> part of the presentation of the gospel in terms of the two Adams… The dying and rising, the putting off and putting on, and the baptism into the death of Christ, are part of incorporation into the new creation in Christ, the second Adam.[57]

This statement indicates that Col. 3.9-10 signifies that putting off the old man and putting on the new man happens in baptism and points to a change from an Adamic being into a Christ-like being. Similarly, C.F.D. Moule in his comment on Col. 3.10 and Eph. 4.24 argues that

> the discarding of clothing before baptism and the reclothing afterwards was recognized as a vividly pictorial symbol of the break with the whole realm of the past, and the *inclusion* of the baptized—the veritable wrapping of him—in a new environment. And that environment was Christ himself, the ultimate Adam. Thus, the conception of Christ as the believers' 'environment' is further evidenced by the clothing metaphor.[58]

If so, we first need to ensure that Col. 3.9-10, to which the metaphor of putting off the old and putting on the new man belongs, really is controlled by the analogy of Adam–Christ. It is true that the author of Colossians does not provide much

---

56. O'Brien, *Colossians, Philemon*, p. 190 sees the adjective νέος (which stands in contrast to παλαιός) as conveying the same sense as the synonym καινός.

57. Yates, 'The Christian Way of Life', pp. 246-47; cf. C.F.D. Moule, *The Origin of Christology* (Cambridge: Cambridge University Press, 1977), p. 88; Martin, *Ephesians, Colossians, and Philemon*, p. 124: 'For Paul, the symbolic universe is set out as "in Adam/in Christ", with Gen. 1.26-27 clearly in the background of our text. Becoming a Christian, for Paul, was nothing short of leaving the old order (in Adam) and being taken up into the new eon determined by Christ's advent as the last Adam'.

58. C.F.D. Moule, *The Origin of Christology*, p. 88.

information about the identity of the old man and the new man. We are not, however, totally in the dark about who these 'men' are, because they are sharply opposed to one another, and in particular, the new man is quite discernibly portrayed by the modifiers. The author describes 'the new man' with the words, ἀνα-καινούμενον εἰς ἐπίγνωσιν κατ᾽ εἰκόνα τοῦ κτίσαντος αὐτόν (Col. 3.10b). Of these words, the pronoun αὐτον obviously points to the new man.[59] M. Black insists that the creator of the new man (τοῦ κτίσαντος αὐτον) is not God but Christ.[60] However, this does not seem to be correct, because the concept of εἰκών (which is modified by τοῦ κτίσαντος αὐτον) seems to allude to Gen. 1.26-27.[61] Beyond doubt, the creation story in Genesis lends support to the idea that τοῦ κτίσαντος is God rather than Christ;[62] God is the creator of the new man. If so, we may interpret 'the image' as 'the image of God';[63] 'it is God who provides the prototype for humanity's renewal'.[64]

However, this is not all that the author intends to express by the concept of εἰκόνα τοῦ κτίσαντος αὐτον. For the specific exhortations in Col. 3.5-17 are derived from the Christological indicatives of Col. 3.1-4. It is, therefore, highly probable that since the image of God points to Christ,[65] κατ᾽ εἰκόνα τοῦ κτίσαντος αὐτόν can be rendered 'after the model of Christ, who is God's image'. C.F.D. Moule contends that κατ᾽ εἰκόνα refers not merely to 'the original creation of man "after God's likeness" (cf. Eph. iv. 24, κατὰ θεόν) but, more specifically, to *Christ* who is the εἰκών of God'.[66]

'The new man', however, cannot be directly equated with Christ himself.[67] If such were the case, we would have to say that Christ (= the new man) has been renewed after his own model, which does not make sense.[68] Of course, one could

59. R. Scroggs, *The Last Adam: A Study in Pauline Anthropology* (Oxford: Blackwell, 1966), pp. 69-70.

60. M. Black, 'The Pauline Doctrine of the Second Adam', *SJT* 7 (1954), pp. 170-79 (175).

61. See C.F.D. Moule, *The Epistles to the Colossians and to Philemon*, pp. 119-20; Scroggs, *The Last Adam*, p. 69.

62. L.B. Radford, *The Epistle to the Colossians and the Epistle to Philemon* (WC; London: Methuen, 1931), p. 268: 'Christ is never described as creator; He is not the source but the agent of creation, Col. i.16, Eph. iii.9, Heb. ii.10, Jn. i.3'.

63. Jervell, *Imago Dei*, p. 249-50; Lohse, *Colossians and Philemon*, pp. 142-43.

64. Martin, *The Church's Lord and the Christian's Liberty*, p. 115.

65. Col. 1.15 states that Christ is the invisible image of God (cf. Col. 1.19; 2 Cor. 4.4). See S.V. McCasland, ' "The Image of God" according to Paul', *JBL* LXIX (1950), pp. 85-100 (especially pp. 87-88).

66. Moule, *The Epistles to the Colossians and to Philemon*, p. 120.

67. M.J. Harris, *Colossians & Philemon: Exegetical Guide to the Greek New Testament* (Grand Rapids: Eerdmans, 1991), p. 152; A.L. Williams (ed.), *The Epistles of Paul the Apostle to the Colossians and to Philemon* (Cambridge: Cambridge University Press, 1907), p. 130; *contra* C.F.D. Moule, 'Colossians and Philemon', p. 994; Lohse, *Colossians and Philemon*, p. 142; Martin, *Colossians and Philemon*, p. 107; Meeks, *The First Urban Christians*, p. 155; Simpson, *Commentary on the Epistles to the Ephesians and the Colossians*, p. 273; R.C. Tannehill, *Dying and Rising with Christ* (Berlin: Verlag Alfred Töpelmann, 1967), pp. 25, 50.

68. Cf. E. Best, *One Body in Christ: A Study in the Relationship of the Church to Christ in the Epistles of the Apostle Paul* (London: SPCK, 1955), pp. 67-68; Williams (ed.), *The Epistles of Paul the Apostle to the Colossians and to Philemon*, p. 130: 'Christ is not ἀνακαινούμενος εἰς ἐπιγωσιν'.

say that in effect the new man can indicate Christ; when the new man points to a being who is regenerated after the pattern of Christ, that being is effectively identified with Christ. When 'the new man' is one in whom the Christ-like nature is being fulfilled, he is someone who is being transformed to a person like Christ.[69] On the basis of this, one could say that the new man symbolizes Christ.[70] But it is still hardly correct to assert that the new man *is* Christ. As a creation the new man is distinguished from Christ whom he should resemble.[71]

Therefore, we affirm that the new man refers to the Christian's new nature which is formed after the pattern of Christ. This new nature may also be called a 'new humanity' or 'new manhood' or 'new character'.[72] H.C.G. Moule properly sees 'the old man' as 'the old state of the unregenerate; the state in Adam, not in Christ; the state of guilt under sentence and of bondage under temptation, with all the subtle "practices" which it fosters in heart and life', and 'the new man' as a being who enters, in the second Adam, on his new state of acceptance and of spiritual victory.[73] Accordingly, it would be legitimate to argue that the new man points to a renewed humanity modelled on Christ, while the old man points to a spoiled humanity modelled on fallen Adam. But why does the author of Colossians use the antithesis between 'the *old* man' and 'the *new* man' rather than the contrast between 'Adam' and 'Christ'? Probably he believes that the antithesis between the old man and the new man more effectively contrasts the old nature (to be taken off) with the new nature (to be put on). The 'old' and 'new' sounds practical, while the 'Adam' and 'Christ' sounds rather doctrinal. By employing the former, the author wishes to make his readers remember that in baptism the old corrupt humanity was taken off and the new regenerated humanity has been adopted. But, for the author, it is clear that the old humanity is inherited from Adam and the new humanity springs from Christ. J. Eadie, who concentrates on the concept of 'the old man', says,

> It [the 'old man'] is a bold personification of our first nature as derived from Adam, the source and seat of original and actual transgression, and called 'old', as existing prior to our converted state.[74]

Eadie's explanations are extremely persuasive, because it is obvious that Col. 3.10b, by referring to the story of Adam's creation in Gen. 1.26-27,[75] describes God's eschatological new creation.

---

69. Bruce, *The Epistles to the Colossians, to Philemon, and to the Ephesians*, p. 147.

70. For exactly the same reason, 'the old man' could be considered as symbolizing the fallen Adam. But this cannot mean that the old man can be directly equated with Adam.

71. *Contra* Martin, *The Church's Lord and the Christian's Liberty*, p. 116.

72. Cf. C.H. Dodd, 'Colossians', in F.C. Eiselen *et al.* (eds.), *ABC* (New York: Abingdon, 1929), pp. 1250-262 (1260); Allen (ed.), *2 Corinthians-Philemon*, p. 246; G.H.P. Thompson, *Letters of Paul to the Ephesians to the Colossians and to Philemon* (ed. P.R. Ackroyd *et al.*; CBC; Cambridge: Cambridge University Press, 1967), p. 152: 'the character and quality of life seen in Jesus'.

73. H.C.G. Moule, *Colossian and Philemon Studies: Lessons in Faith and Holiness* (London: Pickering & Inglis, n.d.), p. 213.

74. J. Eadie, *A Commentary on the Greek Text of the Epistle of Paul to the Colossians* (Grand Rapids: Baker, 1979 [from the 1884 edition]), p. 222; cf. O'Brien, *Colossians, Philemon*, pp. 189-90.

75. Lohse, *Colossians and Philemon*, p. 142; Martin, *Colossians and Philemon*, p. 107; G.E. Sterling,

The phrase, εἰς ἐπίγνωσιν (Col. 3.10b), also suggests that the putting off/on of the old/new man metaphor is connected with the author's understanding of the story of Adam in Genesis. For the author, true 'knowledge' is an important token of those who have experienced investiture with the new man.[76] The word ἐπίγνωσιν may be interpreted as the knowledge of God,[77] that is to say, the knowledge of God's will and his purposes of salvation.[78] The author seems to believe that before the Fall the knowledge of God, which was an important element in the image of God, played the role of being an ethical incentive,[79] thereby preserving a unique relationship with God in faithful obedience to him and that as such, the recovered knowledge of God should play a part in stimulating godly living, thereby sustaining a desirable relationship with God.

Thus when the metaphor of putting off the old man and putting on the new man in Col. 3.9-10 connotes the change from the old Adamic nature to the new Adamic nature, it speaks of restoration to the original state of Adam. Hereby it reflects how the author interprets the first chapters of Genesis, especially the pre-Fall state of Adam. Since he designates this state as one of being clothed (that is, clothed with the new man formed in Christ as the new Adam), he probably maintains that the original Adam was dressed with the image of God.

If this is true, the metaphor could be regarded as a product which results from the author's dialogue with contemporary Jewish Adam traditions, which maintain Adam's pre-Fall clothing, although they are not extant. The probability of the existence of such traditions would be supported by there being Jewish writings which also suggest Adam's pre-Fall clothing. For example, although its date is not

---

' "Wisdom Among the Perfect": Creation Traditions in Alexandrian Judaism and Corinthian Christianity', *NovT* 37 (1995), pp. 355-84 (379); Jervell, *Imago Dei*, pp. 231-48 believes that the teaching of Gen. 1.26-27 plays a decisively significant part in the paraenetic statement of Col. 3.10.

76. Simpson, *Commentary on the Epistles to the Ephesians and the Colossians*, p. 274 holds that 'the "knowledge" that was held out to the Colossians by their would-be teachers was a distorted and imperfect thing in comparison with the full knowledge available to those who, through their union with Christ, had been transformed by the renewing of their minds'; cf. Schweizer, *The Letter to the Colossians*, p. 197: 'in no sense is it ["knowledge"] a matter of Gnostic insight into the nothingness of the material world'. Perhaps, the author argues against the Colossian false teachers' claim that 'knowledge' is to be acquired through mystical experience (Martin, *The Church's Lord and the Christian's Liberty*, p. 117).

77. C.F.D. Moule, *The Epistles to the Colossians and to Philemon*, pp. 159-64; Simpson, *Commentary on the Epistles to the Ephesians and the Colossians*, p. 274.

78. A. Van Roon, *The Authenticity of Ephesians* (NovTSup, 39; Leiden: Brill, 1974), p. 339; Martin, *The Church's Lord and the Christian's Liberty*, p. 116; cf. Williams (ed.), *The Epistles of Paul the Apostle to the Colossians and to Philemon*, p. 131; C.F.D. Moule, 'Colossians and Philemon', p. 994; Pokorný, *Colossians*, p. 169; Lohse, *Colossians and Philemon*, p. 143.

79. The story of the creation of man in Genesis highlights that man was created in the image of God (Gen. 1.26-27). That God's image was implanted into man can be, in a sense, thought of as God himself entering into man. In such a relationship, man's knowledge of God was supreme, on the basis of which he could make a right ethical decision toward God; whether or not to obey God was the most crucial issue for him. But when he was tempted to the Fall, his knowledge of God came to be distorted and malfunctioned. See Chapter 1, §2.3.

clear, whether it is pre-biblical or post-biblical, *Apocalypse of Moses* 20–21 suggests that Adam and Eve's prelapsarian garments consisted of righteousness and
glory.[80] For the author of *Apoc. Mos.*, these two elements were central features of
the image of God in them, and they echo the concept that the new man is to be
formed through ongoing renewal after the absolute image of God, that is, Christ in
Col. 3.10 (cf. Rom. 8.29). Also in post-biblical rabbinic literature, the thought of
Adam's pre-Fall clothing is prevalent.[81] It seems too that the author of *The Hymn
of the Pearl* maintains the thought of Adam's pre-Fall clothing; he speaks of the
protagonist's reinvestiture with his splendid and glorious royal silken garment
(which symbolizes the image of God), which he had worn originally before he left
his Father's kingdom.[82] In particular, the statement that the prince attained a perfect
self-knowledge when he was reclothed in his original garment in verse 77 resembles Col. 3.10, which sees true knowledge as an important feature of the new man.

In relation to the fact that baptism underlies the clothing metaphor in Col. 3.9-
10, the author might relate certain aspects of the rite of baptism to the ritual of the
priest's changing garments (cf. Exod. 29.4-9; Lev. 16.3-4). He perhaps thinks of
the priest becoming a special person, when he wore the holy, priestly garment (cf.
Exod. 29.2, 40). In particular, Urim and Thummim, that is, 'lights' and 'perfections',[83] do not seem remote from the concept of constant renewal implied by the
term, τὸν ἀνακαινούμενον, in Col. 3.10b. R.P. Martin asserts that the latter verse
contains 'the hope that the splendour and glory, which mankind had lost in Adam's
fall, would be restored'.[84]

The fact that the imagery of putting off the old man and putting on the new
delineates a radical change in a person's character could also be compared with a
Roman male's critical change of status when he passes from boyhood to manhood,
taking off the *toga praetexta* and putting on the *toga virilis* in a ceremony.[85]
Further, inasmuch as the putting off/on metaphor in Colossians 3 includes the
notion of ethical regeneration,[86] it could also be compared to the scene in which the
high priest Joshua's dirty garment was replaced by a new one (Zech. 3.3-5), signifying the ethical renewal of the Israelites.

---

80. See Chapter 2, §3.2.
81. See Chapter 2, §5.
82. See Chapter 4, §§3.1 and 3.4.
83. See Chapter 1, §3.2.
84. Martin, *Colossians and Philemon*, p. 107.
85. See Chapter 6.
86. Christians are those who experience an ongoing mortification of their Adamic humanity
and who continuously actualize the Christ-like humanity that already exists in them (cf. Harris,
Colossians & Philemon, p.158). This constant renewal seems to effect the same result as the day-
by-day renewal of the Christians in 2 Cor. 4.16b. Perhaps the author of Colossians believes that the
image of God (in Adam) which was defaced (J. Gnilka, *Der Kolosserbrief*[HTKNT, 10.1; Freiburg:
Herder, 1980], p. 188) by Adam's fall into sin, would be recovered at baptism. In other words, in
baptism Adam's original state of glory, emanating from the image of God in him, is achieved in
'the new man' who is regenerated after the pattern of Christ. Concerning the inclusion of an ethical
significance in the putting off/on metaphor in Col. 3.9-10, see section 2.4.3.1, below.

On the basis of all these observations, we suggest that the clothing-with-the-new-man metaphor in Colossians 3 signifies the believer's baptismal identification with his innermost being, continuously renewed after the image of God, i.e. Christ who is the new Adam, so as to be restored from a post-Fall Adamic personality to a pre-Fall Adamic personality, that is, a Christ-like personality. The author seems to believe that the clothing imagery is well-suited to describe the varied aspects of the change in human nature: a garment manifests its wearer's character, is always in contact with the wearer so as to be virtually part of him/her, and dominates his/her appearance.

2.3.5. Baptismal Incorporation into Ecclesial Oneness in Christ: The New Man as the Ecclesial Locus of Human Equilibrium (Colossians 3.11); One Body (3.15). Adding to the descriptive words for the new man in Col. 3.10b, the author in verse 11 implies that in the new man all the 'accidental distinctions are transcended'.[87] In the new humanity there can be no ethnic (Greek/Jew), religious (circumcised/uncircumcised), cultural (barbarian/Scythian)[88] or social (slave/free) differences (Col. 3.11). The word ὅπου in the verse refers to the new man.[89] The elimination of differences is a crucial theme in 'the baptismal reunification formula' (Gal. 3.28; 1 Cor. 12.13; Gal. 6.15; 1 Cor. 15.28; Eph. 1.23).[90] E. Schweizer holds that Col. 3.11 'takes over from Gal. 3.28 the picture of what baptism really means'.[91] The key idea of Col. 3.11 is 'the exhortation to really live out of the event (which is valid once and for all) of having been called into the new world'.[92]

The author's emphasis is that all people are equal within the new man. If so, 'the new man' is not merely a term for an individual but also a term for a corpus; on the one hand, it refers to an individual nature being continually renewed after the model of Christ who is the image of God, on the other hand to a corporate humanity formed by believers in Christ.[93] The new type of humanity reveals itself in the Christian community, the church.[94] The new humanity is embodied in the church. Since the church is a reality which Christ is establishing by reconciling all human distinctions and forming a new humanity, there cannot be any conflicts in it. In the unity of the church-organism there is no room for the old divisions. Christ encompasses

---

87. Dodd, 'Colossians', p. 1260.

88. These groups are not opposites, as the other pairs are. They have in common that they stood outside the circle of civilized Greek culture, but it seems that the two groups were in grave cultural conflict with each other; for a detailed study on Col. 3.11, see T. Martin, 'The Scythian Perspective in Col. 3.11', *NovT* 37 (1995), pp. 249-61; cf. Martin, *The Church's Lord and the Christian's Liberty*, p. 118; Simpson, *Commentary on the Epistles to the Ephesians and the Colossians*, p. 274.

89. Pokorný, *Colossians*, p. 169; Lohse, *Colossians and Philemon*, p. 146.

90. W.A. Meeks, 'Image of the Androgyne: Some Uses of a Symbol in Earliest Christianity', *History of Religions* 13 (1974), pp. 165-208 (180-83).

91. Schweizer, *The Letter to the Colossians*, p. 196.

92. Schweizer, *The Letter to the Colossians*, p. 196.

93. O'Brien, *Colossians, Philemon*, p. 191; cf. Dodd, 'Colossians', p. 1260; Martin, *Colossians and Philemon*, p. 107; R.W. Wall, *Colossians & Philemon* (ed. G.R. Osborne; The IVP New Testament Commentary Series; Illinois: Intervarity Press, 1993), p. 142.

94. Pokorný, *Colossians*, p. 169; cf. Martin, *Ephesians, Colossians, and Philemon*, p. 123.

the whole of the church and at the same time indwells her; 'Christ is all, and in all'.[95] The Christ who binds his people together in one resides in each of them. As the new man is being formed by the church, he can be thought of as having an ecclesiological aspect. Through baptism believers are incorporated into the church, which is represented by Christ. Like a garment, believers endue themselves with the new man as the ecclesial reality.

In the same vein, the author in Col. 3.15 states that the Colossians have been called 'in one body' (ἐν ἑνὶ σώματι).[96] This phrase corresponds to the concept of the new man in verse 10. As Christians are designated as those who have put on the new man and are at the same time spoken of as those who have been called in one body, it is implied that the clothing-with-the-new-man does not simply refer to an event involving just an individual but to one that involves an organic community. Martin argues that 'one body' in verse 15

> is nothing less than the coming into visible reality of that new man of verse 10; a
> new society is born and grows and is distinguished by a corporate life of 'whole-
> ness' affecting every dimension of the church's existence in the world.[97]

Christians who have abandoned corrupt humanity and have adopted a renewed humanity are those who are called into one body, that is, 'a corporate entity "in Christ" '.[98] In the one-body metaphor, what is emphasized is the idea of unity, 'a unity composed of the complementarity and integrated wholeness of different parts'.[99] There is little doubt that one body indicates the church-community.[100] In Col. 1.18, 24 Paul calls Christ the head of the body which is the church. As the head, Christ has an inseparable relationship with the church as his body. The believers are incorporated into the body of Christ. The life of this body is the Spirit of Christ who dwells in it (Col. 3.11; cf. Gal. 3.20). Yet, insofar as the believers are called in

95. Pokorný, *Colossians*, p. 170 rightly argues that this statement 'does not point to a pantheistic dissolution in the shape of the Risen One'; *contra* L.B. Radford, *The Epistle to the Colossians*, p. 269.

96. Lohse, *Colossians and Philemon*, p. 150 points out that the adjective ἑνί is missing in manuscripts P[46] B1739. If ἐν σώματι be read, he means 'in a community', and if ἑνί be authentic, he means to underline 'the essential oneness of his community' (Williams [ed.], *The Epistles of Paul the Apostle to the Colossians and to Philemon*, p. 141). The emphasis on Christian unity after the reference to putting on the new man (vv. 10-11) seems to match the reading with ἑνί. Further, the stress on the uniting character of love, which should above all be put on by believers (v. 14), also suggests that the reading of ἑνί is more appropriate. Yet there is a possibility that ἑνί might have been inserted by a perceptive scribe.

97. Martin, *The Church's Lord and the Christian's Liberty*, p. 124; C.F.D. Moule, *Worship in the New Testament* (London: Lutterworth, 1961), p. 57: ' "putting on the new humanity" (Eph. 4.24; Col. 3.10) is not only to acquire, individually, a reformed character, but to become incorporated in a new "race" of mankind'; *pace* Schweizer, *The Letter to the Colossians*, p. 208, who holds that 'one body' most probably points to the body of Christ, the church, but argues against the conceptual continuity between 'the new man' and 'one body' by insisting that at v. 15 'the writer abandons the set of images about putting garments on and off'.

98. W. Hendriksen, A *Commentary on Colossians & Philemon* (GSC; London: Banner of Truth, 1971), p. 159.

99. Dunn, *The Epistles to the Colossians and to Philemon*, p. 235.

100. Thompson, *Letters of Paul to the Ephesians to the Colossians and to Philemon*, pp. 154-55.

the one body (Col. 3.15), Christ's Spirit can be thought of as the collective spirit which supplies a corporative life to the one body.

C.F.D. Moule argues in his comment on 'the old man' and 'the new man' that

> these phrases do not merely mean 'one's old, bad character,' and 'the new, Christian character' respectively, as an *individual's* condition: they carry deeper, wider, and more *corporate* associations, inasmuch as they are part of the presentation of the Gospel in terms of the two 'Adams,' the two creations... Thus the terms 'the old humanity', 'the new humanity' derive their force not simply from some individual change of character, but from a corporate recreation of humanity; and what enables the individual to become transformed from selfishness to a growing effectiveness as a useful member of a group is precisely his 'death' in regard to one type of humanity—the great, collectively unredeemed Man—and his 'resurrection' into another: we are back, once more, at the language of baptismal initiation and incorporation.[101]

From all the observations above, we can draw the conclusion that the clothing-with-the-new-man metaphor in Col. 3.10 implies that believers are those who have been incorporated into the church community in baptism. As a garment wraps its wearer as a whole, so the ecclesiological new man embraces the totality of believers. The concept of a garment in its significance of encompassing 'the whole' may be produced by the author's dialogue with the garment traditions of antiquity. As we have repeatedly pointed out, the priestly garment with two onyx stones or twelve precious stones symbolizes the whole Israel (Exod. 28.9-10, 15-21). When the priest adorns himself with the priestly garment, he is identified with the whole Israel as well as God. Thereby, he becomes the representative of Israel and at the same time becomes God's agent.

In his interpretation of the significance of the high priest's garment, Philo (and also Josephus) suggests that it connotes the whole universe. As the high priest dresses himself with the priestly garment, he is identified with the universe, resulting in his being a little universe. In a sense, his identification with the universe can be designated as being identified with God, because for Philo, the universe is to be identified with God. Of course, this does not mean that God loses his own identity and is to be assimilated into the universe. The Colossian concept of an ecclesial garment does not seem to depend on Philo. But when both think of a garment which embraces something as a whole, there is a shared place where they meet together, perhaps in dependence on a common base of tradition.

The idea of a garment as one which envelops totality seems also to be echoed in other Jewish writings. For instance, in *Joseph and Aseneth*, when Aseneth dresses herself in a new linen garment after her conversion to Judaism, the angel states that she shall be 'the City of Refuge' (15.7). Her would-be imitators will find safety and comfort in her. Here her linen garment may be thought of as symbolizing the whole

---

101. C.F.D. Moule, *The Epistles to the Colossians and to Philemon*, pp. 119-20; cf. Schweizer, *The Letter to the Colossians*, p. 197, who, with an overemphasis on the ethical renewal of 'the new man', argues that this concept 'must denote the individual person who lives in faith'; he also insists that the old man can 'only mean the individual person (before one becomes a Christian) along with all that one does'.

people who will convert from paganism to Judaism as Aseneth did. The concept of an ecclesial garment in Colossians 3 could also be compared with the Johannine image of Jesus' untorn tunic, since it symbolizes his people as a whole (Jn 19.23-24). The author of Colossians seems to draw on the contemporary clothing traditions on which the Johannine writings also depend.

Out of all these observations, we can conclude that when the author of Colossians refers to the putting on of the new man, he has in mind the whole Christian unity as the body of Christ. All believers are incorporated into his ecclesial body and enveloped by it.

2.3.6. *Concluding Remarks*

The baptismal language in Col. 3.8-11 and its echo of 2.11-12 implies that the double metaphor of putting-off-the-old-man and putting-on-the-new-man (Col. 3.9-10) describes baptism, the gist of which is one's identification with Christ's death-and-life. This suggests that the metaphor signifies one's inward change after the model of Christ, a change from the old personality to the new. Therefore, the imagery of putting-on-the-new-man connotes that the believer is identified with his or her own innermost being who undergoes a continuous renewal in Christ. In a sense, this means that Adam's original state is recovered, since 'the old man' is connected to the fallen Adam and 'the new man' is bound to Christ as the new Adam.

The author of the putting-on-the-new-man metaphor seems to interpret the pre-Fall state of Adam in the light of Jewish belief that Adam was originally clothed with splendour in terms of the image of God (cf. *Gen. Rab.* 20.12; *Apoc. Mos.* 20–21; *Joseph and Aseneth* 75–77). Whilst maintaining that baptismal change is the centrepiece of the metaphor of putting-on-the-new-man, it does seem also to have been influenced by OT priestly concepts, which are characterized by the priest washing himself with water and investing himself with priestly sacred garments, so becoming a divine person (cf. Exod. 28–29; Lev. 16.3-4; Philo, *Vita Mos.* ii.131). The metaphor could also be understood in conjunction with the idea of the change of status in a Roman male as he takes off his old clothes and puts on the *toga virilis* and the mystery religions' concept of the initiate's identification with a divine being, reflected in *Metamorphoses*, where Lucius becomes an Isis-like person, as he wears the twelve robes after his initiation ritual.

The imagery of putting-on-the-new-man signifies that believers are incorporated into the church community as the one organic body of Christ. This is suggested by the present metaphor's connection with concepts such as human equality, without discrimination between races, classes and sexes (Col. 3.11), and 'one body' (Col. 3.15). As has been argued, an analogy could be found in the priest's garment which symbolizes the whole of Israel (in the OT), the high priest's garment (in Philo's view; *Vita Mos.* ii.133, 135) which is spoken of as symbolizing the whole of the universe, Jesus' untorn tunic (Jn 19.23-24), and Aseneth's new linen robe (*JA* 14–15).

2.4. *Some Contextual Emphases*

2.4.1. *Introductory Remarks.* The clothing-with-the-new-man metaphor in Col. 3.9-10 is undoubtedly influenced by some specific emphases of the context to which each passage belongs. In Col. 3.9-10, the author presents the metaphor specifically from an eschatological and ethical viewpoint, when this passage implies that although a Christ-like humanity has already been given in baptism, it has not yet been fully consummated, so it should be constantly regenerated. In particular, Col. 3.1-4 sets forth an eschatological perspective for the clothing metaphor in verses 9-10. Verses 9 and 12, moreover, are concerned with the matter of the Christian ethic. An investigation of these emphatic elements will be worthwhile in determining the significance of the clothing-with-the-new-man metaphor in Col. 3.10.

2.4.2. *Eschatological Elements (Colossians 3.1-4)*. As was argued in an earlier section,[102] Col. 3.5-17 can be thought of as an explication of 3.1-4, the perspective of which is eschatological. This suggests that the metaphor of clothing-with-the-new-person in 3.10 has an eschatological significance. In Col. 3.1-4 Paul maintains a realized eschatology. He states that Christians have already been raised with Christ, who is seated on high at God's right hand in verse 1 (cf. 2.12; Eph. 2.6). This statement is expanded with two other indicative statements in verses 3-4. The first point is that believers have died and their life is at present concealed with Christ in God;[103] the second point is that at the parousia of Christ, who is their life, they will be joined to him in glory. In fact, the author's exhortation to seek things above (v. 2) is 'an eschatological demand to concentrate on the hidden realities which will characterize them when they are glorified eternally in the world above'.[104] The Christian life is not a static heavenly condition but a historical pilgrimage. In brief, Christians are those who participate in Christ's death (3.3; cf. 2.20), resurrection and ascent to heaven, and in his return.

Thus a Christian's identity should be viewed from the perspective of a realized eschatology. He should live out his ethical life in the recognition that he is already unified with the Christ, who is exalted. Morally, rising with Christ means 'the dominance of new motives and new energies which lift the conduct of life to a higher level'.[105] As the effect of putting off the old man and putting on the new man is identical with what eschatological self-recognition produces, it may be said that this double metaphor points to an eschatological transformation which is to take place in the believer's inmost being. That is, the imagery of clothing-with-the-new-man describes that in baptism the believer attains a heavenly character by means of union with the risen and ascended Christ. This heavenly character is

102. See section 2.2, above.

103. If Christians are unified with Christ, their real life can be considered as being in the realm into which the exalted Christ entered. Bengel, *Gnomon of the New Testament*, IV, p. 180 comments on the words κέκρυπται σὺν τῷ Χριστῷ in Col. 3.3 that 'the world knows neither Christ nor Christians, and Christians do not even know distinctly themselves, i.e. one another'.

104. J.R. Levison, '2 *Apoc. Bar.* 48.42-52.7 and the Apocalyptic Dimension of Colossians 3.1-6', *JBL* 108 (1989), pp. 93-108 (108). He asserts that 'the similarities between 2 *Apoc. Bar.* 48.42-52.7 and Col. 3.1-6 and the solutions which the former offers to the conundrums of the latter indicate that both texts share a common apocalyptic perspective', and that the former 'presents a coherent exposé of an eschatological model...to which the Colossian author alludes' (Levison, '2 *Apoc. Bar.* 48.42-52.7', pp. 93-94).

105. Dodd, 'Colossians', p. 1259; cf. Yates, 'The Christian Way of Life', p. 241.

typified by glory, which is at present hidden in Christ who is the believers' invisible garment (Col. 3.3-4). The author seems to mean that in baptism believers recover the image of God (which gives its owner glory) by being in union with Christ, the new Adam.

It is probable that the clothing-with-the-new-man metaphor is a product of the author's acquaintance with various ancient traditions which associate a garment with the concept of glory. First of all, in the Old Testament there occur several passages which include the concept of a glorious garment. Exod. 28.2, 40 states that the priest's garment is one of divinity, glory and beauty. Ps. 104.2 says that the Lord God covers himself with light as with a garment. Other Jewish documents also share the idea of being clothed with a garment of glory. *1 Enoch* 14.20 calls radiance and whiteness (symbols of glory and holiness) God's garment, which is further described as a sun-like gown; *1 Enoch* 62.15-16 (cf. *2 Enoch* 22.8-10) delineates the heavenly body, which the righteous will receive after their lives on the earth, as 'the garments of glory' or 'the garments of life'. *Apoc. Mos.* 20–21 states that when Adam and Eve originally bore the image of God, they were dressed in righteousness and glory; some rabbinic documents maintain that Adam and Eve wore light before the Fall (e.g. *Gen. Rab.* 20.12). In *Joseph and Aseneth* when Aseneth was adorned with a wedding garment after her conversion to Judaism, her appearance was like light (20.6; 21.5). In *The Hymn of the Pearl* the prince reinvested himself with the royal garment (a symbol for the image of God) which was splendid (vv. 77, 86)[106] and which was identified with the light leading him to his Father's kingdom (cf. vv. 65-66). The concept of being invested with a garment of glory is also found in the mystery religions, which are reflected in Apuleius' *Metamorphoses*. Lucius wears pure linen clothes shining brightly, when he joins the ritual procession (XI.10). When he adorns himself with twelve garments after the initiation ceremony, his appearance becomes sun-like (XI.24).

All these works reflect the fact that in ancient Jewish or mystery-religions circles the idea of being clothed with splendour was prevalent. It is probable that the author of Colossians shares the garment-of-light idea with these documents. Probably he recognized various notions of 'garments of light' in his era; they must have given him insights into the theme of the relationship between believers and Christ, which resulted in his producing the concept of the garment-of-glory. For the author of Colossians, being clothed with the new man signifies that the believers' heavenly identity is at present hidden in Christ through union with him. At the *eschaton* this heavenly identity will be revealed. Presumably the author thinks of the way in which a garment veils its wearer's body, when he speaks of believers' lives being concealed in Christ, who is seated on high and with whom they are united. As was referred to previously, the concept of a garment in its significance of an eschatological change is found in the OT, for example Ps. 102.26b (cf. 51.6), which is quoted in Heb. 1.12 with a slight adaption to the original OT text.

106. See Chapter 4, §3.4.

2.4.3. *Ethical Elements*

2.4.3.1. *'With His [the Old Man's] Deeds' (Colossians 3.9).* Following the exhortation to his audience to abandon all the vices—anger, rage, malice, slander, and filthy language (Col. 3.8), the author further exhorts them, 'Do not lie to one another, seeing that you have put off the old nature with its practices' (3.9). When he adds the phrase 'σὺν ταῖς πράξεσιν αὐτοῦ' to the concept of 'the old man', he undoubtedly imparts an ethical significance to this concept. The old man is inclined to impious conduct; humanity is seen from the perspective of what it does. The old humanity, which cannot help generating vicious actions, should be put aside. Instead, the new humanity must be taken on.

Although the author does not specifically use words about ethical actions for describing 'the new man' in Col. 3.10, yet, since the new contrasts with the old man, it can be regarded as having an ethical significance. S. Schulz, therefore, rightly contends that the two humanities (the old man and the new man) are constituted by their respective actions.[107] It is natural to expect right conduct from the new person who has replaced the old person with its vices. Putting on the new man signifies that one is changed into a new being who can live out the Christian ethic (cf. Col. 3.12). For the author, the fact that the Christian has put on the new humanity is a sufficient reason for manifesting right ethical deeds in his practical life.[108]

2.4.3.2. *Putting on Christian Virtues (Colossians 3.12).* The author's ethical concern with the new man is also expressed in Col. 3.12. In this passage, by using another clothing metaphor, he refers to the qualities the Christian character should include: 'Put on then (οὖν)... compassion, kindness, lowliness, meekness and patience'.[109] This is obviously tied up with ἐνδυσάμενοι τὸν νέον [ἄνθρωπον] in verse 10; the word ἐνδύσασθε (v. 12) takes up the verb ἐνδυσάμενοι (v. 10), but applies the figure to details.[110] The conjunction οὖν marks the logical consequence of the preceding verses; if the Colossians have put on the new humanity, they should manifest its features, that is, virtues which are profitable for maintaining the unification of the Christian community.[111] In brief, the author's appeal to his readers to choose the way of Christian virtues is a continuation of the metaphor of putting off and putting on. R.P. Martin insists that the call to 'put on' the new nature may well have sounded too idealistic and ethereal for Paul's first readers;

107. S. Schulz, *Neutestamentliche Ethik* (Zürich: Theologischer, 1987), p. 566, fn. 54.
108. Cf. Lincoln and Wedderburn, *The Theology of the Later Pauline Letters*, p. 40.
109. Dodd, 'Colossians', p. 1260 asserts that whereas anti-social sins were spoken of in the preceding verses in their negative expression, the virtues which are listed in Col. 3.12 are 'those which have a direct social value (cf. Eph. 4.32-5.2)'.
110. Dunn, *The Epistles to the Colossians and to Philemon*, p. 227; O'Brien, *Colossians, Philemon*, p. 197.
111. Radford, *The Epistle to the Colossians and the Epistle to Philemon*, p. 272; Lincoln and Wedderburn, *The Theology of the Later Pauline Letters*, pp. 54-55; Carson, *The Epistles of Paul to the Colossians and Philemon*, p. 86; Harris, *Colossians & Philemon*, p. 160.

the apostle therefore proceeds to make his appeal more specific and practical as well as more positive.[112]

While the metaphor of putting off the old man and putting on the new man (Col. 3.9-10) stresses the significance of the ontological change due to the faith-union with Christ which baptism ratified, this new clothing metaphor (v. 12) teaches how such a change should be worked out. The spiritual experience of identification with Christ should be realized in the moral effort of obedience to Christ. 'The new man' is a new identity which is to live out a godly life. Christians who have stripped themselves of the old humanity and have put on the new humanity should exemplify godly virtues. As a garment dominates its wearer's external appearance and is always in contact with him, godly virtues must be dominant and continually existent in the humanity of the Christian.

This clothing-with-virtues metaphor corresponds with a number of Old Testament texts, which use clothing images in an ethical way, for example, clothing with righteousness, shame, glory and splendour.[113] In particular, in Zech. 3.3-5 Joshua's taking off his filthy garments and dressing himself in new garments symbolized that Israelites would be transformed from a state of moral iniquity to a state of godliness.[114] A more direct expression of clothing with virtues is found in Philo. He asserts that human beings are destined to be dressed with virtues or vices; virtues are a panoply (παντευχία) of reason, which should control the passion (πάθος) which human beings wear.[115] But this does not necessarily mean that the author of Colossians read and depended upon Philo. While Philo refers to 'virtue' being put on over human beings from a viewpoint of his own philosophical anthropology, the author of Colossians speaks of Christian virtue, which follows the believer's eschatological change in his nature by being united with Christ in baptism. Despite this fundamental difference, the garment-of-virtue concept common to both constitutes an overlapping ground between them. Perhaps the inseparable relationship between human nature and human behaviour induced the author of Colossians to use this imagery of clothing with virtues (Col. 3.12) after his having used the imagery of clothing with the new man in a preceding verse (3.10).

2.4.4. *Concluding Remarks*. The eschatological outlook in Col. 3.1-4, which is maintained also in the imagery of putting-on-the-new-man in 3.9-10, implies that this metaphor refers to the believer's identification with his or her inner self, which is undergoing eschatological change after the model of Christ, the new Adam. Living in the tension between 'already' and 'not yet', believers recognize themselves as beings who are constantly transformed from a fallen to a regenerated nature in Christ, who is the prototype of their renewal. In this concept there is a paradoxical element, that is, in baptism they have already experienced a critical

---

112. Martin, *The Church's Lord and the Christian's Liberty*, p. 119; *idem, Ephesians, Colossians, and Philemon, Interpretation: A Bible Commentary for Teaching and Preaching* (Atlanta: John Knox Press, 1991), p. 124; *idem, Colossians and Philemon* (NCBC; London: Oliphants, 1974), pp. 108-109.
113. See Chapter 1, §1.
114. See Chapter 1, §3.4.
115. See Chapter 2, §5.2.

transformation, and yet it must be continuously repeated. Christians are those who experience more and more their being transformed from the Adamic character into the Christ-like one. The metaphor also signifies that a constant change toward moral perfectness happens in the believer's inner self. As the high priest's filthy garments were replaced by new garments (Zech. 3.3-5), so Christians' morality must be continuously renewed. We have ascertained that this connotation is implied by calling attention to words denoting moral force in Col. 3.9b, 12.

3. *Clothing with the New Man in Ephesians 4.22-24*

3.1. *The Situation of Ephesians' Readers*
Ephesians is another document which most modern scholars look on as 'deutero-Pauline'. Taking up the problems of this letter, for example, its theology, language and style, 'early' catholic features, and relation to other NT documents (especially Colossians), they relinquish the traditional view that it was written by Paul. In this case, however, why 'the verbatim overlap between the references to Tychicus in both letters (Col. 4.7f and Eph. 6.21f)' occurs is not readily explained;[116] it is strange that 'the imitator of the apostle has quoted phrases which are far too situation-related to be re-applicable in a different letter and situation'.[117] An attempt to examine these issues in detail would be beyond the purpose of the present study. Suffice it to say that the view that the similarities in Ephesians and Colossians[118] were the result of one author imitating the other, that is probably incorrect. Rather, these resemblances imply that the two letters are products of the same author on two separate occasions which are not very remote from one another. It is likely that the differences in some points between the two letters are derived from their difference of purpose, which involved different recipients. In fact, the differences between Colossians and Ephesians are not outstanding 'in basic content or even style'.[119] Insofar as the date is concerned, the majority of scholars agree that Colossians is prior to Ephesians; as Ephesians deliberately enriches Colossians' themes with Old Testament traditions, it is probable that Ephesians is a re-written work of Colossians 'for a more Jewish-minded audience'.[120] T. Moritz argues that it is 'by no means implausible to assume that, having written Colossians, the same author decided to address other churches in a similarly syncretic Western Asia Minor environment, albeit with a more Jewish component to it'.[121] If this one-writer theory for Colossians and Ephesians is

116. T. Moritz, *A Profound Mystery: The Use of the Old Testament in Ephesians* (NovTSup, 85; Leiden: Brill, 1996), pp. 219-20.

117. Moritz, *A Profound Mystery*, p. 220.

118. Conzelmann and Lindemann, *Interpreting the New Testament*, p. 207: 'Some references, especially Eph. 1.1/Col. 1.1 and Eph. 6.21f/Col. 4.7f, can only be explained under the assumption of a direct dependence. A similar assessment may also be necessary for Eph. 1.15f/Col. 1.4, 9; Eph. 1.7, 20/Col. 1.14, 20; Eph. 2.20; 3.17/Col. 2.7; Eph. 1.19f/Col. 2.12; Eph. 3.2ff/Col. 1.24ff and Eph. 4.16/Col. 2.19'. Cf. E. Best, 'Who Used Whom? The Relationship of Ephesians and Colossians', *NTS* 43 (1977), pp. 72-96.

119. Moritz, *A Profound Mystery*, p. 220.

120. Moritz, *A Profound Mystery*, p. 220.

121. Moritz, *A Profound Mystery*, p. 220.

to be accepted, it is best to maintain that Ephesians was written by Paul[122] at the period of his imprisonment in Rome (Eph. 3.1; 4.1) toward the end of his life, that is, in the early 60s.[123]

The destination of Ephesians is another difficult issue. The fact that the most ancient MSS do not include the phrase 'in Ephesus' (Eph. 1.1) suggests that the destination might not be Ephesus itself. In fact, Paul speaks of his audience in a neutral way (1.15; 3.2), which is correlated with a lack of his habitual personal greetings. This supports the possibility that the original letter did not contain the phrase 'in Ephesus'. If so, what is meant by the lack of this phrase? And how could a copy, which includes the phrase, have come into existence? It is likely that Ephesians was written as an encyclical letter 'addressed to various churches in the vicinity of Ephesus'.[124] Perhaps the letter to Laodicea, which Paul mentions in Col. 4.16, points to 'Ephesians'. As an encyclical letter 'in its circulation to the churches throughout the region the epistle has reached Laodicea and is about to go to Colossae'.[125] This circulation hypothesis more or less accounts for the lack of 'in Ephesus' in the letter.

Then how did later copies get the phrase 'in Ephesus'? Its presence obviously reflects an intention to connect the letter to Ephesus; someone believed that the whole content of the letter suited the phrase 'in Ephesus' indicating the locale of the recipients. Who did so and on what ground? It is impossible to pinpoint the person who inserted the phrase; we can only imagine that someone who took part in the circulation of the letter did this. He might have thought that the extreme relevance of the letter to the local situation in Ephesus justified the insertion of the phrase 'in Ephesus'. Moreover, inasmuch as Ephesus was included in the cities to which the letter circulated, and inasmuch as Ephesus might have kept it permanently for whatever reason (because Ephesus was the last locale of its circulation?), an insertion of 'in Ephesus' might have been made.

If so, what kind of milieu prevailed the churches in the Lycus Valley in which Ephesus is included? What circumstances in this region are reflected in Ephesians? The intimacy between Colossians and Ephesians urges us to imagine that a situation similar to the one in Colossae might have existed. Presumably the syncretic teaching[126] which had swept the Colossian church also emerged and influenced the churches in the Lycus Valley. Eph. 4.14 speaks of 'every wind of doctrine, by the cunning of men, by their craftiness in deceitful wiles', which echoes the statement of Col. 2.22b, 'human precepts and doctrine'.[127] Christ is the only model after

---

122. I note that a number of well-known scholars argue for the authenticity of Ephesians: see the list in W.G. Kümmel, *Introduction to the New Testament* (Nashville: Abingdon, 1975), p. 357; R.A. Wilson, ' "We" and "You" in the Epistle to the Ephesians', *TU* 87 (1964), pp. 676-80; F. Foulkes, *The Letter of Paul to the Ephesians: An Introduction and Commentary* (TNTC; Leicester: IVP, 1989 [1963]), pp. 40-48; J.W. Bowman, 'The Epistle to the Ephesians', *Int* 8 (1954), pp. 188-204.

123. Those who sees Ephesians as inauthentic usually date it in the period of AD 70–90, when the Pauline corpus was collected.

124. Gundry, *A Survey of the New Testament*, p. 398.

125. Gundry, *A Survey of the New Testament*, p. 398

126. See section 2.1, above.

127. A.T. Lincoln, *Ephesians* (WBC, 42; Dallas: Word Books, 1990), p. 258 maintains that Col. 2.22

which the believers are to be re-created as the new man. Further, if Ephesians is identical with the letter to Laodicea, our hypothesis would gain more substance, because the adjacency of Laodicea to Colossae[128] suggests that Ephesians was written in consideration of the religious milieu in Colossae, which might also have spread to the Ephesian church.

It is highly probable that the emphasis on the Ephesians having been taught in the truth which is in Jesus (Eph. 4.21) is a reaction against the false teaching (4.14), which has become influential in Ephesus. Since Eph. 4.22-24 hinges on Eph. 4.21,[129] which bears in mind the disturbance of the false teaching, the admonition to put on the new man (4.24) probably includes the significance of 'Do not be coloured by heretical doctrine; rather, take to yourself Christ who is the truth itself'.[130] By solidifying their unity with Christ, believers should withstand the false teaching. It is not strange that a clothing metaphor with a military idea in it appears later in Eph. 6.11-17, which seems to echo the implications in 4.14 and the putting-on exhortation in 4.24.[131] The author probably means that the believers should equip themselves with spiritual armour in order to combat the evil powers.[132] Although 4.22-24 does not articulate the military idea as in 6.11-17, the former passage also seems to bear in mind the situation of the readers influenced by false teachings.

3.2. *The Context of Ephesians 4.22-24*
Eph. 4.22-24 belongs to a unit, 4.17-24, which is made up of two parts of exhortation: not to live like Gentiles (vv. 17-20) but to live a life in harmony with the Christian tradition (vv. 21-24).[133] For an appropriate understanding of Eph. 4.22-24, we need to make sense of three infinitives in the passage. In verse 22 ἀποθέσθαι does not appear as a simple infinitive but appears in correlation with the accusative ὑμᾶς,[134] which implies that syntactically Eph. 4.22-24 continues the major idea of verse 21:

---

affects the wording of Eph. 4.14 and argues that the phrase, παντὶ ἀνέμῳ τῆς διδασκαλίας indicates 'false teaching in the guise of the various religious philosophies which threatened to assimilate, and thereby dilute or undermine, the Pauline gospel'; cf. H. Merklein, *Das kirchliche Amt nach dem Epheserbrief* (Munich: Kösel, 1973), p. 107 who is followed by R. Schnackenburg, *Ephesians: A Commentary* (trans. H. Heron; Edinburgh: T. & T. Clark, 1991), p. 186 who holds that probably *the* teaching (ἡ διδασκαλία) designates perverted Christian doctrine, which was possibly damaging to Christian morals (cf. Eph. 5.6-13). But this interpretation does not take into account the tenor of the word 'παντί' (m. dative of πᾶς) between the article ἡ and the term διδασκαλία.

128. Ten miles away (Wright, *Colossians and Philemon*, p. 22).

129. See section 3.2, below.

130. Ephesians does not provide any indication that the clothing-with-the-new-man metaphor in Eph. 4.24 is polemical to a specific recognizable idea drawn from syncretism.

131. In Rom. 13.11-14 the military imagery (= putting on the armour of light) is explicated by the imagery of putting-on-Christ, which corresponds to the imagery of putting-on-the-new-man in Eph. 4.24 (and also Col. 3.10).

132. G. Stoeckhardt, *Ephesians* (trans. M.S. Smooer; CCCS; St. Louis: Publishing House, 1952), p. 205 argues that 'μεθοδεία τῆς πλάνης is a part of the μεθοδίαι τοῦ διαβόλου, 6.11, "the wiles of the devil", who is the author of all religious error and the inspirer of the teachers of error'.

133. Lincoln, *Ephesians*, p. 271.

134. The same usage is found in Eph. 4.17, which uses the form of accusative plus infinitive.

'assuming that you have heard about him and were taught in him' (v. 21a).[135] Thus it seems that the three infinitives in verses 22-24 are epexegetical of ἐδιδάχθητε in verse 21, and so elaborate the content of what was taught.[136] The author highlights three points: to put off the old man, to be renewed in the spirit of the mind, and to put on the new man.

For the contextual connotations of the metaphor, it needs to be borne in mind that there are some important points which are directly or indirectly involved in it. First of all, Eph. 4.22-24 parallels some passages from other Pauline epistles. In particular, it shows a strong connection with Col. 3.8-10. This implies that the metaphor is baptismally 'coloured'. Secondly, Eph. 4.22-24 includes an antithesis similar to that in Col. 3.9-10: ἀποθέσθαι...τὸν παλαιὸν and ἐνδύσασθαι τὸν καινὸν ἄνθρωπον. Both 'the old man' and 'the new man' are followed by modifying words, which differ from those in Colossians. The words suggest that the metaphor is linked with the Adam–Christ motif and specifically with an ethical concern. Thirdly, Eph. 4.22-24 is closely related to the following pericope, so that 4.25 is of consequence when interpreting the present metaphor. In particular, the concept of mutual membership in the verse implies that the metaphor has an ecclesiological nuance.

3.3. *The Meaning of Clothing with the New Man*

3.3.1. *Introductory Remarks.* In this section I will, in the first place, attempt to prove that the clothing-with-the-new-man imagery in Eph. 4.22-24 probably has in mind baptismal practice in the first-century church, so as to signify believers' baptismal identification with Christ.[137] Based on this, I will try to clarify that the metaphor includes various connotations, that is, baptismal union with Christ in his death and exaltation, adoption of a new humanity in Christ who is the new Adam,[138] and incorporation into his ecclesiological body.[139]

135. Schnackenburg, *Ephesians*, p. 195 argues that Eph. 4.21 reveals that the author had an understanding of the church tradition: ' "learning" results from the way of "hearing" (initially in the missionary sermon) and in "instruction" (catechesis in the Church)'.

136. J.A.T. Robinson, *St. Paul's Epistle to the Ephesians* (London: Macmillan, 1904), p. 190; Lincoln, *Ephesians*, pp. 283-84; B.F. Westcott, *St. Paul's Epistle to the Ephesians: The Greek Texts with Notes and Addenda* (London: Macmillan, 1906), p. 67; Schnackenburg, *Ephesians*, p. 199; C.F.D. Moule, *An Idiom Book of New Testament Greek* (Cambridge: Cambridge University Press, 1953), pp. 127, 139; W. Hendriksen, *New Testament Commentary: Exposition of Ephesians* (Grand Rapids: Baker, 1967), p. 213.

137. Eph. 4.22-24 seems to be linked with baptism in the early church, since this passage is in close relationship with Col. 3.8-10, where baptismal traces are detected in its use of baptismal language.

138. As in Col. 3.9-10, in order to attain a proper understanding of putting-on-the-new-man, the term 'the new man' needs to be discerned. The sharp antithesis between putting off the old man and putting on the new man is controlled by the analogy of Adam–Christ and seems to maintain the thought of Adam's pre-Fall investiture found in the Jewish Adam traditions, which are reflected by, e.g. *Apocalypse of Moses*, rabbinic literature and *The Hymn of the Pearl*.

139. The concept of 'one new man' (Eph. 2.15) and mutual membership (Eph. 4.25) implies that the imagery includes a significance of believers' ecclesiological unity with Christ; see section 3.3.4, below.

3.3.2. Baptismal Identification with Christ in His Death-and-Resurrection: Implications of Parallelism of Ephesians 4.22-24 with Other Pauline Clothing-with-a-Person Passages. In Chapter 8[140] and Chapter 9[141] it was emphasized that three Pauline clothing-with-a-person passages, Gal. 3.26-29, Rom. 13.11-14 and Col. 3.9-10, have a baptismal background. Eph. 4.22-24 is similar to these passages, since it uses the same metaphor and particularly shows a very close relationship to Col. 3.9-10. This suggests that baptism may also stand behind Eph. 4.22-24.[142] L. Swain says that the imagery of divestiture and investiture probably reflects 'the early baptismal ceremony (cf. Eph. 1.13; Gal. 3.27; Rom. 13.14) in which the changing of clothes symbolized a transformation of life'.[143] In particular, the baptismal language in Rom. 6.1-11, which is connected to Rom. 13.11-14, seems to share the thought of Eph. 4.22-24. The idea that ὁ παλαιὸς ἄνθρωπος has been crucified with Christ Jesus[144] so that the body of sin might be removed (Rom. 6.6) is similar to the idea that ὁ παλαιὸς ἄνθρωπος should be taken off (Eph. 4.22).[145]

It is not necessary to go into how Eph. 4.22-24 is in affinity with all of its parallels, in order to prove its connection with baptism. I would like to concentrate, in the main, on its similarity to Col. 3.8-10, which uses almost the same ideas and words in order to convey the contrast between the old man and the new man.[146] The parallelism between the two passages may be set out as follows:[147]

	Colossians		Ephesians
3.8	νυνὶ δὲ ἀπόθεσθε καὶ ὑμεῖς...	4.22	ἀποθέσθαι ὑμᾶς κατὰ τὴν προτέραν
3.9	ἀπεκδυσάμενοι τὸν παλαιὸν ἄνθρωπον		ἀναστροφὴν τὸν παλαιὸν ἄνθρωπον...
	σὺν ταῖς πράξεσιν αὐτοῦ		κατὰ τὰς ἐπιθυμίας τῆς ἀπάτης
3.10	καὶ ἐνδυσάμενοι τὸν νέον	4.24	καὶ ἐνδύσασθαι τὸν καινὸν ἄνθρωπον
3.10	τὸν ἀνακαινούμενον εἰς ἐπίγνωσιν	4.23	ἀνανεοῦσθαὶ δὲ τῷ πνεύματι
	τοῦ νοὸς ὑμῶν		
3.10	κατ' εἰκόνα τοῦ κτίσαντος αὐτόν	4.24	τὸν κατὰ θεὸν κτισθέντα

When we follow the theory that Colossians is the antecedent to Ephesians,[148] this arrangement suggests that the author of Ephesians draws on Colossians. The central motif of the old and new man is dependent upon Col. 3.8-10, where 'it is more clearly introduced in a baptismal paraclesis'.[149] Eph. 4.22 must be a variant of

140. Especially §§2.3.2 and 3.3.2.

141. Especially section 2.3.2, above.

142. Cf. Schnackenburg, *Ephesians*, p. 195.

143. L. Swain, 'Ephesians', in *NCCHS* (London: Nelson, 1969 [1953]), pp. 1189-191 (1189); see Chapter 7.

144. This idea is in line with the statement in Rom. 6.3: those who are baptized into Christ Jesus are those who are baptized into his death.

145. It is, of course, true that the crucifixion of the old man and the putting off of the old man manifest a different nuance from one another: while the former underlines union with Christ's death, the latter highlights the removal of the old Adamic identity. Yet, their similarity is so important that it cannot be overlooked.

146. Cf. E. Best, 'Ephesians: Two Types of Existence', *Int* 47 (1993), pp. 39-51 (41).

147. Cf. Lincoln, *Ephesians*, p. 273.

148. See section 3.1, above.

149. Schnackenburg, *Ephesians*, p. 195.

Col. 3.8-9. With the object, 'the old man', the verb ἀποτίθεσθαι is used in place of ἀπεκδύεσθαι, but the former is one which Col. 3.8 employs. The moral conduct of the old man is re-stated in a shortened form, as the list of vices is omitted and instead the phrase κατὰ τὰς ἐπιθυμίας τῆς ἀπάτης is inserted in its place. Col. 3.10 is also imitated by Eph. 4.23-24: the word ἀνακαινούμενον ('being renewed'), which is followed by εἰς ἐπίγνωσιν, is replaced by the similar word ἀνανεοῦσθαι ('to renew'), which is followed by δὲ τῷ πνεύματι τοῦ νοὸς ὑμῶν. 'The new man' is also spoken of again, but for 'new' καινός is employed in place of νέος.[150] The phrase κατ᾽ εἰκόνα is replaced by the phrase κατὰ θεόν; the concept of creation, i.e. κτίσαντος in the form of the aorist participle, is repeated by the word κτισθέντα in the form of the aorist participle passive voice.

If Colossians did indeed pre-date Ephesians, all these observations suggest how deeply Eph. 4.22-24 depends on Col. 3.8-10, and implies that the practice of baptism in the early church lies behind Eph. 4.22-24.[151] As in Col. 3.8-10, the imagery of putting off and putting on seems to reflect the practice of disrobing and rerobing at baptism.[152] R.R. Williams contends that,

> Ephesians then develops—in doublet form—the theme of 'putting off' and 'putting on', an image almost certainly related to the literal putting off of clothes (which eventually developed into the special baptismal robe or *chrisom*).[153]

Of course, the baptismal nuance in Eph. 4.22-24 does not necessarily mean that the fundamental intention of the passage is to describe the manner of the rite of baptism. Rather, the major concern of this passage is one's change from the old to the new humanity. But this does not minimize the significance of the baptismal 'feel' of the passage. Probably the author presupposes that his addressees will recognize that his language has a baptismal connotation. At any rate, when the command to put on the new man indicates a calling to actualize what has taken place in baptism, the metaphor seems to signify that as a garment almost constantly encloses its wearer, so Christ should always be like the believers' garment. In other words, the believers should always be Christ-like people, by being united with Christ. This issue will be considered more fully in the following sections.

3.3.3. *Baptismal Adoption of a New Humanity in Christ the New Adam: Putting off the Old Man/Putting on the New Man (Ephesians 4.22-24).* Also in Eph. 4.22-24, which resembles Col. 3.9-10, the clothing-with-the-new-man-metaphor is part of

150. Bruce, *Paul: Apostle of the Free Spirit*, p. 431, fn. 28 argues that 'no difference in meaning can be pressed here between καινός and νέος'.

151. Apart from a baptismal trace in Eph. 4.22-24 due to its connection with Col. 3.8-10, two other Ephesian passages contain baptismal language: 4.5 presents 'one baptism' as one of seven realities on which the church is established, while 5.25-27 implicitly speaks of baptism (viz. 'washing with water') by which the church has been made a radiant bride of Christ, who gave himself up for her; cf. J.A.T. Robinson, 'The One Baptism as a Category of New Testament Soteriology', *SJT* 6 (1953), pp. 257-74 (especially pp. 257, 267-68).

152. Cf. W.A. Meeks, *The First Urban Christians* (New Haven: Yale University Press, 1983), p. 155.

153. R.R. Williams, 'The Pauline Catechesis', in *Studies in Ephesians* (ed. F.L. Cross; London: Mowbray, 1956), pp. 89-96 (93).

the radical contrast between putting off the old man and putting on the new. In the preceding section,[154] it was argued that this dialectical metaphor is tied up with baptism in the early church. It is highly significant that the baptismal passage includes the Adam–Christ motif (Eph. 4.22-24). It does not seem to be coincidental that other Pauline baptismal clothing-with-a-person passages (i.e. Gal. 3.27; Rom. 13.14; Col. 3.9-10) are equally controlled by the Adam–Christ motif.[155] What Eph. 4.22-24 implies is that baptism involves 'putting on the new man', an event taking place within the scheme of the Adam–Christ typology. Probably the author of Ephesians maintains that in baptism the believer experiences an inner transformation of the whole man, in other words, restoration from the old Adamic character to a new Christ-like character,[156] and that the imagery of clothing-with-the-new-man seems to appropriately portray such an event. In order to validate this hypothesis, it needs to be made clear that Eph. 4.22-24 is controlled by the Adam–Christ analogy.

Certainly, the interpretative words, which are in apposition to the 'old man' (v. 22) and the 'new man' (v. 24) respectively, provide crucial hints as to who these two 'men' are. They also clarify the essence and major characteristics of the two terms.[157] Eadie, in his comment on Eph. 4.22, argues that κατὰ τὴν προτέραν ἀναστροφὴν τὸν παλαιὸν ἄνθρωπον provides 'a bold and vivid personification of the old nature we inherit from Adam, the source and seat of original and actual transgression'.[158] In the first chapters of Genesis the word ἄνθρωπος (LXX Gen. 1.26, 27; 2.7, 8, 15, 18) is applied to the first man Ἀδάμ (LXX Gen. 2.19, 20, 21, 22, 23; 3.9, 10, etc.). The theme of deceitful desires (τὰς ἐπιθυμίας τῆς ἀπάτης) and corruption (φθειρόμενον) in Eph. 4.22 resembles the theme of Adam's deceitful desires and fall in Genesis. By using subtle lies the serpent deceived Eve, and she tempted Adam, which resulted in the Fall. Further, the contrast of the old man (v. 22) to the new man (v. 24), who is associated with Christ, naturally suggests that the Adam Christ motif is at work in the context which includes the two verses. Specifically, the modifying words, τὸν κατὰ θεὸν κτισθέντα ἐν δικαιοσύνῃ καὶ ὁσιότητι τῆς ἀληθείας, which accompany 'the new man' concept, tie up with the Genesis idea (v. 24).

Yet this does not mean that 'the old man' and 'the new man' directly point to the fallen Adam and Christ respectively.[159] Since the terms connote something which is owned by a human being, equating them with Adam and Christ does not seem to be correct. As in Col. 3.9-10, they indicate something involved in one's nature, which is in the model of Adam or Christ. While the old man represents fallen

154. See section 3.3.2, above.

155. See Chapter 8, §§2.3.5; 3.3.4; and Chapter 9, §2.3.4, above.

156. Cf. P.J. Kobelski, 'The Letter to the Ephesians', in *NJBC* (London: Geoffrey Chapman, 1990 [1968]), pp. 883-90 (889); Ridderbos, *Paul*, pp. 63-64.

157. M. Barth, *Ephesians* (AB, 34A; New York: Doubleday, 1974), p. 506.

158. J. Eadie, *A Commentary on the Greek Text of the Epistle of Paul to the Ephesians* (London and Glasgow: Griffin, 1854), p. 323.

159. *Pace* Westcott, *St. Paul's Epistle to the Ephesians*, p. 68; Barth, *Ephesians*, pp. 510, 539; Bruce, *Paul: Apostle of the Free Spirit*, p. 431; cf. Kirby, *Ephesians: Baptism and Pentecost*, p. 27. To equate 'the new man' completely with Christ seems to be incorrect, because the term must connote something that is owned by a human being.

humanity, which is inherited from fallen Adam, the new man indicates recovered humanity in Christ.[160] A.T. Lincoln argues that the old and new men 'are not simply Adam and Christ as representatives of the old and new orders', 'nor more specifically Adam in the inner person and Christ in the inner person'; they rather indicate individuals who 'are identified either with the old or with the new order of existence'.[161] Although the last point is acceptable, the abandonment of the first two points does not seem to be legitimate. Although the author of Ephesians wishes to describe, by using the terms, 'the old man' and 'the new man', individuals in accordance with the old or new order of existence, his interest in their relationship with their representative is also serious, because the idea of Adam–Christ typology significantly emerges in the passage, although not in an overt manner. Further, Lincoln's attempt to distance the names 'Adam' and 'Christ' respectively from 'the old man' and 'the new man', which are symbolic terms about people's innermost beings, does not seem to be appropriate, because the Genesis-inspired words in Eph. 4.22-24 suggest that in this passage the names are indeed significant. As a matter of fact, people who are identified either with the old or the new order of existence cannot be correctly envisaged when the names of Adam and Christ are omitted. While those who are identified with the old order of existence are under the influence of Adam, those who are identified with the new are under the influence of Christ.

Accordingly, we argue that the old man symbolizes humanity's corrupted nature inherited from fallen Adam,[162] what could be called the Adamic nature, while the new man indicates humanity's renewed nature in Christ, that is, the Christ-like nature. As the fallen Adam is the prototype of people of 'the old man', so Christ is the prototype of 'the new man'. 'The new man' is nothing other than a personality which is reshaped after *the image of God* (τὸν κατὰ θεὸν κτισθέντα), that is, after Christ the new Adam.[163] The phrase, κατὰ θεόν, literally indicates 'after God' or 'like God', but since it is a virtual allusion to Gen. 1.27,[164] it may be translated as 'created after God's image'.[165] This interpretation is justified by its parallelism with Col. 3.10, which refers to the creation of the new man after the image of the creator.[166]

160. Cf. Allen (ed.), *2 Corinthians-Philemon*, pp. 160-61; W.R. Newell, *Romans: Verse by Verse* (Chicago: Grace, 1938), p. 496; Martin, *Ephesians, Colossians, and Philemon*, pp. 58-59, 61; Foulkes, *The Letter of Paul to the Ephesians*, p. 139.

161. Lincoln, *Ephesians*, p. 285.

162. A further discussion on this issue will be carried out when we deal with Eph. 4.24. Cf. Jervell, *Imago Dei*, pp. 240-48.

163. Cf. Van Roon, *The Authenticity of Ephesians*, p. 339; Bruce, *Paul: Apostle of the Free Spirit*, p. 205; Dunn, *Christology in the Making*, p. 105.

164. Robinson, *St. Paul's Epistle to the Ephesians*, p. 191; Meyer, *The Epistle to the Ephesians and the Epistle to Philemon*, p. 250; L. Goppelt, *Typos: The Typological Interpretation of the Old Testament in the New* (trans. D.H. Madvig; Grand Rapids: Eerdmans, 1982), p. 132; cf. Barth, *Ephesians*, p. 509; Ridderbos, *Paul*, pp. 72-73, 105.

165. Cf. Lincoln, *Ephesians*, pp. 270, 287.

166. However, T.K. Abbott renders the phrase 'created according to the will of God' (*A Critical and Exegetical Commentary on the Epistles to the Ephesians and to the Colossians* [ICC; Edinburgh: T. & T. Clark, 1897], p. 138). But M. Barth argues against him that this rendering amounts to a

If our hypothesis is correct, as in Colossians 3, the metaphor may be a product of the author's interpretation of the Genesis story of Adam based on his reading of Jewish Adam traditions, which see Adam as having been clothed before the Fall. As was pointed out in section 2.3.4 above, a number of Jewish documents suggest that there have been such Jewish clothing traditions. For instance, *Apocalypse of Moses* 20–21 sees that righteousness and glory, which the first human couple were originally clothed in before the Fall, had been rooted in the image of God. It needs to be noted that the author of Ephesians presents the new man as a being who has been created after the image of God (Eph. 4.24, τὸν κατὰ θεὸν κτισθέντα). The rabbinic thought of Adam and Eve having been dressed in splendour before the Fall in connection with the image of God in them[167] echoes the statement that the new man has been created after God's likeness in Ephesians 4. A similar idea is also found in *The Hymn of the Pearl*, which refers to the prince's eventual reinvestiture with his original radiant garment, which symbolizes his re-union with the image of God.[168]

In view of the underlying baptismal thrust of Eph. 4.22-24, as in Col. 3.9-10, the author probably envisages the priest's changing of garments. This frequently included the ritual of putting off the previous garment, taking a purifying bath and putting on the priestly garment, which was holy, glorious and honourable (Exod. 29.4-9, 40; Lev. 16.3-4). The author probably believes that in baptism the old Adamic humanity is restored to the new Adamic (i.e. Christ-like) humanity.[169] In particular, the priest's clothing himself with Urim ('lights') and Thummim ('perfections') anticipates the idea that the new man has been brought into being through righteousness and the holiness of the truth (Eph. 4.24).[170] Further, the putting off/on imagery in Eph. 4.22-24 emphasizes ethical change (especially vv. 22b-23),[171] and it corresponds to the imagery of the high priest's moral divestiture of the dirty garment and his investiture with a new linen garment in Zech. 3.3-5.

Further, when the putting off/on of the old/new man metaphor depicts the decisive transformation from the old Adamic nature into the new Christ-like nature in Ephesians 4, it resembles a Roman boy's ceremonial replacement of the *toga*

---

tautology, as it is to God alone that the power, will and way of creation is ascribed (Barth, *Ephesians*, p. 509). The word κτισθέντα in the form of the past participle suggests that there has been a divine action of creating the new man before the human action of putting on the new man. Beyond doubt, the subject of the creation work is God. As Adam was created by God, so the new man is also created by God. As the first man was created in God's image, so is the new man.

167. *Gen. Rab.* 20.12; cf. 12.6; *'Abot R. Nat.* 42, 116. See Chapter 2, §5.

168. See Chapter 4, §§3.1 and 3.4.

169. Meeks, *The First Urban Christians*, p. 155: 'baptism suggests a restoration of paradisiac motifs: the lost unity, the lost image, the lost glory'; *pace* Barth, *Ephesians*, pp. 544-45.

170. Of course, the phrase, ἐν δικαιοσύνῃ καὶ ὁσιότητι τῆς ἀληθείας, would first have in mind the quality of the pre-Fall Adam. It seems to be used adverbially, so as to modify the participle κτισθέντα. It, therefore, clarifies how the new man is re-formed. The author seems to present 'righteousness and holiness' (cf. *Wisd. Sol.* 9.3; Lk. 1.75 in the inverted order) as essential features of the new man, because the preposition ἐν 'designates the manifestation or development of the new man' (Eadie, *Ephesians*, p. 329).

171. Concerning this issue, see §§3.4.2.1 and 3.4.2.2, below.

praetexta with the *toga virilis*, symbolizing his change from boyhood immaturity into manhood maturity.

Accordingly, we can infer that the clothing-with-the-new-man metaphor in Ephesians 4 signifies the believer's baptismal restoration from a post-Fall Adamic personality to a pre-Fall Adamic personality, the essence of which is righteousness and holiness.

But why does the author of Ephesians describe this thought by means of the metaphor of changing garments? He probably thinks of the decisive aspect in changing clothes. As changing garments points to parting from the old clothes and being united with the new, so the old Adamic nature is replaced in a rapid way with the new Christ-like humanity. Only when the believers cast out the old nature can they take to themselves the new nature which is being regenerated after the image of God.

Further, the author of Ephesians perhaps thinks of a garment as always being at one with its wearer. Like a garment, the new Adamic nature always remains one with the believer. He also seems to think that a garment reveals its wearer's character and dominates his or her appearance. An Adam-like humanity should be laid aside and instead the Christ-like humanity should be taken on, so that this new humanity may be manifested and pervade the whole of the believer's nature.

3.3.4. Baptismal Incorporation into Ecclesial Oneness in Christ Parallelism of 'the New Man' (Ephesians 4.24) with 'One New Man' (2.15); Mutual Membership (4.25).
The concept of the 'new man' in Eph. 4.24 is also found in 2.15. A. Van Roon assumes that the 'new man' in 4.24 is the same as 'one new man' in Eph. 2.15.[172] While Eph. 2.15 declares that 'one new man'[173] is a corporate reality created by God from the two hostile peoples, viz. Jews and Gentiles, Eph. 4.24 states that 'the new man' is a being who was created after the image of God.[174] It is true that the former conveys ecclesiological connotations in the main, because of the close relationship of 'one new man' with the concept 'body', while the latter forms primarily an anthropological designation, as 'the new man' is contrasted with 'the old man' in the context of Christian conduct. Yet it seems that Eph. 4.22-24 is concerned with how the moral life of the ecclesiological reality ('one new man' in 2.15) is realized. If this is correct, the new man can also be thought of as having an ecclesiological significance.

Our argument is verified by the concept of mutual membership (Eph. 4.25) which immediately follows the concept of putting on the new man (4.24). The conjunction διό at the beginning of Eph. 4.25 suggests that the new pericope, of which this verse is the initial part, is bound up with the ideas in 4.22-24;[175] whereas 4.22-24 presents a fundamental principle as to what a Christian's identity and life should be like,

---

172. Van Roon, *The Authenticity of Ephesians*, p. 339.

173. See W.R. Long, 'Expository Articles: Ephesians 2.11-22', *Int* 45 (1991), pp. 281-83.

174. Cf. Lincoln, *Ephesians*, p. 287; Best, *One Body in Christ*, p. 153; G.D. Ladd, *A Theology of the New Testament* (Grand Rapids: Eerdmans, 1974), p. 480.

175. Cf. Lincoln, *Ephesians*, p. 300; N.A. Dahl, 'Ephesians', in *HBC* (San Francisco: Harper & Row, 1988), pp. 1212-219 (1218).

4.25–5.2 presents more concrete teaching as to what his ethical practice should be.[176] For the author, a transformed humanity must manifest a transformed moral life.

The words ἀποτίθημι and ἀληθείας in Eph. 4.25a are ones which have already been used in 4.22-24. Those who have put off the old nature and put on the new nature are to put off falsehood and instead to speak the truth with their neighbours. The consistent use of ἀποτίθημι[177] seems intended to make the readers continually envisage the significance of the baptism they have received. Those who have put off the old man, who is corrupted by desires springing from deceit, and have put on the new man, who is created in the righteousness and holiness originating from the truth, that is, Jesus Christ, are to banish lies and to tell the truth. The admonition to tell the truth is already present in Eph. 4.15, which states that the building up of the church, namely the body of Christ, is to be achieved by means of speaking the truth in love. This makes it clear that Eph. 4.25 suggests that the clothing-with-the-new-man metaphor involves an ecclesiological significance.

This becomes clearer as Eph. 4.25b[178] underlines that each believer is part of an organic whole; they are members one of another. When the author uses the word μέλη, he bears in mind the concept 'body', which has been used earlier in Ephesians; in fact, the concept 'body' appears in every chapter of Ephesians except chapter 6, viz. 1.23; 2.16; 3.6; 4.4, 12, 16 (twice); 5.23, 30. Beyond a doubt, Eph. 4.16 contains the idea of mutual membership of the one body, as it states that the whole body is to be joined and knitted together when each part performs its own role properly, resulting in its own edification. Undoubtedly, Eph. 4.15 contains the concept of 'members of the body' in a covert manner. Eph. 5.30 directly employs the expression 'members of his [Christ's] body'. The common membership motif in Eph. 4.25 thus indicates membership in the body of Christ, viz. the church.[179]

The author recognizes those who have put off the old humanity and put on the new humanity as members of one organic body. The two-fold action signifies the way in which they become members of the one body of Christ, the church. The author probably assumes that this double action is a condition for ecclesiological membership. In any case, those who have experienced the exchange of the old humanity for the new humanity are thought of as members of Christ's ecclesiological body. H. Ridderbos argues that

> the active 'to have put off' the old and 'to have put on' the new man (Col. 3.10; Eph. 4.24) refers above all to baptism as bidding farewell to the old mode of existence and becoming incorporated into the new being of the church, which Christ has created in himself unto 'one new man' (Eph. 2.15).[180]

176. Schnackenburg, *Ephesians*, p. 206; Barth, *Ephesians*, p. 511.

177. Eph. 4.22, ἀποθέσθαι (2nd aor., infinitive, middle voice); 4.25, ἀποθέμενοι (2nd aor., participle, middle voice).

178. This passage presents a reason why the readers should speak the truth instead of lies: ὅτι ἐσμὲν ἀλλήλων μέλη.

179. Lincoln, *Ephesians*, pp. 300-301; cf. Schnackenburg, *Ephesians*, pp. 206-207; Hendriksen, *Exposition of Ephesians*, p. 217; Kobelski, 'The Letter to the Ephesians', p. 889; Allen (ed.), *2 Corinthians-Philemon*, p. 161.

180. Ridderbos, *Paul*, pp. 223-24.

It may be said that the metaphor of putting on the new man signifies the believer's incorporation into the church community. As a wearer gets into his or her garment, becoming almost one with it, the believers are incorporated into a Christian community, resulting in their identification with one another. Therefore, the new man with which all believers are invested is to have an ecclesiological significance.

If so, it is probable that the author of Ephesians shares the idea of inclusive garment traditions which are reflected in various sources of antiquity. First of all, as two onyx stones (on each of which six names of the sons of Israel are engraved) as well as twelve precious stones, which are attached to the priestly garment, stand for the twelve tribes of Israel (Exod. 28.9-10, 15-21), the garment symbolizes the whole Israel. When the priest wears it, he is unified with the whole of Israel. Further, as it is characterized by the divine sacredness, the wearing of it signifies that its wearer is also identified with God. Therefore, to wear it means to represent the whole of Israel and at the same time to perform a role as God's agent.

Philo (and also Josephus) suggest that the high priest's garment connotes the whole cosmos. When the high priest is clothed with the priestly garment, he is identified with the universe, becoming a microcosm. As God is identified with the cosmos, the wearing of the priestly garment indicates that its wearer is identified with God, becoming a God-like person. For Philo, it is clear that when the high priest wears the priestly garment, he becomes something more than normal people. It is true that Philo's concept of a cosmological priestly garment differs from the Apostle's concept of an ecclesial garment in Eph. 4.24. But in that both present the concept of a garment which embraces 'the whole', they have common ground to share together.

In *Joseph and Aseneth*, Aseneth is clothed with a new linen garment after her conversion from paganism to Judaism, when a man from heaven prophesies that she shall be 'the City of Refuge' (15.7). Her followers will be able to take refuge in her. Here her linen garment is to symbolize the unity of those who will be converted to Judaism. The concept of the new man as an ecclesial garment in Eph. 4 could also be compared with the Johannine concept of Jesus' untorn tunic, since it symbolizes the unity of his people (Jn 19.23-24).

From all these parallels, we can conclude that the putting on of the new man in Ephesians 4 includes the idea that all believers are encompassed by the church community as the body of Christ. All believers are enveloped by Christ's ecclesial body.

3.3.5. *Concluding Remarks*. The verbal resemblance between Col. 3.8-10 and Eph. 4.22-24 imply that the imagery of the putting off and on of clothes in the latter passage describes baptism, the thrust of which is one's participation in Christ's death-and-life. This suggests that the imagery connotes one's inward change modelled on Christ, a transformation from the old humanity to the new. Accordingly, the imagery of putting-on-the-new-man signifies that the believer is identified with his own inner self which experiences a constant regeneration in Christ. This means that the original state of Adam is recovered by being united with Christ as the new Adam.

The author of the clothing-with-the-new-man metaphor seems to presuppose Adam's prelapsarian clothing by depending on the Jewish belief that Adam, as the image of God, had been originally clothed with radiance (cf. *Gen. Rab.* 20.12; *Apoc. Mos.* 20–21; *JA* 75–77). Moreover, whilst the metaphor bears a baptismal nuance, it probably is influenced by the idea of the priest becoming a divine person as he wears the holy, priestly garment (Exod. 28–29; Philo, *Vita Mos.* ii.131). The metaphor could also be thought of as reflecting the idea of the change of status in a Roman male when he replaced the *toga praetexta* with the *toga virilis*, and the mystery faiths' idea of a person being identified with a god or goddess, reflected in Apuleius' *Metamorphoses*, where Lucius' twelve garments worn after the initiation ceremony symbolize his having been united with Isis and become like her.

Further, the metaphor of putting-on-the-new-man connotes that those who have been united with Christ in baptism are incorporated into his body, the church. This is suggested by the present metaphor's connection with such concepts as 'one new man' (Eph. 2.15) and mutual membership (Eph. 4.25). As has been argued, an analogy could be found in the Pentateuch where the priestly garments symbolize the twelve tribes of Israel, in Philo's view of the high priest's garment (*Vita Mos.* ii.133, 135) which sees it as symbolizing the whole of the universe, in the ecclesiological significance of Jesus' untorn tunic (Jn 19.23-24), and in the inclusive character of Aseneth's new linen robe, that is, the robe of 'the City of Refuge' (*JA* 14–15).

3.4. *Some Contextual Emphases*

3.4.1. *Introductory Remarks*. The imagery of clothing with the new man in metaphor in Eph. 4.22-24 seems to be influenced particularly by ethical clements. The passage concentrates on the believer's moral life (especially vv. 22b-23). Although clothing with the new man stands for a Christ-like humanity having already been given in baptism, it still needs to be regenerated continuously. An investigation of this ethical emphasis will be profitable in clarifying the significance of the clothing-with-the-new-man metaphor in Eph. 4.24.

3.4.2. *Ethical Elements*

3.4.2.1. *The Old Man Inclined to Lusts (Ephesians 4.22)*. In understanding the imagery of clothing with the new man in Eph. 4.24, a consideration of Eph. 4.22 is called for, because this passage includes the counterpart of the new man metaphor. As in Col. 3.9, 'the old man' in Eph. 4.22 is also elucidated by ethical concepts: ἀποθέσθαι ὑμᾶς κατὰ τήν προτέραν ἀναστροφὴν τὸν παλαιὸν ἄνθρωπον τὸν φθειρόμενον κατὰ τὰς ἐποθυμίας τῆς ἀπάτης. H.A.W. Meyer holds that 'the pre-Christian moral frame is represented as a person'.[181] The passage demonstrates that the concept of the old man involves an ethical significance, and thereby the concept of the new man also comes to bear an ethical significance, because they are opposites.

---

181. H.A.W. Meyer, *Critical and Exegetical Handbook to the Epistle to the Ephesians and the Epistle to Philemon* (Edinburgh: T. & T. Clark, 1880), p. 247.

For the author, the old man who belongs to the former way of life and who is corrupted by deceptive desires should be taken away. As the old man is what has to be eliminated from individuals, he obviously stands for a human being's whole nature,[182] from which ethical conduct originates. E. Best holds that 'the old self was the self of the preconversion life'.[183] For the author of Ephesians, the old personality from which an evil way of life emerges (cf. Rom. 7.14, 18)[184] must be regenerated. When a person's nature is fallen as characterized by fleshly lusts, he or she cannot help following a wicked lifestyle.

It may be said that ethical conduct is an outward expression of personality; they are closely in contact with each other. The demand to put on godly Christian deeds (Col. 3.12) virtually identifies conduct with personality. The concept of 'putting on' (Col. 3.10, 12; Eph. 4.24), therefore, utilizes the extreme nearness between a garment and its wearer. There is, in fact, nothing that is more constantly in contact with a human being than his or her garment. The new Christ-like personality, which is obtained by abandoning the old Adamic personality, must not only always be triumphant in Christians (as clothing dominating its wearer's appearance), but also must be expressed in ethical behaviour (as clothing identifying its wearer).

3.4.2.2. *Renewal in the Spirit of Mind (Ephesians 4.23)*. In Eph. 4.22-24 putting off the old man and putting on the new man indicates what has already been achieved[185] in baptism, that is to say, the decisive removal of the Adamic self and the adoption of the Christ-like self. But this achieved reality should be actualized in the practical life; it has to be constantly repeated.[186] J.C. Kirby contends that

> what has been done once for all must be done over and over again. What happened at baptism must be a continual experience of the Christian life.[187]

The call for repeated realization is found in Eph. 4.23, which refers to a continuous renewal of the spirit of the mind: ἀνανεοῦσθαι δὲ τῷ πνεύματι τοῦ νοὸς ὑμῶν. Located as it is between 'putting off' and 'putting on', this verse plays a role in providing a supplementary explanation to this two-fold metaphor. A. Van Roon argues,

> The accomplished fact of having put off the old man and put on the new goes together with a renewal which is still continuing in the present.[188]

Similarly, M. Barth also asserts that

> the two verbs 'strip off' and 'put on' appear to denote an external action which is complemented by an internal event, the renewal mentioned in verse 23.[189]

---

182. This word could be exchanged by the words, 'self', 'humanity', 'character', 'personality', etc.

183. Best, 'Ephesians: Two Types of Existence', p. 41.

184. Cf. Abbott, *The Epistles to the Ephesians and to the Colossians*, p. 136.

185. Note that ἀποθέσθαι and ἐνδύσασθαι are aorist infinitives. See J.C. Kirby, *Ephesians: Baptism and Pentecost* (London: SPCK, 1968), p. 159.

186. Kirby, *Ephesians*, p. 145.

187. Kirby, *Ephesians*, p. 159.

188. Van Roon, *The Authenticity of Ephesians*, p. 339.

189. Barth, *Ephesians*, p. 540.

In connection with verse 22, verse 23 suggests that the removal of the fallen nature will be effected by the continuous renewal[190] of the spirit of the believer's mind. Ἀνανεοῦσθαι is in the present tense, which suggests an ongoing change.[191] It is highly probable that, for the author, the essence of this change is the removal of the decayed Adamic nature, and thereby the recovery of the original Adamic nature (probably even more than that).[192] The addition of τοῦ νοὸς ὑμῶν, which is the genitive of the subject,[193] implies that τῷ πνεύματι indicates 'the *human* spirit'.[194] J.A. Bengel asserts that 'the *spirit* is the inmost part of the *mind*'.[195] It has a place in the higher mind.[196] Through it man communes with God; from it his moral judgment is derived. It may, therefore, be called the 'inner self' (cf. Eph. 3.16),[197] or the 'innermost being'.[198] For the author, without a constant renovation of this innermost being, the putting off of the old nature cannot be attained.

In relation to verse 24, verse 23 performs a role which emphasizes that the total newness of personality,[199] which was brought about by God's re-creation, is to be actualized by constant renewal. Without continuous regeneration, what was

190. Abbott, *The Epistles to the Ephesians and to the Colossians*, p. 136.

191. Abbott, *The Epistles to the Ephesians and to the Colossians*, p. 137.

192. It seems that the author does not simply have in mind a return to the state of the first Adam. As Barth, *Ephesians*, p. 508 argues, the eschatological renovation speaks of 'much more than rejuvenation or a restoration of the first Adam and his status'. Cf. S. Brock, 'Clothing Metaphors as a Means of Theological Expression in Syriac Tradition', in *Typus, Symbol, Allegorie bei den östlichen Vätern und ihren Parallelen im Mittelalter* (EB, 4: Abteilung Philosophie und Theologie; Regensburg: Verlag Friedrich Pustet, 1981), p. 16.

193. Meyer, *The Epistle to the Ephesians and the Epistle to Philemon*, p. 248.

194. Meyer, *The Epistle to the Ephesians and the Epistle to Philemon*, pp. 248-49; Robinson, *St. Paul's Epistle to the Ephesians*, p. 191; Foulkes, *The Letter of Paul to the Ephesians*, p. 138. As Lincoln points out (*Ephesians*, pp. 286-87), in view of the fact that there is no use of πνεῦμα in the sense of the human spirit in Ephesians, or of references to the Spirit's control of believers in other Ephesian passages (cf. 1.17; 3.16; 4.3; 5.18; 6.18), some commentators render the Greek word as the holy Spirit (e.g. Allen [ed.], *2 Corinthians-Philemon*, p. 160; Schnackenburg, *Ephesians*, p. 200). If this is the case, Eph. 4.23 must be regarded as speaking about one's renewal by the Spirit in one's mind. However, this cannot be supported by the text, which concerns one's renewal in the spirit of one's mind. The New Testament never calls the divine Spirit the spirit of man's mind (Abbott, *The Epistles to the Ephesians and to the Colossians*, p. 137). Further, the text concentrates on describing the spirit of man's mind, which may be called the sublime moral-principle in man. It is likely that τῷ πνεύματι is the dative of reference rather than the instrumental dative.

195. Bengel, *Gnomon of the New Testament*, IV (Edinburgh: T. & T. Clark, 1858), p. 98; cf. W.R. Schoemaker, 'The Use of רוח in the Old Testament, and of πνεῦμα in the New Testament: A Lexicographical Study', *JBL* 23 (1904), pp. 13-67 (especially, pp. 64-65) who sees the πνεῦμα at Eph. 4.23 'as the seat and source of thoughts and purposes'.

196. Westcott, *St. Paul's Epistle to the Ephesians*, p. 68; C.E. Arnold, *Ephesians: Power and Magic* (SNTSMS, 63; Cambridge: Cambridge University Press, 1989), p. 88; Dodd, 'Ephesians', p. 1234; Eadie, *Ephesians*, pp. 326-27.

197. Arnold, *Ephesians*, p. 88; cf. Kirby, *Ephesians*, p. 27.

198. Barth, *Ephesians*, p. 508.

199. Best, 'Ephesians: Two Types of Existence', p. 41: 'Here [in Eph. 4.24] an absolute is introduced; there is no gradual creation of the new self. The believer is a new self; he or she is not on the way to becoming one'.

achieved by putting on the new man cannot be appropriated and accomplished fully. It is only by ever-repeated renewal that the decisive transformation from the Adamic nature to the Christ-like nature can be attained. The author believes that outward conduct depends upon inward nature. Virtuous behaviour can be derived only from a transformed nature, and the transformed nature can be actualized only by the constant renewal of the innermost being. C.E. Arnold holds that

> the saints are held in a tension between the 'new self' and the 'old self'. They retain characteristics of the 'old self' (4.22) but they are urged to put on the things of the 'new self' (4.23-24), the new life which they already possess but not to its full degree.[200]

The author of Ephesians seems to mean that in baptism a believer is radically stripped of the old Adamic nature and instead clothed with the new Adamic nature, but this does not mean that this new nature has been brought to its final consummation. The action of clothing has been completed, but the garment (i.e. the new man) must be continuously renewed. It is probable that this concept of the constant renewal of a garment is a product of the author's understanding of the concept of a garment not wearing out in Deut. 8.4, which reads, 'Your clothing did not wear out upon you...these forty years'. When the Israelites were in the wilderness on the way to Canaan, their clothes were mystically regenerated. The author of Ephesians seems to have in mind the Jewish garment traditions which included the concept of a garment's regeneration. This idea seems to be also shared by *The Hymn of the Pearl*. After returning to his father's kingdom, the prince re-invested himself with his original garment (i.e. his own self, namely the image of God), which had been energized (*HPrl* 93). The prince states that all the royal feelings rested on him as the energy of his original garment increases. For the author of *HPrl*, the prince's garment is not simply a metaphysical reality but a quasi-physiological reality which can dynamically function in relation to its owner. The concept of the energization of the prince's original garment (God's image in him) could be compared with the concept of renewal of the new man (who has been created after the image of God) as the Christian's garment. What the author of Ephesians maintains is that the new nature has been given to Christians, but the old nature is still at work in them, so the new nature must be victorious more and more.

It is also probable that the author ponders how human beings, when their clothes become dirty, repeatedly exchange them with other clean clothes. This idea of changing garments matches the concept of replacement of the high priest Joshua's filthy garment with a new garment. Further, it is also probable that when he links the concept of renewal with the putting off/on imagery, the author bears in mind the sacredness of the priestly garments referred to in several OT passages. For instance, when they are to be ordained, Aaron and his sons are required to be first cleansed with water before wearing the sacred priestly garments (Exod. 29.4-9; par. 40.12-15), and Aaron is commanded to bathe himself in water prior to entering the holy area to make an offering on the day of atonement (Lev. 16.3-4, 23-24); the

---

200. Arnold, *Ephesians*, p. 97; cf. J.D.G. Dunn, *Unity and Diversity in the New Testament: An Inquiry into the Character of Earliest Christianity* (London: SCM Press, 1977), p. 23.

reason for all this is that only a purified body is allowed to wear the holy, priestly garments.[201]

3.4.3. *Concluding Remarks.* The ethical viewpoint in Eph. 4.22, 23, which is implicitly maintained also in the imagery of putting-on-the-new-man in 4.24, suggests that Christians' baptismal union with Christ should be constantly realized in their practical lives. A constant change toward moral perfection should persistently take place in the believer's inner self. As a dirty garment is repeatedly replaced by a clean garment (Zech. 3.3-5), so a Christian's nature has to be constantly renewed. We have ascertained that this implication of the metaphor is directly or indirectly made by drawing attention to words connoting moral force in Eph. 4.22, 23.

4. Conclusion to Chapter 9

In Col. 3.9-10 and Eph. 4.22-24, the metaphor of putting off the old man and putting on the new seems to be linked with the real practice of baptism in the primitive church. The imagery of putting-on-the-new-man in both passages, therefore, fundamentally indicates the believer's baptismal change from an old corrupted to a new godly nature. In both passages 'the new man' seems to indicate an individual's innermost being, which is modelled on Christ, rather than directly indicating Christ himself. The parallelism between Col. 3.8-11 and 2.11-12, in particular, implies that the essence of baptismal transformation from the old nature to the new lies in one's identification with Christ's death-and-resurrection.

Yet the Genesis-inspired words in Col. 3.9-10 and Eph. 4.22-24 suggest that the metaphor of putting-off and putting-on is controlled by the typology between Christ and Adam. That is, the double metaphor of putting off the old man and putting on the new do not simply point to abandoning an old and adopting a new nature. It rather indicates the need to eradicate the depraved nature which is influenced by fallen Adam and to assume a godly nature constantly renewed after the pattern of Christ, the new Adam. In other words, the metaphor points to movement from an Adamic nature to a Christ-like one. As this idea is suggested by the metaphor of putting off/on, the metaphor of clothing-with-the-new-man seems to maintain that Adam was clothed before the Fall. If this is true, this metaphor probably shares also the Jewish concept of Adam before the Fall being dressed in light, righteousness and glory, which reflects the image of God in him (cf. *Apoc. Mos.* 20–21; *Gen. Rab.* 20.12; *The Hymn of the Pearl*).

Yet, when the metaphor of putting off/on connotes a believer's radical change in baptism, the metaphor of clothing-with-the-new-man also seems to correspond to the transition from boyhood to manhood which was experienced by a Roman male and which was accompanied by the laying aside of the *toga praetexta* and the wearing of the *toga virilis*. The putting off/on metaphor also echoes traditions similar to those found in the concept of the change from a pagan to a Jewish personality, which happened to Aseneth, when she took off her idolatrous garments

201. See Chapter 1, §§3.2 and 3.3.

and put on a new and eventually a wedding garment; and the concept of Lucius' becoming an Isis-like being, when he put on twelve garments after the initiation ritual. However, above all, the metaphor seems to correspond to the ritual of the OT priest's putting off his previous garment, bathing, and putting on the priestly garment, which signified his becoming a holy being, because of the sacred character of the priestly garment (cf. Exod. 28–29; Lev. 6).

Further, insofar as the clothing-with-the-new-man metaphor is controlled by the motif of Adam–Christ and at the same time has a close relationship with ecclesiological concepts (Col. 3.11, 15; Eph. 2.15), it indicates the believers' incorporation into the church as a collective whole, enveloped by Christ as a corporate person. A similar thought can be found in the description of the priest's garment, which includes two onyxes and twelve precious stones, both of which stand for the whole of Israel; in the Philonic concept of the high priest's garment which is thought of as symbolizing the whole cosmos; in the description of the new linen robe of Aseneth as 'the City of Refuge'; and in the Johannine description of Jesus' untorn tunic. In any case, our point is that the new man does not only indicate an individual's humanity but also the Christian community as a whole; the new man emerges in the life of the church (cf. Col. 3.11, 15).

Further, the contextual emphases of Col. 3.9-10 and Eph. 4.22-24 imply that the imagery of putting-on-the-new-man connotes believers' baptismal identification with their inner-beings, which are experiencing ongoing renewal after the new Adam, namely, after Christ who is the focal point of eschatological times and the moral standard for all believers.

Chapter 10

CLOTHING WITH THE RESURRECTION BODY

1. *Introduction*

This final major chapter deals with the two Pauline passages that use clothing imagery when describing the change from the present to the future mode of existence: 1 Cor. 15.49-54 and 2 Cor. 5.1-4. In order to uncover the significance of the metaphor of clothing with the resurrection body in these passages, as in Chapters 8 and 9, we will deal with each of the two passages in a separate sub-chapter. Although the imagery's fundamental significance seems to be almost the same in the two epistles, yet since some expressions, which establish it, are different, there may well be some differences in its nuance between the two letters. When we look into each passage, we will first look into the circumstances of the Corinthian church. We will then move on to an examination of the context of the relevant passage. Then we will attempt to investigate the meaning of the clothing imagery in it. In so doing, we will also be concerned with how the background documents can contribute to unveiling the imagery's significance. Yet we will not assign a specific section for contextual emphases as with Chapters 8 and 9, because the metaphor of clothing with the resurrection body in the suggested passages is not seriously influenced by other contextual themes, which are to affect the metaphor's meaning. Of course, we will include in our investigation of the presented passages all the important concepts within them, which are related to the present metaphor.

2. *Clothing with the Resurrection Body in 1 Corinthians 15.49, 50-54*

2.1. *The Situation of 1 Corinthians' Readers*

1 Corinthians was written by Paul during his third missionary journey. He wrote 1 Corinthians in Ephesus early in AD 55,[1] in order to deal with various problems in

---

1.   While Paul sojourned in Corinth on his second missionary journey, he was attacked by Jewish unbelievers, shortly after Gallio arrived there as a proconsul of Achaia (Acts 18.12), around AD 50/51, attested to by 'the Gallio stone, an inscription from Delphi'. After the dismissal of Jewish accusations against him, Paul stayed in Corinth for a while, then sailed for Syria probably in the spring of AD 52 (Acts 18.18); he arrived at Ephesus, but after staying there for some time, he left, then via Caesarea went to Antioch where he spent some time (Acts 18.19-22); then, he started his third missionary journey; passing through the region of Galatia and Phrygia he came back to Ephesus (Acts 18.23; 19.1), where he resided for about two and a half years (Acts 19.8, 10, 22).

the church. Through this letter, we are informed of how many problems the Corinthian believers were embroiled in. Discerning from his double reference to the issue of resurrection in 1 Corinthians 15 and 2 Corinthians 5,[2] Paul seems to have believed that it was one of the most crucial problems in the Corinthian church. He might also have thought that their mistaken view of resurrection engendered their immoral conduct.

   The Corinthian 'spirituals' seem to have believed not only in Jesus' resurrection from the dead but also in their own future resurrection. However, regarding their present status, they maintained an extremely realized eschatology. They thought that they had already attained 'resurrection' in a spiritual sense, so they believed that this realized resurrection governed their current existence. 'What they will be at the end is nothing other than what they are now, minus their physical body'.[3] It seems that such a dichotomous view of their present existence was influenced by a Greek dualistic view of man which thought that the soul is imprisoned in the body. Specifically, the Corinthian dichotomy might have been indebted to a neo-Platonic dualism, in which an embryo of later Gnosticism was fostered.[4] When Paul, by using the clothing imagery, emphasizes the consistency of the bodily state both in the present and in the resurrection mode of existence, and suggests resurrection as the great event of the parousia, he seems to argue against the Corinthian spirituals' view of 'body' and of an extremely realized eschatology. W.A. Meeks believes that, against the Corinthian *pneumatikoi* who believed their bodies to be already perfected spiritually, Paul, by using apocalyptic language predominantly in the future tense emphasizes 'the imperfection of the present status of Christians and the necessity for mutual responsibility'.[5]

   2.   Regarding similarities between 1 Cor. 15.50-57 and 2 Cor. 5.1-5, see J. Gillman, 'A Thematic Comparison: 1 Cor. 15.50-57 and 2 Cor. 5.1-5', *JBL* 107.3 (1988), pp. 439-54.
   3.   D.A. Carson, D.J. Moo and L. Morris, *An Introduction to the New Testament* (Grand Rapids: Zondervan, 1992), p. 281.
   4.   Carson *et al.*, *An Introduction to the New Testament*, pp. 279-80. As Carson points out, W. Schmithals, *Gnosticism in Corinth: An Investigation of the Letters to the Corinthians* (trans. J.E. Steely; Nashville: Abingdon, 1971), especially pp. 259-75, and a few others, e.g. R. Jewett, *Paul's Anthropological Terms: A Study of Their Use in Conflict Settings* (AGAJU, 10; Leiden: Brill, 1971), pp. 119-34, 254-87, 352-56, and *passim*, hold that Paul argues against Gnosticism in the Corinthian church. But this is hardly supportable, because it is anachronistic to see the Corinthian letters from a viewpoint of Gnosticism which flourished in the second and third centuries AD. Arguing against Schmithals, C.K. Barrett, 'Paul's Opponents in II Corinthians', *NTS* 17 (1971), pp. 233-54 (236) says that 'there is fairly wide agreement that he was wrong'. R.McL. Wilson, 'Gnosis at Corinth', in M.D. Hooker and S.G. Wilson (eds.), *Paul and Paulinism* (Festschrift C.K. Barrett; London: SPCK, 1982), pp. 102-112 argues that only in a 'broad' definition of Gnosticism (cf. E.M. Yamauchi, *Pre-Christian Gnosticism: A Survey of the Proposed Evidences* [London: Tyndale, 1973], pp. 13-21), may the Corinthian correspondence be thought of as polemical to 'a kind of *gnosis*'.
   5.   W.A. Meeks, *The First Urban Christians: The Social World of the Apostle Paul* (New Haven: Yale University Press, 1983), p. 179; R.A. Horsley, ' "How Can Some of You Say that There is No Resurrection of the Dead?" Spiritual Elitism in Corinth', *NovT* 20 (1978), pp. 203-231 (especially pp. 229-31); cf. W.D. Davies, *Paul and Rabbinic Judaism: Some Rabbinic Elements in Pauline Theology* (London: SPCK, 1979 [1948]), p. 49.

2.2. *The Context of 1 Corinthians 15.49, 50-54*

1 Cor. 15.49 belongs to a unit, 1 Cor. 15.45-49, where Paul seeks to verify what he has already argued in the preceding passage, verses 36-44 (especially v. 44),[6] on the basis of scripture, and at the same time to seize an opportunity to return to the analogy between Adam and Christ previously referred to in an abbreviated fashion in verses 21-22.[7] By using two pairs of designations, each of which is applied to both Adam and Christ, Paul propounds the certainty of a change from the present body to the new body.[8] The first pair of designations is that Adam is a living soul (ψυχή), while Christ is a life-giving spirit (πνεῦμα, v. 45). While a *living soul* under-lines the fact that Adam was made with a physical body, a *life-giving Spirit* high-lights the fact that Christ has risen with a spiritual body.[9] By recognizing these two kinds of bodies, Paul would like to assure his readers that there will be a trans-formation from the physical into the spiritual (cf. vv. 42-44).

The second pair of definitions is that whereas Adam is the earthly man, Christ is the heavenly man (vv. 47-49). In verse 47 Paul calls Adam and Christ the first *man*[10] and the second *man*[11] respectively. The first man comes from earth; the second man comes from heaven.[12] Whereas verses 21-22 stress that a man Adam and a man

6.   On the basis of two metaphors (i.e. 'seeds' and 'bodies'), Paul affirmed that there would surely be an event of transformation from a physical body (σῶμα ψυχικόν) to a spiritual body (σῶμα πνευματικόν). J.D.G. Dunn, 'I Corinthians 15.45—Last Adam, Life-Giving Spirit', in B. Lindars and S. Smalley (eds.), *Christ and Spirit in the New Testament* (Festschrift C.F.D. Moule; Cambridge: Cambridge University Press, 1973), pp. 127-41 (129) believes that Paul has taken over 'the ψυχικός/ πνευματικός antithesis from his opponents' at Corinth but 'subtly transposes it into his own terms, σῶμα ψυχικόν and σῶμα πνευματικόν'; cf. Jewett, *Paul's Anthropological Terms*, pp. 352-56.

7.   With the Adam–Christ typology, vv. 21-22 present the principle that believers will be raised in the structure of everyone-in-Christ, while vv. 45-49 present a formula that their resurrection body will be like the risen Christ.

8.   J. Jeremias, '᾽Αδάμ', *TDNT*, I (1964), pp. 141-43.

9.   The words 'soul' (ψυχή) and 'Spirit' (πνεῦμα) in v. 45 are the cognate nouns from which the adjectives 'physical' (ψυχικόν) and 'spiritual' (πνευματικόν) in v. 44 are respectively derived. Verse 46 states that the physical comes first, then the spiritual. This perhaps includes the notion that Adam's physical body comes first, then Christ's spiritual body. However, Paul seems to be more concerned about the significance of the sequence of the two states of the body in relation to the believer's mode of existence. Concerning the meaning of the spiritual body, R.J. Sider, 'The Pauline Conception of the Resurrection Body in 1 Corinthians XV. 35-54', *NTS* 21 (1975), pp. 428-39 (434) argues that it contains the sense of 'a total person controlled by God's Spirit'; see also J.H. Neyrey, 'Body Language in 1 Corinthians: The Use of Anthropological Models for Under-standing Paul and His Opponents', *Semeia* 35 (1986), pp. 129-70 (161).

10.   This is a variant of 'the first man Adam' (v. 45).

11.   This is a variant of 'the last Adam [= Christ]' (v. 45). The change of modifying words, viz. from 'last' to 'second' suggests that there is no other representative person not only between Adam and Christ but also after Christ.

12.   As C.K. Barrett, *The First Epistle to the Corinthians* (BNTC; Peabody: Hendrickson, 1968), pp. 374-75 argues, Paul probably knew some such exegesis on Gen. 1.27 and 2.7 as that of Philo (cf. *Wisd. Sol.* 2.23-24), who implies two kinds of men (*Leg. Al.* i.31): (1) a heavenly, archetypal man, a Platonic idea of man (Gen. 1.27); (2) the historic Adam created out of dust (Gen. 2.7); see also S. Kim, *The Origin of Paul's Gospel* (WUNT, 2.4; Tübingen: Mohr, 1981), p. 172; M.C. de Boer, *The Defeat of Death: Apocalyptic Eschatology in 1 Corinthians 15 and Romans 5* (JSNTSup, 22;

196

Christ respectively originated death and life,[13] our present verse emphasizes that 'the first *man*, Adam' originates from earth, while 'the second *man*, Adam' (Christ) originates from heaven (v. 47).[14] This last comparison intends to suggest that the nature of Adam's body is physical, while that of Christ's *resurrected* body is spiritual.[15] It is clear that the first man from earth corresponds with a *living soul* (= the physical body) and the second man from heaven corresponds with a *life-giving Spirit* (= the spiritual body). What Paul envisages must be that the existence of such different kinds of bodies provides a solid ground for a belief in the resurrection change from the physical to the spiritual.[16]

Paul further advances this idea in verse 48. Adam is not the only being who has a physical body; Christ is not the only being who has a spiritual body. There are many who are like Adam; there are many who are like Christ. Neither of the two men is simply a private individual; each is an *Adam*, a representative man; what each is, others become.[17] Each is the head of those who inherit their attributes. Paul probably has in mind the idea of all-in-Adam and all-in-Christ from verses 21-22. The emphasis is on the fact that as people have a physical body like Adam, so believers will have a spiritual body like Christ. Paul, therefore, is convinced that believers will be transformed from the physical to the spiritual. Verse 49, by using the term φορέω, expresses such a belief.

Verse 50 concludes verses 45-49, and simultaneously prepares for the final paragraph (verses 51-58[18]) which draws the long argument of 1 Corinthians 15 to a

Sheffield: JSOT Press, 1988), pp. 99-101. It is likely that Paul uses Philonic terminology in a different way for his own purpose; for Paul, the heavenly man is an eschatological figure of the spiritual body, i.e. the risen Christ, and not a Platonic pattern of humanity. Cf. Davies, *Paul and Rabbinic Judaism*, pp. 47-48, 51-52; A.T. Lincoln, *Paradise Now and Not Yet* (SNTSMS, 43; Cambridge: Cambridge University Press, 1981), pp. 46-47; M. Black, 'The Pauline Doctrine of the Second Adam', *SJT* 7 (1954), pp. 170-79 (especially pp. 171-72).

13. John Calvin, *The First Epistle of Paul the Apostle to the Corinthians* (CC; Edinburgh: Oliver and Boyd, 1960 [Lat. 1546]), p. 323; R. Scroggs, *The Last Adam: A Study in Pauline Anthropology* (Oxford: Blackwell, 1966), p. 83.

14. Cf. J.H. Moulton and G. Milligan, 'ἐκ', in BAGD (Chicago and London: University of Chicago, 2nd edn, 1979), pp. 234-36 (235); S.E. Porter, *Idioms of the Greek New Testament* (BLG, 2; Sheffield: JSOT Press, 1994), pp. 154-55; C.F.D. Moule, *An Idiom Book of New Testament Greek* (Cambridge: Cambridge University Press, 1953), pp. 71-74; G. Lüdemann, 'ἐκ (ἐξ)', in H. Balz and G. Schneider (eds.), *EDNT*, I (Grand Rapids: Eerdmans, 1990), pp. 402-403. Paul refers to their origin in order to manifest the nature of their bodies. There is no doubt that the thought of man's earthly origin is rooted in Gen. 2.7, because 1 Cor. 15.47a is a simple paraphrase of Gen. 2.7, employing some of the words of the LXX (cf. Dunn, '1 Corinthians 15.45', p. 130). The thought of Christ's heavenly origin is presumably dependent upon the vision of the one like a son of man as seen in Dan. 7.13. Some documents from Paul's day, e.g. *1 Enoch* 46.1-3; *4 Ezra* 13.3, include a reference to a heavenly man, who lived in heaven (cf. Barrett, *The First Epistle to the Corinthians*, pp. 375-76).

15. Cf. Scroggs, *The Last Adam*, p. 88.

16. Dunn, '1 Corinthians 15.45', p. 128 (see also pp. 135-39).

17. Barrett, *The First Epistle to the Corinthians*, pp. 376-77; G.D. Fee, *The First Epistle to the Corinthians* (NICNT; Grand Rapids: Eerdmans, 1987), pp. 789, 794; see Dunn, '1 Corinthians 15.45', pp. 135-39.

18. Fee, *The First Epistle to the Corinthians*, pp. 797-98; B.A. Pearson, *The Pneumatikos-*

close. Further to the statement in verse 49, verse 50 lays down the principle that the earthly body cannot receive the kingdom of God nor the resurrection life in it, which is an introductory remark to the discussion on the resurrection body in verses 50-54. As the idea of transformation from the present physical body into a new spiritual body runs throughout verses 50-54, this passage forms a unit. It consistently expresses the apocalyptic Christian hope of a triumph over death. Verses 51-52 affirm that there will be a radical change in Christian existence from ψυχικόν to πνευματικόν.[19] Syntactically, verse 53 provides a reason for the argument in verses 51-52;[20] but, in context, it states what is necessary in order that the argument in verses 51-52 may be sustained. It makes sure that the dominant idea in the use of clothing imagery is the transformation of the believer's mode of existence from the present to the future. Verse 54 refers to what will happen at the time of transformation described in verse 53. Repeating the reference to the present body being clothed with the future body (v. 54ab), verse 54c stresses the concept of life's victory over death.

2.3. *The Meaning of Bearing the Image of the Heavenly Man (v. 49); Clothing with Imperishability/Immortality (vv. 50-54)*

2.3.1. *Introductory Remarks.* Regarding the metaphor of clothing with the resurrection body in 1 Corinthians 15, there are several important points, which need to be specifically investigated. Verse 49 refers to the concept of believers' bearing the image of the heavenly man; verses 50-52 emphasize that the physical, corruptible body must be changed into the spiritual, incorruptible body, in order to inherit the eternal kingdom of God (v. 50), and that at the parousia the dead will undergo a resurrection-change, and those who are alive, a transformation-change (vv. 51-52). Verses 53-54a state that the present body, which is dominated by perishability and mortality, will be clothed with imperishability and immortality. Verse 54b clarifies the imagery of resurrection-clothing by the concept of life's triumph over death.

2.3.2. *Identification with the Image of the Heavenly Man (v. 49).* By using the concept of clothing, Paul in 1 Cor. 15.49 depicts that a radical change will happen in the mode of the believer's existence.

Psychikos Terminology in 1 Corinthians: A Study in the Theology of the Corinthian Opponents of Paul and Its Relation to Gnosticism (SBLDS, 12; Missoula: Scholars, 1973), p. 15; H. Ridderbos, *Paul: An Outline of His Theology* (trans. J.R. de Witt; Grand Rapids: Eerdmans, 1975), p. 546; cf. A.C. Perriman, 'Paul and the Parousia: 1 Corinthians 15.50-57 and 2 Corinthians 5.1-5', *NTS* 35 (1989), pp. 512-21 (514); J. Jeremias, 'Flesh and Blood cannot Inherit the Kingdom of God', *NTS* 2 (1955–56), pp. 151-59 (151); E.S. Fiorenza, '1 Corinthians', in *HBC* (San Francisco: Harper, 1988), pp. 1168-189 (1188).

19. A. Robertson and A. Plummer, *A Critical and Exegetical Commentary on the First Epistle of St. Paul to the Corinthians* (ICC; Edinburgh: T. & T. Clark, 1967 [1911]), p. 375.

20. H. Conzelmann, *1 Corinthians* (Philadelphia: Fortress, 1969), p. 292.

καὶ καθὼς ἐφορέσαμεν τὴν εἰκονα τοῦ χοϊκοῦ φορέσομεν καὶ τὴν εἰκόνα τοῦ ἐπουρανίου.

Just as we have borne the image of the man of dust, we shall also bear the image of the man of heaven.

This statement indicates that the believer's physical mode of existence will be transformed into a spiritual one. The word φορέω[21] means to wear something as a garment; it is almost synonymous with the word ἐνδύω in verses 53-54 (cf. 2 Cor. 5.1-4).[22] The close link between verse 49 and verses 53-54 implies that the phrase εἰκόνα τοῦ ἐπουρανίου is connected with the concept of the resurrection body. Believers wear a perishable form of existence as a garment at present, but they will wear the imperishable form of existence as a garment at the resurrection.[23]

It is likely that this language of the wearing of the heavenly man's image reflects the concept of being clothed with garments of glory that is attested in Jewish apocalyptic literature (e.g. *1 Enoch* 62.15-16; *2 Enoch* 22.8-10).[24] These documents use the imagery of clothing to describe the righteous and Enoch receiving a heavenly and immortal mode of existence. Furthermore, it should be noticed that, like the preceding verses, verse 49 has been influenced by the Adam story in Genesis. The words τοῦ χοϊκοῦ seem to correspond with the story of Adam's creation out of the dust in Gen. 2.7, while the concept of εἰκών is reminiscent of the concept of the image of God in Gen. 1.27.[25] The concept of bearing the heavenly man's image probably echoes the concept of Adam's clothing in Gen. 3.21,[26] which takes up the

---

21. This word occurs six times in the New Testament, i.e. Mt. 11.8; Jn 19.5; Rom. 13.4; 1 Cor. 15.49a and b; Jas 2.3. Lincoln, *Paradise Now and Not Yet*, p. 50 observes that among the major manuscripts B reads φορέσομεν, while P⁴⁶ ℵ A C D G support φορέσωμεν which is 'the better attested reading in verse 49'.

22. Cf. Lincoln, *Paradise Now and Not Yet*, p. 51; Fee, *The First Epistle to the Corinthians*, p. 794, fn. 34; J. Moffatt, *The First Epistle of Paul to the Corinthians* (London: Hodder & Stoughton, 1959 [1938]), p. 267 argues in his comment on 1 Cor. 15.53 that 'the metaphor of being clothed or invested with immortality...carries on the thought of wearing or bearing the likeness of the heavenly Man (v. 49)'. See also C.F.D. Moule, 'St. Paul and Dualism: The Pauline Conception of Resurrection', *NTS* 12 (1965–66), pp. 106-23 (especially pp. 117-18).

23. K. Weiss, 'φορέω', in H. Balz and G. Schneider (eds.), *EDNT* III (Grand Rapids: Eerdmans, 1993), p. 436.

24. See also *Apoc. Abr.* 13; *Asc. Isa.* 4.16-17; 8.14-15; 9.9.

25. This contrast is similar to the Philonic distinction between the earthly man and the heavenly man. Yet, it fundamentally depends upon Paul's own analogy between the first man Adam and the second man Adam, i.e. Christ. Concerning the meaning of the image of God, see Pate, *Adam Christology*, pp. 65-66, fn. 2, who accepts C.K. Stockhausen's suggestion made in 'Moses' Veil and the Glory of the New Covenant: The Exegetical and Theological Substructure of II Corinthians 3.1-4.6' (unpublished PhD dissertation; Marquette University, 1984), pp. 298-32, 349-71. Stockhausen observes that after the Fall Adam was stripped of 'glory', which is related to 'image', though not identical with it; that 'glory' is the centrepiece of the image of God in Adam.

26. Of course the concept of a believer's wearing Adam's image (1 Cor. 15.49a) is different from the concept of Adam's being clothed with garments of skin (Gen. 3.21). But as the concept of clothing in Gen. 3.21 is connected with the mode of existence, in that the garments of skin may be a sign of Adam's recovery of his original state, and as the idea of all people being included in

themes of 2.25 and 3.7.[27] For Paul, believers at present wear the εἰκών of Adam who was made of dust, but they will eventually wear the εἰκών of Christ who is from heaven.[28] Undoubtedly τοῦ χοϊκοῦ points to Adam, while τοῦ ἐπουρανίου points to Christ.

If the concept of the image of God lies behind the concept of εἰκών, the term signifies more than simply an external form; 'εἰκών has the connotation of "essential character," and can be understood as equivalent to μορφή'.[29] As Adam's descendants, believers once bore his likeness, i.e. his physical nature; but now as Christ's people, they shall hereafter bear his likeness, i.e. his spiritual nature. A. Robertson and A. Plummer rightly argue that

> what Adam was, made of dust to be dissolved into dust again, such are all who share his life; and what Christ is, risen and eternally glorified, such will be all those who share His life. A body, conditioned by ψυχή, derived from Adam, will be transformed into a body conditioned by πνεῦμα, derived from Christ.[30]

At present, believers bear the image of Adam in his physicality, but they will ultimately bear the image of Christ in his spirituality. The present mortal body which is like Adam's body will be clothed with (as it were, changed into) the glorious spiritual body, which is like Christ's risen body (cf. vv. 53-54).[31] The resurrection of Jesus Christ is 'the proper prototype of the resurrection of believers'.[32] 'Whether it be those who die and experience decay or those who are alive at the Parousia, nevertheless their *mortal nature*, their σῶμα ψυχικόν is transformed'.[33] A.T. Lincoln insists that this change will result in a more exalted mode of existence than that which Adam had first possessed.

> The terminology of 'heaven' in connection with that of 'image' provides one way for Paul of expressing the fact that conformity to Christ's image is not simply a

Adam is maintained, the thought of believers wearing Adam's image (in the sense that they are doomed to be like Adam) would not be unnatural.

27. G.A. Anderson, 'Garments of Skin, Garments of Glory' (unpublished paper, n.d.), pp. 1-42 (especially, pp. 1-2, 5, 23).

28. Kim, *The Origin of Paul's Gospel*, p. 144 argues that 'in Rom. 8.29; 1 Cor. 15.45ff. Εἰκών-Christology is Adam–Christology'.

29. Pearson, *The Pneumatikos-Psychikos*, p. 25. For the likeness of the first Adam, see Gen. 5.3. Regarding the likeness of Christ, cf. *Wisd. Sol.* 7.26, which refers to Wisdom as having existed in the image of God; however, the thought of the 'likeness' of the heavenly man, viz. Christ, is essentially that of Rom. 8.29; Phil. 3.21. For Jewish, early Christian, and Gnostic interpretations of Gen. 1.26-27, see H-M. Schenke, *Der Gott 'Mensch' in der Gnosis* (Göttingen: Vandenhoeck & Ruprecht, 1962), pp. 120-43; for the history of the Christian interpretation of Gen. 1.26-27, see C. Westermann, *Genesis I* (BKAT, I/1; Neukirchen: Neukirchener Verlag, 1974), pp. 203-214. For a comprehensive survey of Jewish and Gnostic conceptions of the 'image of God', see J. Jervell, *Imago Dei: Gen. 1,26f. im Spätjudentum, in der Gnosis und in den paulinischen Briefen* (FRLANT, 76; Göttingen: Vandenhoeck & Ruprecht, 1960).

30. Robertson and Plummer, *The First Epistle of St. Paul to the Corinthians*, p. 374.

31. Cf. D.E.H. Whiteley, *The Theology of St. Paul* (Oxford: Blackwell, 1964), p. 252.

32. Carson *et al.*, *An Introduction to the New Testament*, p. 261.

33. Sider, 'The Pauline Conception of the Resurrection Body', p. 438.

restoration of something lost by the first Adam but involves a distinctly new element, a new quality of existence.[34]

Paul perhaps shares with Jewish Adam traditions the thought that Adam had been originally clothed with heavenly qualities. This thought is reflected in a number of Jewish documents. For example, *Apocalypse of Moses* 20–21 maintains that Adam and Eve were dressed in righteousness and glory. *Genesis Rabbah* 20.12 presents the pre-Fall Adam as clothed with light. *The Hymn of the Pearl* describes how the prince (the symbol of Adam) has been re-clothed with his splendid royal garment, that is, his original self, namely the image of God (vv. 75-78, 86). *The Hymn of the Pearl* seems to show the closest analogy to the concept of 'change' from the image of the earthly man to the image of the heavenly man (1 Cor. 15.49). In line with the Jewish idea of Adam's pre-Fall clothing, Paul seems to speak of human beings' restoration to the original Adamic state by using the imagery of clothing.

2.3.3. *The Change from the Physical, Perishable Body to the Spiritual, Imperishable Body (vv. 50-52)*

2.3.3.1. 'σὰρξ καὶ αἶμα' *against* βασιλεία θεου; φθορά/ἀφθαρσία *(v. 50)*. Verse 50 does not include the concept of clothing, but since this passage has an inseparable relationship with the clothing imagery in verses 49, 50-54, it needs to be properly investigated.

> σὰρξ καὶ αἶμα βασιλείαν θεοῦ κληρονομῆσαι οὐ δύναται οὐ δὲ ἡ φθορὰ τὴν ἀφθαρσίαν κληρονομεῖ.

> flesh and blood cannot inherit the kingdom of God, nor does the perishable inherit the imperishable.

Paul emphasizes the unfitness of the present body for the heavenly order, and so suggests the necessity of its transformation.[35] This implies that the clothing imagery in verses 49-54 connotes that the physical, perishable body will be dressed in the spiritual, imperishable body. J. Jeremias believes that the first clause refers to those living at the parousia, and the second clause to those who are dead at the parousia.[36] For him, the Semitism 'flesh and blood' indicates those who survive at Jesus' second coming, while the perishable points to those who died before that event. He asserts that 'the parallelism is thus not synonymous, but synthetic and the meaning of v. 50 is: neither the living nor the dead can take part in the Kingdom of God—as they are'.[37]

---

34. Lincoln, *Paradise Now and Not Yet*, pp. 51-52; cf. Kim, *The Origin of Paul's Gospel*, pp. 320-21.

35. Pearson, *The Pneumatikos-Psychikos*, pp. 25-26.

36. Jeremias, 'Flesh and Blood', p. 152, who is followed by Barrett, *The First Epistle to the Corinthians*, pp. 379-80.

37. Jeremias, 'Flesh and Blood', p. 152. He argues that every verse of the four following verses, viz. 51-54 also contains the contrast between the living and the dead, although the terms are different (Jeremias, 'Flesh and Blood', pp. 153-54). But his interpretation of τὸ φθαρτὸν as the dead

However, Jeremias's view is hardly supportable, because ' "this" perishable, as Paul expresses it in verse 53, obviously refers, just as "this" mortal, to the existing earthly life and earthly body, and not to that which is in process of decomposition in the grave'.[38] Further, his view does not match the context, the focal point of which is the great eschatological change from the earthly into the heavenly body and not the sameness of destiny for the living and the dead at the parousia.[39] Even in verses 51-52, which obviously contain the concept of the living and the dead, Paul's primary concern is the transformation from the earthly into the heavenly body.

Furthermore, it is not reasonable to see the concept of the imperishable as one which can be absorbed into that of the kingdom of God, because each term seems to retain its own significance.[40] Probably Paul wishes to make the concept of the imperishable, which is determined by that of the perishable, to be a term which at the same time describes the nature of the kingdom of God. Accordingly, we hold that verse 50 rather constitutes a synonymous parallelism: the present physical body, composed of flesh and blood, cannot inherit the kingdom of God, nor can the present corruptible body inherit the resurrection life which is essential to God's kingdom.[41] Both 'flesh and blood' and 'the perishable' most likely indicate the same reality, viz. the present earthly body, which is subject to physicality and corruptibility (vv. 42, 52-54).[42]

2.3.3.2. Resurrection and Transformation (vv. 51-52). In establishing the clothing imagery in 1 Cor. 15.50-54, verses 51-52 play a crucial part. The central point of verses 51-52 is that all believers, whether through death or not, will undergo the eschatological change at the parousia. Verse 51 states, by way of introduction: 'Lo! I tell you a mystery. We shall not all sleep, but we shall all be changed'.[43] The

and τὸ θνητόν as the living is scarcely acceptable. See Perriman, 'Paul and the Parousia', p. 514.

38. Ridderbos, *Paul*, p. 546.

39. *Contra* Conzelmann, *1 Corinthians*, p. 291. For an argument against Jeremias, see Sider, 'The Pauline Conception of the Resurrection Body', pp. 436-37.

40. Jeremias, 'Flesh and Blood', p. 152; cf. Robertson and Plummer, *The First Epistle of St. Paul to the Corinthians*, p. 376. In the view of G.D. Fee, both 'the kingdom of God' and 'the imperishable' point to the heavenly existence (*The First Epistle to the Corinthians*, pp. 798-99). The latter concept may be interpreted as such, but the former may not, because such an interpretation drastically reduces the significance of 'the kingdom of God'. There is no specific reason to interpret 'the imperishable' as the 'final heavenly existence' (*The First Epistle to the Corinthians*, p. 799). Already in 1 Cor. 6.9-10 the terminology, 'the kingdom of God', was used for its own significance, viz. in the sense of the divine order which will eventually be accomplished at the Last Day; it must also be borne in mind in 6.24-28 since Paul depicts the age to come in terms of Christ's handing over the kingdom to God the Father after he has destroyed all his enemies, the last of which is death. Further, in v. 58 also the same concept may be detected, as the passage anticipates that believers' labour in the Lord will be compensated in the coming age.

41. Cf. Perriman, 'Paul and the Parousia', p. 514.

42. G.G. Findlay, 'St. Paul's First Epistle to the Corinthians', in *EGT*, II (London: Hodder & Stoughton, 1900), pp. 729-953 (940); Moffatt, *The First Epistle of Paul to the Corinthians*, p. 265: 'flesh and blood (as in Gal. 1.16) means human nature as opposed to the divine'; Moffatt does not comment on the concept of 'the perishable'.

43. For a number of variants of this text, see Barrett, *The First Epistle to the Corinthians*, pp. 380-81.

word 'mystery' indicates 'a previously concealed truth now revealed' (cf. Rom. 11.25).[44] There can be no doubt that 'sleep' refers to death (cf. 1 Thess. 4.14; 1 Cor. 7.39; 15.6, 8, 20, etc.).[45] The first clause, therefore, signifies that death will not be experienced by all Christians; there will be those who are alive at the parousia.[46] The pronoun 'we', which is used in both clauses, indicates believers in general, both those who are dead and those who survive until the parousia.[47] Accordingly, verse 51 can be paraphrased as follows: 'At the parousia, some will be dead, others will be alive, but all will undergo the great transformation'.[48] All Christians, whether dead or alive at Jesus' second coming, will be changed.[49] The word 'change' (ἀλ-λάσσω)[50] must not be applied only to those who are alive at the return of Christ. Fee correctly points out,

> The contrasts that have been set up, however, are not between the corpse of the dead and their reanimated bodies, but between bodies in their present earthly expression vis-à-vis their transformation into the likeness of Christ's glorified body.[51]

Verse 52 clarifies verse 51: 'in a moment, in a twinkling of an eye, at the last trumpet. For the trumpet will sound, and the dead will be raised imperishable, and we shall be changed'. The three phrases imply that the great change through either transfiguration or resurrection will take place in a moment. 'The dead' and 'we' (i.e. the living) must be two different classifications, according to verse 51a.[52] However, the change which both are to experience will be the same. Both the dead and the living will simultaneously experience a startling change at the parousia: the former, the resurrection from death to life; the latter, the transformation from

---

44. D.H. Stern, *Jewish New Testament Commentary* (Clarksville: Jewish New Testament Publications, 1992), p. 489; cf. J.D.G. Dunn, *Jesus and the Spirit* (London: SCM Press, 1975), p. 230; Ridderbos, *Paul*, p. 547.

45. C.S. Keener, *Bible Background Commentary: New Testament* (Downers Grove: IVP, 1993), p. 488.

46. Barrett, *The First Epistle to the Corinthians*, p. 380.

47. L. Morris, *The First Epistle of Paul to the Corinthians* (Leicester: IVP, 1976 [1958]), pp. 232-33 sees the first 'we' as 'Christians alive at that day', and the second 'we' as all believers, whether they be dead or alive at the parousia. But his interpretation of the first 'we' is not supportable, because it would mean that Christians who are alive at the parousia will not all be dead, which does not make any sense. On the other hand, Barrett, *The First Epistle to the Corinthians*, p. 380 seems to consider the first 'we' to be all believers, dead or alive at the parousia, and the second 'we' as those who are alive only. But the latter is not acceptable, because it seems to be based on an improper interpretation of v. 51. Further, such an interpretation does not give a proper explanation to the conjunction 'but' (δέ). Conzelmann, *1 Corinthians*, p. 290 argues that 'The second πάντες again means all believers'.

48. Cf. Moffatt, *The First Epistle of Paul to the Corinthians*, p. 266; J.J. O'Rourke, '1 Corinthians', in *NCCHS* (London: Nelson, 1969 [1953]), pp. 1143-160 (1159); Findlay, 'St. Paul's First Epistle to the Corinthians', p. 941.

49. Fee, *The First Epistle to the Corinthians*, pp. 800-801.

50. This word is used only here and in v. 52 in the New Testament in order to describe the resurrection change (Fee, *The First Epistle to the Corinthians*, p. 800).

51. Fee, *The First Epistle to the Corinthians*, p. 799.

52. Conzelmann, *1 Corinthians*, p. 291; Jeremias, 'Flesh and Blood', p. 153.

physical to spiritual.[53] The present passage treats resurrection and transformation as corresponding terms.[54] The effects of these parts of a two-fold phenomena will be, of course, identical in that they will result in the glorious body.[55] G.G. Findlay rightly holds that,

> the certainty of change in *all* who shall 'inherit incorruption' is declared (51), and the assurance is given that while this change takes place in 'the dead' who are 'raised incorruptible', at the same time 'we' (the assumed living) shall undergo a corresponding change (52; cf. 2 Cor. v. 2ff.).[56]

What has been made clear from our observations is that verses 51-52 characterize the imagery of clothing-with-the-resurrection-body as a radical change. The earthly mode of existence will be transformed into a heavenly one. When Paul describes this resurrection change by means of clothing imagery, he probably has in mind contemporary clothing metaphors which picture a critical change in the mode of human existence. *1* and *2 Enoch* are documents that evidence the existence of such metaphors. *1 Enoch* 62.15-16 says that the righteous, who have escaped from an earthly condition and entered into a heavenly one, are to be clothed with garments of glory or life, namely a heavenly immortal body. *2 Enoch* 22.8-10, in order to portray that *Enoch*'s earthly body has been changed into a heavenly glorious body, states that he took off earthly and put on heavenly garments. In both passages the clothing imagery describes that as a worn-out garment is exchanged for a new garment, so the earthly body will be replaced by the heavenly glorious body, and that as a garment dominates the appearance of its wearer, so life and glory will characterize the appearance of the future body of the righteous. Paul believes that when the present corruptible body is changed into a future incorruptible body at the parousia, this new mode of existence will be pervaded by life and glory. The resurrection body will be dominated by these features.

2.3.4. *The Replacement of the Perishable/Mortal Body with the Imperishable/ Immortal Body (vv. 53-54a).* In 1 Cor. 15.53-54a, by making direct use of clothing imagery, Paul describes the parousia change in the mode of existence, which has been mentioned in verses 51-52. In order to be transfigured, Christians, whether living or dead at the parousia, need to put on imperishability/immortality.

> 53 Δεῖ γὰρ τὸ φθαρτὸν τοῦτο ἐνδύσασθαι ἀφθαρσίαν καὶ τὸ θνητὸν τοῦτο ἐνδύσασθαι ἀθανασίαν. 54a ὅταν δὲ τὸ φθαρτὸν τοῦτο ἐνδύσηται ἀφθαρσίαν, καὶ τὸ θνητὸν τοῦτο ἐνδύσηται ἀθανασίαν...

> 53 For this perishable nature must put on the imperishable, and this mortal nature must put on immortality. 54a When the perishable puts on the imperishable, and the mortal puts on immortality...

---

53. Cf. Robertson and Plummer, *The First Epistle of St. Paul to the Corinthians*, p. 377; Ridderbos, *Paul*, p. 537.

54. Cf. C.S.C. Williams, 'I and II Corinthians', in *PCB* (London: Nelson, 1975 [1962]), pp. 954-72 (965).

55. Cf. Whiteley, *The Theology of St. Paul*, pp. 253-54.

56. Findlay, 'St. Paul's First Epistle to the Corinthians', p. 941.

As in verse 50, the two clauses of verse 53 (which is repeated in 54a) seem to be in synonymous parallelism.[57] The word δεῖ implies that our passage recapitulates the principle stated in verse 50; while the need for change is negatively declared in verse 50 (viz. the present body cannot receive the kingdom of God and life in it), it is now reaffirmed in a positive manner.[58] For the resurrection change, our present corruptible/mortal[59] body has to put on incorruptability/immortality (ἀφθαρσία/ ἀθανασία).

Both ἀφθαρσία and ἀθανασία may be thought of as indicating an identical reality, namely the heavenly resurrection life. Ἀφθαρσία indicates the incorruptible character of the resurrection body. For Paul, incorruptibility can also be applied to God (Rom. 1.23; cf. 1 Tim. 1.17). Ἀθανασία points to the immortal character of the resurrection body. One of the important aspects in the culmination of resurrection immortality is the transformation of the immortal soul's transformation into its heavenly mode.[60] J. Barr argues that the centrality of the resurrection in the New Testament does not indicate the denial or the marginalization of the idea of the soul's immortality; he imagines that the scheme of two kinds of bodies in 1 Cor. 15.42-54 is that 'the soul lives on and is transformed into the "spirit" which actuates the transformation of the body'.[61] He believes that immortality and resurrection are in a relationship of complementarity and not of conflict. In any case, ἀφθαρσία and ἀθανασία indicate everlasting domination by the resurrection life, which will be accomplished at the parousia. Imperishability and immortality are not a reality that belongs to the

57. Fee, *The First Epistle to the Corinthians*, p. 802; Conzelmann, *1 Corinthians*, p. 292.

58. Findlay, 'St. Paul's First Epistle to the Corinthians', p. 941.

59. τὸ φθαρτόν is more comprehensive than τὸ θνητόν (Robertson and Plummer, *The First Epistle of St. Paul to the Corinthians*, p. 377). While the former focuses on human nature as liable to decomposition, the latter focuses on human nature as subject to death. But both have this in common: that they refer to one and the same reality, i.e. the earthly body, the 'present mortal corruptible existence' (J. Héring, *The First Epistle of Saint Paul to the Corinthians* [trans. A.W. Heathcote and P.J. Allcock; London: Epworth Press, 1962], p. 181).

60. Cf. Mt. 10.28 which reads, 'And do not fear those who kill the body but cannot kill the soul; rather fear him who can destroy both soul and body in hell'. Paul seems to maintain the idea of the soul's immortality and at the same time he believes that at the parousia it will take on a new quality. He recognizes immortality as putting on the resurrection body. On the other hand, dualistic Greek anthropology does not believe in a resurrection immortality. It only believes in the immortality of the soul, which is a natural endowment of humanity (Fee, *The First Epistle to the Corinthians*, pp. 802-803; W.F. Orr and J.A. Walther, *I Corinthians: A New Translation* [AB, 32; New York: Doubleday, 1976], p. 350; cf. *Wisd. Sol.* 2.23-24). For the Greek philosophical concept of the immortality of the soul, see J.L. Price, 'The First Letter of Paul to the Corinthians', in *IOCB* (London: Collins, 1971), pp. 795-812 (812); O. Cullmann, *Immortality of the Soul or Resurrection of the Dead?* (London: Epworth, 1958), pp. 19-39; G.W.E. Nickelsburg, *Resurrection, Immortality, and Eternal Life in Intertestamental Judaism* (HTS, 26; Cambridge: Harvard University Press, 1972), pp. 177-80 argues that Cullmann's essay 'presupposes a continuity between the Jewish and Christian viewpoints'; K. Stendahl, *Meanings: The Bible as Document and as Guide* (Philadelphia: Fortress, 1984), p. 196; Dunn, *Jesus and the Spirit*, pp. 120-22; E.R. Goodenough, *Jewish Symbols in the Greco-Roman Period* IX (Bollingen Series, 37; New York: Pantheon Books, 1964), p. 167.

61. J. Barr, *The Garden of Eden and the Hope of Immortality* (Minneapolis: Fortress, 1993), pp. 94-96, 110-11.

present mode of existence but a reality that will be embodied in the future mode of existence when the great change will take place.

The verb ἐνδύσασθαι is 'the usual word for putting on clothing'.[62] It conveys 'the thought of wearing or bearing the likeness of the heavenly Man (49)'.[63] At the parousia, the present physical body will be clothed with the new spiritual body.[64] Paul does not seem to be concerned about two different kinds of bodies at the parousia, viz. the body of the dead and that of the living, as in verses 51-52. His interest is that the believer's earthly corruptible body, whether alive or dead at the return of Jesus Christ, will be transformed into a heavenly incorruptible body in order to receive the resurrection life. Therefore, the view that 'Paul and his converts expected the Parousia to occur before their death'[65] does not seem to do justice to our passage. A.C. Perriman asserts that 1 Corinthians 15 'effectively precludes the possibility that Paul is thinking in terms of a significant proportion of Christians who will escape death'.[66]

If so, why does Paul use the imagery of clothing with ἀφθαρσία/ἀθανασία to depict the resurrection change? As was already pointed out,[67] this imagery shows a close affinity to the idea of the attirement of the righteousness (who rise from the earth, that is, enter the heavenly order by escaping from the earthly order) with garments of glory or life (*1 Enoch* 62.15-16). The imagery also resembles the description of *Enoch*'s transformation from an earthly to a heavenly mode of existence as his replacing of earthly with heavenly clothes (*2 Enoch* 22.8-10). These parallels suggest that the resurrection-clothing imagery in 1 Corinthians 15 is probably a product of Paul's recognition of the contemporary Jewish transformation idea, described by clothing symbolism.

Yet this would not be a sufficient explanation of Paul's use of the present clothing imagery. It should be remembered that Paul has used the Adam–Christ typology in establishing his resurrection theory. For him, the resurrection will take place according to the formula of all-in-Adam/all-in-Christ (vv. 21-22). Although believers as Adam's descendants bear the image of Adam at present, in the long run, they will bear the image of Christ at the parousia (vv. 45-49). As they have borne the same earthly mortal body as Adam's, so they will bear the same heavenly immortal body as Christ's. For Paul, the perishable/mortal body's being covered over by the imperishable/immortal body means that the Adamic earthly body is covered over by the new Adamic heavenly body, which resembles Christ's glorious body after his resurrection.

62. Morris, *The First Epistle of Paul to the Corinthians*, p. 234; cf. A. Barnes, *Notes on the New Testament V.1 Corinthians* (London: Blackie, n.d.), p. 321; A.T. Robertson, *Word Pictures in the New Testament. IV. The Epistles of Paul* (Nashville: Broadman, 1931), p. 198.

63. Moffatt, *The First Epistle of Paul to the Corinthians*, p. 267.

64. E. Stauffer, *New Testament Theology* (trans. J. Marsh; London: SCM Press, 1955), p. 211; W.G. Kümmel, *Theology of the New Testament* (trans. J.E. Steely; London: SCM Press, 1980 [1973]), p. 237; cf. Morris, *The First Epistle of Paul to the Corinthians*, p. 234: 'The body now is but the garb of the real man. In the life to come the real man will put on another suit.'

65. Williams, 'I and II Corinthians', p. 965.

66. Perriman, 'Paul and the Parousia', pp. 512-13.

67. See section 2.3.3.2, above.

If thus Paul's resurrection-clothing imagery is inseparably bound up with the idea of the Adam–Christ typology, it is highly probable that the imagery is built up on the basis of his interpretation of the Adam story in Genesis 1–3. As was noted in an earlier section,[68] there is little doubt that the concept of ἐνδύω in 1 Cor. 15.53-54 is in line with the concept of φορέω in verse 49, where the Adam motif is explicitly employed. These two verbs are interchangeable.[69] In fact, crucial concepts in 1 Cor. 15.53-54 have their equivalents in the Genesis story of Adam. The concept of corruptibility/mortality of the present body echoes the concept of death which has come to be dominant in the fallen Adam (cf. Gen. 2.17; 3.3, 19); the concept of life which will characterize the resurrection body corresponds to the concept of divine life which Adam originally received (Gen. 2.7); and the concept of the corruptible/mortal body being clothed with an incorruptible/immortal one looks back on the event of Adam and his wife having been clothed with garments of skins as a sign of their restoration to life and glory (Gen. 3.21), which reflect the image of God (Gen. 1.26-27). That the perishability/mortality caused by Adam will be endued with imperishability/immortality by Christ as the antitype of Adam points to restoration from the fallen Adamic state to the original Adamic state.[70] Paul probably envisages that Adam's body in its original state was clothed with divine life which might have been preserved, had he not forfeited it by deliberate disobedience to God.

However, since Genesis certainly does not mention Adam's pre-Fall clothing, we need to designate how Paul came to maintain the thought of Adam's pre-Fall clothing. As the concept of prelapsarian clothing is frequently found in ancient documents, it is probable that Paul's thought about Adam's pre-Fall clothing comes from his acquaintance with ancient Jewish traditions rather than from his own independent imagination. In his interpretation of the Adam narrative in the first three chapters of Genesis, he seems to have employed current ideas which he thought of as throwing light on the subject. He did not have any reason to blindly exclude all contemporary ideas. As has already been suggested, some documents of antiquity such as *Apocalypse of Moses* (chapters 20–21),[71] rabbinic literature[72] and *The Hymn of the Pearl* (vv. 75-78, 86)[73] regard Adam as being clad in splendid garments before the Fall. These works reflect the fact that in ancient Jewish circles the idea of Adam being adorned with radiance prior to his fall was prevalent. Perhaps Paul shares the idea of Adam's pre-Fall clothing with these documents.

Finally, Paul's use of clothing imagery for the description of the resurrection change in 1 Cor. 15.53-54a may perhaps be related to his perception of the human

---

68. See section 2.3.2, above.

69. See Weiss, 'φορέω', p. 436.

70. For Paul, this point seems to be clear, when he holds that people are dead in Adam who fell from life to death, but believers will be raised in Christ who was raised from death to life (vv. 21-22), and when he argues that although believers bear the image of fallen Adam at present, they will ultimately bear the image of the risen Christ (v. 49). The same point may also be found in the concept of life's victory over death (v. 54), death being the sentence imposed on Adam after the fall.

71. See Chapter 2, §§3.2 and 3.3.

72. See Chapter 2, §5.

73. See Chapter 4, §§3.1 and 3.4.

custom of clothing. Clothing imagery provides a graphic depiction of the nature of the change from a previous to a later mode of existence.[74] In connection with this clothing imagery, two dialectical points may be highlighted. First, clothing imagery implies continuity between the present and the future body.[75] As a change of clothing does not involve a change in its wearer, so the transformation of the body from the physical into the spiritual does not involve a change in the identity of its owner.[76] Robertson and Plummer provide a crucial statement:

> ἐνδύσασθαι...is a metaphor which implies that there is a permanent element continuing under the new conditions. In a very real sense it is the same being which is first corruptible and then incorruptible.[77]

Secondly, the clothing imagery implies discontinuity between the present and the future body. As clothing dominates its wearer's external appearance, the spiritual body will govern the future mode of Christian existence. The corruptible present body will be changed and replaced with the incorruptible new body, by which the nature of believers will be represented. In fact, clothing even reflects its wearer's character.

2.3.5. Life's Victory over Death (v. 54b). In order to clarify the significance of the resurrection-clothing metaphor, in 1 Cor. 15.54b Paul introduces another metaphor: life's swallowing up of death. This is a supplementary addition to the imagery of the present body being clothed with the future body. This manner of developing a specific issue is similar to the way in which the author of Colossians employs the imagery of clothing-with-virtue (3.12), in order to specify the significance of the clothing-with-the-new-man metaphor (3.10).

By citing Isa. 25.8,[78] 1 Cor. 15.54b refers to what will happen at the time of transformation described in verses 53-54a: τότε γενήσεται ὁ λόγος ὁ γεγραμμένος, κατεπόθη ὁ θάνατος εἰς νῖκος ('then shall come to pass the saying that is written: "Death is swallowed up in victory"'). The conquest of death, the last enemy, is the climax to which 1 Corinthians 15 has been heading.[79] The subjugation of death will be the essential element in the resurrection change. For Paul, the radical change from the physical to the spiritual body will be decisively achieved by life's victory

---

74. M.E. Dahl, *The Resurrection of the Body* (London: SCM Press, 1962), p. 113.

75. Cf. Héring, *The First Epistle of Saint Paul to the Corinthians*, p. 181: ' "To put on" is well chosen to suggest the idea of a new corporeal existence, which will, however, not be without a link with the old'; Whiteley, *The Theology of St. Paul*, pp. 249-50, 251-52; Dahl, *The Resurrection of the Body*, p. 15; Ridderbos, *Paul*, pp. 549-50.

76. Cf. J.P. Lange, *Commentary on the Holy Scripture. X. Romans and Corinthians* (Grand Rapids: Zondervan, 1960), p. 347: 'The maintenance of a personal identity, with a change in the quality of the vestiture, is here unmistakably implied'; John Calvin, *The First Epistle of Paul the Apostle to the Corinthians* (CC; Edinburgh: Oliver and Boyd, 1960), p. 344.

77. Robertson and Plummer, *The First Epistle of St. Paul to the Corinthians*, p. 377.

78. See O'Rourke, '1 Corinthians', p. 1160; de Boer, *The Defeat of Death*, pp. 46-47; Orr and Walther, *I Corinthians*, pp. 350-51.

79. J.D.G. Dunn, *1 Corinthians* (NTG; Sheffield: Sheffield Academic Press, 1995), p. 86.

over death, the last enemy. Transformation without the complete destruction of death is unimaginable.

The image of swallowing up plays a role that is secondary to the image of clothing. These two images are similar in that each implies not only a dominant but also a subordinate party. As something swallowed up is totally subsumed by its eater, so death will be thoroughly conquered by life. The resurrection change will not only bring about the present body being hidden by the new body, but also cause the mortal substance of the earthly body to be conquered by life, resulting in death's annihilation. E.S. Fiorenza properly asserts that 'whereas in baptism believers have been freed from the power of sin and of the law, in the Parousia they will be freed from the power of death' (1 Cor. 15.56-57).[80] In short, for Paul, the physical body's being clothed with incorruptibility and with immortality implies that the element of death in the body will be totally vanquished by life. When he thus supports the idea of resurrection-clothing by means of the swallowing up metaphor, he seems to concentrate on how a garment dominates its wearer's appearance. In an earlier chapter, we examined how many examples of antiquity show such a function of a garment.[81]

On the other hand, Paul's thinking of life's conquest of death as the centrepiece of the resurrection change also implies that the clothing imagery in 1 Corinthians 15 is controlled by the Adam–Christ motif. For Paul, the resurrection is a reversal of human destiny determined by Adam's fall from life to death (vv. 21-22). Such an event will happen when this present earthly body is clothed with imperishability and immortality. When this takes place, life will completely conquer death. The train of Paul's thought on the resurrection shows that he thinks of the life that will ultimately be gained as being the result of a reversal of the judgment pronounced on Adam in Gen. 3.19. Robertson and Plummer rightly hold,

> He knows that all death will be swallowed up now that Christ has conquered death by rising again. The doom pronounced upon Adam (Gen. iii.19) is removed; and the result (εἰς) is victory, absolute and everlasting triumph. Death is annihilated, and God is all in all.[82]

In conclusion, the metaphor of life swallowing death links the metaphor of the corruptible, mortal body's being clothed with the incorruptible, immortal body with life's total victory over death. In turn this implies restoration to something more than Adam's original state, which was characterized by divine life. The resurrection life of Christ who is the second and last Adam will pervade the resurrection body of the believer.

2.3.6. *Concluding Remarks*. The clothing imagery in 1 Corinthians 15 describes what will happen to the mode of existence of believers, whether alive or dead, at the parousia. First of all, the imagery connotes that the present body, which is dominated by the fallen Adamic physicality, will be replaced by the resurrection body, which is pervaded by the second Adamic (that is, the risen Christ's) spirituality

---

80. Fiorenza, '1 Corinthians', p. 1188.
81. See Chapter 8, §2.3.3.
82. Robertson and Plummer, *The First Epistle of St. Paul to the Corinthians*, p. 378.

(v. 49). Secondly, the imagery depicts that the present perishable body will be changed into the imperishable resurrection body in order to inherit God's kingdom. The present body's physicality (which is symbolized by 'σὰρξ καὶ αἷμα') and mortality will be changed into a quality suitable to the kingdom of God; Paul states that at the parousia, the deceased Christians will undergo a resurrection-change, and those who are alive, a transformation-change (vv. 50-52). Thirdly, the imagery portrays that the present body, which is characterized by φθαρτός/θνητός, will be changed into a body which is characterized by ἀφθαρσία/ἀθανασία (vv. 53-54a). Finally, the imagery signifies that the present body, which is subject to death, will be transfigured into a body which is subject to life (v. 54b).

3. *Clothing with the Resurrection Body in 2 Corinthians 5.1-4*

3.1. *The Situation of 2 Corinthians' Readers*
2 Corinthians was also written by Paul during his third missionary journey. After having sent 1 Corinthians to the church in Corinth in AD 55, he wrote 2 Corinthians in Macedonia in the following year or so (2 Cor. 2.12-13; 7.5; 8.1-5; 9.2). In contrast to 1 Corinthians which had been written in order to answer many questions of the church, 2 Corinthians was written in response to Titus' favourable report. In particular, judging from his re-reference to the theme of resurrection in 2 Corinthians 5 which was spoken of in 1 Corinthians 15, it seems that Paul thought of it as one of the most important issues for the Corinthian believers. As he suggested that the final consummation of the resurrection body would happen in the future, that is, at the parousia, he perhaps believed that the so-called spirituals, who were borne in mind when 1 Corinthians was written, were still influential in the church. As previously mentioned, they tended to despise the human body, against which Paul, by using the concept of 'putting on over', insisted on the bodily resurrection of believers.

3.2. *The Context of 2 Corinthian 5.1-4*
2 Cor. 5.1-4, on which we will specifically concentrate with regard to the concept of clothing, is part of the unit 5.1-10,[83] the theme of which is death and life. This is the issue which is prominent in 4.7-18 and which is expanded in 5.1-10.[84] 2 Cor. 5.1-4 can be considered to be a pericope in that it is consistently concerned with the question of the future mode of Christian existence. In order to establish this very idea, Paul uses three pairs of antitheses. The first pair is 'the earthly tent and the heavenly house' (v. 1); when the former is dismantled, the latter will be established. The second pair is 'being naked or unclothed and being clothed' (vv. 2-4b).

---

83. This passage is in turn part of a wider unit, 4.7–5.21; see C.M. Pate, *Adam Christology as the Exegetical & Theological Substructure of 2 Corinthians 4.7-5.21* (New York: University Press of America, 1991), p. 2.

84. Γάρ in 2 Cor. 5.1 implies that 5.1-5 furthers what has been said in the preceding part, which must be specifically 4.7-18. In fact, 2 Cor. 5.1-5 is an extension of the theme of 4.16-18, which includes contrasts between the outer man and the inner man, the temporary and the eternal (twice in vv. 17-18), the seen and the unseen (v. 18). See R.P. Martin, *2 Corinthians* (WBC, 40; Texas: Word Books, 1986), pp. 97, 102.

Believers yearn to be clothed with the heavenly building, in order that they may avoid being naked. The third pair is mortality versus life (v. 4c). That believers are clothed with the heavenly building will be confirmed by life's swallowing up of mortality (v. 4c). It is probable that behind all these contrasting pairs the Adam motif stands; this will be investigated when these verses are dealt with. What is particularly underlined by the use of clothing imagery throughout verses 2-4 is that the change in the believer's mode of existence at the parousia will be characterized by life's triumph over mortality. The concept of mortality and life is concealed even in verse 1, which mentions the possession of a heavenly house after the decomposition of an earthly tent.[85]

3.3. *The Meaning of Clothing with the Heavenly Building*

3.3.1. *Introductory Remarks.* In relation to the resurrection-clothing metaphor in 2 Corinthians 5, there are several crucial points to be noted. They are similar to those found in 1 Corinthians 15. 2 Cor. 5.1-2 elucidates the resurrection change as the earthly tent's being covered over by the heavenly building; verses 3-4ab, as nakedness' being covered over by the heavenly body; verse 4c explains it as mortality's being swallowed up by life.

3.3.2. *Replacement of the Earthly Body with the Heavenly Body (vv. 1-2)*

1 οἴδαμεν γὰρ ὅτι ἐὰν ἡ ἐπίγειος ἡμῶν οἰκία τοῦ σκήνους καταλυθῇ, οἰκοδομὴν ἐκ θεοῦ ἔχμεν, οἰκίαν ἀχειροποίητον, αἰώνιον ἐν τοῖς οὐρανοῖς 2 καὶ γὰρ ἐν τούτῳ στενάζομεν, τὸ οἰκήριον ἡμῶν τὸ ἐξ οὐρανοῦ ἐπενδύσασθαι ἐπιποθοῦντες

1 We know that if the earthly tent we live in is destroyed, we have a building from God, a house not made with hands, eternal in the heavens. 2 Here indeed we groan, and long to put on our heavenly dwelling.

In order to describe the believer's resurrection change, Paul first employs building imagery, and then mixes it with clothing imagery. It would, therefore, be reasonable to consider first the significance of the building imagery, then of the clothing imagery in its mixture with the former. While believers live in their earthly tent,[86] they groan,[87] longing to be clothed with a heavenly dwelling. Paul does not

---

85. Further, v. 5 refers to the guaranteed change from mortality to life; vv. 6 and 8 respectively refer to 'being at home in the body' and 'being away from the body and at home with the Lord', which echo v. 1.

86. I interpret ἐν τούτῳ as 'in the tent'. This interpretation is on the ground that the antecedent of the demonstrative is probably σκῆνος. Further, ἐν τούτῳ in 5.4 is immediately followed by τῷ σκήνει (see Lincoln, *Paradise Now and Not Yet*, p. 65). The translation of NIV and P.E. Hughes (*Paul's Second Epistle to the Corinthians* [NICNT; Grand Rapids: Eerdmans, 1962], p. 167, fn. 27), which render ἐν τούτῳ as 'meanwhile', is inappropriate because it does not match the context.

87. Groaning (στενάζειν) has two nuances, one negative and the other positive (Lincoln, *Paradise Now and Not Yet*, p. 65). The negative nuance is that Paul recognizes that he dwells in an earthly tent-body, which is subject to destruction. Inasmuch as he has a physical body (5.1, 2, 4), he cannot avoid suffering and even death (cf. 4.7-18). The positive nuance is that he recognizes that he is to have a heavenly house-body, which is imperishable. Earthly distresses, even death, can

elucidate what is meant by these two images and their being mixed. Rather, he thinks that his readers know what he means. There is little doubt that the two words ὀικία and οἰκοδομή,[88] which play a decisive role in forming the building imagery, refer to the body.[89] In the first-century Greek world, ὀικία was used in the sense of the external shell of the soul or real self.[90] Of course, this passage does not mean to speak of the release of the soul from the captivity of corporeal existence, but so far as ὀικία connotes 'body', the passage can be looked on as being tangentially connected with a Greek view of man. However, it is noteworthy that in the Gospel of John, Jesus Christ states, 'Destroy this temple, and I will raise it again in three days' (Jn 2.19), in which the temple points to Jesus' body (Jn 2.21).[91] Furthermore, Paul himself teaches that the Christians' body is the temple of the Holy Spirit (1 Cor. 6.19). Perhaps various notions of this kind have permeated Paul's mind, cross-fertilized with each other, and eventually crystallized as the building imagery in 2 Cor. 5.1-2.

Yet, an important question is why Paul mixes the building with the clothing imagery. It is unlikely that this mixture was alien to his readers. We can find a similar device in Philo, who mixes the concept of being clothed with that of residing in a house; for Philo, the garment of skin in Gen. 3.21 connotes the physical human body, which is the residence of a soul, the reality which results from the man-of-dust (= the first mind, Adam) having been inbreathed by the divine life (= the sense, Life).[92] That is, for him the human body functions as the soul's garment and at the same time as its abode. Further, the mixture of the concept of 'house' with that of 'clothing' is also present in Jewish traditions that see the temple as God's garment (*Pesiq. Rab Kah.* 15.3; *Lev. Rab.* 6.5; *Lam. Rab.* 15.3). Furthermore, the mixture

no longer dominate in this immortal body. The positive aspect in Paul's groaning seems to overwhelm the negative aspect (cf. Martin, *2 Corinthians*, p. 104; C.K. Barrett, *The Second Epistle to the Corinthians* (BNTC; Peabody: Hendrickson, 1973), p. 152; V.P. Furnish, *II Corinthians* [New York: Doubleday, 1984], pp. 295-96). In particular, in v. 4a the word βαρούμενοι, 'being burdened', is appended to the idea of groaning. In the light of the context, this word seems to mean 'to be weighed down by the corruptibility of the earthly body' (cf. 4.7, 12, 16; 5.1).

88. Since the two words can be placed in apposition with each other (v. 1b), Paul obviously means them to be synonymous. Whiteley, *The Theology of St. Paul*, p. 256; cf. R. Berry, 'Death and Life in Christ: The Meaning of 2 Cor. 5.1-10', *SJT* 14 (1961), pp. 60-76 (62) who asserts that 'the word οἰκοδομή...suggests a building still in course of erection'.

89. K. Schelkle, *The Second Epistle to the Corinthians* (London: Burns & Oates, 1969), p. 74; W. Lillie, 'An Approach to II Corinthians', *SJT* 30 (1977), pp. 59-70 (67); F.F. Bruce, 'Paul on Immortality', *SJT* 24 (1971), pp. 457-72 (470); Lincoln, *Paradise Now and Not Yet*, 61; T.F. Glasson, '2 Corinthians V. 1-10 versus Platonism', *SJT* 43 (1990), pp. 145-55 (146). On the other hand, Pate, *Adam Christology*, p. 121 argues that Paul in his expression of 'we know' of 2 Cor. 5.1 shares with his audience the tradition of the temple theme, as seen in, e.g. *2 Bar.* 4.2-7; *1 Enoch* 90.28-42; *4 Ezra* 10.44-59. However, in these Jewish apocalyptic traditions the temple imagery has nothing to do with the idea of 'body'.

90. See Plato, *Crat.* 403 B; *Gorg.* 523 E, 524 D; Philo, *Praem.* 120; *Som.* i.122; *Leg. Al.* ii.55-57; *Quae. Gen.* i.28; cf. *Wisd. Sol.* 9.15.

91. In Mk 14.58 Jesus' accusers argued that they heard him say that he would destroy the man-made Jerusalem temple and in three days would build another, not made with hands.

92. Cf. *Quae. Gen.* i.53 which deals with Gen. 3.21; see Chapter 2, §5.2.

was probably not strange to the readers, as they lived in the Graeco-Roman world, where the original meaning of the name of the *casula*, the garment of the poorer classes, is ' "little house"—a diminutive of *casa*'.[93]

Paul perhaps believes that the mixture of images expresses well what he would like to say in 2 Cor. 5.1-4. He appears to think that there is an analogy between 'house' and 'garment', in that both accommodate the human beings inside them, although the manner of their so doing is not identical. Perhaps he also thinks that they perform a supplemental function with one another. Whereas the building image simply refers to the *fact* that the earthly body will be exchanged with a heavenly body, the clothing image concentrates on the *way* in which the earthly body is replaced by the heavenly body. In verses 2-4, the building imagery seems to be secondary; it seems to be employed in order to underline the significance of the clothing imagery. Inasmuch as the concept of building stands for 'body', its use implies that the 'clothing' refers to a change that will happen to the body. At any rate, as ὀικία and οἰκοδομή point to 'body', the clothing metaphor in 2 Cor. 5.1-2 expresses a strong belief[94] that the present inferior body will be replaced by a future superior body. It seems that the earthly tent-house indicates the physical body in its temporary nature, while the heavenly house indicates the spiritual resurrection body in its permanent character.[95] For Paul, clothing with the heavenly building[96] means that the heavenly body will be given to the believer after his or her earthly body is destroyed.

But this does not seem to be all that Paul wishes to describe with the mixed metaphor; there is a probability that behind it the Adam motif is at work. E.E. Ellis asserts that 'the "tent-house" (2 Cor. 5.1) envisions primarily not the individual self (although this is included) but the whole ἐν Ἀδάμ corporeity which stands under death'.[97] It is indeed likely that the contrast between the earthly body (= tent-house) and the heavenly body (= building from God) echoes 1 Cor. 15.47-49, where Adam and Christ are respectively called a man from earth and a man from heaven. As

---

93. R.A.S. MacAlister, *Ecclesiastical Vestments: Their Development and History* (London: Elliot Stock, 1896), p. 44. The *toga* as the outdoor costume (see Chapter 6) was so inconvenient that a more convenient form of the garment was developed, resulting in variations appearing, e.g. the *paenula*, the *casula* and the *planeta* (MacAlister, *Ecclesiastical Vestments*, pp. 42-43).

94. The present tense ἔχομεν expresses Paul's assurance that the heavenly house will without doubt be given in the future, viz. at the parousia. The word cannot mean that Christians now possess this heavenly house in the sense of living in it, for v. 2 speaks of a desire to be clothed with it. See M.J. Harris, '2 Corinthians 5.1-10: Watershed in Paul's Eschatology?', *TB* 22 (1971), pp. 32-57 (41); Lillie, 'An Approach to II Corinthians', p. 67; Lincoln, *Paradise Now and Not Yet*, pp. 63-64.

95. H.A.W. Meyer, *Critical and Exegetical Handbook to the Epistles to the Corinthians* (CECNT, 2; Edinburgh: T. & T. Clark, 1879), pp. 251-53; Martin, *2 Corinthians*, p. 102; Harris, '2 Corinthians 5.1-10', p. 39; *idem, Raised Immortal: Resurrection and Immortality in the New Testament* (London: Morgan & Scott, 1986), pp. 219-21; Lincoln, *Paradise Now and Not Yet*, p. 61.

96. In significance there is no difference between the concept of 'οἰκοδομὴν ἐκ θεοῦ…, οἰκίαν… ἐν τοῖς οὐρανοῖς' (2 Cor. 5.1) and the concept of 'τὸ οἰκητήριον…τὸ ἐκ οὐρανοῦ' (2 Cor. 5.2), which Paul and his readers desire to wear.

97. E.E. Ellis, 'II Corinthians V. 1-10 in Pauline Eschatology', *NTS* 6 (1959–60), pp. 211-24 (218).

was argued above,[98] this opposition suggests an interaction with the Philonic concept of the earthly man and the heavenly man, which is based on an interpretation of Gen. 2.7/1.27. For Paul, the Adam-man, the man from earth, is a man of physical body, while Christ, the man from heaven, is a man of spiritual body. Perhaps Paul would also like to establish an anthropology on the basis of his interpretation of the first three chapters of Genesis.

In fact, as the clothing idea (2 Cor. 5.2, 3, 4) indicates the believer's acquiring resurrection life, it seems to reflect the clothing image in Gen. 3.21, which symbolizes the restoration of the original divine life. Further, the concept of being naked and unclothed (2 Cor. 5.3, 4) seems to echo Adam's naked state after the Fall (Gen. 3.7-11). The concept of life's swallowing up of death (2 Cor. 5.4) also seems to signify that the life which had been lost at the Fall (cf. Gen. 2.17) is to be recovered. In addition, 2 Cor. 5.11-15, which is adjacent to the passage under study, uses the idea of the one and the many: in his death and resurrection Christ represents all believers. Behind this statement the Adam–Christ typology seems to stand. Paul probably thinks that the quality of the believer's present body is inherently the same as that of Adam's postlapsarian body, because all mankind is united to him. Paul, however, believes that in the case of Christians, the life of the risen Christ already operates even in such a mortal body (2 Cor. 4.10-12, 14, 16-18). In the long run, this body will be turned into an immortal heavenly body like Christ's risen body (cf. 1 Cor. 15.50-54). In brief, clothing with the heavenly house after the earthly has been destroyed means that the present mortal body modelled on the fallen Adam will be replaced by the future eternal body modelled on the risen Christ as the new Adam.

If the mixed imagery in 2 Cor. 5.1-2 thus connotes the believer's restoration to the original Adamic state, it is probable that Paul maintains the idea of Adam's prelapsarian clothing, in keeping with the Jewish thought that Adam had been clothed with divine qualities before the Fall.[99]

If so, when is the heavenly body given to believers? Verse 1 underlines that the heavenly body is one which can be possessed only when the present earthly body has died. The word καταλυθῇ obviously describes the earthly tent-body, which represents man's present mode of existence, being dismantled.[100] The collapse of the tent-body clearly points to death.[101] Working from a concept of death as the soul's departure from the body (v. 8), Paul appears to expect his readers to understand verse 1a as referring to death, the decomposition of the body. R. Martin is probably right when he refutes a dualistic understanding of 2 Cor. 5.1a: to see this passage as describing the soul's separation from the body is to 'press Paul to argue for a dualistic appraisal of man'.[102] However, he does not clearly suggest what

---

98. See section 2.2, above.

99. See Chapter 2, §§3.2, 3.3, 5; Chapter 4, §§3.1, 3.4; Chapter 10, §2.3.4.

100. J.J. Lias, *The Second Epistle of Paul the Apostle to the Corinthians* (CGTSC; Cambridge: Cambridge University Press, 1892), p. 67; cf. L. Brun, 'Zur Auslegung von II Kor 5.1-10', *ZNW* 28 (1929), pp. 207-209 who argues that the word indicates Paul's suffering in this life.

101. K. Hanhart, 'Paul's Hope in the Face of Death', *JBL* 88 (1969), pp. 445-57 (447).

102. Martin, *2 Corinthians*, p. 105.

Paul's view of man's constitution is and what his view of the afterlife is. When Martin states that 'the interim period is a bodiless one (1 Cor. 15.35-38)',[103] he himself seems to take a dualistic view of man. It would be more appropriate to acknowledge the dualistic aspect of Paul's anthropology,[104] and to try to discover the way in which it differs from other dualistic views, for example from Greek dichotomical anthropology or from primitive Gnosticism. In Pythagoreanism the body is the soul's prison-house, so the soul's escape from the body is to be desired.[105] The same thought is maintained not only in Platonism[106] but also in Paul's contemporary Philo (*Leg. Al.* ii.57, 59). However, Paul never speaks of the soul's happy escape from the body. Rather, the thought that the heavenly house-body is to be *put on over* the earthly tent-body (vv. 2-3)[107] suggests that he was opposed to such a Greek philosophy.[108] J. Murphy-O'Connor states that,

> As his teaching on resurrection indicates (1 Cor. 15), the body was an essential component of the person. In opposition to the Greeks, who saw the body as a prison from which the soul had to be liberated, he viewed the body as the only sphere in which the commitment of the spirit to Christ became real.[109]

As was suggested in an earlier section,[110] if a proto-Gnosticism were at work in the Corinthian church, it was undoubtedly opposed to Paul's thought. R. Bultmann asserts that Paul's thought of *putting on over* (2 Cor. 5.2, 4) contains an 'indirect polemic against a Gnosticism, which teaches that the naked self soars aloft free of any body'.[111] Paul never thinks of a soul's separation from a body as a desirable state, as Gnosticism insists, because the body is essential for the full expression of humanity.[112] Rather, Paul considers the believer's future mode of existence as the state of the present body being covered over by the future body. There is continuity between the two bodies.

If so, does Paul mean that the change from the earthly tent-body into the heavenly house-body will happen immediately at death, apart from the parousia? R.F. Hettlinger, who believes that between 1 Corinthians 15 and 2 Corinthians 5 'Paul's thought underwent a significant development', argues that the latter passage asserts

---

103. Martin, *2 Corinthians*, p. 106.

104. Paul seems to believe that in a person co-exist σῶμα and πνεῦμα, which are not in any disharmony (cf. 1 Cor. 5.3). See Whiteley, *The Theology of St. Paul*, pp. 38-39; cf. Lillie, 'An Approach to II Corinthians', pp. 62-63; cf. R.H. Gundry, *'Soma' in Biblical Theology* (SNTSMS, 29; Cambridge: Cambridge University Press, 1976), pp. 135-58.

105. Glasson, '2 Corinthians V. 1-10 versus Platonism', pp. 146-47.

106. Plato, *Gorg.* 524 D; cf. *Gorg.* 523 E, *Crat.* 403 B.

107. For the meaning of ἐπενδύσασθαι, see section 3.3.3, below.

108. See F. Young and David F. Ford, *Meaning and Truth in 2 Corinthians* (BFT; London: SPCK, 1987), pp. 130-31; H.L. Goudge, *The Second Epistle to the Corinthians* (WC; London: Methuen, 1927), p. 47.

109. J. Murphy-O'Connor, *The Theology of the Second Letter to the Corinthians* (NTT; Cambridge: Cambridge University Press, 1991), p. 49.

110. See sections 2.1 and 3.1, above.

111. R. Bultmann, *Theology of the New Testament*, I (trans. K. Grobel; London: SCM Press, 1983 [1952]), p. 202; cf. Schmithals, *Gnosticism in Corinth*, pp. 261, 263.

112. Cf. Ridderbos, *Paul*, p. 549.

that the believer will receive a spiritual heavenly body at the moment of death.[113] However, as R. Berry points out,[114] Hettlinger's theory of development amounts to 'a flat contradiction' between 1 Corinthians 15 and 2 Corinthians 5. The context never implies that death automatically brings about a new life. For Paul, the question of when the earthly body is transformed into the heavenly body depends upon when the parousia comes.[115] When Paul was threatened with death, he looked forward to eternal glory; he fixed his eyes on what was unseen but eternal (4.17-18). The heavenly body will be eternal (5.1); at the parousia eternity will be realized in the present body. Moreover, if, as we have argued, the analogy between Adam and the risen Christ lies behind verse 1, our hypothesis gains credence. For it will be at the parousia that the transition from the mortal earthly body (that is like Adam's) to the immortal heavenly body (that is like the risen Christ's) will be achieved. Further, when Paul affirms that the mortal will be swallowed up by life (5.4), he is thinking of the end of the world, at which believers will experience a great change from a corruptible to an incorruptible mode of existence. The parallel passage, 1 Cor. 15.54, undoubtedly envisages the resurrection-change at the parousia.

Paul seems to acknowledge an intermediate state for those who have died before the parousia.[116] They will rather be 'away from the body and at home with the Lord' (v. 8). For Paul, who desires the parousia change and is under the threat of death, this statement is not unnatural. He wishes to speak of the believer's existence in the interim period.[117] This verse has been taken by some to refer to an immediate change at death from the present into the future body.[118] However, this is not necessarily meant by the passage. Rather, it means that although believers die, they will be with

113. R.F. Hettlinger, '2 Corinthians 5.1-10', *SJT* 10 (1957), pp. 174-94 (185). Among those who take the same view are, Hettlinger enumerates, Davies, *Paul and Rabbinic Judaism*, pp. 310-11; Bultmann, *Theology of the New Testament*, I, p. 201, etc. See also Whiteley, *The Theology of St. Paul*, p. 259; Bruce, 'Paul on Immortality', pp. 468-71; Glasson, '2 Corinthians V. 1-10 versus Platonism', p. 148.

114. Berry, 'Death and Life in Christ', p. 60; see also L.S. Thornton, *The Common Life in the Body of Christ* (London: Dacre, 1963 [1942]), pp. 284-86; Goudge, *The Second Epistle to the Corinthians*, pp. 45-55; Lincoln, *Paradise Now and Not Yet*, p. 64; cf. Ellis, 'II Corinthians V 1-10', p. 224.

115. Cf. Meyer, *The Epistles to the Corinthians*, p. 252; Goudge, *The Second Epistle to the Corinthians*, p. 47; Ridderbos, *Paul*, p. 501; D.A. Oepke, 'δύω κτλ', *TDNT*, II (1964), pp. 318-21 (321).

116. Ridderbos, *Paul*, p. 550; cf. W.L. Craig, 'Paul's Dilemma in 2 Corinthians 5.1-10: A "Catch-22"', *NTS* 34 (1988), pp. 145-47. Some reject the idea that in 1 Cor. 15 Paul has the intermediate state in mind; see D.A. Oepke, 'γυμνός', *TDNT*, I (1964), pp. 773-75; 'δύω κτλ', *TDNT*, II (1964), pp. 318-21; 'παρουσία κτλ', *TDNT*, V (1967), pp. 858-71. J.N. Sevenster, 'Short Studies: Einige Bemerkungen Über Den 'Zwischenzustand' Bei Paulus', *NTS* 1 (1954–55), pp. 291-96 also believes on the basis of 2 Cor. 5.8 and Phil. 1.23 in the main that Paul conceives of an intermediate state; but he points out that σὺν Χριστῷ εἶναι (Phil. 1.23) and ἐνδημῆσαι πρὸς τὸν κύριον (2 Cor. 5.8) may not exclusively refer to the intermediate state; he says, 'Es könnte auch sein—obwohl es m.E. nicht wahrscheinlich ist—, daß Paulus in gewissem Sinne proleptisch von der Herrlichkeit des Tages des Herrn spricht' (p. 296).

117. Hanhart, 'Paul's Hope in the Face of Death', p. 447 rightly affirms that 2 Cor. 5.8 'hardly refers to the resurrection of the dead'; Cullmann, *Immortality*, pp. 52-57 implies that whereas 2 Cor. 5.1-5 refers to events at the parousia, 5.6-9 speaks of life after death.

118. F.F. Bruce (ed.), *1 and 2 Corinthians* (NCBC; London: Oliphants, 1971), p. 200.

Christ even in the intermediate state. For Paul, who believes that in the present body life already operates (4.10-11, 16), the idea that Christians in their intermediate state are with Christ is natural.[119] Accordingly, verse 1 signifies that even though the present earthly body decomposes, a heavenly body will be given at the parousia.[120]

What are the characteristics of the future heavenly body? As 2 Cor. 5.1 shows, the future body will be so superior to the present body as to be beyond comparison. This is manifested in the modifying words used for each. While the words ἐκ θεοῦ, ἀχειροποίητον, αἰώνιον and ἐν τοῖς οὐρανοῖς modify the future body, the words ἐπίγειος and τοῦ σκήους describe the present body. H.A.W. Meyer rightly says that ἐκ θεου and ἐν τοῖς οὐρανοῖς correspond with ἐπίγειος, while ἀχειροποίητον and αἰώνιον correspond with τοῦ σκήους.[121] Four modifying words describe the features of the future body.[122] First, the future body will be spiritual. Whereas the present body originates from earth and has a physical nature, the future body will originate from God and have a spiritual nature. Probably the preposition ἐκ of the phrase ἐκ θεοῦ expresses not merely origin or source but also nature (cf. Jn 3.6).[123] Secondly, the future body will be indestructible. The present body can be easily destroyed, but the future body will be unbreakable. Thirdly, the future body will be characterized by eternity. Whereas the present body is temporary, the future body will be permanent. It cannot be attacked by death. Fourthly, the future body will be supernatural. While the present body is one which is suitable to the earthly dimension, the future body will be one which fits the heavenly dimension.[124]

3.3.3. *Nakedness' Being Covered over by Heavenly Glory (vv. 3-4ab).* 2 Cor. 5.3-4ab designates the clothing with the resurrection body as nakedness' being covered over by the heavenly body.

> 3 εἴγε καὶ ἐνδυσάμενοί, οὐ γυμνοὶ εὑρεθησόμεθα. 4ab καὶ γὰρ οἱ ὄντες ἐν τῷ σκήνει στενάζομεν βαρούμενοι, ἐπειδὴ οὐ θέλομεν ἐκδύσασθαι ἀλλ' ἐπενδύσασθαι

> 3 so that by putting it on we may not be found naked. 4ab For while we are still in this tent, we sigh with anxiety; not that we would be unclothed, but that we would be further clothed.

In this pericope, the word γυμνός and the compound ἐπενδύσασθαι need to be specifically examined, because γυμνός is contrasted with the concept of being clothed and ἐπενδύσασθαι is the major word in the clothing language.

---

119. The following might be Paul's scheme of Christian existence: (a) the earthly body in the present time, (b) the intermediate identity in the interim time, and (c) the heavenly body at the parousia. (A), the physical nature, will be transformed into (b), the spiritual nature, which does not have physical aspects; then (b) will be changed into (c), the perfected spiritual nature, which includes even physical aspects. At this final stage, Christian existence will be represented by the glorified spiritual body, viz. the heavenly body.

120. See J. Osei-Bonsu, 'Does 2 Cor. 5.1-10 Teach the Reception of the Resurrection Body at the Moment of Death?', *JSNT* 28 (1986), pp. 81-101.

121. Meyer, *The Epistles to the Corinthians*, p. 253.

122. Whiteley, *The Theology of St. Paul*, pp. 258-59.

123. Lüdemann, 'ἐκ (ἐξ)', p. 403.

124. Lincoln, *Paradise Now and Not Yet*, p. 61.

The word γυμνός[125] in v. 3 is 'synonymous with that expressed by ἐκδύσασθαι in verse 4'.[126] A separate examination of ἐκδύσασθαι will not be necessary; γυμνός only seems to have priority to ἐκδύσασθαι. Γυμνός does not seem simply to reflect the fear of nakedness that was common to ancient Jews.[127] Some view that this term denotes a bodiless state;[128] they believe that Paul speaks of an immediate transformation from the present body to the future body without undergoing death; they insist that Paul thinks that being clothed indicates a bodily state and being naked indicates a bodiless state. But this is subtly misleading. Paul's major concern is not whether the believer will be in a body or bodiless but whether or not his present body will be transformed into a heavenly body. When the believer's present body is turned into a heavenly body, he will not be left naked; but while his present body remains unchanged into a heavenly body, he will be left naked.[129] The point being made is that nakedness indicates the state of being unclothed with a heavenly body at the parousia, in other words, the state of being in an earthly mode of existence at the parousia when the earthly body has failed to be changed into the heavenly mode of existence.[130]

E.E. Ellis perceptively comments:

125. For the use of the word γυμνός in the New Testament and in the LXX, see Whiteley, *The Theology of St. Paul*, p. 257.

126. Lincoln, *Paradise Now and Not Yet*, p. 66. However, P.W. Van Der Horst, 'Short Studies: Observations on a Pauline Expression', *NTS* 19 (1972–73), pp. 181-87 (183) asserts that 'the absolute use of ἐκδύσασθαι in II Cor v. 4 perhaps may be explained also as "putting off the body", i.e. dying', but this interpretation is not supported by the context; Oepke, 'δύω κτλ', p. 318. Paul focuses on the concept of putting on the heavenly body over the earthly body rather than the concept of putting off the earthly body and putting on the heavenly body. Of course, Paul does not mean to cover the earthly body as it is with the heavenly body; the earthly body's being over-clothed with the heavenly body includes the significance of transformation from the former body to the latter body.

127. Barrett, *The Second Epistle to the Corinthians*, p. 153; Martin, *2 Corinthians*, pp. 99, 100; cf. C.L. Mitton, 'Paul's Certainties: V. The Gift of the Spirit and Life beyond Death—2 Corinthians v. 1-5', *ExpT* 69 (1957–58), pp. 260-63 (260); M.E. Thrall, *The First and Second Letters of Paul to the Corinthians* (Cambridge: Cambridge University Press, 1965), p. 143; Bruce (ed.), *1 and 2 Corinthians*, p. 203.

128. Cullmann, *Immortality*, pp. 51-54; Berry, 'Death and Life in Christ', pp. 64-66; Goudge, *The Second Epistle to the Corinthians*, p. 47; Plummer, *The Second Epistle of St. Paul to the Corinthians*, pp. 147-49; Hughes, *Paul's Second Epistle to the Corinthians*, pp. 169, 171, 173; Schelkle, *The Second Epistle to the Corinthians*, p. 75; Harris, *Raised Immortal*, pp. 222-23; cf. Lillie, 'An Approach to II Corinthians', p. 63; Craig, 'Paul's Dilemma', p. 145; Glasson, '2 Corinthians V. 1-10 versus Platonism', pp. 145-46. In Plato (*Crat.* 403 B) γυμνός is used for describing the bodiless soul, which is to the Greek an enviable condition, but to the Jews a dreadful condition (cf. Barrett, *The Second Epislte to the Corinthians*, p. 153; Martin, *2 Corinthians*, pp. 99-101). However, in 2 Cor. 5.3-4 γυμνός is far from refering to the soul without the body. The word describes the condition of the body when the parousia has come.

129. Cf. Plummer, *The Second Epistle of St. Paul to the Corinthians*, p. 147.

130. Note that 2 Cor. 5.2-4 unmistakingly reflects Paul's concern, not lest he should be disembodied before the parousia, but lest he should be denied a part in the resurrection and fall to the fate of unbelievers at the parousia; M.E. Dahl, *The Resurrection of the Body: A Study of 1 Corinthians 15* (Studies in Biblical Theology, 36; London: SCM Press, 1962), p. 29.

> Both γυμνός and ἐκδύω in II Cor v have the judgment scene in view. The opposite of being clothed upon by the house from heaven, i.e. the righteous Body of Christ, is not to be disembodied but to stand in the judgment ἐν Ἀδάμ, i.e. in the Body that is naked in guilt and shame.[131]

This implies that nakedness points to the condition (at the Last Day) of a body which is like Adam's post-Fall body, which has lost its righteousness and glory.[132] Similarly, C.M. Pate holds that what Paul wants to avoid experiencing is 'Adam's nakedness', viz. the state of having stripped from him the divine glory with which he was originally clothed.[133] Nakedness, then, signifies a fallen-Adamic, bodily state that is without glory because of its failure to be changed into a spiritual resurrection body at the parousia. Accordingly, we can conclude that the metaphor of clothing with the heavenly body signifies that the believer's present body is turned into a glorious resurrection body which resembles the risen body of Christ as the second and last Adam.

As has been already suggested, the compound ἐπενδύσασθαι[134] underlines that he who is already wearing something goes on to put on something else over it. Believers already wear the earthly tent-body, but they desire to put on the heavenly house-body over it.[135] Here the earthly body being covered over by the heavenly body

131. Ellis, 'II Corinthians V. 1-10', p. 221; cf. Murphy-O'Connor, *The Theology of the Second Letter to the Corinthians*, p. 52; D. Wenham, 'Being "Found" on the Last Day: New Light on 2 Peter 3.10 and 2 Corinthians 5.3', *NTS* 33 (1987), pp. 477-79 (478).

132. See Ellis, 'II Corinthians V. 1-10', pp. 223-24.

133. Pate, *Adam Christology*, p. 115. Pate argues that this understanding of the Adam story parallels some Jewish documents of Paul's day; he suggests *3 Bar.* 6.16; *2 Enoch* 22.8 and 30.12; *Gen. Rab.* 20.12; *Apoc. Mos.* 20.1. However, *3 Bar.* 6.16 and *2 Enoch* 30.12 do not use the concept of clothing. *Gen. Rab.* 20.12 and *Apoc. Mos.* 20.1 are of consequence in relation to the background of 2 Cor. 5. *2 Enoch* 22.8 has something to do with Adam, and seems to be crucial in that it significantly uses the clothing metaphor in relation to a change in the mode of existence. Cf. Ridderbos, *Paul*, p. 503: ' "not to be found naked" and "to be clothed" (vv. 2-4) mean not only: no longer to be bodiless, but: to share in the full glory of God, undoubtedly because of receiving the new glorified "body" '.

134. While v. 3 uses ἐνδυσάμενοι, vv. 2 and 4 use ἐπενδύσασθαι. As Hettlinger, '2 Corinthians 5.1-10', pp. 178-79 argues, there do not seem to be serious differences between these two words. He points out that in 1 Cor. 15.53 'Paul uses ἐνδύσασθαι for the putting on of the Resurrection Body.' A similar view is maintained by Berry, 'Death and Life in Christ', p. 64. Considering that the idea ἐνδυσάμενοι in v. 3 ties in with ἐπενδύσασθαι in v. 2, the former has the same significance as that of the latter (Oepke, 'δύω κτλ', p. 320; Bruce [ed.], *1 and 2 Corinthians*, p. 203). In v. 3 Paul perhaps considers that a word which is more properly contrasted with the word γύμνος is ἐνδυσάμενοι. Yet, in v. 4 when he re-uses ἐπενδύσασθαι, this word seems to be in the forefront of Paul's mind as a major term which aptly manifests his thought of the parousia change. With this word Paul is perhaps inclined to highlight continuity between the present body and the resurrection body.

135. Barrett, *The Second Epistle to the Corinthians*, pp. 152-53; Hughes, *Paul's Second Epistle to the Corinthians*, p. 168; Furnish, *II Corinthians*, pp. 295-96; Whiteley, *The Theology of St. Paul*, pp. 254-55; Lincoln, *Paradise Now and Not Yet*, pp. 65-66. In contrast, Hanhart, 'Paul's Hope in Face of Death', p. 451, holds that the word ἐπενδύεσθαι does not refer to 'the putting on of a new heavenly body over the old one like a pullover or a topcoat, as if Paul indeed was trying to solve an anthropological puzzle of the afterlife'. For Hanhart, while ἐνδύεσθαι refers to the life of the Spirit, which is received at baptism and in daily renewal, ἐπενδύεσθαι refers to receiving the 'full measure

emphasizes the continuity of bodily existence and at the same time stands for the transformation from one into the other,[136] of which Paul also speaks in 1 Cor. 15.53-54. The earthly tent-body will be replaced by the glorious resurrection body at the parousia.[137]

C.F.D. Moule, in his comment on ἐπενδύσασθαι, argues that Paul's concept in 1 Corinthians 15 of a sudden change at the parousia from mortal to immortal life has changed in 2 Corinthians 5 into the concept of a progressive transformation from the old man into the new man.[138] For Moule, Paul has forsaken his former opinion (cf. 1 Corinthians 15); he now believes that at death there ends a spiritual process of mortification of the old man and a progressive occupation of the new man, thereby the renewed inner man starts living a new life.[139] But it is unlikely that Paul changed his views so radically that he completely abandoned his former expectation of the parousia and instead taught a Greek idea of the soul's immortality, that is, a resurrection immediately at the time of death. It is highly likely that Paul wrote 2 Cor. 5.1-4 expecting the Corinthians to remember his previous teaching in 1 Cor. 15.53-54. As a matter of fact, there is no fundamental contradiction between the idea in 2 Cor. 5.1-4 and the apocalyptic vision of 1 Corinthians 15.[140]

Paul, rather, yearns for the speedy arrival of the parousia so that the believers' earthly body may be transformed into a heavenly body. Inasmuch as the reality of the heavenly dwelling (v. 2) is the same as that of the 'building from God', viz. the eternal heavenly house (v. 1), and inasmuch as the great transformation will take place at the parousia, the wearing of the heavenly building (v. 2) will happen at Jesus Christ's second coming.[141] To be clothed with the desired heavenly house (v. 2)

of this life of the Spirit with which he [Paul] was already endowed' (Hanhart, 'Paul's Hope in Face of Death', p. 455). Hanhart's argument that ἐπενδύεσθαι may not concern the issue of afterlife seems to be right. But his view that those clothing-words describe the life of the Spirit does not seem to be acceptable, because those words are used to describe a change in the mode of existence from that of the present into that of the future. Cf. Glasson, '2 Corinthians V. 1-10 versus Platonism', pp. 149-50.

136. Cullmann, *Immortality*, pp. 51-54; Hughes, *Paul's Second Epistle to the Corinthians*, p. 168.

137. Pate, *Adam Christology*, p. 121.

138. Moule, 'St. Paul and Dualism', pp. 106-108, 118. Cf. Harris, '2 Corinthians 5.1-10', p. 57 who asserts that '2 Corinthians 5.1-10 marks a watershed in the development of Paul's eschatology', and that 'in 2 Corinthians 5 he [Paul] envisages his own receipt of a σῶμα πνευματικόν comparable to Christ's as occurring at the time of his death'. But this cannot be acceptable, because the Christian dead are hardly considered as possessing a similar body to the spiritual body of Christ which was able to manifest itself even as a physical form.

139. Moule, 'St. Paul and Dualism', pp. 118-19.

140. Young and Ford, *Meaning and Truth in 2 Corinthians*, p. 133; J. Héring, *The Second Epistle of Saint Paul to the Corinthians* (trans. A.W. Heathcote and P.J. Allcock; London: Epworth Press, 1967), p. 38; C.K. Barrett, 'Immortality and Resurrection', in *Resurrection and Immortality: A Selection from the Drew Lectures on Immortality* (ed. C.S. Duthie; London: Samuel Bagster, 1979), p. 86: 'we must put 2 Corinthians 5 along with 1 Corinthians 15, not to contradict it but to supplement it'; M. Goulder, 'The Unity of the Corinthian Correspondence' (a seminar paper read at British New Testament Conference, Aberdeen, 1996), pp. 15-20.

141. Goudge, *The Second Epistle to the Corinthians*, p. 47; R. Bultmann, *Exegetische Probleme*

undoubtedly has the same significance as that of the change from the present earthly body into the future heavenly body (v. 1).

Is Paul's wish for the parousia's quick arrival so that he may survive until then and so experience the great transfiguration without death?[142] There is little doubt that he believed at an earlier stage of his ministry that the parousia would come soon, so he might be able to welcome it whilst he was still alive (1 Thess. 4.15-17).[143] However, the present passage does not seem to express such an expectation of an imminent parousia. It rather suggests that Paul will probably be taken away before the parousia.[144] In the face of a situation that threatens his life (4.8-12), Paul envisages the probability that he will die fairly soon. He is sure that even if he dies before the parousia, he will be at home with the Lord (v. 8). He seems to believe that even in the intermediate state he would enjoy being at home with Christ.[145] But he is so ardent in his desire to undergo the great change at the parousia that he earnestly wishes the parousia would come soon.[146] The question of whether he lives until the parousia or not is not the major concern of the passage. The key-note is that even if the present body decomposes, the heavenly body will undoubtably replace it at the parousia.

In sum, the verb ἐπενδυσασθαι discloses two dialectical aspects. One aspect is that of continuity between the present and the future body.[147] Although one puts on one garment over another that has already been put on, the identity of the wearer him/herself is not changed. When the [high] priest dresses himself with manifold priestly garments (as it were, the ephod is put on over a blue robe, which is in turn put on over a woven tunic of fine linen, which is in turn put on over linen undergarments),[148] this does not mean that he undergoes manifold changes in his identity. Similarly, the person who owns the present body will be the very same person who will have the future body.[149] But there is also an aspect of discontinuity between the present body and the future body. When someone who has already put on one

des zweiten Korintherbriefes (SBU, 9; Uppsala, 1947; Darmstadt: Wissenschaftliche Buchgesellschaft, 1963), p. 12; F.V. Filson and J. Reid, 'Second Corinthians', in *IB* X (Nashville: Abingdon, 1953), pp. 265-425 (327); Ellis, 'II Corinthians V. 1-10', p. 221.

142. Cf. Hughes, *Paul's Second Epistle to the Corinthians*, p. 169. Hughes argues that Paul is expressing his personal desire to be transformed into a heavenly body without the process of the collapse of his physical body.

143. Harris, '2 Corinthians 5.1-10', p. 36; Hanhart, 'Paul's Hope in Face of Death', p. 449. However, Paul's expectation of Christ's imminent return does not necessarily mean that he has not yet attained to such a thought of the 'change' as spoken of in 1 Cor. 15.52 (Ridderbos, *Paul*, p. 535).

144. Harris, '2 Corinthians 5.1-10', p. 35.

145. In Paul's scheme of human existence both for the present and the future, there can be an interim state between death and the parousia. But the present passage never postulates anything like a transformation from an intermediate state into a heavenly body. Paul simply intimates that there will be an interim state which will be, to deceased Christians, a happy one (5.8); he goes no further with this idea. See Ridderbos, *Paul*, pp. 504-508.

146. Cf. R.H. Strachan, *The Second Epistle of Paul to the Corinthians* (London: Hodder & Stoughton, 1935), p. 100.

147. Hughes, *Paul's Second Epistle to the Corinthians*, p. 168; Mitton, 'Paul's Certainties', p. 261.

148. See Chapter 1, §3.2.

149. Cf. Moule, 'St. Paul and Dualism', p. 116.

garment puts another over it, his external appearance will be changed as he does so. The last garment to be put on will be the one which dominates his appearance. In a similar manner, the form of the present body will differ from that of the future body. There will be a radical change between the two. Whereas the present body is dominated by physicality, the future body will be dominated by spirituality (cf. 1 Cor. 15.42-44).

3.3.4. *Life's Subjugation of Mortality (v. 4c)*. Verse 4c presents the ultimate goal in the desire to put the heavenly body on over the present body: ἵνα καταποθῇ τὸ θνητὸν ὑπὸ τῆς ζωῆς ('so that what is mortal may be swallowed up by life'). Through the contrast between mortality and life, Paul suggests that clothing with the resurrection body connotes being endowed with the perfected body, which will be one which has overcome the element of mortality in the earthly body. That is to say, the earthly body is subject to death, but the heavenly body will be subject to life. At the parousia, death will be entirely conquered by life.

There is little doubt that the concept of clothing with the resurrection body as life's swallowing up of mortality also takes the Adam motif as its background. The first three chapters of Genesis relate that Adam first received the divine life (cf. Gen. 1.27; 2.7), but because of his sin (Gen. 3.6) he fell into death (cf. Gen. 2.17; 3.19). People are first born into the last, fallen state of Adam, so that they commit iniquities and live under the rule of death, but those who are in Christ eventually recover life. If the story of the life-then-death of Adam is extended to the story of the death-then-life of Christians who have started out in Adam, the statement about mortality being swallowed up by life can be regarded as having its background in the Adam story.

In brief, clothing with the resurrection body indicates the believer's being enveloped by the heavenly body. This body will be the product of a victory over death (a death that is the predominant factor in the corruptible body), so that it will be overpowered by life.

3.3.5. *Concluding Remarks*. The clothing imagery in 2 Corinthians 5 describes how the resurrection change will take place at the parousia. In the first place, the imagery denotes that the earthly body will be covered over by the heavenly body (vv. 1-2). Paul seems to use the word ἐπενδύσασθαι deliberately (v. 2). This covering over has two elements: one is a change from destructibility to indestructibility, the other is the consistency of the bodily mode (although the present body is physical and the resurrection body is spiritual). Secondly, the imagery indicates that at the final consummation, the spiritual nakedness of the present body will be covered over by heavenly qualities, resulting in a glorious body (vv. 3-4ab). The verb ἐπενδύσασ-θαι is found again in verse 4. Adamic shamefulness (cf. Gen. 3.7-10) in the present body will disappear and instead the heavenly glory, which was radiant in the risen Christ, will predominate in the resurrection body. Finally, the imagery connotes that the present physical body, subject to death, will be replaced by the spiritual body that has a capacity for eternal life (v. 4c).

4. *Conclusion to Chapter 10*

Paul's clothing imagery in 1 Cor. 15.49, 50, 51-54 and 2 Cor. 5.1-4 is associated with his strong assurance that believers will experience a great change in their existence at the parousia. The imagery connotes that their earthly physical body will be changed into a heavenly spiritual body, whether through transfiguration or through resurrection, at the parousia. Since the use of the concept of 'house' as a figure for 'body' was common in the Graeco-Roman world, Paul's concept of the replacement of the earthly tent-house with the heavenly building (2 Cor. 5.1-2), in particular, would be understood as referring to a resurrection-change in 'body' as a full expression of one's person. For his resurrection-clothing metaphor, Paul seems to reflect Jewish traditions such as those found in *1 Enoch* 62.15-16 and *2 Enoch* 22.8-10, where clothing imagery is used as a metaphor for a change in the mode of existence.

Paul's clothing metaphor in 1 Corinthians 15 and 2 Corinthians 5 seems to high-light that the parousia change involves two dialectical elements: continuity in person and discontinuity in form. The metaphor suggests that the owner of the future resurrection body will be the very same person who has owned the present physical body. The metaphor specifically underlines that bodiliness, which is the central aspect of the present mode of existence, will also be an important element even in the resurrection body. This thought is eminently reflected in the concept 'putting on over' (ἐπενδύσασθαι) in 2 Cor. 5.2, 4. Paul is possibly being polemical against the Corinthian spirituals, who were perhaps affected by a Greek dualistic anthropology which despised the 'body', so that they believed that they had already attained the supreme state of existence spiritually. On the other hand, Paul's parou-sia-clothing imagery suggests that there will be huge differences in quality between the present body and the resurrection body. For him, the present body is pervaded by physicality (1 Cor. 15.49), destructibility (2 Cor. 5.1), nakedness (i.e. shameful-ness due to the lack of glory with life; 2 Cor. 5.3-4), corruptibility and mortality (1 Cor. 15.50, 53-54ab), but this body will be transformed into one which is characterized by spirituality, indestructibility, clothedness (i.e. the glory that results from restoration to life), incorruptibility and immortality.

It is highly probable that Paul's resurrection-clothing image signifies that the fallen Adamic mode of existence is to be changed into the risen Christ-like mode of existence. Paul probably formulates his 'clothing' theology on the basis of the Adam story in Genesis. The wider context to which 1 Cor. 15.49, 50-54 belongs makes it explicit that the passage is controlled by the Adam–Christ typology. The fact that 2 Cor. 5.1-4 includes several concepts which are found in the story of Adam in Genesis implies that the Adam motif operates in the passage. Paul reflects the story that Adam was created in the image of God, inbreathed with life, and warned that he would die if he disobeyed God's command. Further, he seems to think that there is significance in the antithesis between being naked and being clothed.

As the concept of parousia-clothing in 1 Corinthians 15 and 2 Corinthians 5 connotes restoration to the pre-Fall Adamic state, Paul seems to bear in mind the idea of Adam being clothed before the Fall with garments of glory due to his divine life. Paul probably shares the Jewish idea of Adam's pre-Fall clothing which is postulated by documents such as *Apoc. Mos.* 20–21; *Gen. Rab.* 20.12; *HPrl* 75–78, 86. When Adam fell, he forfeited this glory, resulting in his spiritual death. However, Christ as the second and last Adam has conquered death through his resurrection. Those who belong to Christ will at the parousia receive a heavenly spiritual body like his glorious body. To possess a heavenly body is to recover Adam's original body, which was pervaded by divine life.

CONCLUSION TO PART II

We have so far considered Pauline clothing passages by categorizing them into three, that is, clothing with (1) Christ (Gal. 3.26-29, Rom. 13.14), (2) the new man (Col. 3.9-10, Eph. 4.22-24) and (3) the resurrection body (1 Cor. 15.49, 50-54, 2 Cor. 5.1-4).

In fact, the imagery of clothing with Christ and the new man are virtually identical in their significance, although their emphases vary subtly according to the context to which each passage belongs. This imagery fundamentally describes the baptismal unity with Christ and its effects. The doublet of 'putting off' and 'putting on' (Col. 3.9-10; Eph. 4.22-24) matches the picture of the baptisand's disrobing before baptism and rerobing after baptism, which seems to have been a significant part of the baptismal practice of the primitive church.[1] Probably the imagery of putting-on-Christ in Rom. 13.14 has in mind the baptismal statement in 6.3-4. In particular, Gal. 3.27 identifies the concept of baptism into Christ with the concept of clothing with Christ. This passage specifically underlines the believer's change in status through baptismal union with Christ, resulting in obtaining sonship of God, in other words, heirship of his kingdom. Paul seems here to draw on the Roman custom of clothing with a *toga virilis* at the time of transition from boyhood to manhood.[2] Perhaps he also has in mind the high priest's garment which symbolizes his union with God, or mystery religions clothing ideas, which are reflected in Lucius' twelve-fold garment which stands for his identification with Isis.

Yet the imagery of putting on the new man or Christ in Col. 3.9-10, Eph. 4.22-24 and Rom. 13.14 seems to stress a change in the believer's nature. By being united with Christ, he has already experienced the eradication of the fallen Adamic nature and identification with a new Adamic nature, that is, a Christ-like nature. 'Christ', with whom the believer is united, is not merely a normal human being or a religious genius but a person who distinctly stands over against the fallen Adam; he is the new prototype into whom the believer is being moulded. 'The new man', which the believer should wear, points to the innermost self which is being renewed after the pattern of Christ as the counter-figure to the fallen Adam. What was lost because of Adam's fall is restored in baptism by being united with Christ as the second Adam. Human nature, which was spoiled at Adam's fall, is recovered at baptism by being incorporated into Christ. The metaphor of putting on a person develops a theology of restoration in connection with baptism. As this clothing

1. See Chapter 7.
2. See Chapter 6.

imagery hinges on the Adam–Christ typology,[3] it seems to be a product of dialogue with the Jewish thought of Adam's prelapsarian clothing.[4] In particular, for the author of *The Hymn of the Pearl*, which reflects early Jewish Adam traditions, the protagonist's splendid royal silken robe symbolizes his original self, that is, the image of God. This symbolism seems to be the closest to the Pauline 'clothing with a person' language.

He who has entered this state of wearing Christ as if he were a garment (that is, the state of union with Christ) should manifest an ethical change in his practical life. Rom. 13.14, Col. 3.9-10 and Eph. 4.22-24 focus on the fact that right deeds can only derive from a renovated humanity. Gal. 3.27-28 implicitly expresses that the sublimation of Christian ethics is achieved when all human conflicts are banished in Christian communities that are united into Christ at baptism. The author of the metaphor seems to have in mind the influence a garment exerts on what its wearer does. Of course, the selection of a garment depends on its wearer's decision, but once it is worn, it tends, in turn, to influence its wearer. In *Joseph and Aseneth*, when Aseneth adorned herself with extravagant idolatrous garments, she was boastful, but when she replaced them with a black mourning tunic for remorse, she became humble. In *The Hymn of the Pearl*, when the royal prince (= Adam) clothed himself with an Egyptian-style garment, he became engrossed in worldly Egyptian foods. But when he took off the apparel, he was motivated to return to the Father's kingdom.

In addition, the clothing-with-a-person imagery connotes the believers' incorporation into the church community, which is embraced and represented by Christ, an inclusive personality. As a garment wraps its wearer as a whole, so Christ envelops the church as a whole. This analogy is found not only in the normal way in which human beings dress, but also in the symbolism of priestly garments for all Israel in the OT, in Philo's concept of the high priest's garment as a symbol of the universe, in the new linen garment of Aseneth, 'the City of Refuge', and in Jesus' untorn tunic.

The imagery of clothing with the heavenly man's image (1 Cor. 15.49) or incorruptibility/immortality (1 Cor. 15.50-54) and its sister imagery, clothing with the heavenly building (2 Cor. 5.1-4), connote the parousia change, that is, the transformation of those who are alive or the resurrection of those who are dead at Christ's second coming. Probably Paul's emphasis on the bodiliness of the resurrection mode of existence argues against a Greek dualistic anthropology, an embryonic-Gnostic dichotomy, which had disturbed the church in Corinth. As he also underlines that this change in Christian existence will happen at the parousia, he seems to be controverting the teaching of the arrogant spirituals in the church.

When Paul uses clothing imagery to describe the parousia change, he seems to reflect an idea seen for example in *1 Enoch* 62.15-16 and *2 Enoch* 22.8-10, where resurrection transformation is symbolized by clothing imagery. It is also probable that he applies his insights into the symbolic image of human clothing to his

---

3. E. Peterson, 'Theologie des Kleides', *BM* 16 (1934), pp. 347-56 (especially pp. 347-50, 353).
4. See Chapter 2, §5.

teaching about Christian existence in the future. As the concept of putting one garment over another (cf. ἐπενδύσασθαι in 2 Cor. 5.2, 4) includes elements of both discontinuity and continuity, so the parousia change will manifest the same elements. The present body's physicality, perishability and mortality will be changed into spirituality, imperishability and immortality. But, as a human being may change his clothes, yet himself remain unchanged, so the believer himself remains the same person, although his present body will be changed into the future one. Further, when Paul uses clothing imagery in 1 Corinthians 15 and 2 Corinthians 5, he seems to have in mind the believer's restoration to the original Adamic state which is characterized by life and unashamedness, reflecting the image of God. This is implied by the concept of the believer's future bearing of the image of the man from heaven, Christ (1 Cor. 15.49), as well as by that of the believer's veiling of his or her nakedness (the fallen Adamic state) with a heavenly body and his being dominated by eternal life at the parousia (2 Cor. 3–4). This theory seems to be drawn from Paul's interpretation of the story of Adam in the first three chapters of Genesis, whilst perhaps also bearing in mind the Jewish traditions that Adam was clothed with 'righteousness and glory' (*Apoc. Mos.* 20–21) or 'light' (*Gen. Rab.* 20.12; cf. *Hprl* 75–78, 86).

GENERAL CONCLUSION

We have, in Part I, concentrated on examining the history-of-religions background to Pauline clothing imagery and then, bearing in mind the result of this examination, we have attempted, in Part II, to uncover the meaning of the metaphor in three groups of Pauline clothing passages: (1) Gal. 3.27 and Rom. 13.14; (2) Col. 3.9-10 and Eph. 4.22-24; and (3) 1 Cor. 15.49-54 and 2 Cor. 5.1-5. The clothing metaphor in the first two categories springs from the same well of ideas; both categories refer to putting-on-a-person (putting on Christ in Gal. 3.27 and Rom. 13.14; putting on the new man in Col. 3.10 and Eph. 4.24). Undoubtedly, the clothing metaphor in the third category also derives from the same pool of ideas, since the two relevant passages (1 Cor. 15.49-54; 2 Cor. 5.1-4) both speak of putting on a transformed resurrection body.

However, this does not mean that Gal. 3.27, Rom. 13.14, Col. 3.9-10 and Eph. 4.22-24, with their clothing-with-a-person metaphor, simply express one uniform idea whilst 1 Cor. 15.49-54 and 2 Cor. 5.1-5, with their clothing-with-the-resurrection-body metaphor, simply express another uniform idea. In each case, one passage fundamentally stands on the same basis as the other passages, and yet simultaneously, according to the context to which it belongs, brings forth ideas which are peculiar to it and which suit the context. Accordingly, it is not strange that clothing passages in the same category sometimes reveal an overlapping thought and sometimes manifest a different nuance.

1. In Gal. 3.27, Rom. 13.14, Col. 3.9-10 and Eph. 4.22-24, those elements which are essential and put these passages into the same category, are the idea of baptism and an Adam–Christ typology. In connection with these two major elements, the clothing-with-a-person metaphor seems to basically take as its background the practice of baptism of the ancient church and the significance contained in this practice. If the significance of the early church's baptismal practice is thought of as being in continuity with that of its background rituals (e.g. priestly washing), then the Pauline clothing-with-a-person metaphor must also be linked with clothing ideas from other sources. This metaphor, in fact, involves various nuances and emphases, which seem to be linked with various facets of the history-of-religions background, whether they be oral traditions, written literature, customs or ritual practices.

There is little doubt that the putting on of Christ basically indicates baptismal union with Christ. This is evidenced by the identification of baptism into Christ[1] with putting on Christ in Gal. 3.27 and the correspondence between Gal. 2.19-20

---

1. In Chapter 8, §2.3.2, it was highlighted that this concept bears in mind the actual praxis of baptism in the earliest church.

and 3.20; the link between Rom. 13.11-14 and 6.1-5 through the bridge of 6.12-13; the presence of baptismal language in Col. 3.8-11; and a probable link between Col. 2.11-12 and 3.8-11. The putting-on-a-person metaphor did not seem strange or unfamiliar to those who heard it. It is highly probable that they understood that the putting-on metaphor was related to the contemporary practice in the primitive church of putting clothing off and on at baptism.

Thus, for the earliest Christians, it would not be difficult to link the concept of putting off/on with baptism. Various pieces of evidence[2] suggest that in the first century Jewish proselyte baptism, where the actual putting off/on had a significant meaning (that is, the eradication of the past heathen life and rebirth with a new nature), was already being practised.[3] In particular, the idea of a baptismal change in human nature could be compared with a similar thought in Christian baptism.

There are documents which echo earliest Christian baptismal practice. For example, *Gos. Thom.* 37, *Apos. Trad.* 21, *Gos. Phil.* 101 and *Epis. Fab.* 19 imply that the baptisand's putting off of clothing before baptism indicates the removal of his or her old nature, while putting on a different garment afterward signifies the adoption of a new nature. In particular, in *Gos. Thom.* 37 this renewal is achieved by identification with 'the Son of the Living One'; in *Gos. Phil.* 101, with 'the living man'; and in *Epis. Fab.* 19, with 'Christ'. These instances are similar to the concept of clothing with Christ (Gal. 3.27; Rom. 13.14) or with the new man (Col. 3.10; Eph. 4.24).

Furthermore, *Gos. Thom.* 37 and *Epis. Fab.* 19 imply that the early church imparted the Adam motif to the putting off and putting on of clothing in baptism. The concepts of 'undressing without ashamedness' (*Gos. Thom.* 37) and 'taking off the tunics of skin' (*Epis. Fab.* 19) must have been derived from the story of Adam in Genesis 2–3. Probably the author of *The Gospel of Thomas* and Jerome, the writer of *Epistle to Fabiola*, think that in baptism fallen human nature is restored to Adam's original state. As was argued in Chapter 7, if these documents include a description of the early church's baptismal practice, then the Pauline clothing-with-a-person metaphor may also be thought of as containing a description of baptism. For this metaphor seems to describe the significance of baptism from the perspective of the Adam–Christ typology. Accordingly, I argue that the Pauline clothing-with-a-person metaphor has in mind the early church's actual practice of baptism and its significance, which centred on the spiritual transformation from the fallen Adamic nature to a Christ–like one. Without doubt the Adam–Christ contrast is dominant in the Pauline clothing-with-a-person passages.[4] Therefore, we argue that the essence of this metaphor is believers' baptismal identification with Christ, who is the new Adam.

---

2.   Epictetus Book II, IX. 20-21; *Sib. Ora.* 3.592-93; 4.165-66; *b. Yebam.* 22a, 46a, 47ab, 48b; 97b; *Pesaḥ.* 8.8; '*Ed.* 5.2.

3.   See Chapter 7. In particular, the story of Aseneth's conversion to Judaism in *Joseph and Aseneth* informs us of a picture of Jewish proselyte baptism, which may be a reflection of its earlier practice (see Chapter 3).

4.   See Chapter 8, §§2.3.5, 3.3.4; Chapter 9, §§2.3.4, 3.3.3.

The metaphor, which is thus dominated by the Adam–Christ motif, seems to presuppose that Adam had originally been clothed with divine elements in the image of God, but that he was stripped of these elements at the Fall; that although all human beings have been born to this fallen state, those who are united with Christ in baptism are restored to the original Adamic state. The story of Adam in Genesis implies that Adam originally had divine life and glory, which were associated with the image of God, but it does not include a direct reference to his prelapsarian clothing. It is probable that the idea of Adam's pre-Fall clothing suggested in the Pauline clothing-with-a-person imagery draws on the Jewish Adam tradition, which maintains that Adam possessed divine attributes and this is reflected in later Jewish documents such as *Apocalypse of Moses*, *Genesis Rabbah* and *The Hymn of the Pearl*.

The central idea on baptismal unity with Christ, which is signified by the clothing-with-a-person metaphor, is a participation in Christ's death-and-resurrection.[5] The metaphor implies wearing a symbolic garment associated with death or life. Such a concept may have been current in the first century. It is reflected in various documents, for example *Joseph and Aseneth* (the idolatrous garment and the black mourning tunic/the wedding garment) and *Metamorphoses* (an ass-mask/white linen garments worn after Lucius has been transformed and immediately before his initiation to Isis, as well as twelve-fold garments worn afterwards). A similar concept can also be detected in *The Hymn of the Pearl* (AD ca. 200–225), which includes the contrast between an Egyptian-style garment and the brilliant royal silken garment.

The baptismal nuance in the clothing-with-a-person metaphor is possibly the product of a dialogue with the concept of identification with a divine being through ritual bathing and clothing, which is also found in other documents. Although there are many differences between Christian baptism and Isiac initiation, the idea that an initiate is reborn to a new life and achieves oneness with Isis through ritual bathing, the presence of an initiation ceremony, and the motif of clothing with twelve-fold garments are elements that are similar to those in Christian baptism. The apostle of the Gentiles would not have found it difficult to perceive what was happening in other religions and to draw on this knowledge for his own purpose. Further, a similar case is found in the Pentateuch, where the priest is united with God and becomes a quasi-divine being through the ritual of washing-then-clothing (cf. Exod. 29.4-9; par. 40.12-15; Lev. 16.3-4). If the apostle bears in mind the ritual of the priestly change of clothes, he probably compares Christ (= the believers' garment) to the priestly garment. Christ's righteousness (which is the source of his followers' righteousness) is analogous to the sacredness of the priestly garment. This analogy seems to be borne in mind, since the apostle stresses right ethical conduct with his metaphor of putting-on-Christ (or the new man).[6] He seems to postulate that human conduct can be influenced by clothing, although the decision to put it on is made in the first place by the wearer. For example, when Aseneth in *Joseph and Aseneth*

---

5. See Chapter 8, §§2.3.3, 3.3.3; Chapter 9, §§2.3.3, 3.3.2.
6. See Chapter 8, §3.4.3; Chapter 9, §§2.4.3, 3.4.2.

was dressed in an extravagant pagan garment, her behaviour was boastful; and when the prince in *The Hymn of the Pearl* was clothed in an Egyptian-style garment, he indulged himself in Egyptian food.

In particular, the imagery of clothing with Christ in Gal. 3.27 connotes a baptismal unity with Christ's Spirit.[7] The imagery seems to be influenced by the concept of God's Spirit's clothing himself with a specific human being in the Old Testament.[8] In Judg. 6.34, 1 Chron. 12.18 and 2 Chron. 24.20 God's being clothed with a person is the reverse of the concept of a person's being clothed with Christ. But when, in practice, a person's being clothed with Christ means that Christ dwells in that person, then the concept seems to be very close to the passages in the OT. In fact, God's Spirit's clothing himself with a man shows the same effect as a man's clothing himself with the Spirit. Further, they are identical in that they both refer to a unity between God and man. If the clothing-with-a-person metaphor thus contains the notion of a believer's oneness with a divine being, namely Christ as the real image of God (cf. Col. 3.10; Eph. 4.24; 2 Cor. 4.4), probably it also reflects the ancient notion of man's unity with God, which is found in the priest's identification with God's sacredness in the OT (cf. Philo, *Vita Mos.* ii.131) as he wears the priestly holy garment. A similar theme is perhaps found when Lucius is identified with Isis after his initiation.

Further, when the image of clothing-with-Christ indicates a critical change in a believer's status, that is, the acquisition of sonship of God by being united with God's son Christ (particularly Gal. 3.27), the metaphor seems to draw on the Roman male's custom of exchanging the *toga praetexta* for the *toga virilis* at the transition from boyhood to manhood.

Above all, the clothing-with-a-person metaphor denotes that believers who have undergone baptismal union with Christ are incorporated into his body, the church. This idea seems to teach the spiritual significance of the priestly garment, which symbolizes the whole of Israel and which encloses its wearer, who represents all the Israelites. The image of inclusive clothing can also be found in the Johannine concept of Jesus' untorn tunic. A similar image also occurs in *Joseph and Aseneth* where Aseneth's new linen garment symbolizes the totality of Aseneth's would-be imitators, as she becomes 'the City of Refuge' to them.

The combination of the concept of clothing with that of change occurs in Ps. 102.26 (cf. Isa. 51.6). This passage concentrates on the theme of an eschatological transformation of the cosmos. The idea of change in the clothing-with-a-person metaphor may echo this psalm, or at least the sort of idea that is reflected in it. Indeed the notion of eschatology in this passage probably dominates the passages in the Pauline epistles, giving an eschatological significance to the metaphor of clothing-with-a-person. This eschatological clothing imagery is prominent particularly in Gal. 3.27 and Rom. 13.14. Yet as far as Col. 3.9-10 and Eph. 4.22-24 are dominated by the analogy between Adam and Christ, these passages can also be seen from the same viewpoint.

---

7.   See Chapter 8, §2.3.4.1.
8.   See Chapter 1, §4.

2. In 1 Cor. 15.49-54 and 2 Cor. 5.1-4, the clothing metaphor describes the eschatological change which will happen in a believer's existence, a change either through the transformation of those who are still alive or through the resurrection of those who have died, at Christ's second coming. Again, in these Corinthian passages the parousia change which believers will experience is seen from the perspective of the analogy between Adam and Christ. In 1 Cor. 15.49-54, the concept of εἰκών and the 'earthly man' (in contrast to the 'heavenly man'), the antithesis between life and death, and the concept of being clothed, all find their equivalents in the first three chapters of Genesis (cf. 1.26-27; 2.7, 9, 17; 3.19, 21, 22). The Adam motif also significantly operates in 2 Cor. 5.1-4; the contrast between nakedness and being clothed and between death and life seem to be reminiscent of the story of Adam in Genesis.

As the typology between Adam and Christ predominates in 1 Corinthians 15 and 2 Corinthians 5, the metaphor of clothing with the resurrection body indicates that the believer's body is changed into one which is glorious and Christ-like at the parousia. In other words, it will be transfigured to the original Adamic state. The essence of this change is to be restored to the image of God (cf. 1 Cor. 15.49).[9] If so, it is highly probable that the metaphor of clothing with a resurrection body shares the thought of the early Jewish Adam traditions, such as those found in *The Hymn of the Pearl*. In this document, the prince's being re-clothed with his royal garment connotes that he is re-united with his own self, namely the image of God which was once lost (vv. 75-78, 86).

Further, the identification of clothing with the resurrection body with restoration to the pre-Fall state of Adam denotes that our Corinthian passages presuppose Adam's pre-Fall clothing. As has been suggested above, this results from Paul's understanding of the story of Adam in Genesis. Yet as Genesis does not directly include the concept of pre-Fall clothing, Paul probably draws on the idea of Adam's pre-Fall clothing from other clothing traditions, which are reflected, for example, in *Apoc. Mos.* 20–21 and rabbinic literature (particularly *Gen. Rab.* 20.12). *Apoc. Mos.* 20–21 suggests that before the Fall Adam and Eve were clothed with 'righteousness and glory', which appear to be inseparable correlatives. *Gen. Rab.* 20.12 sees Gen. 3.21 as stating that God had clothed Adam and Eve with 'light' before the Fall.

Above all, we note that our Corinthian passages describe the future parousia change by the metaphor of clothing. The present corruptible/mortal body will be clothed with a future incorruptible/immortal body (1 Cor. 15.53-54). The earthly physical body will be clothed with the heavenly spiritual body (2 Cor. 5.1-2). At the parousia, the present body in its state of fallen 'nakedness' will be covered over by a heavenly glory (cf. 2 Cor. 5.3) so that it will be pervaded by eternal, divine life (cf. 1 Cor. 15.54; 2 Cor. 5.2-4). When the parousia transfiguration is thus described by means of clothing imagery, it is highly probable that Paul shares the

---

9.   Note that Paul regularly combines the concept of 'glory' with that of 'image' (Rom. 1.23; 8.29-30; 1 Cor. 11.7; 2 Cor. 3.18; 4.4), which suggests that these words are substantially synonymous. Cf. Jervell, *Imago Dei*, pp. 108-109; G. Bray, 'The Significance of God's Image in Man', *TB* 42.2 (1991), pp. 195-225 (205).

idea of changing garments that is found in the Jewish clothing traditions in *1 Enoch* 62.15-16 and *2 Enoch* 22.8-10. In these documents, the resurrection change, viz. a change from the earthly mode of existence to a heavenly one, is depicted by the metaphor of taking off the earthly garment and putting on the heavenly. The transformed body will be typified by 'glory', which is the quintessential attribute of God (*1 Enoch* 14.20).

As the reference of the clothing-with-the-resurrection body in 1 Corinthians 15 and 2 Corinthians 5 is to the most crucial event of the *eschaton*, it may reflect the clothing imagery in Ps. 102.26. In this psalm, the eschatological transformation of the cosmos is described by the image of changing garments.

2 Cor. 5.2, moreover, depicts the parousia change by means of the metaphor of being clothed with a heavenly building. As this image of building symbolizes the body, the passage implicitly stresses that the future mode of existence will continue to be a bodily one. If this is so, Paul is perhaps being polemical against the Corinthian *pneumatikoi*, who were influenced by the Greek idea of the body as the soul's prison, and who seem to have indulged in an extremely realized eschatology. Further, the concept of ἐπενδύω (2 Cor. 5.2, 4) also seems to support the physical and material aspect of the glorious resurrection body. The concept of a believer's being covered over by a heavenly body signifies the corporeality of this resurrection existence. This body will, of course, be the result of a critical change in the earthly body (2 Cor. 5.1; cf. 1 Cor. 15.53-54). The concept 'putting on over' possibly draws on the ritual of the priest's undergarments being covered over by outer garments. This concept can also be found in Lucius' being clothed with twelve-fold garments.

Finally, it needs to be remembered that the Corinthian clothing imagery describes not only continuity of person (the one dressed in the present body will also be dressed in the future body), but also discontinuity of form (the body's character will be changed from corruptible/mortal to incorruptible/immortal).

Apart from the Pauline clothing metaphor's being associated with the history-of-religions background, it probably also reflects various inherent qualities of clothes. Clothing not only dominates its wearer's appearance but also reveals its wearer's character. Clothing covers and is closely in contact with its wearer; the two virtually become identified with each other. Yet, despite this closeness between them, clothing, even when being worn, continues to be an independent item; it is paradoxically separated from its wearer. Further, clothing can be exchanged for other clothing. Clothing once worn also tends to influence its wearer's behaviour. Above all, clothing functions not only to cover nakedness but also to manifesting its wearer's status. Most of these implications seem to be at work in the clothing-with-a-person metaphor. In the clothing-with-the-resurrection-body metaphor, the implications of covering and changing seem to be particularly prominent.

In sum, the Pauline clothing imagery describes not only the baptismal change of being united with Christ in his death and resurrection (Gal. 3.27; Rom. 13.14; Col. 3.9-10; Eph. 4.22-24) but also the parousia change in the mode of Christian existence, namely the transformation of the present earthly body to the future heavenly body, which will happen at the *eschaton* (1 Cor. 15.49, 50-54; 2 Cor. 5.1-4). It is at *baptism* that believers experience the new creation of their nature, in which new life is inaugurated and so begins to operate; it is at the general *resurrection* at the parousia that they will fully achieve a glorious body, in which the heavenly life is predominant.

BIBLIOGRAPHY

Abbott, T.K., *A Critical and Exegetical Commentary on the Epistles to the Ephesians and to the Colossians* (ICC; Edinburgh: T. & T. Clark, 1897).

Abrahams, I., 'How Did the Jews Baptize?', *JTS* 12 (1911), pp. 609-612.

Adam, A., *Die Psalmen des thomas und das Perlenlied als Zeugnisse vorchristlicher Gnosis* (BZNW, 24; Berlin: W. de Gruyter, 1959).

Allen, C.J. (ed.), *2 Corinthians-Philemon* (BBC, 11; Nashville: Broadman, 1971).

Althaus, P., *Der Brief an die Römer* (Göttingen: NTD, 1966).

Andersen, F.I., '2 (Slavonic Apocalypse of) Enoch', in J.H. Charlesworth (ed.), *OTP*, I (London: Darton, Longman & Todd, 1983), pp. 91-213.

Anderson, G.A., 'Garments of Skin, Garments of Glory' (unpublished paper, n.d.), pp. 1-42.

—'The Exaltation of Adam and the Fall of Satan', *JJTP* 6 (1997), pp. 105-134.

Argall, R.A., 'The Source of a Religious Error in Colossae', *CTJ* 22.1 (1987), pp. 6-20.

Arnold, C.E., *Ephesians: Power and Magic* (SNTSMS, 63; Cambridge: Cambridge University Press, 1989).

Asselin, D.T., 'The Notion of Dominion in Genesis 1-3', *CBQ* 16 (1954), pp. 277-94.

Aune, D.E., 'Religions, Greco-Roman', in *DPL* (Leicester: IVP, 1993), pp. 786-96.

Badke, W.B., 'Baptism into Moses—Baptized into Christ: A Study in Doctrinal Development', *EQ* 88.1 (1988), pp. 23-29.

Balsdon, J.P., and B.M. Levick, 'Claudius', in S. Hornblower and A. Spawforth (eds.), *The Oxford Classical Dictionary* (Oxford: Oxford University Press, 1996), pp. 337-38.

Barclay, J.M.G., 'Mirror-Reading a Polemical Letter: Galatians as a Test Case', *JSNT* 31 (1987), pp. 73-93.

—*Obeying the Truth: A Study of Paul's Ethics in Galatians* (Edinburgh: T. & T. Clark, 1988).

—*Jews in the Mediterranean Diaspora: From Alexander to Trajan (323 BCE-117 CE)* (Edinburgh: T. & T. Clark, 1996).

Barnes, A., *Notes on the New Testament. V: 1 Corinthians* (London: Blackie, n.d.).

Barr, J., *The Garden of Eden and the Hope of Immortality* (Minneapolis: Fortress, 1993).

Barrett, C.K., *The First Epistle to the Corinthians* (BNTC; Peabody: Hendrickson, 1968).

—'Paul's Opponents in II Corinthians', *NTS* 17 (1971), pp. 233-54.

—*The Second Epistle to the Corinthians* (BNTC; Peabody: Hendrickson, 1973).

—'Immortality and Resurrection', in C.S. Duthie (ed.), *Resurrection and Immortality: A Selection from the Drew Lectures on Immortality* (London: Samuel Bagster, 1979), pp. 68-88.

—*The New Testament Background: Selected Documents* (London: SPCK, 1987 [1956]).

—*A Commentary on the Epistle to the Romans* (BNTC; Peabody: Hendrickson, 1991 [1957]).

Barrosse, T., 'Death and Sin in Saint Paul's Epistle to the Romans', *CBQ* 15 (1953), pp. 438-59.

Barth, K., *Christ and Adam: Man and Humanity in Romans 5* (trans. T.A. Smail; Edinburgh: Oliver & Boyd, 1963 [1956]).

Barth, M., *Ephesians* (AB, 34A; New York: Doubleday, 1974).

Bartsch, H.W., 'Die historische Situation des Römerbriefes' (*SE*, 4, TUGAL 102; Berlin: Akademie-Verlag, 1968), pp. 281-91.

Beasley-Murray, G.R., *Baptism in the New Testament* (Grand Rapids: Eerdmans, 1990 [1962]).

Beet, J.A., *A Commentary on St. Paul's Epistle to the Romans* (London: Hodder & Stoughton, 1887).

Beker, J.C., 'Colossians', in *HBC* (San Francisco: Harper & Row, 1988), pp. 1226-229.

Belleville, L.L., ' "Under Law": Structural Analysis and the Pauline Concept of Law in Galatians 3.21-4.11', *JSNT* 26 (1986), pp. 53-78.

Bengel, J.A., *Gnomon of the New Testament*, IV (Edinburgh: T. & T. Clark, 1858).

Berchman, R.M., 'Philo of Alexandria', in E. Ferguson *et al.* (eds.), *EEC* (New York: Garland, 1990), pp. 726-27.

Berry, R., 'Death and Life in Christ: The Meaning of 2 Cor 5.1-10', *SJT* 14 (1961), pp. 60-76.

Best, E., *One Body in Christ: A Study in the Relationship of the Church to Christ in the Epistles of the Apostle Paul* (London: SPCK, 1955).

—'Who Used Whom? The Relationship of Ephesians and Colossians', *NTS* 43 (1977), pp. 72-96.

—'Ephesians: Two Types of Existence', *Int* 47 (1993), pp. 39-51.

Betz, H.D., *Galatians* (Philadelphia: Fortress, 1979).

Bevan, A.A., 'The Hymn of the Soul', *TS* 5.3 (Cambridge: Cambridge University Press, 1897), pp. 1-40.

Black, M., 'The Pauline Doctrine of the Second Adam', *SJT* 7 (1954), pp. 170-79.

—*The Book of Enoch or 1 Enoch* (Leiden: Brill, 1985).

Bligh, J., *Galatians: A Discussion of St. Paul's Epistle* (HC, 1; London: St. Paul Publications, 1969).

Boadt, L., 'Ezekiel', in *NJBC* (London: Geoffrey Chapman, 1993), pp. 305-328.

Boucher, M., 'Some Unexplored Parallels to 1 Cor 11, 11-12 and Gal 3, 28: The NT on the Role of Women', *CBQ* 31 (1969), pp. 50-58.

Bowman, J.W., 'The Epistle to the Ephesians', *Int* 8 (1954), pp. 188-204.

Braude, W.G., *Jewish Proselyting: In the First Five Centuries of the Common Era the Age of the Tannaim and Amoraim* (Providence: Brown University, 1940).

Bray, G., 'The Significance of God's Image in Man', *TB* 42.2 (1991), pp. 195-225.

Brenner, A., *Colour Terms in the Old Testament* (JSOTSup, 21; Sheffield: JSOT Press, 1982).

Briscoe, D.S., *Genesis* (ComC; Waco: Word Books, 1987 [1979]).

Brock, S., 'Jewish Traditions in Syriac Sources', *JJS* 30.2 (1979), pp. 212-32.

—'Clothing Metaphors as a Means of Theological Expression in Syriac Tradition', in M. Schmidt (ed.), *Typus, Symbol, Allegorie bei den östlichen Vätern und ihren Parallelen im Mittelalter* (EB, 4: Abteilung Philosophie und Theologie; Regensburg: Verlag Friedrich Pustet, 1981), pp. 11-38.

Bromiley, G.W., 'Aspects of Luther's Doctrine of Baptism', *EQ* 17 (1945), pp. 281-95.

Brooks, O.S., 'A Contextual Interpretation of Galatians 3.27', *SB*, 3 [1978], JSNTSup, 3 [1980]), pp. 47-56.

Brown, R.E., *The Death of the Messiah: From Gethsemane to the Grave—A Commentary on the Passion Narratives in the Four Gospels*, II (ABRL; New York: Doubleday, 1994).

Bruce, F.F., *The Epistle of Paul to the Romans: An Introduction and Commentary* (TNTC; Leicester: IVP, 1983 [1863]).

—'Paul on Immortality', *SJT* 24 (1971), pp. 457-72.

—*Commentary on the Book of the Acts* (NICNT; Grand Rapids: Eerdmans, 1977).

—*Paul: Apostle of the Free Spirit* (Carlisle: Paternoster, 1980 [1977]).

—*The Epistles to the Colossians, to Philemon, and to the Ephesians* (NICNT; Grand Rapids: Eerdmans, 1984).

—*The Epistle to the Galatians: A Commentary on the Greek Text* (NIGTC; Grand Rapids: Paternoster/Eerdmans, 1992 [1982]).

Bruce, F.F. (ed.), *1 and 2 Corinthians* (NCBC; London: Oliphants, 1971).

Brueggemann, W., 'From Dust to Kingship', *ZAW* 84 (1972), pp. 1-18.

Brun, L., 'Zur Auslegung von II Kor 5.1-10', *ZNW* 28 (1929), pp. 207-209.

Brunner, E., *The Letter to the Romans: A Commentary* (London: Lutterworth, 1959).

Buck, C.H., 'The Date of Galatians', *JBL* 70 (1951), pp. 113-22.

Bullough, S., 'Zechariah', in R.C. Fuller *et al.* (eds.), *NCCHS* (London: Nelson, 1969 [1953]), pp. 724-37.

Bultmann, R., *Exegetische Probleme des zweiten Korintherbriefes* (SBU, 9; Upssala, 1947; Darmstadt: Wissenschaftliche Buchgesellschaft, 1963).

—*Theology of the New Testament*, I (trans. K. Grobel; London: SCM Press, 1983 [1952]).

Burch, V., 'Notes and Studies: A Commentary on the *Syriac Hymn of the Soul*', *JTS* 19 (1918), pp. 145-61.

Burchard, C., *Untersuchungen zu Joseph und Aseneth* (WUNT, 8; Tübingen: Mohr, 1965).

—'Ein Vorlaufinger griechischer Text von Joseph und Aseneth', *DBAT* 14 (1979), pp. 1-53.

—'Joseph and Aseneth', in J.H. Charlesworth (ed.), *OTP*, II (New York: Doubleday, 1985), pp. 177-247.

—'The Importance of Joseph and Aseneth for the Study of the New Testament: A General Survey and a Fresh Look at the Lord's Supper', *NTS* 33 (1987), pp. 102-134.

Burkert, W., *Ancient Mystery Cults* (Cambridge: Harvard University Press, 1987).

Burkitt, F.C., *Early Eastern Christianity* (London: Murray, 1904).

—'Notes and Studies: *Toga* in the East', *JTS* 23 (1922), pp. 281-82.

Burton, E.D., *A Critical and Exegetical Commentary on the Epistle to the Galatians* (ICC; Edinburgh: T. & T. Clark, 1921).

Calvin, John, *The First Epistle of Paul the Apostle to the Corinthians* (CC; Edinburgh: Oliver and Boyd, 1960 [Lat. 1546]).

Cannon, G., *The Use of Traditional Materials in Colossians* (Macon: Mercer University Press, 1983).

Caragounis, C.C., 'Romans 5. 15-16 in the Context of 5. 12-21: Contrast or Comparison?', *NTS* 31 (1985), pp. 142-48.

Carley, K.W., *Ezekiel* (Cambridge: Cambridge University Press, 1974).

Carlson, R.P., 'The Role of Baptism in Paul's Thought', *Int* 47 (1993), pp. 255-66.

Carrington, P., *The Primitive Christian Catechism* (Cambridge: Cambridge University Press, 1940).

Carson, D.A., D.J. Moo, and L. Morris, *An Introduction to the New Testament* (Grand Rapids: Zondervan, 1992).

Charles, R.H., *The Book of Enoch* (Oxford: Clarendon, 1893).

—*The Book of Enoch or 1 Enoch* (Oxford: Clarendon, 1912).

—'Enoch, Book of the Secrets of', in J. Hastings (ed.), *DB*, I (Peabody: Hendrickson, 1988 [orig. Edinburgh: T. & T. Clark, 1898]), pp. 708-11.

Charlesworth, J.H., 'Seminar Report: The SNTS Pseudepigrapha Seminars at Tübingen and Paris on the Books of Enoch', *NTS* 25 (1979), pp. 315-23.

—*The Pseudepigrapha and Modern Research with a Supplement* (SBLSCSS, 7S; Michigan: Scholars Press, 1981).

Chesnutt, R.D., 'The Social Setting and Purpose of Joseph and Aseneth', *JSP* 2 (1988), pp. 21-48.

—*From Death to Life: Conversion in Joseph and Aseneth* (JSPSup, 16; Sheffield: Sheffield Academic Press, 1995).

Chilton, B.D., 'Galatians 6.15: A Call to Freedom before God', *ExpT* 89 (1977–78), pp. 311-13.

Clark, R.T.R., *Myth and Symbol in Ancient Egypt* (London: Thames & Hudson, 1959).

Clements, R.E., 'Leviticus', in Clifton J. Allen (ed.), *Leviticus-Ruth* (BBC, 2; London: Marshall, Morgan & Scott, 1971), pp. 1-74.

Clines, D.J.A., 'The Image of God in Man', *TB* 19 (1968), pp. 53-103.

Cole, R.A., *The Epistle of Paul to the Galatians: An Introduction and Commentary* (Grand Rapids: Eerdmans, 1975 [1965]).

Collins, J.J., 'Sibylline Oracles', in J.H. Charlesworth (ed.), *OTP*, I (London: Darton, Longman & Todd, 1983), pp. 317-472.

—*Between Athens and Jerusalem: Jewish Identity in the Hellenistic Diaspora* (New York: Crossroad, 1983).

Colson, F.H. and G.H. Whitaker (trans.), *Philo* (LCL; 10 vols. of major works and 2 vols. of supplement; London: William Heinemann, 1962).

Conybeare, F.C., 'On the Apocalypse of Moses', *JQR* 7 (1895), pp. 216-35.

Conzelmann, H., *1 Corinthians* (Philadelphia: Fortress, 1969).

Conzelmann, H., and A. Lindemann, *Interpreting the New Testament* (trans. S.S. Schatzmann; Peabody: Hendrickson, 1988).

Cousar, C.B., *Galatians, Interpretation: A Bible Commentary for Teaching and Preaching* (Louisville: John Knox Press, 1982).

Craig, W.L., 'Paul's Dilemma in 2 Corinthians 5.1-10: A "Catch-22" ', *NTS* 34 (1988), pp. 145-47.

Cranfield, C.E.B., *A Critical and Exegetical Commentary on the Epistle to the Romans* (ICC; 2 vols.; Edinburgh: T. & T. Clark, 1975–1979).

—*Romans: A Shorter Commentary* (Grand Rapids: Eerdmans, 1992 [1985]).

Cross, F.L. (ed.), 'Philo', in *ODCC* (London: Oxford University Press, 1963 [1957]), pp. 1065-66.

Cullmann, O., *The Christology of the New Testament* (London: SCM Press, 1959).

—'The Gospel of Thomas and the Problem of the Age of the Tradition Contained Therein: A Survey', *Int* 16 (1962), pp. 418-38.

—*Salvation in History* (London: SCM Press, 1967).

—*Immortality of the Soul or Resurrection of the Dead?* (London: Epworth, 1968).

Curtis, E.L., *A Critical and Exegetical Commentary on the Books of Chronicles* (ICC; Edinburgh: T. & T. Clark, 1952 [1910]).

Dahl, M.E., *The Resurrection of the Body* (London: SCM Press, 1962).

Dahl, N.A., *Studies in Paul: Theology for the Early Christian Mission* (Minneapolis: Augsburg, 1977).

—'Ephesians', in *HBC* (San Francisco: Harper & Row, 1988), pp. 1212-219.

Danby, H., *The Mishnah* (Oxford: Oxford University Press, 1933).

Daube, D., 'Appended Note: Participle and Imperative in 1 Peter', in E.G. Selwyn, *The First Epistle of St. Peter* (London: Macmillan, 1952 [1946]), pp. 467-88.

—*The New Testament and Rabbinic Judaism* (Peabody: Hendrickson, 1956).

Davies, W.D., *Invitation to the New Testament: A Guide to Its Main Witnesses* (London: Darton, Longman & Todd, 1967).

—*Paul and Rabbinic Judaism: Some Rabbinic Elements in Pauline Theology* (London: SPCK, 1979 [1948]).

de Boer, M.C., *The Defeat of Death: Apocalyptic Eschatology in 1 Corinthians 15 and Romans 5* (JSNTSup, 22; Sheffield: JSOT Press, 1988).

Delling, G., 'Einwirkungen der Sprache der Septuaginta in "Joseph and Aseneth" ', *JSJ* 9 (1978), pp. 29-56.

Dibelius, M., 'The Isis Initiation in Apuleius and Related Initiatory Rites', in F.D. Francis and W.A. Meeks (eds.), *Conflict at Colossae: A Problem in the Interpretation of Early*

Christianity Illustrated by Selected Modern Studies (SBS, 4; Missoula: SBL & Scholars, 1975), pp. 61-121.

Dodd, C.H., 'Colossians', in F.C. Eiselen *et al.* (eds.), *ABC* (New York: Abingdon, 1929), pp. 1250-262.

—'Ephesians', in F.C. Eiselen *et al.* (eds.), *ABC* (New York: Abingdon, 1929), pp. 1222-237.

—*The Epistle of Paul to the Romans* (MoffNTC; London: Hodder & Stoughton, 1947 [1932]).

Douglas, R.C., 'Liminality and Conversion in Joseph and Aseneth', *JSP* 3 (1988), pp. 31-42.

Dow, J., 'Galatians', in F.C. Eiselen *et al.* (eds.), *ABC* (New York: Abingdon, 1929), pp. 1207-221.

Drijvers, J.W., 'The Acts of Thomas', in W. Schneemelcher (ed.), *New Testament Apocrypha*, II (Cambridge: Clarke, 1992 [Tübingen: Mohr, 1989]), pp. 322-411.

Dummelow, J.R. (ed.), 'Judges', in *CHB* (London: Macmillan, 1920 [1909]), pp. 155-72.

Duncan, G., *The Epistle of Paul to the Galatians* (London: Hodder & Stoughton, 1939 [1934]).

Dunn, J.D.G., *Baptism in the Holy Spirit* (London: SCM Press, 1970).

—'I Corinthians 15.45: Last Adam, Life-Giving Spirit', in B. Lindars and S. Smalley (eds.), *Christ and Spirit in the New Testament* (Festschrift C.F.D. Moule; Cambridge: Cambridge University Press, 1973), pp. 127-41.

— *Jesus and the Spirit* (London: SCM Press, 1975).

—*Unity and Diversity in the New Testament: An Inquiry into the Character of Earliest Christianity* (London: SCM Press, 1977).

—'Salvation Proclaimed VI. Romans 6.1-11: Dead and Alive', *ExpT* 93 (1982), pp. 259-64.

—*Romans 9–16* (WBC, 38A; Dallas: Word Books, 1988).

—*Christology in the Making* (London: SCM Press, 1989 [1980]).

—'Paul's Understanding of the Death of Christ as Sacrifice', in S.W. Sykes (ed.), *Sacrifice and Redemption: Durham Essays in Theology* (Cambridge: Cambridge University Press, 1991), pp. 35-52.

—'Echoes of Intra-Jewish Polemic in Paul's Letter to the Galatians', *JBL* 112.3 (1993), pp. 459-77.

—*The Epistle to the Galatians* (BNTC; Peabody: Hendrickson, 1993).

—*The New Testament Theology: The Theology of Paul's Letter to the Galatians* (Cambridge: Cambridge University Press, 1993).

—*1 Corinthians* (NTG; Sheffield: Sheffield Academic Press, 1995).

—*The Epistles to the Colossians and to Philemon* (NIGTC; Grand Rapids: Eerdmans, 1996).

Eadie, J., *A Commentary on the Greek Text of the Epistle of Paul to the Ephesians* (London and Glasgow: Griffin, 1854).

—*A Commentary on the Greek Text of the Epistle of Paul to the Colossians* (Grand Rapids: Baker, 1979 [orig. 1884]).

Easton, B.S., 'Critical Notes: Self-Baptism', *AJT* 24 (1920), pp. 513-18.

Easton, B.S. (trans.), *The Apostolic Tradition of Hippolytus* (Cambridge: Cambridge University Press, 1934).

Ebeling, G., *The Truth of the Gospel: An Exposition of Galatians* (Philadelphia: Fortress, 1985 [1912]).

Edersheim, A., *The Life and Times of Jesus the Messiah*, II (London: Longmans, 1883).

Edwards, D.R., 'Dress and Ornamentation', in D.N. Freedman *et al.* (eds.), *ABD*, II (New York: Doubleday, 1992), pp. 232-38.

Eissfeldt, O., *The Old Testament: An Introduction* (Oxford: Basil Blackwell, 1965).

Elliott, J.K. (ed.), *The Apocryphal New Testament: A Collection of Apocryphal Christian Literature in an English Translation Based on M.R. James* (Oxford: Clarendon, 1993).

Ellis, E.E., 'II Corinthians V. 1-10 in Pauline Eschatology', *NTS* 6 (1959–60), pp. 211-24.

Epstein, I., *The Babylonian Talmud* (18 vols.; London: Soncino Press, 1948).

Evans, J.M., *Paradise Lost and the Genesis Tradition* (Oxford: Clarendon, 1968).

Evans, P.W., *Sacraments in the New Testament* (London: Tyndale, 1946).

Fee, G.D., *The First Epistle to the Corinthians* (NICNT; Grand Rapids: Eerdmans, 1987).

Feltoe, C.L., 'Notes and Studies: *Toga* and *Togatus* in the Books of the Mozarabic Rite', *JTS* 23 (1922), pp. 57-59.

Ferguson, E., *Backgrounds of Early Christianity* (Grand Rapids: Eerdmans, 1993).

Ferguson, J., *The Religions of the Roman Empire* (London: Thames & Hudson, 1970).

Filson, F.V., and J. Reid, 'Second Corinthians', in *IB*, X (Nashville: Abingdon, 1953), pp. 265-425.

Findlay, G.G., 'St. Paul's First Epistle to the Corinthians', in *EGT*, II (London: Hodder & Stoughton, 1900), pp. 729-953.

Finegan, J., *Myth & Mystery* (Grand Rapids: Baker, 1989).

Fiorenza, E.S., '1 Corinthians', in *HBC* (San Francisco: Harper, 1988), pp. 1168-189.

Fitzmyer, J.A., 'The Letter to the Galatians', in *NJBC* (London: Geoffrey Chapman, 1990 [1968]), pp. 780-90.

Foulkes, F., *The Letter of Paul to the Ephesians: An Introduction and Commentary* (TNTC; Leicester: IVP, 1989 [1963]).

Freedman, H., and M. Simon (ed.), *Midrash Rabbah: Genesis*, I (trans. H. Freedman; London: Soncino Press, 1939).

Fuller, R.H., *The Foundations of New Testament Christology* (London: Lutterworth, 1965).

Fung, R.Y.K., *The Epistle to the Galatians* (ed. G.D. Fee; NICNT; Grand Rapids: Eerdmans, 1953).

Furnish, V.P., *II Corinthians* (New York: Doubleday, 1984).

Gillman, J., 'A Thematic Comparison: 1 Cor 15.50-57 and 2 Cor 5.1-5', *JBL* 107.3 (1988), pp. 439-54.

Ginzberg, L., *The Legends of the Jews*, V (Philadelpha: The Jewish Publication Society of America, 1954).

Glasson, T.F., '2 Corinthians V. 1-10 versus Platonism', *SJT* 43 (1990), pp. 145-55.

Gnilka, J., *Der Kolosserbrief* (HTKNT, 10.1; Freiburg: Herder, 1980).

Godet, F., *Commentary on St. Paul's Epistle to the Romans*, II (trans. A. Cusin; Edinburgh: T & T. Clark, 1884).

Goodenough, E.R., *An Introduction to Philo Judaeus* (Oxford: Blackwell, 1962).

—*Jewish Symbols in the Greco-Roman Period*, IX (Bollingen Series, 37; New York: Pantheon Books, 1964).

—*By Light, Light: The Mystic Gospel of Hellenistic Judaism* (Amsterdam: Philo Press, 1969).

Goppelt, L., *Typos: The Typological Interpretation of the Old Testament in the New* (trans. D.H. Madvig; Grand Rapids: Eerdmans, 1982).

Gordon, T.D., 'The Problem at Galatia', *Int* 41 (1987), pp. 32-43.

Gottstein, A.G., 'The Body as Image of God in Rabbinic Literature', *HTR* 87.2 (1994), pp. 171-95.

Goudge, H.L., *The Second Epistle to the Corinthians* (WC; London: Methuen, 1927).

Goulder, M., 'The Unity of the Corinthian Correspondence' (a seminar paper read at British New Testament Conference, Aberdeen, 1996), pp. 1-21.

Granger-Taylor, H., 'Toga', in S. Hornblower and A. Spawforth (eds.), *The Oxford Classical Dictionary* (Oxford: Oxford University Press, 1996), p. 1533.

Grant, R.M., *Gods and the One God* (LEC, 1; Philadelphia: The Westminster Press, 1986).

Grayston, K., *The Epistles to the Galatians and to the Philippians* (London: Epworth, 1957).

—*Dying, We Live: A New Enquiry into the Death of Christ in the New Testament* (New York and Oxford: Oxford University Press, 1990).

Griffiths, J.G. (ed.), *Apuleius of Madauros the Isis-Book.Metamorphoses, Book* XI (Leiden: Brill, 1975).
Gundry, R.H., '*Soma*' *in Biblical Theology* (SNTSMS, 29; Cambridge: Cambridge University Press, 1976).
—*A Survey of the New Testament* (Grand Rapids: Zondervan, 1994).
Guthrie, D. (ed.), *Galatians* (CBNS; London: Nelson, 1969).
Guyot, C.H., 'The Chronology of St. Paul', *CBQ* 6 (1944), pp. 28-36.
Hanhart, K., 'Paul's Hope in the Face of Death', *JBL* 88 (1969), pp. 445-57.
Hansen, G.W., *Abraham in Galatians: Epistolary and Rhetorical Contexts* (JSNTSup, 29; Sheffield: Sheffield Academic Press, 1989).
Harris, M.J., '2 Corinthians 5.1-10: Watershed in Paul's Eschatology?', *TB* 22 (1971), pp. 32-57.
—*Raised Immortal: Resurrection and Immortality in the New Testament* (London: Morgan & Scott, 1986).
—*Colossians & Philemon: Exegetical Guide to the Greek New Testament* (Grand Rapids: Eerdmans, 1991).
Hatch, E., and H.A. Redpath, *A Concordance to the Septuagint*, I (Grand Rapids: Baker, 1987 [orig. Oxford: Clarendon, 1897]).
Hawkins, R.M., 'The Galatian Gospel', *JBL* 59 (1940), pp. 141-46.
Hays, R.B., *The Faith of Jesus Christ: An Investigation of the Narrative Substructure of Galatians 3.1-4.11* (SBLDS, 56; Chico: Scholars, 1983).
—'Christology and Ethics in Galatians: The Law of Christ', *CBQ* 49 (1987), pp. 268-90.
Heil, J.P., *Romans-Paul's Letter of Hope* (AnB, 112; Rome: Biblical Institute, 1987).
Hendriksen, W., *New Testament Commentary: Exposition of Ephesians* (Grand Rapids: Baker, 1967).
—*A Commentary on Colossians & Philemon* (GSC; London: Banner of Truth, 1971).
Héring, J., *The First Epistle of Saint Paul to the Corinthians* (trans. A.W. Heathcote and P.J. Allcock; London: Epworth Press, 1962).
—*The Second Epistle of Saint Paul to the Corinthians* (trans. A.W. Heathcote and P.J. Allcock; London: Epworth Press, 1967).
Hess, R.S., 'Genesis 1-2 in Its Literary Context', *TB* 41.1 (1990), pp. 143-53.
Hettlinger, R.F., '2 Corinthians 5.1-10', *SJT* 10 (1957), pp. 174-94.
Hicks, R.D. (trans.), *Diogenes Laertius*, II (Cambridge: Harvard University Press; London: William Heinemann, 1970).
Himmelfarb, M., *Ascent to Heaven* (Oxford: Oxford University Press, 1993).
Hodge, C., *Commentary on the Epistle to the Romans* (Grand Rapids: Eerdmans, 1955).
Holtz, T., 'Christliche Interpolationen in "Joseph und Aseneth"', *NTS* 14 (1968), pp. 482-97.
Hooker, M.D., 'Were There False Teachers in Colossae?', in B. Lindars and S.S. Smalley (eds.), *Christ and Spirit in the New Testament* (Festschrift C.F.D. Moule; Cambridge: Cambridge University Press, 1973), pp. 315-31.
—*Pauline Pieces* (London: Epworth, 1979).
Horgan, M.P., 'The Letter to the Colossians', in *NJBC* (London: Geoffrey Chapman, 1990 [1968]), pp. 876-82.
Horsley, R.A., ' "How Can Some of You Say that There Is no Resurrection of the Dead?" Spiritual Elitism in Corinth', *NovT* 20 (1978), pp. 203-231.
Howard, G., *Paul: Crisis in Galatia* (SNTSMS, 35; Cambridge: Cambridge University Press, 1979).
Howard, J.K., *New Testament Baptism* (London: Pickering & Inglis, 1970).
Hughes, P.E., *Paul's Second Epistle to the Corinthians* (NICNT; Grand Rapids: Eerdmans, 1962).

Hunt, J.P.W., 'Colossians 2.11-12, The Circumcision/Baptism Analogy, and Infant Baptism', *TB* 41.2 (1990), pp. 227-44.

Hunter, A.M., *The Epistle to the Romans* (London: SCM Press, 1955).

Idelsohn, A.Z., *Jewish Liturgy and Its Development* (New York: Henry Holst, 1932).

Isaac, E., '1 (Ethiopic Apocalypse of) Enoch', in J.H. Charlesworth (ed.), *OTP*, I (London: Darton, Longman & Todd, 1983), pp. 5-89.

Isenberg, W.W., 'The Gospel of Philip (II,3)', in J.M. Robinson (ed.), *The Nag Hammadi Library in English* (San Francisco: Harper, 1990 [1978]), pp. 139-60.

Jackman, D., *Judges, Ruth* (ed. L.J. Ogilvie; ComC; Dallas: Word Books, 1991).

Jeremias, J., 'Flesh and Blood cannot Inherit the Kingdom of God', *NTS* 2 (1955–56), pp. 151-59.

—*Infant Baptism in the First Four Centuries* (London: SCM Press, 1960).

—*The Parables of Jesus* (London: SCM Press, 1963).

—''Αδάμ', *TDNT*, I (1964), pp. 141-43.

—*Jerusalem in the Time of Jesus* (London: SCM Press, 1969).

Jervell, J., *Imago Dei: Gen 1, 26f. im Spätjudentum, in der Gnosis, und in den paulinischen Briefen* (FRLANT, 76; Göttingen: Vandenhoeck & Ruprecht, 1960).

Jewett, R., *Paul's Anthropological Terms: A Study of Their Use in Conflict Settings* (AGAJU, 10; Leiden: Brill, 1971).

Johnson, M.D., 'Life of Adam and Eve', in J.H. Charlesworth (ed.), *OTP*, II (New York: Doubleday, 1985), pp. 249-95.

Jonas, H., *The Gnostic Religion* (London: Routledge, 1958).

Käsemann, E., *Leib und Leib Christi: Eine Untersuchung zur paulinischen Begrifflichkeit* (BHT, 9; Tübingen: Mohr [Paul Siebeck], 1933).

—*Commentary on Romans* (trans. G.W. Bromiley; London: SCM Press, 1980).

Kaye, B.N., 'Βαπτίζειν εἰς with Special Reference to Romans 6' (*SE*, 6, TUGAL, 112; Berlin: Akademie-Verlag, 1973), pp. 281-86.

Keck, L.E., *Paul and His Letters, Proclamation Commentaries* (ed. G. Krodel; Philadelphia: Fortress, 1988).

Kee, H.C., 'The Socio-Religious Setting and Aims of "Joseph and Aseneth"', *SBLSPS* 10 (1976), pp. 183-92.

—'The Socio-Cultural Setting of Joseph and Aseneth', *NTS* 29 (1983), pp. 394-413.

Keener, C.S., *Bible Background Commentary: New Testament* (Downers Grove: IVP, 1993).

Kertelge, K., *'Rechtfertigung' bei Paulus* (Münster: Aschendorff, 1967).

Kilpatrick, G.D., 'Living Issues in Biblical Scholarship: The Last Supper', *ExpT* 64 (1952–53), pp. 4-8.

Kim, S., *The Origin of Paul's Gospel* (WUNT, 2.4; Tübingen: Mohr, 1981).

Kirby, J.C., *Ephesians: Baptism and Pentecost* (London: SPCK, 1968).

Kirk, K.E., *The Vision of God: The Christian Doctrine of the Summum Bonum* (London: Longmans, 1932).

Klijn, A.F.J., 'The So-called Hymn of the Pearl', *Vigiliae Christianae* 14 (1960), pp. 154-64.

—*The Acts of Thomas: Introduction—Text—Commentary* (NovTSup, 5; Leiden: Brill, 1962).

Knibb, M.A., *The Ethiopic Book of Enoch*, II (Oxford: Clarendon, 1978).

—'The Date of the Parables of Enoch: A Critical Review', *NTS* 25 (1979), pp. 345-59.

—'*1 Enoch*', in H.F.D. Sparks (ed.), *AOT* (Oxford: Clarendon, 1984), pp. 169-320.

Knox, D.B., 'The Date of the Epistle to the Galatians', *EQ* 13 (1941), pp. 262-68.

Kobelski, P.J., 'The Letter to the Ephesians', in *NJBC* (London: Geoffrey Chapman, 1990 [1968]), pp. 883-90.

Kraftchick, S.J., 'Seeing a More Fluid Model', in D.M. Hay (ed.), *Pauline Theology* II: *1 & 2 Corinthians* (Minneapolis: Fortress, 1993), pp. 18-34.

Kruse, H., 'The Return of the Prodigal, Fortunes of a Parable on Its Way to the Far East', in *Orientalia* (Nova Series, 47; Roma: Pontificium Institutum Biblica, 1978), pp. 163-214.

Kümmel, W.G., *Introduction to the New Testament* (Nashville: Abingdon, 1975).

—*Theology of the New Testament* (trans. J.E. Steely; London: SCM Press, 1980 [1973]).

Ladd, G.D., *A Theology of the New Testament* (Grand Rapids: Eerdmans, 1974).

Lähnemann, J., *Der Kolosserbrief* (Gerd Mohn: Gütersloher Verlagshaus, 1971).

Lambden, S.N., 'From Fig Leaves to Fingernails: Some Notes on the Garments of Adam and Eve in the Hebrew Bible and Select Early Postbiblical Jewish Writings', in P. Morris and D. Sawyer (eds.), *A Walk in the Garden: Biblical, Iconographical and Literary Images of Eden* (JSOTSup, 136; Sheffield: JSOT Press, 1992), pp. 74-90.

Lampe, G.W.H., '*Baptisma* in the New Testament', *SJT* 5 (1952), pp. 163-74.

Lange, J.P., *Commentary on the Holy Scripture. X. Romans and Corinthians* (Grand Rapids: Zondervan, 1960).

Layton, B., *The Gnostic Scriptures* (London: SCM Press, 1987).

Leaney, A.R.C., *The Jewish & Christian World 200 BC to AD 200* (CCWJCW, 7; Cambridge: Cambridge University Press, 1989 [1984]).

Leenhardt, F.J., *The Epistle to the Romans: A Commentary* (London: Lutterworth, 1961).

Levison, J.R., *Portraits of Adam in Early Judaism: From Sirach to 2 Baruch* (JSPSup, 1; Sheffield: JSOT Press, 1988).

—'*2 Apoc. Bar.* 48.42-52.7 and the Apocalyptic Dimension of Colossians 3.1-6', *JBL* 108 (1989), pp. 93-108.

—'Adam and Eve, Life Of', in *ABD*, I (New York: Doubleday, 1992), pp. 64-66.

Lias, J.J., *The Second Epistle of Paul the Apostle to the Corinthians* (CGTSC; Cambridge: Cambridge University Press, 1892).

Lightfoot, J.B., *St. Paul's Epistle to the Galatians* (London: Macmillan, 10th edn, 1890 [1865]).

—*Colossians and Philemon* (London: MacMillan, 1900 [1875]).

Lillie, W., 'An Approach to II Corinthians', *SJT* 30 (1977), pp. 59-70.

Lilly, J.L., 'Exposition of the Missal Epistles from Romans', *CBQ* 3 (1941), pp. 349-55.

Lincoln, A.T., *Paradise Now and Not Yet* (SNTSMS, 43; Cambridge: Cambridge University Press, 1981).

—*Ephesians* (WBC, 42; Dallas: Word Books, 1990).

Lincoln, A.T., and A.J.M. Wedderburn, *The Theology of the Later Pauline Letters* (NTT; Cambridge: Cambridge University Press, 1993).

Littmann, E., 'Enoch, Books Of (Ethiopic and Slavonic)', in I.K. Funk *et al.* (eds.), *JE*, V (New York and London: Funk and Wagnalls, 1903), pp. 179-82.

Lohse, E., *Colossians and Philemon* (trans. W.R. Poehlmann and R.J. Karris; Philadelphia: Fortress, 1971).

Long, W.R., 'Expository Articles: Ephesians 2.11-22', *Int* 45 (1991), pp. 281-83.

Longenecker, R.N., *Galatians* (WBC, 41; Dallas: Word Books, 1990).

Luck, G., *ARCANA MUNDI: Magic and the Occult in the Greek and Roman Worlds* (Baltimore: John Hopkins University Press, 1985).

Lüdemann, G., 'ἐκ (ἐξ)', in H. Balz and G. Schneider (eds.), *EDNT*, I (Grand Rapids: Eerdmans, 1990), pp. 402-403.

Lührmann, D., *Galatians: A Continental Commentary* (Minneapolis: Fortress, 1992).

Luther, Martin, *A Commentary on St. Paul's Epistle to the Galatians: A Revised and Completed Translation Based on the 'Middleton' Text Prepared by P.S. Watson* (Cambridge: Clarke, 1978 [orig. 1535]).

MacAlister, R.A.S., *Ecclesiastical Vestments: Their Development and History* (London: Elliot Stock, 1896).

Manson, T.W., 'Romans', in M. Black and H.H. Rowley (eds.), *PCB* (London: Nelson, 1963), pp. 940-53.

Marcus, J., ' "Let God Arise and End the Reign of Sin!" A Contribution to the Study of Pauline Parenesis', *Biblica* 69 (1988), pp. 386-95.

Marshall, J.T., 'Adam, Books Of', in J. Hastings (ed.), *DB* I (Peabody: Hendrickson, 1988 [Edinburgh: T. & T. Clark, 1898]), pp. 37-38.

Martin, R.P., *Worship in the Early Church* (Grand Rapids: Eerdmans, 1964).

—*Colossians: The Church's Lord and the Christian's Liberty* (Exeter: Paternoster, 1972).

—*Colossians and Philemon* (NCBC; London: Oliphants, 1974).

—*Reconciliation: A Study of Paul's Theology* (London: Morgan & Scott, 1981).

—*2 Corinthians* (WBC, 40; Texas: Word Books, 1986).

—*Ephesians, Colossians, and Philemon, Interpretation: A Bible Commentary for Teaching and Preaching* (Atlanta: John Knox, 1991).

Martin, T., 'The Scythian Perspective in Col 3.11', *NovT* 37 (1995), pp. 249-61.

Martyn, J.L., 'A Law-Observant Mission to Gentiles: The Background of Galatians', *SJT* 38 (1985), pp. 307-324.

—'Events in Galatia: Modified Covenantal Nomism versus God's Invasion of the Cosmos in the Singular Gospel. A Response to J.D.G. Dunn and B.R. Gaventa', in J.M. Bassler (ed.), *Pauline Theology* I: *Thessalonians, Philippians, Galatians, Philemon* (Minneapolis: Fortress, 1991), pp. 160-79.

Matera, F.J., *Galatians* (SPS, 9; Collegeville: The Liturgical Press, 1992).

McCasland, S.V., ' "The Image of God" according to Paul', *JBL* 69 (1950), pp. 85-100.

McKnight, S., *A Light Among the Gentiles: Jewish Missionary Activity in the Second Temple Period* (Minneapolis: Fortress, 1991).

McNeile, A.H., *The Book of Exodus* (London: Methuen, 1908).

Mearns, C.L., 'Dating the Similitudes of Enoch', *NTS* 25 (1979), pp. 360-69.

Meeks, W.A., 'The Image of the Androgyne: Some Uses of a Symbol in Earliest Christianity', *History of Religions* 13.3 (1974), pp. 165-208.

—*The First Urban Christians: The Social World of the Apostle Paul* (New Haven: Yale University Press, 1983).

—*The Moral World of the First Christians* (LEC, 6; Philadelphia: The Westminster Press, 1986).

Meggitt, J.J., *Paul, Poverty and Survival* (ed. J. Barclay, J. Marcus and J. Riches; SNTIW; Edinburgh: T. & T. Clark, 1998).

Merklein, H., *Das kirchliche Amt nach dem Epheserbrief* (Munich: Kösel, 1973).

Meyer, H.A.W., *Critical and Exegetical Handbook to the Epistle to the Galatians* (Edinburgh: T. & T. Clark, 1873).

—*Critical and Exegetical Handbook to the Epistles to the Corinthians* (CECNT, 2; Edinburgh: T. & T. Clark, 1879).

—*Critical and Exegetical Handbook to the Epistle to the Ephesians and the Epistle to Philemon* (Edinburgh: T. & T. Clark, 1880).

Meyer, M.W., 'Mystery Religions', in *ABD*, IV (New York: Doubleday, 1992), pp. 941-45.

Meyer, P.W., 'Romans', in *HBC* (San Francisco: Harper & Row, 1988), pp. 1130-167.

Meyers, C.L., *Haggai, Zechariah 1-8* (AB; Grand Rapids: Doubleday, 1987).

Mitchell, H.G., *A Critical and Exegetical Commentary on Haggai, Zechariah, Malachi and Jonah* (ICC; Edinburgh: T. & T. Clark, 1937 [1912]).

Mitton, C.L., 'Paul's Certainties: V. The Gift of the Spirit and Life beyond Death—2 Corinthians v. 1-5', *ExpT* 69 (1957–58), pp. 260-63.

Moffatt, J., *The First Epistle of Paul to the Corinthians* (London: Hodder & Stoughton, 1959 [1938]).

Momigliano, A., *Claudius* (Cambridge: Cambridge University Press, 1961).

Moore, G.F., *A Critical and Exegetical Commentary on Judges* (ICC; Edinburgh: T. & T. Clark, 1918 [1895]).

—*Judaism in the First Centuries of the Christian Era: The Age of the Tannaim*, I (Cambridge: Harvard University Press, 1927).

Morfill, W.R., *The Book of the Secrets of Enoch* (Oxford: Clarendon, 1896).

Morgan, R., *Romans* (NTG; Sheffield: Sheffield Academic Press, 1995).

Moritz, T., *A Profound Mystery: The Use of the Old Testament in Ephesians* (NovTSup, 85; Leiden: Brill, 1996).

Morris, L., *The First Epistle of Paul to the Corinthians* (Leicester: IVP, 1976 [1958]).

Motyer, J.A., 'Urim and Thummim', in J.D. Douglas (ed.), *NBD* (Grand Rapids: Eerdmans, 1973 [1962]), p. 1306.

Moule, C.F.D., *An Idiom Book of New Testament Greek* (Cambridge: Cambridge University Press, 1953).

—*Worship in the New Testament* (London: Lutterworth, 1961).

—*The Epistles of Paul the Apostle to the Colossians and to Philemon* (Cambridge: Cambridge University Press, 1962).

—'Colossians and Philemon', in M. Black and H.H. Rowley (eds.), *PCB* (London: Nelson, 1963), pp. 990-95.

—'St. Paul and Dualism: The Pauline Conception of Resurrection', *NTS* 12 (1965–66), pp. 106-123.

—*The Origin of Christology* (Cambridge: Cambridge University Press, 1977).

Moule, H.C.G., *Colossian and Philemon Studies: Lessons in Faith and Holiness* (London: Pickering & Inglis, n.d.).

Moulton, J.H., '"It is His Angel"', *JTS* 3 (1902), pp. 514-27.

Moulton, J.H., and G. Milligan, 'κοσμέω', in BAGD (Chicago and London: University of Chicago Press, 2nd edn, 1979), p. 445.

—'ἐκ', in BAGD (Chicago and London: University of Chicago Press, 2nd edn, 1979), pp. 234-36.

Mozley, J.H., 'Documents: the "Vita Adae"', *JTS* 30 (1929), pp. 121-49.

Murphy, J.G., *A Critical and Exegetical Commentary on the Book of Genesis* (Edinburgh: T. & T. Clark, 1863).

Murphy-O'Connor, J., *The Theology of the Second Letter to the Corinthians* (NTT; Cambridge: Cambridge University Press, 1991).

Murray, J., *The Epistle to the Romans*, II (ed. F.F. Bruce; NICNT; Grand Rapids: Eerdmans, 1965).

Myers, J.M., *I Chronicles* (AB; New York: Doubleday, 1979 [1965]).

Myers, J.M., and P.P. Elliott, 'Judges', in *IB* II (New York: Abingdon, 1956), pp. 677-825.

Newell, W.R., *Romans: Verse by Verse* (Chicago: Grace, 1938).

Neyrey, R.H., 'Body Language in 1 Corinthians: The Use of Anthropological Models for Understanding Paul and His Opponents', *Semeia* 35 (1986), pp. 129-70.

Nickelsburg, G.W.E., *Resurrection, Immortality, and Eternal Life in Intertestamental Judaism* (HTS, 26; Cambridge: Harvard University Press, 1972).

—'Some Related Traditions in the Apocalypse of Adam, The Books of Adam and Eve, and *1 Enoch*', in B. Layton (ed.), *The Rediscovery of Gnosticism* II: *Sethian Gnosticism* (SHR, 41; Leiden: Brill, 1981), pp. 515-39.

Nock, A.D., *Conversion: The Old and the New in Religion from Alexander the Great to Augustine of Hippo* (Oxford: Clarendon, 1933).

O'Brien, P.T., *Colossians, Philemon* (WBC, 44; Waco: Word Books, 1982).

Oden, R.A., 'Grace or Status? YHWH's Clothing of the First Humans', in J.J. Collins (ed.), *The Bible Without Theology: The Theological Tradition and Alternatives to It* (San Francisco: Harper & Row, 1987), pp. 92-105.

Oepke, D.A., *Der Brief des Paulus and die Galater* (THKNT; Leipzig: Deichertsche Verlagsbuchhandlung, 1937).

—'βάπτω κτλ', *TDNT*, I (1964), pp. 529-46.

—'γυμνός', *TDNT*, I (1964), pp. 773-75.

—'δύω κτλ', *TDNT*, II (1964), pp. 318-21.

—'παρουσία κτλ', *TDNT*, V (1967), pp. 858-71.

Oesterley, W.O.E., *The Books of the Apocrypha* (London: Roxburghe House, 1914).

—'Judges', in F.C. Eiselen *et al.* (eds.), *ABC* (New York: Abingdon, 1929), pp. 357-76.

—*A History of Israel*, II (Oxford: Clarendon, 1945 [1932]).

Oldfather, W.A. (trans.), *Epictetus: The Discourses as Reported by Arrian, the Manual, and Fragments* I (ed. E. Capps *et al.*; LCL; London: Heinemann, 1926).

O'Neill, J.C., *The Recovery of Paul's Letter to the Galatians* (London: SPCK, 1972).

Orchard, D.B., 'Galatians', in *NCCHS* (London: Nelson, 1969 [1953]), pp. 1173-80.

O'Rourke, J.J., '1 Corinthians', in *NCCHS* (London: Nelson, 1969 [1953]), pp. 1143-160.

Orr, W.F., and J.A. Walther, *I Corinthians: A New Translation* (AB, 32; New York: Doubleday, 1976).

Osei-Bonsu, J., 'Does 2 Cor 5.1-10 Teach the Reception of the Resurrection Body at the Moment of Death?', *JSNT* 28 (1986), pp. 81-101.

Pate, C.M., *Adam Christology as the Exegetical & Theological Substructure of 2 Corinthians 4.7-5.21* (New York: University Press of America, 1991).

Payne, J.B., 'תָּמַם', in R.L. Harris *et al.* (eds.), *TWOT*, II (Chicago: Moody Press, 1980), pp. 973-74.

Pearson, D.A., *The Pneumatikos-Psychikos Terminology in 1 Corinthians: A Study in the Theology of the Corinthian Opponents of Paul and Its Relation to Gnosticism* (SBLDS, 12; Missoula: Scholars, 1973).

Pennington, A., '2 Enoch', in H.F.D. Sparks (ed.), *AOT* (Oxford: Clarendon, 1984), pp. 321-62.

Perriman, A.C., 'Paul and the Parousia: 1 Corinthians 15.50-57 and 2 Corinthians 5.1-5', *NTS* 35 (1989), pp. 512-21.

Pervo, R.I., 'Joseph and Aseneth and the Greek Novel', *SBLSPS* 10 (1976), pp. 171-81.

Peterson, E., 'Theologie des Kleides', *BM* 16 (1934), pp. 347-56.

Philonenko, M., *Joseph et Aséneth: Introduction, Text Critique, Traduction et Notes* (Studia Post-Biblica, 13; Leiden: Brill, 1968).

Pokorný, P., *Colossians: A Commentary* (Peabody: Hendrickson, 1991).

Porter, S.E., 'The Argument of Romans 5: Can a Rhetorical Question Make a Difference?', *JBL* 110.4 (1991), pp. 655-77.

—*Idioms of the Greek New Testament* (BLG, 2; Sheffield: JSOT Press, 1994).

Price, J.L., 'The First Letter of Paul to the Corinthians', in *IOCB* (London: Collins, 1971), pp. 795-812.

—'Romans 6.1-14', *Int* 34 (1980), pp. 65-69.

Quispel, G., 'Gnosticism and the New Testament', in J.P. Hyatt (ed.), *The Bible in Modern Scholarship* (Nashville and New York: Abingdon, 1965), pp. 252-71.

Radford, L.B., *The Epistle to the Colossians and the Epistle to Philemon* (WC; London: Methuen, 1931).

Reif, S.C., *Judaism and Hebrew Prayer: New Perspectives on Jewish Liturgical History* (Cambridge: Cambridge University Press, 1993).

Reitzenstein, R., *Das iranische Erlösungsmysterium. Religionsgeschichtliche Untersuchungen* (Bonn, 1921).

—*Hellenistic Mystery-Religions: Their Basic Ideas and Significance* (trans. J.E. Steely; Pittsburgh: Pickwick, 1978).

Rendall, F., 'The Epistle to the Galatians', in W.R. Nicoll (ed.), *EGT*, III (London: Hodder & Stoughton, 1903), pp. 123-200.

Rengstorf, K.H., 'ποταμός κτλ', *TDNT*, VI (1968), pp. 595-623.

Richardson, A., *An Introduction to the Theology of the New Testament* (London: SCM Press, 1979 [1958]).

Ridderbos, H., *Paul: An Outline of His Theology* (trans. J.R. de Witt; Grand Rapids: Eerdmans, 1975).

—*The Epistle of Paul to the Churches of Galatia* (London: Marshall, Morgan & Scott, 1976 [3rd edn, 1967]).

Robertson, A., and A. Plummer, *A Critical and Exegetical Commentary on the First Epistle of St. Paul to the Corinthians* (ICC; Edinburgh: T. & T. Clark, 1967 [1911]).

Robertson, A.T., *Word Pictures in the New Testament. IV. The Epistles of Paul* (Nashville: Broadman, 1931).

Robinson, J.A.T., *St. Paul's Epistle to the Ephesians* (London: Macmillan, 1904).

—'The One Baptism as a Category of New Testament Soteriology', *SJT* 6 (1953), pp. 257-74.

—*Wrestling with Romans* (London: SCM Press, 1979).

Robinson, W., 'Historical Survey of the Church's Treatment of New Converts with Reference to Pre- and Post-Baptismal Instruction', *JTS* 42(1941), pp. 42-53.

Rost, L., *Judaism Outside the Hebrew Canon* (Nashville: Abingdon, 1976).

Sanday, W., and A.C. Headlam, *Critical and Exegetical Commentary on the Epistle to the Romans* (ICC; Edinburgh: T. & T. Clark, 1925 [1895]).

Sanders, J.N., 'Galatians', in M. Black and H.H. Rowley (eds.), *PCB* (London: Nelson, 1963), pp. 973-79.

Sandmel, S., *Philo of Alexandria: An Introduction* (Oxford: Oxford University Press, 1979).

Sandys, J.E. (ed.), *A Companion to Latin Studies* (Cambridge: Cambridge University Press, 1943 [1910]).

Sawyer, J.F.A., 'Notes and Studies: The Meaning of בְּצֶלֶם אֱלֹהִים ("In the Image of God") in Genesis I-XI', *JTSNS* 25 (1974), pp. 418-26.

Schelkle, K., *The Second Epistle to the Corinthians* (London: Burns & Oates, 1969).

Schenke, H.-M., *Der Gott 'Mensch' in der Gnosis* (Göttingen: Vandenhoeck & Ruprecht, 1962).

—'The Gospel of Philip', in W. Schneemelcher (ed.), *New Testament Apocrypha* I: *Gospels and Related Writings* (trans. R.McL. Wilson; Cambridge: Clarke, 1991), pp. 179-208.

Schlam, C.C., *The Metamorphoses of Apuleius* (London: Duckworth, 1992).

Schlier, H., *Der Brief an die Galater* (KEKNT, 7; Göttingen: Vandenhoeck & Ruprecht, 1971).

Schmithals, W., *Gnosticism in Corinth: An Investigation of the Letters to the Corinthians* (trans. J.E. Steely; Nashville: Abingdon, 1971).

—*Paul and the Gnostics* (New York: Abingdon, 1972).

Schnackenburg, R., *Das Heilsgeschehen bei der Taufe nach dem Apostel Paulus* (München: K. Zink, 1950).

—*Ephesians: A Commentary* (trans. H. Heron; Edinburgh: T. & T. Clark, 1991).

Schneider, G., *The Epistle to the Galatians* (London: Burns & Oates, 1969).

Schoemaker, W.R., 'The Use of רוּחַ in the Old Testament, and of πνεῦμα in the New Testament: A Lexicographical Study', *JBL* 23 (1904), pp. 13-67.

Schulz, S., *Neutestamentliche Ethik* (Zürich: Theologischer, 1987).

Schürer, E., *The History of the Jewish People in the Age of Jesus Christ* (175 B.C.-A.D. 135) III/1 (Edinburgh: T. & T. Clark, 1986 [1885]).

—*The History of the Jewish People in the Age of Jesus Christ* (175 B.C.-A.D. 135) III/2 (Edinburgh: T. & T. Clark, 1987 [1885]).

Schweizer, E., 'Dying and Rising with Christ', *NTS* 14 (1967), pp. 1-14.

—*The Letter to the Colossians: A Commentary* (London: SPCK, 1982).

Scott, E.F., *The Epistles of Paul to the Colossians, to Philemon and to the Ephesians* (MoffNTC; London: Hodder & Stoughton, 1942 [1930]).

Scroggs, R., *The Last Adam: A Study in Pauline Anthropology* (Oxford: Blackwell, 1966).

Scroggs, R., and K. Groff, 'Baptism in Mark', *JBL* 92 (1973), pp. 531-48.

Segelberg, E., 'The Baptismal Rite according to Some of the Coptic Gnostic Texts of Nag-Hammadi', in *Studia Patristica*,V (TUGAL 80; Berlin: Akademie- Verlag, 1962), pp. 117-28.

Segundo, J.L., *The Humanist Christology of Paul* (New York: Orbis Books, 1986).

Selwyn, E.G., *The First Epistle of St. Peter* (London: Macmillan, 1952 [1946]).

Sevenster, J.N., 'Short Studies: Einige Bemerkungen Über Den "Zwischenzustand" Bei Paulus', *NTS* 1 (1954–55), pp. 291-96.

Seyffert, O., *A Dictionary of Classical Antiquities: Mythology, Religion, Literature & Art* (London: Swan Sonnenschein, 1899).

Sharp, D.S., *Epictetus and the New Testament* (London: Kelly, 1914).

Sharpe, J.L., 'The Second Adam in the Apocalypse of Moses', *CBQ* 35 (1973), pp. 35-41.

Sider, R.J., 'The Pauline Conception of the Resurrection Body in 1 Corinthians XV. 35-54', *NTS* 21 (1975), pp. 428-39.

Simpson, E.K., *Commentary on the Epistles to the Ephesians and the Colossians* (ed. F.F. Bruce; NICNT; Grand Rapids: Eerdmans, 1972 [1957]).

Singer, S. (trans.), *The Authorized Daily Prayer Book* (London: Eyre and Spottiswoode, 1962).

Skinner, J., *Critical and Exegetical Commentary on Genesis* (ICC; Edinburgh: T. & T. Clark, 1910).

Smith, J.Z., *Map Is Not Territory: Studies in the History of Religions* (ed. J. Neusner; SJLA, 23; Leiden: Brill, 1978).

Snaith, N.H., 'Leviticus', in M. Black and H.H. Rowley (eds.), *PCB* (London: Nelson, 1962), pp. 241-53.

Speiser, E.A., *Genesis* (AB, 1; New York: Doubleday, 1964).

Spittler, R.P., 'Testament of Job', in J.H. Charlesworth (ed.), *OTP*, I (London: Darton, Longman & Todd, 1983), pp. 829-68.

Stalker, D.M.G., 'Exodus', in M. Black and H.H. Rowley (eds.), *PCB* (London: Nelson, 1975 [1962]), pp. 208-40.

Stanley, C.D., ' "Neither Jew Nor Greek": Ethnic Conflict in Graeco-Roman Society', *JSNT* 64 (1966), pp. 101-124.

Stauffer, E., *New Testament Theology* (trans. J. Marsh; London: SCM Press, 1955).

Stendahl, K., *Meanings: The Bible as Document and as Guide* (Philadelphia: Fortress, 1984).

Sterling, G.E., ' "Wisdom Among the Perfect": Creation Traditions in Alexandrian Judaism and Corinthian Christianity', *NovT* 37 (1995), pp. 355-84.

Stern, D.H., *Jewish New Testament Commentary* (Clarksville: Jewish New Testament Publications, 1992).

Stern, M. (ed.), *Greek and Latin Authors on Jews and Judaism*. I. *From Herodotus to Plutarch* (PIASH; Jerusalem: IASH, 1974).

Stockhausen, C.K., 'Moses' Veil and the Glory of the New Covenant: The Exegetical and Theological Substructure of II Corinthians 3.1-4.6' (unpublished PhD dissertation; Marquette University, 1984).

Stoeckhardt, G., *Ephesians* (trans. M.S. Smooer; CCCS; St. Louis: Concordia, 1952).

Stone, M., 'The Death of Adam: An Armenian Adam Book', *HTR* 59 (1966), pp. 283-91.

Stone, S., 'The Toga: From National to Ceremonial Costume', in J.L. Sebesta and L. Bonfante (eds.), *The World of Roman Costume* (Wisconsin: The University of Wisconsin, 1994), pp. 13-39.

Strachan, R.H., *The Second Epistle of Paul to the Corinthians* (London: Hodder & Stoughton, 1935).

Strack, H.L., and P. Billerbeck, *Kommentar zum Neuen Testament aus Talmud und Midrasch*, I (Munich: Beck'sche, 1926).

Strack, H.L., and G. Stemberger, *Introduction to the Talmud and Midrash* (Edinburgh: T. & T. Clark, 1991).

Stuhlmacher, P., *Paul's Letter to the Romans: A Commentary* (Louisville: Westminster/John Knox, 1994).

Suter, D.W., *Translation and Composition in the Parables of Enoch* (SBLDS, 47; Missoula: Scholars, 1979).

Swain, L., 'Ephesians', in *NCCHS* (London: Nelson, 1969 [1953]), pp. 1189-191.

Tannehill, R.C., *Dying and Rising with Christ* (Berlin: Verlag Alfred Töpelmann, 1967).

Taylor, P.M., '"Abba, Father" and Baptism', *SJT* 11 (1958), pp. 62-71.

Thompson, G.H.P., *Letters of Paul to the Ephesians to the Colossians and to Philemon* (ed. P.R. Ackroyd *et al.*; CBC; Cambridge: Cambridge University Press, 1967).

Thompson, M., *Clothed with Christ: The Example and Teaching of Jesus in Romans 12.1–15.13* (JSNTSup, 59; Sheffield: JSOT Press, 1991).

Thornton, L.S., *The Common Life in the Body of Christ* (London: Dacre, 1963 [1942]).

Thrall, M.E., *The First and Second Letters of Paul to the Corinthians* (Cambridge: Cambridge University Press, 1965).

Tobin, T.H., *The Creation of Man: Philo and the History of Interpretation* (CBQMS, 14; Washington: CBAA, 1983).

Torrance, T.F., 'Proselyte Baptism', *NTS* 1.2 (1954), pp. 150-54.

Torrey, C.C., *The Apocryphal Literature: A Brief Introduction* (New Haven: Yale University Press, 1953 [1945]).

Tregelles, S.P. (trans.), *Gesenius' Hebrew and Chaldee Lexicon* (Milford: Mott Media, 1979).

Tyson, J.B., 'Paul's Opponents in Galatia', *NovT* 10 (1968), pp. 241-54.

Van der Horst, P.W., 'Short Studies: Observations on a Pauline Expression', *NTS* 19 (1972–73), pp. 181-87.

Van Roon, A., *The Authenticity of Ephesians* (NovTSup, 39; Leiden: Brill, 1974).

Vaughan, C.J., *St. Paul's Epistle to the Romans* (London: Macmillan, 1890).

Vogel, H., 'The First Sacrament: Baptism', *SJT* 7 (1954), pp. 41-58.

Vout, C., 'The Myth of the Toga: Understanding the History of Roman Dress', in I. McAuslan and P. Walcot (eds.), *Greece & Rome* (Second Series, 42; Oxford: Oxford University Press, 1995), pp. 204-220.

Wall, R.W., *Colossians & Philemon* (ed. G.R. Osborne; The IVP New Testament Commentary Series; Illinois: Intervarsity Press, 1993), p. 142.

Walsh, J.T., 'Genesis 2.4b-3.24: A Synchronic Approach', *JBL* 96.2 (1977), pp. 161-77.

Walsh, P.G., *The Roman Novel: The 'Satyricon' of Petronius and the 'Metamorphoses' of Apuleius* (Cambridge: Cambridge University Press, 1970).

Walters, H.B., *A Guide to the Exhibition Illustrating Greek and Roman Life* (London: Clowes, 1929).

Walton, F.R., 'Athens, Eleusis, and the Homeric Hymn to Demeter', *HTR* 45 (1952), pp. 105-14.

Wedderburn, A.J.M., 'Adam in Paul's Letter to the Romans' (*SB*, 3 [1978], JSNTSup, 3 [1980]), pp. 413-30.

—'The Soteriology of the Mysteries', *NovT* 29 (1987), pp. 53-72.

—*Baptism and Resurrection: Studies in Pauline Theology against Its Graeco-Roman Background* (Tübingen: Mohr, 1987).

Weima, J.A.D., 'Gal 6.11-18: A Hermeneutical Key to the Galatian Letter', *CTJ* 28 (1993), pp. 90-107.

Weiss, K., 'φορέω', in H. Balz and G. Schneider (eds.), *EDNT*, III (Grand Rapids: Eerdmans, 1993), p. 436.

Wells, L.S.A., 'The Books of Adam and Eve', in R.H. Charles (ed.), *APOT*, II (Oxford: Clarendon, 1913), pp. 123-54.

Wells, L.S.A (trans.) and M. Whittaker, (rev.), 'The Life of Adam and Eve', in H.F.D. Sparks (ed.), *AOT* (Oxford: Clarendon, 1984), pp. 141-68.

Wenham, D., 'Being "Found" on the Last Day: New Light on 2 Peter 3.10 and 2 Corinthians 5.3', *NTS* 33 (1987), pp. 477-79.

Wenham, G.J., *Genesis 1-15* (WBC, 1; Dallas: Word Books, 1987).

West, S., '*Joseph and Aseneth*: A Neglected Greek Romance', *CQNS* 24 (1974), pp. 70-81.

Westcott, B.F., *St. Paul's Epistle to the Ephesians: The Greek Texts with Notes and Addenda* (London: Macmillan, 1906).

Westermann, C., *Genesis*, I (BKAT, I/1; Neukirchen: Neukirchener Verlag, 1974).

Wevers, J.W. (ed.), *Ezekiel* (CBNS; London: Nelson, 1969).

Whiston, W. (trans.), *The Works of Josephus* (Peabody: Hendrickson, 1987).

Whiteley, D.E.H., *The Theology of St. Paul* (Oxford: Blackwell, 1974).

Wifall, W., 'The Breath of His Nostrils: Gen 2.7b', *CBQ* 36 (1974), pp. 237-40.

Wilckens, U., *Der Brief an die Römer*, III (EKKNT; 3 vols.; Zürich: Benziger/Neukirchen: Neukirchener Verlag, 1978, 1980, 1982).

Williams, A.L. (ed.), *The Epistles of Paul the Apostle to the Colossians and to Philemon* (Cambridge: Cambridge University Press, 1907).

Williams, C.S.C., 'I and II Corinthians', in M. Black and H.H. Rowley (eds.), *PCB* (London: Nelson, 1975 [1962]), pp. 954-72.

Williams, R.R., 'The Pauline Catechesis', in F.L. Cross (ed.), *Studies in Ephesians* (London: Mowbray, 1956), pp. 89-96.

Wilson, L.M., *The Roman Toga* (ed. D.M. Robinson; JHUSA, 1; Baltimore: Johns Hopkins University Press, 1924).

—*The Clothing of the Ancient Romans* (ed. D.M. Robinson; JHUSA, 24; Baltimore: Johns Hopkins University Press, 1938).

Wilson, R.A., 'Ezekiel', in *HBC* (San Francisco: Harper, 1988), pp. 652-94.

—' "We" and "You" in the Epistle to the Ephesians', *TU* 87 (1964), pp. 676-80.

Wilson, R. McL., 'Gnostics—in Galatia?', *SE*, IV (TUGAL, 102; Berlin: Akademie-Verlag, 1968), pp. 358-67.

—'Gnosis at Corinth', in M.D. Hooker and S.G. Wilson (eds.), *Paul and Paulinism* (Festschrift C.K. Barrett; London: SPCK, 1982), pp. 102-114.

Winston, D., *Philo of Alexandria: The Contemplative Life, the Giants, and Selections* (London: SPCK, 1981).

Witherington, B., 'Rite and Rights for Women—Galatians 3.28', *NTS* 27 (1981), pp. 593-604.

Wolf, H., 'אוֹר', in R.L. Harris *et al.* (eds.), *TWOT*, I (Chicago: Moody Press, 1980), p. 26.

Wolfson, H.A., *Philo: Foundations of Religious Philosophy in Judaism* (2 vols.; Cambridge: Harvard University Press, 1947).

Wright, N.T., 'Adam in Pauline Christology', *SBLSPS* 22 (Chico: Scholars, 1983), pp. 359-89.

—*Colossians and Philemon* (TNTC; Leicester: IVP, 1986).

Wuest, K.S., *Galatians in the Greek New Testament: For the English Readers* (Grand Rapids: Eerdmans, 3rd edn, 1948).

Yamauchi, E.M., *Pre-Christian Gnosticism: A Survey of the Proposed Evidences* (London: Tyndale, 1973).

Yates, R., 'Colossians and Gnosis', *JSNT* 27 (1986), pp. 49-68.

—'The Christian Way of Life: The Paraenetic Material in Colossians 3.1-4.6', *EQ* 63.3 (1991), pp. 241-51.

Young, F., and D.F. Ford, *Meaning and Truth in 2 Corinthians* (BFT; London: SPCK, 1987).

Zeilinger, F., *Der Erstgeborene der Schöpfung: Untersuchungen zur Formalstruktur und Theologie des Kolosserbriefes* (Wien: Verlag Herder, 1974).

Zerafa, P., 'Exodus', in *NCCHS* (London: Nelson, 1969), pp. 173-92.

Ziesler, J., *The Epistle to the Galatians* (London: Epworth, 1992).

INDEXES

INDEX OF REFERENCES

BIBLE

Habakkuk	
2.14	33
3.3	33
3.13	12

Zephaniah	
2.14	12

Zechariah	
2.5	33
3	49
3.3-5	4, 8, 11, 12, 18, 24, 26, 29, 102, 121, 143, 149, 166, 174, 175, 183, 191
3.4	24
3.9	24
13.4	11

Apocrypha
2 Esdras

3.21-22	141
4.30	141

Judith	
5.23	111
7.27	111

Wisdom of Solomon	
1.53	211
2.23-24	195
7.1	15, 42
7.16-17	111
7.26	199
9.1-3	15, 42
9.3	183
10.1-2	15

Sirach	
17.1-7	15
17.4	42
37.13-14	111
38.1-2	111

1 Maccabees	
11.10	111

New Testament
Matthew

10.19-20	111
10.28	204
11.8	198
13.45-46	72, 73
13.45	73

Mark	
1.15	132

Luke	
1.75	183
8.29	111
15.11-32	72

John	
1.3	163
2.19	211
2.21	211
3.6	216
5.21-22	111
8.42	111
19.5	198
19.23-24	125, 144, 170, 186, 187
19.23	125

Acts	
2.15	111
15	109
16.2	108
16.6	108
18.12	193
18.18	193
18.19-22	193
18.23	108, 193
19.1	193
19.8-10	153
19.8	193
19.10	193
19.22	193
20.3	133

Romans	
1.5-6	133
1.13	133
1.16	146
1.23	204, 231
2.5-11	135
2.17–3.8	133
3.12	135
3.14	17, 135
3.21-31	133
3.26	146
5.1	141
5.6	132
5.12-21	3, 39, 140-42
5.14	141
6–8	3
6	139
6.1–7.6	133
6.1-23	141
6.1-14	126, 141
6.1-11	96, 115, 117, 136, 138, 141, 179
6.1-6	3
6.1-5	139, 228
6.2-11	117
6.3-5	139, 140
6.3-4	224
6.3	96, 113, 139, 141, 145, 179
6.4-7	157
6.4	139, 160
6.6	179
6.11	138
6.12-14	136, 138, 141
6.12-13	136, 138, 140, 228
6.12	138
6.13	138, 140
6.14	111
7.7	39
7.14	188
7.18	188
8.2-3	111

Numbers			22.18	125		23.6	10
20.26	10		29.11	10		27.3	10
20.28	10		34.13	10		27.4	10
			34.26	10		27.7	10
Deuteronomy			64.6	10		38.4	10
22.11	10		64.12	10		42.14	10
			70.13	10		44.17	10
Judges			72.6	10			
6.34	10		92.1	10		*Daniel*	
			103.1	10		7.9	32
2 Samuel (2 Kgdms)			108.18	10			
6.14	10		108.19	10		*Jonah*	
			108.29	10		3.5	10
1 Kings (3 Kgdms)			131.9	10		3.6	10
17.5	10		131.16	10			
17.38	10		131.18	10		*Micah*	
22.30	10		146.8	10		7.10	10
2 Kings (4 Kgdms)			*Proverbs*			*Zephaniah*	
1.24	10		16.23	11		1.8	10
13.18	10		23.21	10			
14.2	10		31.21	10		*Zechariah*	
			31.25	10		3.4	10
1 Chronicles						3.5	10
12.18	10		*Song of Songs*			3.6	10
			5.3	10		13.4	10
2 Chronicles							
6.41	10		*Isaiah*			**Hebrew Bible**	
24.20	10		3.24	10		*Genesis*	
28.15	10		4.1	10		3.21	10
			11.5	10			
Esther			22.21	10		*Exodus*	
4.1	10		49.18	10		28.40-41	10
5.1	10		50.3	10			
			51.9	10		*Leviticus*	
Job			59.17	10		6.3-4	10
8.22	10		61.10	10			
10.11	10					*Jeremiah*	
13.26	10		*Jeremiah*			49.3	10
29.14	10		4.8	10			
31.19	10		10.9	10		*Zechariah*	
39.19	10		30.3	10		3.3	10
39.20	10					3.4	10
40.5	10		*Ezekiel*			3.5	10
			7.27	10			
Psalms			9.2	10		*Psalms*	
17.32	10		16.10	10, 11		18.32	10
17.39	10		16.11	10		18.39	10

22.19	125	73.6	10	132.16	10
30.11	10	93.1	10	132.18	10
35.13	10	104.1	10	147.8	10
35.26	10	109.18	10		
65.6	10	109.19	10	*Job*	
65.12	10	109.29	10	40.10	10
71.13	10	132.9	10		

OTHER ANCIENT REFERENCES

Pseudepigrapha

1 Enoch

1–36	31, 33	91.13	33	16.4	33
1.9	30	102.3	33		
14	34	106–108	31	*3 Enoch*	
14.8-25	32			24.22	33
14.18-21	32	*2 Syriac Baruch*			
14.19	33	4.2-7	211	*4 Ezra*	
14.20	20, 30, 32-	14.17-19	15, 42	2.39	34
	36, 42, 56,	48.42–52.7	171	2.45	34
	103, 118,			6.45-46	15
	172, 232	*2 Enoch*		6.53-59	15
14.21	32	1–68	31	7.91	33
22.14	33	1–2	31	8.21	33
25.7	33	3–21	31	10.44-59	211
27.3	33	22–38	31	13.3	196
36.4	33	22	34		
37-71	30, 31, 34	22.8-10	8, 30, 33,	*5 Apocryphal Syriac*	
40.3	33		35, 103,	*Psalms*	
46.1-3	196		172, 198,	2	33
62	34		203, 205,		
62.13	34		222, 225,	*Apocalypse of Abraham*	
62.15-16	8, 30, 34,		232	13	198
	35, 37, 42,	22.8	36, 37, 56,		
	56, 102,		218	*Apocalypse of Elijah*	
	172, 198,	22.15	35	1.3	33
	203, 205,	30.10-15	15, 42		
	222, 225,	30.12	218	*Apocalypse of Moses*	
	232	31.3	15, 42	7.1	40
62.15	34-36	39–66	31	8.2	40
62.16	35, 36	44.1-2	15, 42	10.3	41
63.2	33	58.1-3	15, 42	12.1	41
71.11	34	67	31	13.15	40
72–82	31	68	31	14.2	39, 42
75.3	33	69–73	31	15–30	39
83–90	31			15–23	39
83.8	33	*3 Baruch*		17.1	39, 41
90.28-42	211	6.12	33	19.3	39
91–105	31	6.16	218	20–21	8, 39, 42-
		7.2	33		44, 56,
		11.2	33		

INDEX OF AUTHORS